AN INTRODUCTION TO
INTERNATIONAL
ECONOMICS

AN INTRODUCTION TO INTERNATIONAL ECONOMICS

STEPHEN A. BAKER

STEPHEN A. BAKER
Capital University

HARCOURT BRACE JOVANOVICH, PUBLISHERS

San Diego   New York   Chicago   Austin   Washington, D.C.
London   Sydney   Tokyo   Toronto

Requests for permission to make copies of any part of this work should be mailed to: Copyright and Permissions Department, Harcourt Brace Jovanovich, Publishers, Orlando, Florida 32887.

ISBN: 0-15-542185-9

Library of Congress Catalog Card Number: 89-84685

Printed in the United States of America

For Maria

PREFACE

Interest in international economic issues is growing. Discussions are frequent in the popular media, and it is now difficult to imagine a student graduating with a degree in economics who has not taken a course in international economics. Furthermore, student interest in international economic issues is not confined to economics majors: most classes contain students from other disciplines, such as business, political science, and international relations. *An Introduction to International Economics* is designed to meet the need for a comprehensive, up-to-date text that can be used by students with a wide range of academic backgrounds and interests.

There are many international economics textbooks that claim to be appropriate for students with a limited economics background, and many that claim to describe fully techniques that are not usually found in a principles course. It has been my experience, however, that when the presentation of new material relies heavily on techniques with which students are not familiar, there is a tendency to devote more time to mastering the mechanics of the techniques than to trying to understand the relevant economics issues. Therefore, I have designed this presentation to be essentially nonmathematical, and I have used diagrams and tables primarily to illustrate and reinforce points made in the text. Students who have taken a standard course in economics principles will be familiar with most of the techniques and diagrams used.

An Introduction to International Economics is divided into three sections dealing with, respectively, principles of international economics, history of international economics, and special topics. This structure allows students to progress from learning principles to the application of those principles in economic analysis. After the principles section, the historical chapters offer a comprehensive critical survey of the development of the international monetary system and the history of commercial policy. Although the lessons of history are often clear, unfortunately they are also often forgotten. So these chapters are designed to show how historical experience is relevant to current concerns and hence to deepen students' understanding of current issues and policies. The special topics section is a novel feature of this book. Here is in-depth treatment of subjects I have found to be of high student interest: the Eurocurrency market; the European Economic Community and the plan to establish a single European market by 1992; less developed countries (with a focus on trade, international development, and international debt); and multinational corporations.

An Introduction to International Economics is structured so that instructors can cover either trade and commercial policy (Chapters 1–5) or international finance and open economy macroeconomics (Chapters 6–10) first. The history chapters and special topics can be used throughout the course to illustrate the principles of international economics, or they can be left until nearer the end of the course and used selectively as time and interest permit. One of the main objectives has been to ensure that this text can be used in a wide variety of ways, to answer a wide variety of instructor needs and student backgrounds.

ACKNOWLEDGMENTS

I would like to thank my friends and colleagues for their support and encouragement, especially Roger Van Tassel and Howard Nicholson.

I have benefited from many valuable comments made by reviewers of the manuscript. I accept full responsibility for the imperfections that remain, but the reviewers deserve much of the credit for the appealing parts of the text. The reviewers are Betty Chu, San Jose State University; Denise Dimon, University of San Diego; Daniel Himarios, University of Texas at Arlington; Peter Kressler, Glassboro State College; Timothy Fries, University of Florida; Charles Engel, University of Virginia; Susan Ranney, University of Washington; Robert Stern, University of Michigan; and Henry Thompson, Auburn University.

Special thanks go to Ed Stuart of Northeastern Illinois University, who red the entire manuscript and provided extensive and very helpful comments that went far beyond the call of duty.

And thanks must go to the book team at HBJ: John Carey, acquistions editor; David Dexter, manuscript editor; Brett Smith, production editor; Avery Hallowell, art editor; Kim Turner, production manager; and Cathy Reynolds, designer, for their hard work and dedication to this project.

CONTENTS

HISTORICAL EXPERIENCE   221

P A R T   T H R E E
TOPICS IN INTERNATIONAL ECONOMICS   321

AN INTRODUCTION TO
INTERNATIONAL
ECONOMICS

THE IMPORTANCE

OF

INTERNATIONAL

ECONOMICS

International trade is a significant and growing part of most economies. In some sectors, imported goods dominate. For example, most radios, televisions, and videocassette recorders sold in the United States are imported. Foreign brand names have become familiar and popular. Could we survive without Sony products? (Yes, but life would not be so enjoyable.) Even when imports seem unimportant, potential foreign competition can be a major influence on the prices and output of domestic manufacturers. Consumers throughout the world are affected by changes in the prices of products such as coffee, wheat, and particularly oil.

An indication of the importance and growth of trade is given by the ratio of imports to national income, shown in Table I.1. But trade is even more important than this ratio suggests. The international sector is dynamic and its performance often has a major influence on overall economic performance. Changes in the component of GNP accounted for by net exports can be a large part of the overall change in GNP.

As Table I.2 shows, trade accounts for 12.6 percent of employment in American manufacturing. The proportion of international trade varies among states and among industries. In some states, export-related employment accounts for over 20 percent of employment in an industry. The industries accounting for the most exports in 1984 were: non-electrical machinery, transportation equipment, electric and electronic equipment, chemical products, and primary metals. These five industries accounted for 65 percent of

TABLE I.1   Imports as a Percentage of GNP

	1955	1965	1975	1985	1988
Canada	20.3	19.2	24.5	26.4	26.3
France	13.2	11.6	17.8	23.3	20.6
Germany	17.8	19.0	23.4	30.7	26.1
Italy	13.9	13.0	22.3	22.8	18.4
Japan	10.8	9.8	13.7	12.7	8.9
United Kingdom	22.9	19.2	27.1	28.5	26.9
United States	4.2	4.4	7.6	10.0	10.7

Source: IMF, *International Financial Statistics, 1988,* June 1989.

export-related sales of manufactures, and for 58 percent of export-related employment.

Trade creates jobs in the export sector, but imported goods can also lead to the collapse of domestic firms. How should we view the growth of international trade? Is it a threat or a benefit? We shall see that perhaps the most important conclusion from international economics is that international trade is beneficial. It is easy to see that individual countries have gained—the importance of international trade for the German and Japanese economies is well known, and for some newly industrialized countries, such as Hong Kong, Singapore, South Korea, and Taiwan, trade has been a vital part of their economic growth.

One of the most interesting features of international trade is that countries can gain without other countries losing. The reason is that international trade increases economic efficiency. Basically, international trade is the same as trade between individuals within a country. Few people argue that trade between New York and California should be restricted, and yet trade over much shorter distances, which happens to be across a national boundary, is often a major economic and political issue. For example, freer trade between Canada and the United States was a major issue in the 1988 Canadian election.

Another issue that leads to heated debate is the effects of international capital flows. Over the last few decades, improved communications and the removal of restrictions on capital flows have led to increased capital mobility. Although this capital mobility may have contributed to exchange rate instability, the development of a global capital market has helped increase incomes and employment by facilitating international investment. For example, an interesting recent development is the creation of employment by flows of foreign capital into the American economy. (Similar capital flows helped the development of the American economy in the nineteenth century.)

TABLE I.2   Exports and Related Employment in U.S. Manufacturing, 1986 (percentage of employment in each sector)

SIC	Industry	U.S.A.	Calif.	Texas	Ohio	Michigan	New York
20	Food and products	4.0	4.6	3.9	2.2	2.7	1.9
21	Tobacco products	14.8					
22	Textile mill products	7.9			12.3		5.3
23	Apparel and products	2.4	2.1	1.4	2.2	11.0	2.0
24	Lumber, wood products	7.4	6.0	3.5	4.5	8.3	
25	Furniture and fixtures	2.6	2.0	1.4	1.9	2.4	2.6
26	Paper and products	11.1	10.6	10.0	9.3	9.9	9.7
27	Printing and publishing	4.1	3.8	4.0	4.7	3.4	4.2
28	Chemicals and products	16.3	13.6	23.0	15.2	19.0	14.7
29	Petrol and coal products	8.4	9.1	9.2	4.0	11.1	
30	Rubber and plastics	12.6	11.7	11.8	13.3	13.5	13.5
31	Leather and products	4.5		6.8			4.0
32	Stone, clay, glass products	7.7	6.3	3.8	11.7	8.9	10.6
33	Primary metal industries	23.1	22.2	26.1	22.7	22.4	22.6
34	Fabricated metal products	13.3	12.7	13.8	15.5	18.2	12.5
35	Non-electrical machinery	20.3	27.7	23.9	16.4	14.3	23.0
36	Electric and electronic equipment	23.7	28.5	21.4	19.2	18.8	26.9
37	Transportation equipment	12.7	10.5	19.7	14.5	12.2	11.5
38	Scientific instruments and products	17.8	18.1	11.9	21.5	16.5	18.4
39	Miscellaneous manufacturing industries	6.7	7.0	3.7	4.0	4.2	5.3
	Total manufacturing	12.6	14.7	13.5	13.9	13.3	12.7
	Exports ($ billions)	294.3	31.4	21.2	20.2	18.1	17.1

Source: U.S. Department of Commerce, Bureau of the Census, "Exports from Manufacturing Establishments: 1985 and 1986," Manufacturing Analytical Report Series, AR86-1, issued January 1989.

International trade and investment are motivated by the same forces as domestic trade and investment. Why, if this is so, is international economics different from standard domestic macroeconomics and microeconomics? The answer is the world is divided into national markets with separate governments. Non-economic factors such as differences between languages and cultures have contributed to market separation, but there are also economic explanations of market separation. First, labor and capital have traditionally been much more mobile among regions within a country than among countries. Second, differences between national markets have been accentuated by restrictions on the movement of goods, labor, and capital. Third, people in different countries use different currencies, so international transactions can be affected by changes in the value of currencies.

Some questions in international economics relate to whether national markets are too closely linked or too divided: Should international trade and capital flows be restricted? Does exchange rate variability reduce welfare? Other interesting questions in international economics include: Is trade really beneficial? Can trade help developing countries grow? What are the effects of trade and capital flows on domestic economic policy? Are multinational corporations a threat to welfare? These are just a few of the many questions we shall consider.

PART ONE

PRINCIPLES
OF
INTERNATIONAL
ECONOMICS

1

THE CAUSES AND EFFECTS OF INTERNATIONAL TRADE

INTRODUCTION 1.1

A reasonable starting point for the study of international economics is to ask: Why do countries trade? The question can be answered quite simply: Countries trade because the prices of goods and services vary across countries, and foreign goods and services are often less expensive than domestic goods and services. However, this does not tell us much about the effects of trade, or why some goods and services cost less in one country than another. These are the two basic economic questions we shall be concerned with in this and the following two chapters. Although the discussion focuses on trade in goods (merchandise trade), the present analysis could be extended to cover trade in services as well.

THE GAIN FROM TRADE 1.2

If countries trade voluntarily, we might presume that they gain from trade. This presumption is correct.

The gains from trade can be shown by considering the relationship between consumption and work. It might be possible for one person to produce everything he or she needs, but it is unlikely. And even if such economic independence were possible, it would probably not be appealing to most people because they would be forced to live poorly with a narrow range of goods.

Individuals in modern economies do not try to produce exactly what they consume. Normally, people work in return for money, which in turn is used for consumption purposes. Although a person usually only helps in the production or distribution of a few goods, the range of products available for consumption is much wider; people specialize in the production of certain items, and obtain other goods through trade. Trade is necessary if the full benefits of *specialization* are to be enjoyed. Even towns or regions are not completely self-sufficient; it might be technically feasible in some climates, but the people would be worse off because both the variety and total quantity of goods would be reduced if trade were prevented.

People gain by trading with one another. Hence, it is not surprising that trade takes place naturally without any deliberate action needed to encourage it. Trade also takes place naturally between countries—we would not expect the gains from trade to stop at national boundaries. The effects of trade between countries are analogous to the effects of trade between individuals: specialization increases the overall quantity of goods and trade allows countries to consume a greater quantity and variety of goods than they could without trade.

1.3 ABSOLUTE ADVANTAGE

In this section we introduce the concept of *absolute advantage.* This is used to show how a country gains through specialization when resources are moved from one sector to another and the country takes part in trade. Although the concept of absolute advantage is an imperfect explanation of the reason for trade, it is useful as a background to the concept of comparative advantage, which is examined in the next section.

Adam Smith's View

The gain from trade and specialization was recognized by Adam Smith in his book *An Inquiry into the Nature and Causes of the Wealth of Nations,* first published in 1776.[1] His argument was as follows:

> It is the maxim of every prudent master of a family, never to make at home what it will cost him more to make than to buy. The taylor does not attempt to make his own shoes, but buys them of the shoemaker. The shoemaker does not attempt to make his own cloaths, but employs a taylor. The farmer attempts to make neither one nor the other, but employs those different artificers. All of

---

[1] Smith's book was an attack on mercantilist views, which were the basis for British economic policy of the time. Mercantilists argued that imports should be restricted so that gold would be received from foreign countries in payment for the excess of exports over imports. Increasing the stock of gold was seen as a way to increase the wealth and power of a country.

them find it for their interest to employ their whole industry in a way in which they have some advantage over their neighbours, and to purchase with a part of its produce . . . whatever else they have occassion for.

What is prudence in the conduct of every private family can scarce be folly in that of a great kingdom. If a foreign country can supply us with a commodity cheaper than we ourselves can make it, better buy it of them with some part of the produce of our own industry, employed in a way in which we have some advantage. . . .

The natural advantages which one country has over another in producing particular commodities are sometimes so great, that it is acknowledged by all the world to be in vain to struggle against them. By means of glasses, hotbeds, and hotwalls, very good grapes can be raised in Scotland, and very good wine too, can be made of them at about thirty times the expense for which at least equally good wine can be brought from foreign countries. Would it be a reasonable law to prohibit the importation of all foreign wines merely to encourage the making of wine in Scotland? But if there be a manifest absurdity in turning towards any employment thirty times more of the capital and industry of the country than would be necessary to purchase from foreign countries an equal quantity of the commodities wanted, there must be an absurdity, though altogether not so glaring, yet exactly of the same kind, in turning towards any such employment a thirtieth, or even a three hundredth part more of either. Whether the advantages which one country has over another be natural or acquired, is in this respect of no consequence.[2]

Adam Smith's view was based on the concept of absolute advantage. A country is said to have an absolute advantage in the production of a commodity if it uses fewer resources than another country to produce the commodity. In a simple economy where labor is the only factor of production, the cost of production is determined by the amount of labor used. In such a simple world, if one country uses less labor than other countries to make a good, that country is said to have an absolute advantage in making the good.

Absolute advantage is illustrated in Table 1.1. The United States has an absolute advantage in wheat because to produce a ton of wheat fewer hours are needed in the U.S. than in the EEC. By similar reasoning, the EEC has

TABLE 1.1   Number of Hours per Unit of Output

	Wheat	*Cars*
EEC	400	200
U.S.	200	300

[2] Smith, Adam, *An Inquiry into the Nature and Causes of the Wealth of Nations,* Modern Library College Editions, Random House, 1985, pp. 226–28.

an absolute advantage in cars in this example. What happens when trade takes place?

Introducing Trade

Let us assume that 1 car can be exchanged for 1 ton of wheat through international trade. If the U.S. gives up the production of 1 car, 300 fewer hours are neeed for car production, and 1½ more tons of wheat can be produced instead. If the U.S. exports 1 ton of wheat and imports 1 car, it replaces the car that was given up, and still has ½ ton of wheat left. Similarly, if the EEC gives up 1 ton of wheat, 400 fewer hours are needed for wheat production, and 2 extra cars can be produced. By exporting 1 car and importing 1 ton of wheat the EEC can replace the lost wheat and still have 1 car left. In this example, each country gains by exporting the good in which it has an absolute advantage, and importing the other good.

Provided that we believe every country is the most efficient producer of some good, we seem to have a plausible explanation of trade. Production costs differ because of differences in labor requirements among goods, and people trade in order to obtain goods at lower cost. In the example used above, more labor is required to produce cars in the U.S. than in the EEC, so the U.S. imports cars from the more efficient producer. The EEC imports wheat because more labor is required there to produce wheat than in the U.S.

Although this explanation is plausible, it is too limited. It is true that countries can gain from trade by exporting goods in which they have an absolute advantage, but a country does not need to have an absolute advantage in producing a good in order to be able to export it. This is shown in the following section.

1.4 OPPORTUNITY COST AND COMPARATIVE ADVANTAGE

The *opportunity cost* of producing 1 unit of a good is the amount of the other good (in our two-good model) that could have been produced using the same resources. For example, using the data shown in Table 1.1, because it takes 400 hours to produce a ton of wheat in the EEC and only 200 hours to produce a car, the opportunity cost of producing a ton of wheat is 2 cars. The opportunity costs of domestic production derived from the data in Table 1.1 are shown in Table 1.2.

Opportunity Cost and the Incentive to Trade

Countries gain from trade because the opportunity cost of imported goods is less than the opportunity cost of domestic goods. If world prices allow the exchange of 1 car for 1 ton of wheat, the U.S. imports cars because it only gives up 1 ton of wheat for an imported car whereas the opportunity cost of a domestically produced car is 1½ tons of wheat (see Table 1.2). The EEC

TABLE 1.2   Domestic Opportunity Costs

	Wheat	Cars
EEC	2 cars	1/2 ton of wheat
U.S.	2/3 car	1½ tons of wheat

imports wheat because the opportunity cost of a ton of imported wheat (1 car) is less than the opportunity cost of producing a ton of wheat (2 cars).

In the example above, each country has an absolute advantage in one of the goods. What happens if one country has an absolute advantage in both goods? Is mutually beneficial trade possible?

Table 1.3 shows an example in which the U.S. has an absolute advantage in both wheat and car production. Let us continue to assume that it is possible to exchange 1 ton of wheat for 1 car through international trade. Even though the labor requirements for U.S. production in Table 1.3 are half of what they are in Table 1.1, the cost of cars in terms of wheat is exactly the same as before: the U.S. gives up 1½ tons of wheat for each car it produces and the opportunity cost of an imported car is 1 ton of wheat. Therefore, the incentive for the U.S. to trade is the same: the opportunity cost of an imported car is less than the opportunity cost of a domestically produced car. The fact that the EEC uses more labor to produce a car is irrelevant—in other words, absolute advantage is irrelevant.

The labor requirements for the EEC are the same in Table 1.3 as in Table 1.1, and the incentive for the EEC to trade is the same: the opportunity cost of imported wheat (1 car per ton) is less than the opportunity cost of domestically produced wheat (2 cars per ton). Therefore, both countries gain from trade.[3]

TABLE 1.3   Number of Hours per Unit of Output

	Wheat	Cars
EEC	400	200
U.S.	100	150

[3] We have shown that countries benefit from international trade because the opportunity cost of imported goods is less than the opportunity cost of domestic goods. In view of this, it is not surprising that countries that have pursued liberal trade policies have usually grown faster than countries that have attempted to increase self-sufficiency by restricting imports. We examine the relationship between trade and economic growth in Chapter 18.

Comparative Advantage

The concept of opportunity cost is the basis for the concept of *comparative advantage*. A country is said to have a comparative advantage in a good if its opportunity cost of producing the good is lower than that of other countries. It has a comparative disadvantage in a good if its opportunity cost of production is higher than that of other countries. Thus, a country will export the good in which it has a comparative advantage, and import the good in which it has a comparative disadvantage.

In the preceding example, the EEC has a comparative advantage in car production, and the U.S. has a comparative disadvantage, because the EEC's opportunity cost of producing cars (½ ton of wheat) is less than that of the U.S. (1½ tons of wheat). Similarly, the U.S. has a comparative advantage in wheat production, and the EEC has a comparative disadvantage, because the opportunity cost of producing wheat in the U.S. (⅔ car) is less than the opportunity cost of producing wheat in the EEC (2 cars).

Both countries can gain from trade, because when they specialize in goods in which they have a comparative advantage world output increases. As before, assume that the U.S. produces more wheat and fewer cars, and that the EEC produces more cars and less wheat. The changes in output resulting from specialization are shown in Table 1.4. It is clear that world output increases. How the extra output is distributed between the countries depends on world prices, because these determine the rate at which cars and wheat are exchanged (the terms of trade). The determination of the terms of trade is discussed in Section 1.5.

A Diagrammatic Approach

The gains from trade can be shown diagrammatically by using a *production possibility frontier (PPF)*. This shows how much of two goods a country can produce using the limited resources it has available. Assume that the EEC has 2,000 hours of labor that can be used to produce wheat or cars, and that the labor requirements are as shown in Table 1.3. If all the labor is used in wheat production and no cars are produced, 5 tons of wheat can be produced. If all the labor is used to produce cars, 10 cars can be produced. A combination of the two goods may be produced, but for every ton of wheat

TABLE 1.4   The Change in Output Resulting from Specialization

	Wheat	Cars
EEC	−1	+2
U.S.	+1.5	−1
World	+0.5	+1

produced the EEC gives up 2 cars. The production possibility frontier in Figure 1.1 shows the combinations of wheat and cars that can be produced by the EEC using all the labor available.

Since the slope of a line is the vertical movement accompanying a horizontal movement of 1 unit, we see that the slope of a production possibility frontier is the amount of the good represented on the vertical axis (cars) that is lost when 1 extra unit of the good represented on the horizontal axis (wheat) is produced. Therefore, the slope of the EEC's production possibility frontier is the opportunity cost of producing wheat. The opportunity cost of imported wheat is shown by the slope of the *trade line (TT)*: for every ton of imported wheat, the EEC must export 1 car (we assume that 1 car is worth 1 ton of wheat at world prices).

In the absence of trade the EEC can only consume what it produces, so consumption must take place on or below the production possibility frontier. However, if the EEC trades with the U.S., it is possible for it to consume more of one or both goods. For example, if the EEC specializes in car pro-

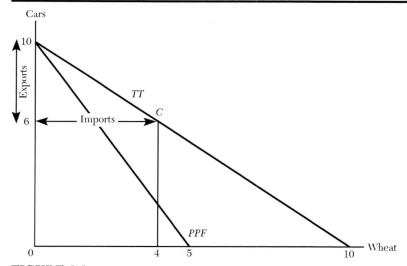

FIGURE 1.1

The EEC's Gains from Trade

The EEC has 2,000 hours of labor available. This labor can be used to produce 10 cars or 5 tons of wheat, or any combination of cars and wheat shown by the production possibility frontier *(PPF)*. For each ton of wheat produced the EEC gives up 2 cars. In the absence of trade, the EEC can only consume on or below the production possibility frontier. If it specializes in car production, the EEC can consume at points along the trade line *(TT)* trading cars for wheat at the rate of 1:1. For example, consumption may take place at point *C* if the EEC produces 10 cars and exports 4 cars in return for 4 tons of wheat.

duction and trades 4 cars for 4 tons of wheat, it will be possible for it to have 6 cars and 4 tons of wheat. This would not have been possible without trade.

The EEC can consume anywhere along the trade line by producing cars and trading cars for wheat. The trade line passes through the point on the axis showing the EEC's production after specialization. For every point on the production possibility frontier, except the intercept with the vertical axis, there is a point on the trade line that represents more of both goods. Therefore, the EEC must be better off if it can consume along the trade line instead of being restricted to points along its production possibility frontier. The EEC gains from trade because the opportunity cost of imported wheat (the slope of the trade line) is less than the opportunity cost of domestic wheat (the slope of the production possibility frontier). If the opportunity costs were the same, there would be no gain from trade.

Figure 1.2 shows the production possibility frontier for the U.S. based on the data shown in Table 1.3 and using the assumption that 3,000 hours of labor are available. By producing wheat and trading wheat for cars, the U.S. is able to consume along the trade line and is clearly better off. The slope of the production possibility frontier shows the cost of wheat in terms of cars.

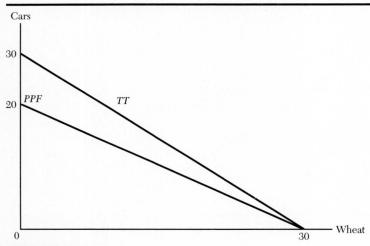

FIGURE 1.2

The U.S.'s Gains from Trade

The U.S. has 3,000 hours of labor available. This labor can be used to produce 30 tons of wheat, or 20 cars, or any combination of cars and wheat shown by the production possibility frontier *(PPF)*. For each car produced the U.S. gives up 1½ tons of wheat. In the absence of trade the U.S. can only consume on or below the production possibility frontier. If it specializes in wheat production, the U.S. can consume along the trade line trading wheat for cars at the rate of 1:1.

TABLE 1.5 **Number of Hours per Unit of Output**

	Wine	Cloth
Portugal	80	90
England	120	100

The reciprocal of the slope shows the cost of cars in terms of wheat: the opportunity cost of cars. The U.S. gains from trade because the opportunity cost of imported cars (the reciprocal of the slope of the trade line) is less than the opportunity cost of domestic cars (the reciprocal of the slope of the production possibility frontier).

Ricardo's Example of Comparative Advantage

David Ricardo, in "On the Principles of Political Economy and Taxation," first published in 1817, was the first person to recognize the importance of comparative advantage, and the irrelevance of absolute advantage. His example is worth considering to strengthen the understanding gained from the preceding discussion. Using Portugal and England as examples, Ricardo assumed that Portugal could produce wine and cloth using less labor than England; thus Portugal had an absolute advantage in producing both goods. His example is shown in Table 1.5.

In order to determine the pattern of trade we must calculate the opportunity costs of production. The data are shown in Table 1.6. Portugal has a comparative advantage in wine production, and England has a comparative advantage in cloth production. Assume that 1 unit of wine can be exchanged for 1 unit of cloth through trade. If Portugal imports 1 unit of cloth it costs 1 unit of wine, but it would have cost $9/8$ units of wine to produce a unit of cloth in Portugal, so Portugal gains from trade. Similarly, the opportunity cost of producing wine in England is $12/10$ units of cloth, imported cloth costs 1 unit of wine, so England gains by importing wine. Even though Portugal has an absolute advantage in both wine and cloth, trade is beneficial for both countries.

TABLE 1.6 **Domestic Opportunity Costs**

	Wine	Cloth
Portugal	8/9 units of cloth	9/8 units of wine
England	12/10 units of cloth	10/12 units of wine

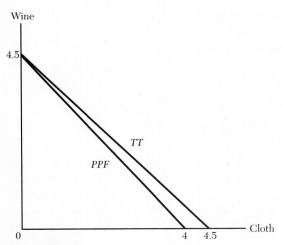

FIGURE 1.3

Portugal's Gains from Trade

Portugal has 360 hours of labor available. This labor can be used to produce 4.5 units of wine, or 4 units of cloth. In the absence of trade Portugal can only consume on or below the production possibility frontier *(PPF)*. If it specializes in wine production, Portugal can consume along the trade line *(TT)* trading wine for cloth at the rate of 1:1.

The gains from trade can be shown diagrammatically as before. Assume that Portugal has 360 hours of labor available, and England has 600 hours available. Portugal's production possibility frontier is shown in Figure 1.3. If Portugal specializes in wine production, it can trade wine for cloth, and consume along the trade line rather than the production possibility frontier below it. Similarly, specialization in cloth production and participation in trade permit England to consume along the trade line shown in Figure 1.4.

Absolute and Comparative Advantage

Obviously, some countries cannot produce goods as efficiently as other countries, and yet they still take part in international trade. Therefore, absolute advantage, which rests on the implicit assumption that all trading countries are world leaders in the production of their exported goods, is a less accurate explanation of trade than comparative advantage. Also, in the theory of absolute advantage, the cost of a good is incorrectly related to the amount of inputs (e.g., number of hours) used to make the good. When a country imports a good, consumers do not ask what the inputs required to make the good were; they do not care whether the process used was efficient or not. The relevant question for consumers is: What is the price of the good?

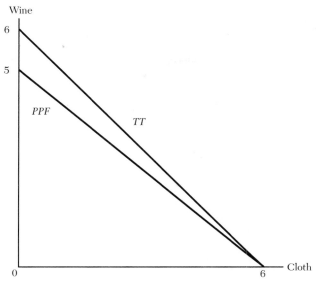

FIGURE 1.4

England's Gains from Trade
England has 600 hours of labor available. This labor can be used to produce 5 units of wine or 6 units of cloth. In the absence of trade England can only consume on or below the production possibility frontier *(PPF)*. If it specializes in cloth production, England can consume at points along the trade line *(TT)* trading cloth for wine at the rate of 1:1.

DOMESTIC PRICES, WORLD PRICES, AND THE DIRECTION OF TRADE   1.5

In a barter model the price of one good is the amount of the other good that must be given up, therefore the price of a good is its opportunity cost. We have seen that trade can be explained by the difference between the opportunity cost of imported and domestic goods. Allowing for the fact that people use money instead of engaging in barter does not change the basic analysis. The relative dollar prices of goods are indicators of their opportunity costs. To be precise, the opportunity cost of X in terms of Y is the ratio of the price of X to the price of Y (P_X/P_Y). For example, if radios cost \$80 and tickets to see the Boston Celtics cost \$20, the opportunity cost of a radio is 4 tickets. Let us examine the explanation of trade in terms of relative prices.

Pre-Trade Prices and Relative Cost

In the model we have used so far, there is competition, labor is the only input, and the input requirements are fixed. In such a model, the domestic price ratio before trade takes place (the *pre-trade price ratio*) will be determined by and equal to the relative cost of production. For example, if it takes twice as much labor to produce cloth as it does to produce wheat, the price of cloth will be twice that of wheat, that is, the price ratio will equal 2.

To understand why, consider an example in which the price ratio is not equal to the relative cost. If the relative cost of producing cloth is 2 units of wheat, and the price ratio is 1, producers find it profitable to switch from cloth production to wheat production (cloth costs twice as much to produce as wheat, but they sell for the same amount). The decrease in the supply of cloth, and the increase in the supply of wheat, cause the price of cloth to rise relative to the price of wheat, thus the price ratio rises. Similarly, if the price ratio is 3, it is profitable to switch from wheat to cloth production, and the price ratio falls. Adjustment continues until the price ratio equals the relative cost of production. [4]

Price Differences and Trade

Returning to the discussion of Table 1.1, we saw that the U.S. gains because the opportunity cost of an imported car (1 ton of wheat) is less than the opportunity cost of a domestic car (1½ tons of wheat). The domestic opportunity cost of cars equals the ratio of the domestic pre-trade price of cars to the domestic pre-trade price of wheat. The opportunity cost of imported cars is shown by the ratio of the world price of cars to the world price of wheat. Therefore, the conclusion could be reworded as follows: The U.S. gains from trade because the *world price ratio* differs from the domestic pre-trade price ratio.

Diagrammatically, the difference between the pre-trade price ratio and the world price ratio is shown by the difference between the slopes of the production possibility frontier and the trade line. Recall that the slope of a production possibility frontier equals the opportunity cost of the good represented on the horizontal axis (X) expressed in terms of the good represented on the vertical axis (Y). Because the opportunity cost equals the pre-trade price ratio, the slope of the production possibility frontier is also equal to the pre-trade price ratio (P_X/P_Y). The steeper the production possibility frontier, the higher the pre-trade price ratio.

We can describe price ratios in terms of the good on the vertical axis or the good on the horizontal axis. The reciprocal of the slope is the cost of the good represented on the vertical axis expressed in terms of the good on the

---

[4]There is no role for demand in the determination of the price ratio because the relative cost is constant. In the next chapter we examine a model in which there are increasing costs and the price ratio is determined by the interaction of supply and demand.

horizontal $(P_Y/P_X = 1/(P_X/P_Y))$. As the ratio P_X/P_Y rises, the ratio P_Y/P_X falls; in other words, as X becomes more expensive relative to Y, Y becomes less expensive relative to X.

As an example, consider the lines in Figure 1.4. The slope of the production possibility frontier is ⅚ and the slope of the trade line is 1. The pre-trade price of wine in terms of cloth is greater than the world price of wine, whereas the pre-trade price of cloth in terms of wine is less than the world price of cloth.

Price Differences and the Gain from Trade

If the world price ratio differs from the pre-trade price ratio, the slope of the trade line differs from the slope of the production possibility curve. A country is able to gain by specializing (producing at one of the intercepts of the production possibility frontier) and then consuming at a point along the trade line. The greater the divergence between the pre-trade price ratio and the world price ratio, the greater the gain from trade. This is shown in Figure 1.5. As the world price ratio rises, the slope of the trade line increases, and

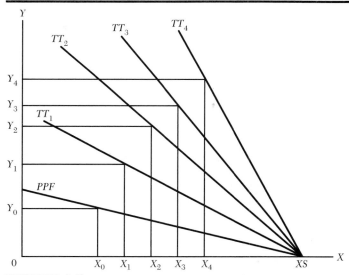

FIGURE 1.5

The Gains from Trade and World Prices

As the world price ratio (P_X/P_Y) increases, the slope of the trade line (TT) increases. The gains from trade increase as the difference between the pre-trade domestic price ratio (shown by the slope of PPF) and the world price ratio increases. The gains from trade are shown by the increase in the quantity available of both goods. At pre-trade prices the country might produce and consume the combination of goods X_0Y_0. At world price ratios shown by the slopes of TT_1, TT_2, TT_3, and TT_4, the country produces XS and could consume X_1Y_1, X_2Y_2, X_3Y_3, and X_4Y_4, respectively.

the quantities of X and Y that can be consumed increase. For example, if the trade line shifts from TT_1 to TT_4, the quantities of X and Y consumed could increase from X_1Y_1 to X_4Y_4. Because our model does not include demand, we cannot say what the quantities consumed actually are. However, we have shown that the country could consume more of both goods, and this is sufficient for us to see that there is a gain from trade. If the world price ratio is the same as the domestic price ratio, engaging in trade will not make a country better off because the trade line and the production possibility frontier coincide.

World Prices and the Direction of Trade

Using the data shown in Table 1.5 and Table 1.6, it is useful to consider what would happen if, at world prices, 2 units of wine were worth 1 unit of cloth. Cloth would be more expensive on world markets than in either country, and thus producers in both countries would find it profitable to export cloth. Similarly, wine would be cheaper on world markets than in either country, and both would import wine. In a two-country model this clearly would not be possible: Where would the imports come from and the exports go?

If world prices are such that both countries try to supply cloth, there will be an excess supply of cloth, and the price of cloth (in terms of wine) will fall. The price will continue falling until the excess supply is removed. This will happen when the world price of cloth falls below the domestic price of cloth in one of the countries; that country then stops exporting cloth and exports wine instead. Similarly, consider what happens if both countries want to import wine. The price of wine (in terms of cloth) will rise, and one country will begin to export wine rather than import it. Thus, the world price will change so that the two countries will want to export and import different goods.

This analysis suggests that, in a two-country model, the world price ratio must lie between the two domestic pre-trade price ratios. In Table 1.7 we have extended the example above by showing three world price ratios—A, B, and C. At world price ratio A, both countries will want to export cloth and import wine, and the price of cloth will tend to fall relative to the price of

TABLE 1.7   World Price Ratios

	Price of Wine in Units of Cloth	Price of Cloth in Units of Wine
World price ratio A	1/2	2/1
Portugal	8/9	9/8
World price ratio B	1/1	1/1
England	12/10	10/12
World price ratio C	2/1	1/2

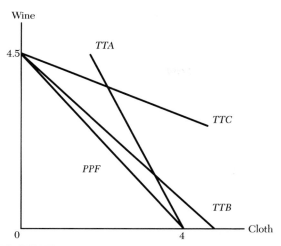

FIGURE 1.6

The Effect of Changing World Prices on Portugal's Production and Trade
The production possibility frontier *(PPF)* is the same as in Figure 1.3. The slopes of
the trade lines *TTA*, *TTB*, and *TTC* show the world price ratios *A*, *B*, and *C*, respectively, from Table 1.7. At world price *A*, Portugal produces 4 units of cloth, exports
cloth, and imports wine. At world prices *B* and *C*, Portugal produces 4.5 units of wine,
exports wine, and imports cloth.

wine. At world price ratio *C*, both countries will want to export wine and
import cloth, and the price of cloth will tend to rise relative to the price of
wine. At world price ratio *B*, Portugal will export wine and import cloth,
whereas England will export cloth and import wine.

The production possibility frontiers of Portugal and England are shown in
Figures 1.6 and 1.7, respectively. The pattern of trade described in the previous paragraph can be derived by comparing the slopes of the production
possibility frontiers of Portugal and England with the slopes of the trade lines.
If the trade line is steeper than the production possibility frontier, the world
price of cloth in terms of wine is higher, and the world price of wine in terms
of cloth is lower than the pre-trade price. In this case the country will export
cloth, for example, as Portugal does when facing world price ratio *A*. If the
trade line is flatter than the production possibility frontier, the world relative
price of cloth is lower and the world relative price of wine is higher than the
pre-trade price. In this case the country will export wine, for example, as
Portugal does when facing world price ratios *B* or *C*.

The Determination of the Terms of Trade

The world price ratio is called the *terms of trade*. The *equilibrium terms
of trade* are those at which the quantities of goods that countries would like
to trade are equal. If the actual terms of trade differ from the equilibrium

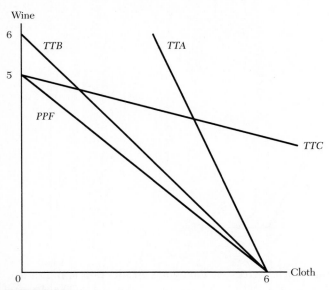

FIGURE 1.7

The Effect of Changing World Prices on England's Production and Trade
The production possibility frontier *(PPF)* is the same as in Figure 1.4. The trade lines
TTA, *TTB*, and *TTC* have the same slopes as the trade lines in Figure 1.6, and show
the world price ratios *A*, *B*, and *C*, respectively, from Table 1.6. At world prices *A*
and *B*, England produces 6 units of cloth, exports cloth, and imports wine. At world
price *C*, England produces 5 units of wine, exports wine, and imports cloth.

terms of trade, excess demand or excess supply will force the terms of trade
to change. Although it is clear that in a two-country model the equilibrium
terms of trade must lie between the two pre-trade price ratios, we cannot say
exactly what the equilibrium will be. To predict the terms of trade requires a
model including both demand and supply, because the amount of a good that
a country exports or imports is the difference between domestic demand and
supply. The model used so far only includes supply.

Offer Curves[5]

If we assume that we know how much a country produces and consumes
at different price ratios, we can use *offer curves* to show how the terms of
trade are determined by the demand and supply of traded goods. An offer
curve shows the relationship between the terms of trade and the quantities of

---

[5]The following intuitive introduction to offer curves is sufficient to illustrate how demand and
supply determine the terms of trade. A more rigorous analysis is presented in the next chapter.

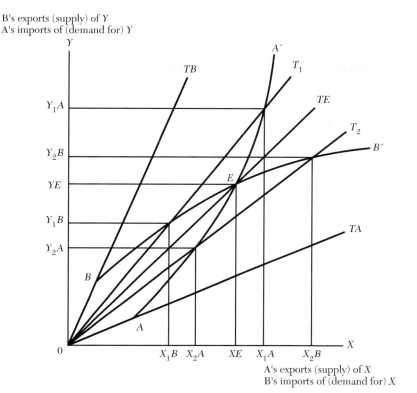

FIGURE 1.8

The Determination of the Terms of Trade

The quantities traded by countries A and B at different terms of trade are shown by the offer curves $0AA'$ and $0BB'$. At the point of intersection (E) the supply and demand of X and Y are equal. The slope of the line $0TE$, passing through E, shows the equilibrium terms of trade.

exports supplied and imports demanded. In Figure 1.8, country A's supply of exports is shown on the horizontal axis, and A's demand for imports is shown on the vertical axis. The terms of trade are shown by the slope of a line from the origin to a point showing the quantitites traded. For example, at point E country A exports XE in exhange for YE, thus the world price of X in terms of Y is YE/XE, the slope of $0TE$.

    The terms of trade line $0TA$ represents the terms of trade that equal country A's pre-trade price ratio. Country A is willing to trade if the terms of trade differ from this ratio, point A showing the quantities that A trades if the difference is infinitesimal. (For convenience, point A is drawn on $0TA$.) As the relative price of X increases, and the terms of trade line becomes steeper, country A is willing to supply more exports of X in exchange for imports of Y. For example, the amount that A is willing to trade on $0T_1$ $(X_1A$ for $Y_1A)$ is greater than on $0TE$ $(XE$ for $YE)$. The curve $0AA'$ is A's offer curve.

B's offer curve can be added to the diagram. Notice that A's exports are B's imports, and A's imports are B's exports. B's pre-trade price ratio is $0TB$, and point B represents B's trade when the terms of trade differ infinitesimally from B's pre-trade price ratio. As the price of X in terms of Y decreases, the price of Y in terms of X increases, the terms of trade line becomes flatter, and country B exports more Y in exchange for X. B's offer curve is $0BB'$.

The Equilibrium Terms of Trade

The quantities that the countries want to trade are equal when the terms of trade line is $0TE$. If the terms of trade line is above $0TE$, for example $0T_1$, A's supply of X (X_1A) exceeds B's demand (X_1B), and A's demand for Y (Y_1A) is greater than B's supply of Y (Y_1B). Thus, the price of X in terms of Y falls. If the terms of trade line is below $0TE$, for example $0T_2$, B's demand for X (X_2B) exceeds A's supply of X (X_2A), A's demand for Y (Y_2A) is less than B's supply (Y_2B), and the relative price of X rises.

Offer curves show how the terms of trade adjust to equate the demand and supply of traded goods for two countries. Obviously in the real world there are many countries, and two or more countries may export the same good if a third country is the buyer. However, the major conclusion remains relevant: countries export goods in which they have a comparative advantage (their opportunity cost is lower than that implied by the terms of trade). When an excess supply or excess demand exists, the terms of trade change to equate demand and supply.

Domestic Prices and Trade

The discussion above shows that a good is exported when the world price is higher than the country's pre-trade price, and imported when the world price is lower than the country's pre-trade price. However, when trade takes place, domestic prices change. Because exporters can sell their output at world prices, domestic consumers of exported goods must pay world prices. As the world prices of exported goods exceed their pre-trade prices, the introduction of trade causes the domestic prices of exports to rise above their pre-trade prices. Similarly, the availability of imports at world prices below pre-trade prices forces the domestic prices of imports below their pre-trade prices. In this way prices in different countries are equalized by trade, because they all adjust towards world prices.

We have seen that trade results from differences in opportunity costs, which are shown by differences in pre-trade prices. We would not expect post-trade prices to differ much because of the tendency for prices to be equalized through trade. In reality, prices in different countries are not exactly equal because of various barriers. For example, transport costs and trade restrictions prevent the free movement of goods and thus break the unity of the market.[6]

MAKING THE MODEL MORE REALISTIC   1.6

The Overall Gain from Trade

The preceding section showed that there is a gain from trade because the total quantity of goods available expands as a result of a more efficient allocation of resources. Not everybody gains equally though, unless a policy of income redistribution is carried out. Consider what happens when imports suddenly become available, which is not unrealistic for it is essentially what happens when an import ban is removed or a very high tariff on imports is reduced. Producers in the import-competing sector now face competition from imports. Perhaps some will go bankrupt because they cannot compete, perhaps others will experience lower profits and be forced to pay lower wages. Other sectors of the economy may also suffer because workers in the import-competing sector are customers of firms in those other sectors.

The unemployment and loss of income resulting from an increase in trade will not normally last forever; labor will move into other activities. The faster labor moves, the less significant the adverse effects of imports will be. Economists differ in their judgment of how fast the adjustment process will be, hence there is disagreement about the size and duration of the costs to society resulting from an increase in imports. The analysis of absolute advantage and comparative advantage ignores these costs of adjustment. Whereas we would normally expect a gain from trade in the long term, in the short term, when increases in imports cause job losses and lower profits in some sectors, the overall gain from trade may not be perceived by the people involved.

Specialization

The Ricardian model's prediction that countries will specialize completely is not realistic. The reason the model leads to this prediction is that the opportunity costs of the goods remain constant (because the labor inputs remain constant). If it is worth transferring 1 unit of labor from X production to Y production, it is worth transferring all the labor. Although the Ricardian model's prediction of the extent of specialization is unrealistic, the prediction that countries will become more specialized when trade takes place is realistic. In Chapter 2 we will see that if we assume that the costs of production increase with increased output (increasing costs), complete specialization does not necessarily result.

---

[6]See the discussion of purchasing power parity in Chapter 6.

The Determination of Opportunity Cost

The theory of comparative advantage should not be criticized because of its simplistic approach to the determination of production costs, namely, that labor is the only input and cost is solely determined by the amount of labor used. The labor requirements are used merely to show the relative production costs and relative prices so that opportunity costs can be determined. In the real world there are many different inputs, and we would expect these to influence product prices. For example, a major influence on the prices of some goods is the price of energy. The fact that many inputs are used does not change the basic analysis though: a country's comparative advantage is determined by how much of one good is given up for another. We do not need to use inputs to derive the relative value of goods if we know market prices.

Normally, we would expect the market price of a good to be influenced by both demand and supply. In the simple model presented in this chapter, supply conditions determine the pre-trade price ratio, and if demand were included it would determine the pre-trade quantities sold.[7] In the next chapter a more complete model is presented in which the pre-trade price ratio and the quantities produced and consumed are determined by the interaction of supply and demand.

Exchange Rates

In the domestic market, the use of a single currency leads to the unification of markets: prices in New York, Washington, Chicago, and so on, are comparable because they are all expressed in dollars. The prices of foreign goods can be compared with the prices of domestic goods by using exchange rates to convert prices expressed in foreign currencies into domestic currency. The price of a foreign good changes in domestic currency if the exchange rate changes. Therefore, exchange rate changes can affect a country's comparative advantage. In Chapter 6 this issue is examined in detail, but it can already be seen that the exchange rate is potentially of great significance to domestic producers and consumers.

Summary of Main Points

People do not usually attempt to achieve full self-sufficiency because they are able to consume a greater quantity and variety of goods by trading with other people. Similarly, countries gain from international trade because specialization increases the overall quantity of goods and trade allows countries to consume more goods and a greater variety of goods than they could consume without trade.

Adam Smith used the concept of *absolute advantage* to explain interna-

---

[7] Section 2.2 shows how demand determines the pre-trade quantities in a model where cost is constant.

tional trade. A country has an absolute advantage in a good if it uses fewer resources to produce the good than other countries. Although this explanation is still commonly used, it is flawed because absolute advantage is neither necessary nor sufficient for a country to export a product.

Ricardo provided the basis for the modern explanation of international trade by explaining trade using the concept of *comparative advantage*. A country has a comparative advantage in producing a good if the opportunity cost of producing the good is lower than in other countries.

The *opportunity cost* of producing a good is the quantity of the other good(s) that could have been produced with the same resources. In the Ricardian model, labor inputs are used to calculate the opportunity cost of a good. Market prices can also be used to derive opportunity costs because relative prices show how much one good is worth relative to other goods.

The opportunity cost of domestic production is shown by the *pre-trade price ratio*. The opportunity cost of goods on world markets is shown by the *world price ratio*. Countries gain from international trade if the opportunity cost of domestically produced goods differs from the opportunity cost of goods on world markets, that is, if the pre-trade price ratio differs from the world price ratio.

The gains from trade can be shown diagrammatically. The pre-trade price ratio is shown by the slope of the *production possibility frontier*. The world price ratio is shown by the slope of the *trade line*. Countries gain from trade if the slope of the production possibility frontier differs from the slope of the trade line.

The price of exports relative to the price of imports is called the *terms of trade*, which are determined by international demand and supply. The *equilibrium terms of trade* are where the demand and supply of traded goods are equal. If demand and supply are not equal, the terms of trade will change.

Study Questions

1. It takes 20 hours to produce X domestically, and 30 hours to produce Y. Calculate the opportunity cost of X in terms of Y. If X is available for $\frac{1}{2}Y$ on world markets, what is the saving (in terms of Y) from importing 1 unit of X?

2. Alex is a lawyer and owns a house that needs painting. Alex can paint twice as fast as a professional painter and does the same quality of work. The hourly earnings of lawyers are three times the earnings of painters. Should Alex paint the house or have a professional painter do it?

3. a. In the table, which country has an absolute advantage in bicycles? Which country has an absolute advantage in cars? Which country has a comparative advantage in bicycles and which in cars?
   b. If trade takes place at 6 cars per 100 bicycles, which countries export which commodities?

	Number of Hours Per Unit	
	Bicycles	Cars
Holland	50	1,000
England	100	1,500

    c. How much does each country gain if 100 bicycles are exported in exchange for 6 cars? (Express the gain to the car exporter in bicycles, and the gain to the bicycle exporter in cars.)

    d. Explain how the gains from specialization are shown in your answer to this question.

4. The table below shows the number of hours of labor needed to produce goods X and Y in countries A and B.

	Number of Hours Per Unit of Output	
	X	Y
A	5	4
B	2	3

    a. Assuming that labor is paid an hourly wage equal to the amount labor produces in an hour, compare wages in A and B expressed first in X per hour and then in Y per hour.

    b. If the terms of trade (P_X/P_Y) equals 1, which goods do the countries export?

    c. Assuming trade takes place, calculate the amount of imports that can be obtained from 1 hour's work. (Hint: use the terms of trade to convert the amount of exports per hour into the amount of imports per hour.) Compare this figure with the quantity of the imported good that could be produced domestically in 1 hour, and comment on how this illustrates a gain from trade.

5. A country has a total of 500 hours of labor, which it uses to produce 100 watches and 100 shirts: it takes 2 hours to produce a shirt and 3 hours to produce a watch. Shirts are worth $4 at world prices, and watches are worth $8. The country has been producing this combination of watches and shirts for some time, and the resources used in one industry cannot be used in the other industry. Does this mean that the country should not trade? If there is a gain from trade, why does it occur? Show the importance of the assumption of factor mobility (that labor can move freely from one sector to another) by considering how the gains from trade change as increased factor mobility allows the country to specialize. (Draw the production possibility frontier and show the consumption possibilities using appropriate trade lines.)

6. a. Why do countries trade?
   b. What are the effects of trade on
      1) consumers?
      2) domestic producers of import substitutes?
      3) producers of exports?

7. Critically evaluate the argument that small countries cannot gain by trading with the United States because the U.S. is large and has a technological advantage.

8. The labor inputs for the United States and the rest of the world (ROW) are shown in the table below. Critically evaluate the argument that the ROW is exploited if it trades with the U.S. because the labor used to make the ROW's exports is greater than the labor used to make the ROW's imports from the U.S.

Number of Hours per Unit of Output		
	Wheat	*Fruit*
U.S.	20	30
ROW	40	50

Selected References

Bhagwati, J. N. "The Gains from Trade Once Again." *Oxford Economic Papers* 20 (July 1968): 137–48.

Chacholiades, M. C. *International Trade Theory and Policy.* New York: McGraw-Hill, 1978.

Chipman, J. S. "A Survey of the Theory of International Trade, Part 1, The Classical Theory." *Econometrica* 33 (July 1965): 477–519.

Kemp, M. C. "Some Issues in the Analysis of Trade Gains." *Oxford Economic Papers* 20 (July 1968): 149–61.

Kemp, M. C. *The Pure Theory of Trade and Investment.* Englewood Cliffs, N.J.: Prentice-Hall, 1969.

Ricardo, D. "On the Principles of Political Economy and Taxation." In *The Works and Correspondence of David Ricardo,* edited by P. Sraffa. New York: Cambridge University Press, 1951.

Samuelson, P. A. "The Gains from International Trade." *Canadian Journal of Economics and Political Science* 5 (May 1939): 195–205.

Smith, A. *An Inquiry into the Nature and Causes of the Wealth of Nations.* New York: Modern Library College Editions, Random House, 1985.

2

MODERN TRADE

THEORY

2.1 **INTRODUCTION**

In the Ricardian model, which was discussed in Chapter 1, comparative advantage is explained solely by differences in labor productivity. In this chapter the determinants of trade are examined in more detail. We shall see that trade can result from differences between countries' tastes for goods and from differences in their relative factor endowments. We begin by discussing how demand can be represented by indifference curves. Then we examine the role of supply. The assumption of constant costs that was used in the first chapter is replaced by the assumption of increasing costs, and the importance of factor endowments is discussed. Finally, we consider the determination of the terms of trade.

2.2 **INTRODUCING DEMAND**

Consumer Indifference Curves

Welfare maximization for a country can be examined using the same techniques that are used to examine utility maximization for an individual. In consumer theory, it is assumed that a consumer's tastes can be represented by indifference curves.[1] An *indifference curve* shows the combinations of two goods (X and Y) that yield a particular level of satisfaction or utility to the consumer. An indifference curve is similar to a contour line on a map, which shows points having the same height, but indifference curves cannot be labeled to show the level of satisfaction because satisfaction cannot be quanti-

---

[1] The following discussion of indifference curves provides the minimum information needed to understand their use in international economics. A more detailed discussion can be found in any intermediate microeconomics textbook.

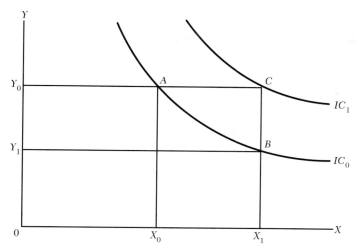

FIGURE 2.1

Consumer Indifference Curves

Indifference curves represent combinations of X and Y that yield particular levels of satisfaction or utility. They are convex and slope downwards from left to right. If consumption changes from point A to point B on indifference curve IC_0, consumption of X increases (from X_0 to X_1), thus consumption of Y must fall (from Y_0 to Y_1) if the level of satisfaction is to remain constant. Point C on IC_1 represents a higher level of satisfaction than points A and B because IC_1 is further from the origin than IC_0.

fied (unlike contour lines, which can be labeled according to the height represented). The numbering of the indifference curves, as shown in Figure 2.1 (IC_0 and IC_1), is merely for identification.

Indifference curves slope downward from left to right because as a person's consumption of one good decreases consumption of the other good must increase if the level of satisfaction is to remain constant. For example, in Figure 2.1, the consumer's level of satisfaction is the same at point A as it is at point B because A and B lie on the same indifference curve (IC_0); more X and less Y are consumed at point B than at point A. If the amount of Y consumed does not fall when consumption of X increases, for example when consumption changes from A to C, the level of satisfaction increases, and the consumer moves to an indifference curve (IC_1) further from the origin, representing a higher level of satisfaction.

Indifference curves represent different levels of satisfaction. They do not intersect because one combination of goods cannot provide two levels of satisfaction.

The amount of one good that a consumer must give up when an additional unit of the other good is consumed in order that satisfaction remains constant is called the *marginal rate of substitution*. It is shown by the slope of an indifference curve.[2] We assume that the marginal rate of substitution declines as we move around an indifference curve; therefore, indifference curves will be convex to the origin.

The assumption of a diminishing marginal rate of substitution may be justified by the *law of diminishing marginal utility*.[3] As the quantity of X consumed increases, the consumer is willing to give up less Y for an additional unit of X for two reasons. First, additional units of X become less valuable as the quantity of X consumed increases. Second, the units of Y that are given up become more valuable as the quantity of Y consumed decreases.

There are an infinite number of indifference curves that can be drawn, representing different levels of satisfaction. (These indifference curves form an "indifference curve map.") The objective for a consumer interested in maximizing satisfaction is to consume on the highest indifference curve attainable from a given level of income.

The Budget Line

With an income (or budget) of B, the maximum amount of X a person may consume is B/P_X, provided no Y is consumed. If no X is consumed, the maximum amount of Y a person may consume is B/P_Y. The line joining these two points, as in Figure 2.2, is called the *budget line*. It shows the combinations of X and Y that cost the same amount as the consumer's income. Points above the budget line are unattainable because these combinations of X and Y would cost more than the consumer's income. Points below the budget line show combinations of X and Y that cost less than the consumer's income. Since satisfaction increases with spending, the consumer continues spending until all the income available is used up.[4] Thus, the consumer does not consume combinations of goods represented by points below the budget line.

Consumer Maximization of Satisfaction

The maximum level of satisfaction is provided by the combination of goods where an indifference curve is tangential to the budget line. The indifference curve at this point is the highest that can be reached with the available income. For example, in Figure 2.2, satisfaction is maximized at point C.

Recall that the slope of an indifference curve is the marginal rate of substitution. The slope of the budget line is the price ratio (P_X/P_Y).[5] Therefore, the maximization of satisfaction leads to the equality of the marginal rate of substitution and the price ratio.

---

[2] The marginal rate of substitution is negative because Y decreases as X increases, but usually the minus sign is omitted for convenience.

[3] This assumption is sufficient but not necessary. The marginal rate of substitution declines, even if the marginal utility of X increases when the consumption of X increases and the consumption of Y declines, provided that the increase in the marginal utility of Y is proportionally greater than the increase in the marginal utility of X.

[4] Saving can be considered to be a good for the purposes of this analysis.

[5] Moving from the vertical intercept to the horizontal intercept, the vertical change divided by the horizontal change is: $-(B/P_Y)/(B/P_X)$, which equals $-P_X/P_Y$. The minus sign is omitted for convenience.

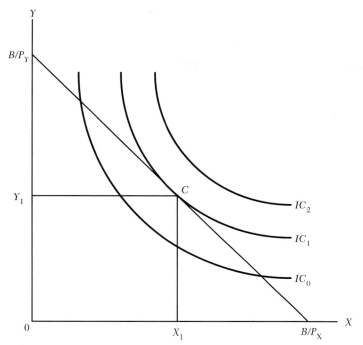

FIGURE 2.2

Consumer Welfare Maximization

The maximum amounts of X and Y that can be purchased from a given income are B/P_X and B/P_Y, respectively. The line connecting these points is the budget line. The consumer maximizes welfare by consuming at point C where the budget line is tangential to an indifference curve (IC_1).

Social Indifference Curves

We assume that the welfare of a country can be represented by a set of *social indifference curves,* in the same way that an individual's satisfaction can be represented by a set of consumer indifference curves.[6] However, social indifference curves are not the same as consumer indifference curves in all respects. Society's welfare may be affected by changes in the distribution of income as well as by the amount of goods available. For example, we would not expect two policies that result in the same increase in the amount of goods available to be equally attractive if one policy makes poor people poorer and rich people richer, and the other policy makes rich people poorer and poor people richer. Changes in the distribution of income may affect welfare and

---

[6]The assumption that society's preferences can be described by a set of social indifference curves, which do not change when trade is introduced or the level of trade regulated, is discussed in detail by Chacholiades (1978).

change the position or shape of social indifference curves. If the indifference curves change, we cannot assess the effects of trade using indifference curve analysis. Therefore, for expositional convenience, we adopt the standard assumption that the income distribution is unaffected by trade or is maintained constant by government policies.

Welfare Maximization

A country's welfare is maximized by consuming on the highest possible social indifference curve. The constraint a country faces is that if it does not engage in trade it can only consume what it produces. This constraint is analogous to the income constraint a consumer faces. The quantities of X and Y available are shown by the production possibility frontier. In the Ricardian model, the production possibility frontier is a straight line resembling a consumer's budget line. In the absence of trade, the maximum welfare level is achieved at the point of tangency of the production possibility frontier and a social indifference curve.

In Figure 2.3, the pre-trade equilibrium is shown by point C_1 on the production possibility frontier *(PPF)*. At this point, the slope of the social indifference curve (SIC_1) is equal to the slope of the production possibility frontier. Therefore, the marginal rate of substitution is equal to the opportunity cost of domestically produced goods. Consumption at other points on the production possibility frontier would lead to a lower welfare; for example, consumption at point B leads to the level of welfare shown by indifference curve SIC_0.

The Gain from Trade: Fixed Opportunity Cost

When international trade is introduced, the country is no longer restricted to points along the production possibility frontier because consumption may take place along the terms of trade line *(TT)*. Welfare is maximized when a social indifference curve is tangential to the terms of trade line. In Figure 2.3, welfare is maximized at C_2. YS is produced, X_2 and Y_2 are consumed, thus YS minus Y_2 is exported and X_2 is imported. There is a gain from trade because a higher social indifference curve (SIC_2) can be reached by consuming along the terms of trade line than can be reached if consumption is confined to points along the production possibility frontier.

Deriving the Ricardian Offer Curve

The Ricardian offer curve, which was discussed at the end of Chapter 1, can be derived using indifference curves. At the pre-trade price ratio the country consumes at point C_1 in Figure 2.4. If the pre-trade price ratio is greater than the terms of trade, the country specializes in good Y and produces at point YS, the intercept of the production possibility frontier on the vertical axis. The points of consumption on the terms of trade lines are determined by the positions of the indifference curves, in other words by the nature of the demand for the goods. Post-trade consumption takes place at points

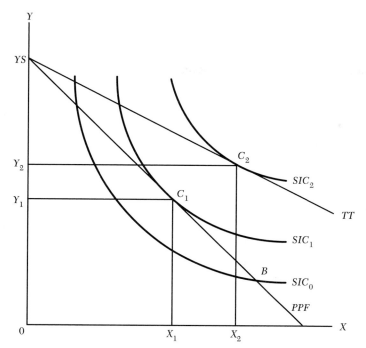

FIGURE 2.3

The Gain from Trade: Fixed Opportunity Costs

Before trade, consumption can take place on or below the production possibility frontier *(PPF)*. Welfare is maximized at point C_1 on the social indifference curve SIC_1. When trade is introduced, by specializing in Y production and consuming along the trade line *(TT)*, the welfare level of SIC_2 may be attained at C_2. The combination of goods consumed when the country trades (X_2Y_2) could not be achieved without trade because it lies above the production possibility frontier.

C_2, C_3, and so on, depending on the terms of trade. The difference between domestic consumption and production is trade, and can be plotted to form the Ricardian offer curve.

The Gain from Trade and Indifference Curve Analysis

The use of indifference curves to show the gain from trade must be defended for pragmatic reasons and not because indifference curves are realistic. However, the proposition that there is a gain from trade does not depend on the acceptability of the use of indifference curves. It should be remembered that the gain from trade can be shown without them.

The discussion in Chapter 1 showed that a country gains from trade because trade increases the quantities of goods the country can consume. To be more specific, the consumption possibilities along the terms of trade line are

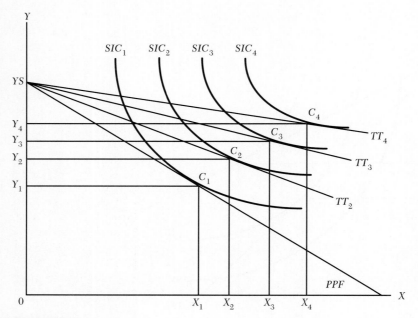

FIGURE 2.4

The Quantity of Trade and the Terms of Trade: Fixed Costs

As in Figure 2.3, the country specializes in Y production and consumes along the trade line. As the terms of trade fall, the country consumes more X. Since the country does not produce X, imports of X are shown by the amounts of X consumed. The quantity of Y exported is the difference between domestic production and consumption. For example, at the terms of trade shown by TT_2, the country imports X_2, produces YS and consumes Y_2, thus it exports $YS - Y_2$.

greater than the consumption possibilities along the production possibility frontier (except at the point of intersection). By introducing indifference curves into the analysis, we can determine the amount of trade at different terms of trade, and the location of the Ricardian offer curve. However, the introduction of indifference curves does not alter the reason for the gain from trade: Trade is beneficial because it increases the quantities of goods a country can consume.

2.3 INCREASING OPPORTUNITY COST

The assumption of constant opportunity cost used in Chapter 1 implies that as labor is transferred from one sector to another, the changes in the outputs of the sectors are the same for each unit of labor transferred, regardless of how large a transfer takes place. However, the labor used to produce one good may not be equally suitable for the production of other goods. Also, the capital used to produce a good may be inappropriate for the production of other goods. For example, labor skills required in the textile industry may be of little value in the automobile industry, and machines used in the construction industry may be of little use in electronics.

A more realistic assumption, reflecting the lack of homogeneity of factors of production, is that the opportunity cost of producing a good rises with the quantity of the good produced.[7] When a small quantity of X is produced, large increases in the quantity of X can be obtained by giving up small amounts of Y, because the factors of production that increase X production most, and reduce Y production least, can be transferred from Y to X. As the production of X expands, it becomes progressively more difficult to increase X production by transferring factors of production from Y to X, and the amount of Y that must be sacrificed for each additional unit of X increases. Therefore, the opportunity cost of producing a good increases as the production of the good increases. Recall that the slope of a production possibility frontier shows the opportunity cost of domestic production. A production possibility frontier showing increasing opportunity costs is bowed out from the origin, as in Figure 2.5.

The Gain from Trade Again

In the absence of trade, welfare is maximized when a social indifference curve is tangential to the production possibility frontier. In Figure 2.5 this occurs at the point $C_1 = Q_1$. When trade is introduced, welfare is maximized when consumption takes place at C_3 and production at Q_3. At these points, the slope of the social indifference curve (SIC_3) and the slope of the production possibility frontier (PPF) are equal to the slope of the terms of trade line (TT_3). Therefore, welfare maximization leads to the equality of the marginal rate of substitution, the opportunity cost of domestic production, and the terms of trade.

It is interesting to note that as domestic production changes opportunity cost changes, and the rate of transformation is equated to the terms of trade without specialization necessarily arising. This result contrasts with that of the Ricardian model where specialization occurs because the opportunity costs of production are constant.

The Consumption Gain and the Production Gain

The gain from trade can be separated into two parts: a *consumption gain* that occurs because trade allows countries to consume at world prices rather than domestic prices, and a *production gain* that occurs because specialization

---

[7]This is sometimes referred to as a diminishing marginal rate of transformation or technical substitution.

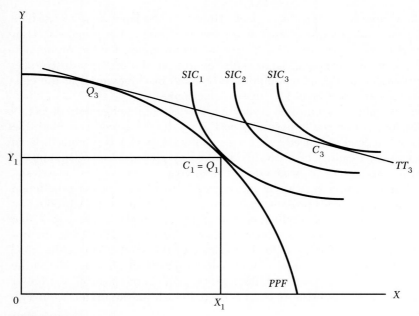

FIGURE 2.5

The Gain from Trade: Increasing Costs

The production possibility frontier is bowed out from the origin because of the assumption of increasing costs. In the absence of trade, welfare is maximized when consumption and production take place at point $C_1 = Q_1$ on SIC_1. When trade is introduced, welfare is maximized if production takes place at Q_3, and consumption takes place at C_3 on SIC_3.

increases when trade takes place. These are shown in Figure 2.6. If the level of production is fixed at Q_1, the consumption gain is shown by the increase in welfare made possible by consumption taking place at C_2 on SIC_2 rather than at C_1 on SIC_1. When production changes from Q_1 to Q_3, a further increase in welfare occurs because of the benefits of increased specialization. The production gain is shown by the movement from C_2 on SIC_2 to C_3 on SIC_3.

The division of the gain from trade into the consumption and production gains leads to an interesting result: A country gains from trade even if it cannot change its production. The explanation of this result is that welfare increases if trade takes place between countries that have different pre-trade price ratios. In the example shown in Figure 2.6, the gain from trade arises because other countries value Y more highly relative to X than the home country. The home country's welfare rises when it consumes less Y and exports Y, because it receives more X than is needed to maintain the initial level of welfare.

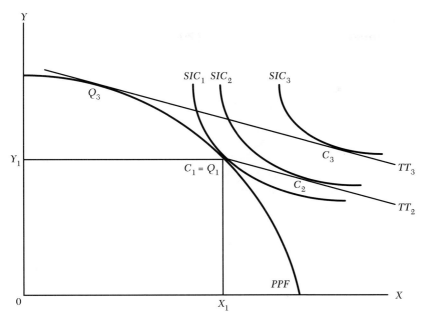

FIGURE 2.6

The Consumption and Production Gains from Trade

Initially, production and consumption take place at C_1. If the production of X and Y does not change when trade is introduced, the gain from trade arising from the opportunity to consume at world prices is shown by the movement from SIC_1 to SIC_2 on TT_2. If production changes from Q_1 to Q_3, a further increase in welfare occurs because the country becomes more specialized. The gain from increased specialization is shown by the movement from SIC_2 to SIC_3.

The Gain from Trade and the Terms of Trade

We can use social indifference curves to show that the gain from trade increases with the size of the disparity between the pre-trade price ratio and the terms of trade. In Figure 2.7, initially the terms of trade are slightly below the pre-trade price ratio; the country imports X and exports Y. As the terms of trade decrease further and the terms of trade line becomes flatter, production switches from X to Y, and higher social indifference curves can be reached. When the terms of trade decrease, the relative price of X (the imported good) falls, and more X is consumed. Since the production of X falls as the terms of trade decrease, it is clear that imports increase.[8]

---

[8] Increased imports do not imply increased exports. The relative price of imports is lower when the terms of trade fall, thus more imports are available for a given amount of exports. If the demand for imports is elastic with respect to the terms of trade, exports increase when the

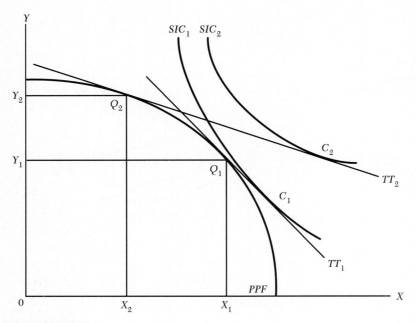

FIGURE 2.7

The Gain from Trade and the Terms of Trade: Increasing Costs

Initially, the country produces at Q_1 and consumes at C_1 on social indifference curve SIC_1. As the terms of trade decrease from TT_1 to TT_2, the country can reach a higher social indifference curve (SIC_2). Production changes from Q_1 to Q_2, thus less X is produced and more Y. However, consumption of X increases (because a decrease in the terms of trade implies that the relative price of the imported good falls). Therefore, imports of X increase. Imports and exports are shown by the difference between domestic production and consumption.

2.4 **THE HECKSCHER-OHLIN THEOREM**

In the Ricardian model, pre-trade price differences reflect differences in labor productivity. In the Heckscher-Ohlin model, disparities between countries' pre-trade price ratios are caused by differences in relative *factor endowments*. Two assumptions are needed to demonstrate the relationship between factor endowments and pre-trade prices. First, we assume that the pattern of demand is similar in the two countries: if the countries face the same prices, the same proportion of income is spent on each good and this proportion does

---

terms of trade fall. If the demand for imports is inelastic, exports decrease when the terms of trade fall. The offer curves shown in the first two chapters are based on the assumption that the demand for imports is elastic.

not change as income increases. Second, we assume that the production functions of the two countries are identical and do not have increasing returns to scale: if the two countries face the same input prices, the same production method will be used.

Factor Endowments and Factor Prices

Assume that there are two factors of production, labor (L) and capital (K), and two countries A and B. If country A has more capital per unit of labor than country B $(KA/LA > KB/LB)$, country B must have more labor per unit of capital than country A $(LA/KA < LB/KB)$. In this case, country A is said to be *capital abundant* and country B is said to be *labor abundant*. Given the assumptions of the model, factor prices will reflect the relative scarcity of the factors of production, and the ratio of the price of capital (R) to the price of labor (W) will be lower in country A than in country B $(RA/WA < RB/WB)$.

Factor price differences lead to differences in the prices of goods. Assume that there are two goods, X and Y, and that X production requires more capital per unit of labor than Y production. In other words, X production is capital-intensive and Y production is labor-intensive. If country A is capital abundant, the capital-labor factor price ratio will be lower in country A than in country B, and in the absence of trade, the ratio of the price of X to the price of Y (P_X/P_Y) will also be lower in country A than in country B. Therefore, the capital abundant country (A) will have a comparative advantage in the capital-intensive product (X) and the labor abundant country (B) will have a comparative advantage in the labor-intensive product (Y).

The Heckscher-Ohlin theorem states that a country has a comparative advantage in the production of the good that uses the country's abundant factor intensively. This is illustrated in Figure 2.8. We assume that country A is capital abundant and country B is labor abundant. The countries have identical tastes, shown by a single indifference map. In the absence of trade, different prices exist because the countries' factor endowments differ; country A consumes at CA_0 and country B consumes at CB_0. When trade takes place both consume at the same point $(CA_1 = CB_1)$. Country A exports X, the capital-intensive product, and B exports Y, the labor-intensive product.

A common example of the Heckscher-Ohlin theorem in practice is agricultural exports. The United States, Australia, and New Zealand are relatively well endowed with high-quality land, have good climates, and export agricultural goods. Another example is exports of labor-intensive products, such as textiles and low-technology manufactured goods, from Hong-Kong, Korea, and Taiwan. These countries are relatively well endowed with unskilled or semi-skilled labor and do not have as high a level of capital and technology as Japan and the United States.

The Potential Importance of Tastes

Taste differences can also give rise to pre-trade price differences and hence to trade. In Figure 2.9, even though both countries have the same factor endowments, the same technology, and thus the same production possibility

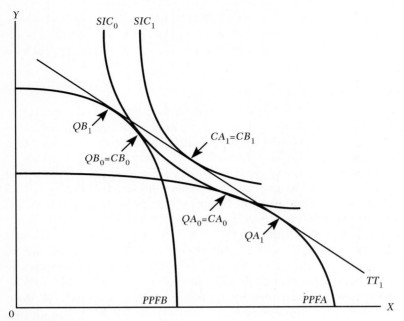

FIGURE 2.8

The Heckscher-Ohlin Theorem with Identical Tastes

Countries A and B have the same tastes (shown by a common set of social indifference curves) and different factor endowments (shown by the production possibility frontiers *PPFA* and *PPFB*, respectively). Before trade, the countries produce and consume at $QA_0 = CA_0$ and $QB_0 = CB_0$, respectively. The relative price of the capital-intensive good (X) is lower in the capital abundant country (A), and the relative price of the labor-intensive good (Y) is lower in the labor abundant country (B). When trade is introduced, the countries export the good that uses intensively their abundant factor: country A exports X and country B exports Y. They consume at the same point $(CA_1 = CB_1)$.

frontiers, the pre-trade price ratios differ because tastes differ. Country A consumes at CA_0 and country B consumes at CB_0. The pre-trade price ratios are shown by the slopes of the production possibility frontiers at CA_0 and CB_0. The price ratio (P_X/P_Y) is higher in A than in B. When trade is introduced, prices are equalized, and because the production possibility frontiers are identical, both countries produce the same quantities of X and Y. However, they do not consume the same amounts because of the difference in tastes: country A consumes at CA_1 and country B at CB_1.

It is possible that differences in tastes will be large enough to offset differences in factor endowments. If a country is capital abundant, but has a strong preference for capital-intensive goods, goods of this type may be more expensive in that country than in the labor abundant country. In this case, the pattern of trade will be the opposite of that predicted by the Heckscher-

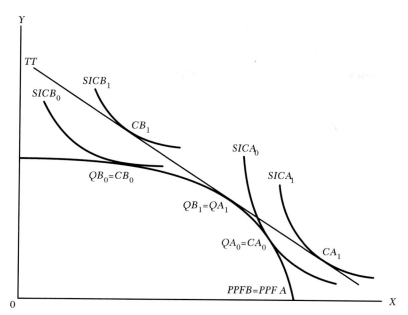

FIGURE 2.9

Taste Differences and Trade

Countries A and B have the same factor endowments shown by a common production possibility frontier *(PPFA = PPFB)*. The countries' pre-trade price ratios differ because their tastes differ: the relative price of X is higher in country A, and the relative price of Y is higher in country B. When trade is introduced, country A imports X and exports Y, and country B imports Y and exports X.

Ohlin theorem. This possibility is shown in Figure 2.10. The price of X is higher in country A than in country B because of a difference in tastes that is large enough to outweigh the effects of the difference in factor endowments.

Factor Price Equalization

It has been shown that factor price differences resulting from different factor endowments can explain pre-trade price differences. Using the assumptions of the Heckscher-Ohlin model it can be shown that the equalization of goods prices leads to the equalization of factor prices.[9] In reality, these assumptions are not fulfilled, and we do not observe complete factor price equalization. However, we should not expect reality to correspond exactly to a model. Although absolute factor price equalization does not take place, trade does generate a tendency towards factor price equalization.

---

[9] A proof of factor price equalization is beyond the scope of this text. See Chacholiades (1978).

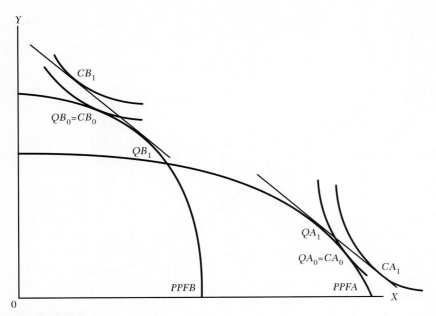

FIGURE 2.10

The Heckscher-Ohlin Prediction Reversed because of a Difference in Tastes

Countries A and B have different factor endowments and different tastes. For simplicity, the social indifference curves have not been labeled. As in Figure 2.8, country A is relatively abundant in capital and country B is relatively abundant in labor. Because of the difference in tastes, the pre-trade relative price of the capital-intensive good (X) is higher in the capital abundant country (A), and the pre-trade relative price of the labor-intensive good (Y) is higher in the labor abundant country (B). In this case the labor-intensive country exports the capital-intensive good, and the capital abundant country exports the labor-intensive good. Thus, the pattern of trade is the opposite of that predicted by the Heckscher-Ohlin theorem.

If a country is labor abundant, it exports labor-intensive goods when trade is introduced. As the output of the export industry increases, its demand for inputs increases. However, the export industry uses more labor per unit of capital than the import-competing sector. Therefore, as resources are released by the import-competing sector, insufficient labor per unit of capital is released. The excess demand for labor relative to capital pushes up the price of labor (the abundant factor) relative to the price of capital. The tendency towards factor price equalization is clear. In the absence of trade, the abundant factor is relatively cheap. Trade leads to an increase in the price of the abundant factor. Therefore, trade tends to equalize factor prices.

The logic may be understood by considering a simple example. The United States is well endowed with land in comparison with most countries. What would happen to the rents paid for American agricultural land if exports of agricultural produce were not allowed? Probably rents would fall because the United States has more agricultural land than is needed to supply produce for the domestic market. Therefore, trade increases the price of land relative to other inputs.

Trade and Factor Mobility

Trade can be viewed as a substitute for factor mobility: trade equalizes factor prices through the prices of goods, factor mobility equalizes factor prices through factor flows. Consider the case of a capital abundant country that is next to a labor abundant country. Labor will be relatively more expensive in the capital abundant country than in the labor abundant country. Thus, there will be an incentive for people to move from the labor abundant country to the capital abundant country. The capital abundant country may choose to limit immigration, perhaps because of fears about the effect of immigration on wages. However, imports from the labor abundant country have a similar effect on wages: imports of labor-intensive products reduce the prices of those products and thus reduce the price of labor (assuming that labor is the factor used intensively in the import-competing sector).

The effects of illegal aliens on wages in sectors using unskilled or semi-skilled labor is often discussed. Also, one often hears complaints about unfair competition from countries with low wages. Essentially, the effect on wages of trade and immigration can be very similar.

Trade and the Distribution of Income

The discussion of the relationship between factor prices and trade suggests that, because trade changes factor prices, the distribution of income will change when trade is introduced. Some people will gain from trade while others may lose. In theory, income could be redistributed in such a way as to ensure that nobody is made worse off by the introduction of trade. However, without such redistribution we cannot say that there has actually been a gain from trade because peoples' welfares cannot be compared. (Interpersonal comparisons of welfare are impossible because welfare cannot be measured.) However, we can conclude that society is potentially better off, because trade increases the quantity of goods available for consumption. In the Ricardian model, it is assumed that opportunity costs remain constant, thus the effect of trade on the distribution of income is not shown in the model.

THE DETERMINATION OF THE TERMS OF TRADE   2.5

Offer Curves and the Terms of Trade

In Section 2.3 it was shown how imports increase and the gain from trade increases with the size of the divergence between the pre-trade price ratio and the terms of trade (see Figure 2.7). The quantities of X and Y traded at

B's exports (supply) of Y
A's imports of (demand for) Y

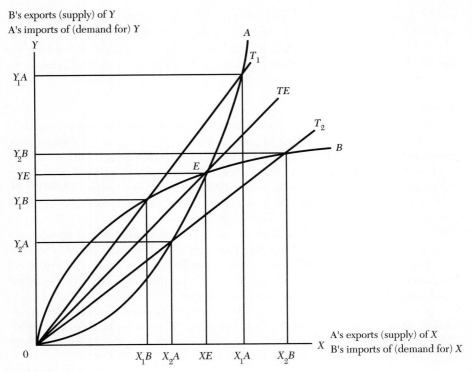

FIGURE 2.11

The Determination of the Terms of Trade

The equilibrium terms of trade are shown by $0TE$, which passes through E, the point of intersection of the offer curves $0A$ and $0B$. At point E, the demand and supply of X and Y are equal. If the terms of trade equal $0T_1$, B's demand for X (X_1B) is less than A's supply of X (X_1A), and the relative price of X, the terms of trade, falls. If the terms of trade equal $0T_2$, B's demand for X (X_2B) is greater than A's supply of X (X_2A), and the terms of trade rise.

different terms of trade can be used to plot an *offer curve*. Country A's offer curve is shown as $0A$ in Figure 2.11.

The terms of trade at a point on the offer curve are equal to the slope of a line from the origin to the point. The amount of trade increases as the terms of trade increase for two reasons: (1) consumption of the imported good increases as the relative price of the imported good falls, and (2) production of the exported good increases and production of the imported good decreases. If the terms of trade equal the pre-trade price ratio, no trade takes place. (This is what is shown by the offer curve passing through the origin.)

The offer curve for another country (country B) is included in Figure 2.11. In a two-country model, the exports of one country are the imports of the other country, and the axes are labeled accordingly. Assuming that the pre-trade price ratio for country B differs from that of country A, the slopes of the offer curves at the origin differ. At the origin, the slope of country A's offer curve is less than the slope of country B's offer curve, thus we can conclude that the pre-trade price ratio is lower in country A than in country B.

The equilibrium terms of trade are the terms of trade at which the quantities of X and Y supplied and demanded by the two countries are equal. In Figure 2.11, the equilibrium terms of trade are shown by the line $0TE$. If the terms of trade are below $0TE$, the quantity demanded of imports of X by country B exceeds the quantity supplied of exports of X by country A, and the relative price of X in terms of Y, the terms of trade, will rise. If the terms of trade are above $0TE$, the quantity demanded of imports of X by country B is less than quantity supplied of exports of X by country A, and the terms of trade will fall. (The equilibrium can also be described in terms of good Y.)

Export-Led Growth and the Terms of Trade

In general, the terms of trade will change if the underlying demand or supply of goods changes. For example, if a country is large enough to influence world prices, an increase in the demand for imports will raise the relative price of imports. A similar effect occurs if technological progress in the export sector increases the supply of exports because the relative price of exports will fall (which is equivalent to an increase in the relative price of imports). The effects of an increase in the supply of exports (or an increase in the demand for imports) are shown in Figure 2.12. When the offer curve of country A moves from $0A_1$ to $0A_2$, the terms of trade change from $0T_1$ to $0T_2$.

When a country's supply of exports increases, the country experiences two conflicting forces: welfare tends to increase because the quantity that can be produced increases, and welfare tends to fall because the relative price of exports tends to fall. It is possible that the country may even lose from growth of the export sector because of the price effects of an increase in the supply of exports. This possibility is referred to as *immiserizing growth* and is shown in Figure 2.13. Growth shifts the production possibility frontier from PPF_1 to PPF_2. Initially, the level of welfare is shown by social indifference curve SIC_1. At constant terms of trade, the country would be better off after growth, because social indifference curve SIC_2 could be reached. However, the decline in the terms of trade, shown by the shift of the terms of trade line from TT_1 to TT_0, means that welfare falls to the level shown by social indifference curve SIC_0.

The price effects of supply changes are illustrated by the experience of the Organization of Petroleum Exporting Countries (OPEC). In 1973 and 1979, OPEC found that by restricting exports members were better off than if they sold all they could. As more nations became oil producers, however, the supply of oil increased faster than the demand for oil, and the world price of oil fell in the early eighties. The general point is that when countries' exports consist of a limited range of products, the effects of supply changes may be significant. This possibility is particularly important for less developed countries, as is shown in Chapter 18.

B's exports (supply) of Y
A's imports of (demand for) Y

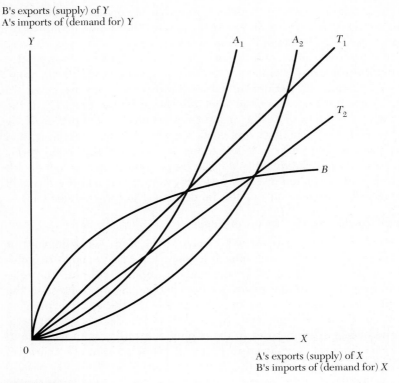

A's exports (supply) of X
B's imports of (demand for) X

FIGURE 2.12

Export-Led Growth and the Terms of Trade

If A's supply of exports increases, the quantity of exports offered per unit of imports increases, and the offer curve moves outwards from $0A_1$ to $0A_2$. The deterioration of the terms of trade is shown by the shift of the terms of trade line from $0T_1$ to $0T_2$.

A decrease in the demand for imports (or fall in the supply of exports) has the opposite effect from an increase in the supply of exports. If the demand for imports falls, the terms of trade tend to improve. Diagrammatically this could be shown by an inwards movement of the offer curve. The fall in demand for imports could be caused by an import restriction. The beneficial terms of trade effect has been used as an argument for tariffs, and is discussed in section 5.3.

Summary of Main Points

A country's welfare can be represented by a set of *social indifference curves*. These are convex and do not intersect. The further a social indifference curve is from the origin, the higher the level of welfare it represents. In the absence of trade, countries are restricted to consuming at points along the production possibility frontier. Introducing trade allows consumption to take

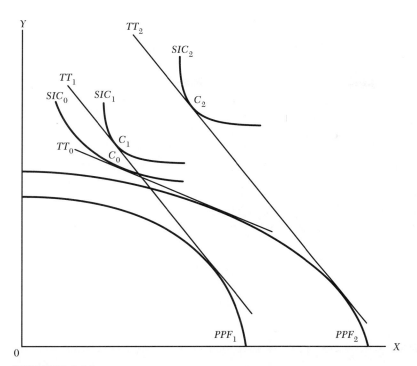

FIGURE 2.13

Immiserizing Growth

Growth is shown by the outward movement of the production possibility curve from PPF_1 to PPF_2. If the terms of trade are constant and shown by the terms of trade line TT_2, which is parallel to TT_1, welfare would increase from the level shown by social indifference curve SIC_1 to that shown by SIC_2. However, because growth is concentrated in the export sector, there is a decline in the terms of trade. This is shown by the shift in the terms of trade line from TT_1 to TT_0. The lower level of welfare resulting from the decline in the terms of trade is shown by SIC_0.

place along the terms of trade line and a higher level of welfare (shown by a higher indifference curve) can be reached.

The gain from trade can be separated into a *consumption gain*, from being able to consume at world prices, and a *production gain*, from specialization. The consumption gain implies that a country will gain from trade even if it cannot change its output.

The *Heckscher-Ohlin theorem* explains the difference between pre-trade prices, that is, comparative advantage, in terms of differences between countries' relative *factor endowments*. The theorem predicts that a country will have a comparative advantage in the good that requires for its production intensive use of the country's abundant factor. A country is relatively well endowed with labor *(labor abundant)* if it has more labor per unit of capital than the other country (the *capital abundant* country). The reason that the labor abundant country has a comparative advantage in the labor-intensive good is that the price of labor relative to the price of capital will be lower in the labor abundant country than in the capital abundant country.

The Heckscher-Ohlin model is based on the assumption that tastes are similar across countries. Differences in tastes can be a cause of international trade (and can offset the influence of factor endowments on trade). It is also assumed that countries have the same production functions.

An interesting prediction of the Heckscher-Ohlin model is that trade will tend to equate relative factor prices. As the output of the export sector expands, the relative price of the factor used intensively in the export sector (the abundant factor) will increase. Since this factor was relatively cheap before trade, trade tends to equalize relative factor prices.

Trade is the difference between production and consumption. Indifference curves can be used to show how much countries produce and consume at different terms of trade. This information can be used to plot *offer curves* representing the demand for imports and the supply of exports at different terms of trade. The equilibrium terms of trade are those at which the demand and supply of traded goods are equal. This equilibrium is shown by the intersection of the offer curves.

An increase in the supply of exports (or an increase in the demand for imports) shifts the offer curve outwards and causes a deterioration in a country's terms of trade. It is possible that the deterioration in the terms of trade will more than offset the benefits of growth in the export sector and that the country's welfare will fall. A tariff reduces a country's demand for imports and shifts the offer curve inwards. In this case the terms of trade improve.

Study Questions

1. Assume that country A is labor abundant, country B is capital abundant, production of good X is labor-intensive, and production of good Y is capital-intensive. What is the pattern of trade?

2. Using the assumptions of the previous question, describe how and why there will be a tendency towards factor price equalization.

3. Using the assumptions of Question 1, discuss how factor flows can lead to factor price equalization in the same way as trade. In the Heckscher-Ohlin model, what would happen if factors were completely mobile?

4. Assuming increasing costs, show the gains from trade diagrammatically for a country that imports Y and exports X. Split the gain into the consumption and production gains.

5. Using social indifference curves, show that an improvement in the terms of trade increases welfare even if production is fixed.

6. Critically evaluate the view that, if all factors of production are fully employed before trade, world output cannot increase when trade begins, and there cannot be mutual benefits from trade.

7. Country A faces a straight-line offer curve from country B. What does this imply? Can A gain from trade? Explain.

8. Why does the Ricardian model predict that countries will be completely specialized and the Heckscher-Ohlin model predict that specialization will increase without complete specialization necessarily occurring?

9. Critically evaluate the view that, because developed countries have more factors of production than less developed countries, mutually beneficial trade is impossible.

Selected References

Bhagwati, J. N. "The Pure Theory of International Trade." *Economic Journal* 74 (March 1964): 1–84.

Caves, R. E., and Johnson, H. G., eds. *Readings in International Economics*. Homewood, Ill.: Richard D. Irwin, 1968.

Chacholiades, M. C. *International Trade Theory and Policy*. New York: McGraw-Hill, 1978.

Chipman, J. S. "A Survey of the Theory of International Trade: Part 3, the Modern Theory." *Econometrica* 34 (January 1966): 18–76.

Clement, M. O., Pfister, R. L., and Rothwell, K. J. *Theoretical Issues in International Economics*. New York: Houghton Mifflin Co., 1967.

Ellis, H. S., and Metzler, L. A. *Readings in the Theory of International Trade*. Homewood, Ill.: Richard D. Irwin, 1949.

Krauss, M. B. *A Geometric Approach to International Trade*. New York: Halstead-Wiley, 1979.

Meade, J. E. *A Geometry of International Trade*. London: Allen and Unwin, 1952.

3

QUALIFICATIONS AND EXTENSIONS OF TRADE THEORY

3.1 **INTRODUCTION**

In this chapter we discuss some qualifications and extensions of trade theory. The object is not to challenge the value of standard trade theory, but rather it is to extend the analysis and show that many factors can influence trade. All economic models are simplifications of reality; one model cannot be expected to explain every possibility. Different models are useful because they yield different insights, and because they are appropriate in different circumstances.

We begin by examining empirical tests of the Heckscher-Ohlin theorem, which have stimulated other explanations of trade.

3.2 **EMPIRICAL TESTS OF THE HECKSCHER-OHLIN THEOREM**

The Structure and Growth of World Trade

The Heckscher-Ohlin theorem is a static explanation of trade because comparative advantage results from factor endowments, which it is assumed do not change. Although the approach may be appropriate for the study of trade in primary products, where endowments of natural resources are clearly of vital importance, factor endowments are not always an adequate explanation of trade in manufactured products. For example, the emergence of

TABLE 3.1   The Structure of World Trade, 1987

		Percentage of Exports from		
		Industrial Market Economies	Developing Countries	Nonmarket Economies
Going to	Industrial market economies	77.9	65.8	25.1
	Developing countries	17.9	25.7	17.2
	Nonmarket economies	3.5	7.7	54.0

Note: Totals may not sum to 100% because of rounding errors and omissions.
Source: Calculated using data from *United Nations Monthly Bulletin of Statistics,* June 1988.

Southeast Asian countries as major exporters of manufactured goods in the last two decades, and the decline in the relative importance of Western countries in world trade, cannot be explained easily using the Heckscher-Ohlin model.

The Heckscher-Ohlin model leads us to expect that there will be a high degree of trade between countries with dissimilar factor endowments. For example, we would expect a large amount of trade between developed countries and less developed countries because less developed countries have more labor per unit of capital than developed countries. Also, less developed countries often have natural resources whereas developed countries have better manufacturing skills and more advanced technology.

Table 3.1 shows that trade between developed countries is much greater than trade between developed countries and less developed countries. This pattern of trade probably cannot be explained by factor endowments, because although the factor endowments of developed countries are not identical, the endowments of developed countries have a closer similarity to each other than they do to the endowments of less developed countries. Geographical proximity may be part of the explanation. Table 3.2 shows that the major trading partner of the United States is Canada, and members of the European Economic Community trade with each other to a large degree. However, geographical proximity cannot fully explain the degree of trade between developed countries, for example, between Japan and the United States or between the European Economic Community and the United States.

Although the Heckscher-Ohlin theorem may not explain all trade, most economists probably would not object to the proposition that factor price differences resulting from factor endowments can be a cause of trade. Whether

TABLE 3.2   Trade between Some Major Trading Areas, 1987

		Percentage of Exports from			
		Canada	EEC	Japan	U.S.
Going to	Canada	—	1.1	2.4	23.4
	EEC	7.4	57.9	15.9	23.3
	Japan	5.4	1.7	—	11.0
	U.S.	75.5	8.7	36.7	—

Source: Calculated using data from *United Nations Monthly Bulletin of Statistics*, June 1988.

factor endowments alone are actually an adequate explanation of trade flows is a question that has been the subject of many empirical studies. One of the most influential studies was undertaken by Wassily Leontief.

The Leontief Paradox

Leontief (1953) tested the Heckscher-Ohlin theorem by comparing the labor and capital needed by the United States to produce $1 million worth of exports and $1 million worth of import substitutes. He found that American export production used more labor per unit of capital than the production of import substitutes. Assuming that import substitutes are produced in the same way as imports, it appeared that the United States imported capital-intensive goods and exported labor-intensive goods. This finding was not what was expected: casual empiricism suggests that the United States is capital abundant and, if the Heckscher-Ohlin theorem is valid, American exports should be more capital-intensive than American imports.

Leontief's first test used 1947 data. Similar results were obtained with 1951 data by Leontief (1956), and with 1962 data by Baldwin (1971). Maskus (1985) also found evidence of paradoxical outcomes for the United States. Studies of the capital-labor ratios of other countries' imports and exports yielded more paradoxes. For example, Tatemoto and Ichimura (1959) found that Japan exported capital-intensive products, even though Japan was one of the most labor abundant industrial countries. However, Japan's trade with the United States was consistent with the predicitons of the Heckscher-Ohlin model. Bharadwaj's (1962) investigation of Indian trade showed that India, a labor abundant country, exported labor-intensive goods as we might expect, but India's exports to the United States were capital-intensive. Wahl (1961) found that Canada, a capital abundant country, exported capital-intensive products, but since most of Canada's trade is with the United States (which is perhaps better endowed with capital than Canada), this result does not clearly support the Heckscher-Ohlin theorem. Finally, in a study of thirty-five countries Baldwin (1979) found that paradoxical outcomes were common.

These studies cast doubt on the general validity and relevance of the

Heckscher-Ohlin theorem. We shall consider the explanations of the Leontief paradox as a way of examining the foundations of the Heckscher-Ohlin theorem in more detail, and as an introduction to other explanations of trade that are discussed in the following sections.

Labor Productivity

Leontief explained the paradox by arguing that American workers are more productive than foreign workers. To be specific, he suggested that American labor is three times more productive than foreign labor. (In effect, this would triple the U.S. labor force.) He did not attribute this difference in productivity to differences in the quality of labor, but rather to American "entrepreneurship, superior organization, and a favorable environment." However, Leontief's explanation cannot be accepted without reservation. Although these factors may increase the productivity of labor, they might also increase the productivity of capital. This explanation is only acceptable to the extent that labor productivity is increased by more than the productivity of capital.

Leontief's explanation relates to the output of homogeneous labor. The paradox can be explained if we drop the assumption that labor is homogeneous. For example, it has been suggested that American workers are more productive because they are more skilled. Thus, one explanation of the paradox is that the United States is relatively abundant in skilled labor and exports products that use skilled labor intensively. This explanation suggests that the emphasis on labor and capital as the only factors of production is unwarranted and that the role of training and education should also be considered.

Research and Development

Training and education are particularly important for research and development. Research and development expenditures have been found to be positively correlated with a sector's export performance. The explanation of Leontief's findings is that the United States has a comparative advantage in technologically advanced products, and the high labor cost in export industries is due to the use of highly educated labor needed for research and development activities. Baldwin's (1971) study, which shows that workers are more highly educated in the export sector than in the import-competing sector, supports this explanation.

Natural Resources

The Leontief paradox has been attributed to the importance of trade in natural resources. The United States is a large importer of natural resources and the extraction of natural resources uses a large amount of capital. Therefore, the paradox can be explained by differences in the type of natural resources with which countries are endowed. This explanation seems to be supported by the evidence. Leontief (1956) found that when natural-resource products are excluded from the data the paradox was removed, and Baldwin

(1971) found that the size of the paradox was reduced. However, the outcome depends on which industries are excluded, and the selection of the industries to be excluded is inevitably arbitrary.

Identical Production Functions

It is assumed in the Heckscher-Ohlin theorem that production functions are identical. If production functions are not identical, Leontief's methodology is not appropriate. Leontief's data were drawn from the input-output table for the United States. He assumed that the inputs used by other countries when they produced America's imports were the same as the inputs used by import-competing firms in the United States. If production functions are not identical, these input data are not an indication of the factors actually used when the goods were produced.

Factor Intensity Reversals

The Heckscher-Ohlin theorem is based on the assumption that factor intensities are not reversible: if a good is produced by a labor-intensive method at one set of factor prices it is not produced by a captial-intensive method at another set of factor prices. A detailed discussion of factor intensity reversals is beyond the level of this text. It is sufficient to note that in deriving the Heckscher-Ohlin result we assumed that one good is capital-intensive and one is labor-intensive. The Heckscher-Ohlin theorem leads us to expect that countries will export goods that use their abundant factors intensively. If one good uses a country's abundant factor intensively at one factor price ratio, and a different good uses the abundant factor intensively at another factor price ratio, the simple relationship between factor abundance and comparative advantage in particular goods is lost.

Factor intensity reversals can explain the Leontief paradox: at pre-trade factor prices the United States may want to import a labor-intensive good; at post-trade factor prices (when the good is imported) the same good may be produced by a capital-intensive method. Attempts to assess the significance of factor intensity reversals have given conflicting results, in part because different types of production functions have been used in empirical work. Unfortunately, trade theories do not specify the appropriate form of production function.

Taste Differences

We have seen that taste differences can be responsible for trade, and may be sufficiently strong to override a production bias resulting from differences in relative factor endowments.[1] For tastes to be used as an explanation of the Leontief paradox, it must be assumed that the United States has a preference for capital-intensive goods. However, this explanation is not supported by the

---

[1] See Figure 2.10.

evidence. Empirical work suggests that taste differences are not great between countries with similar income levels, and, as we have seen, trade is higher between developed countries (which have similar levels of income) than between developed and less developed countries.

Barriers to Trade

Another explanation of the Leontief paradox is that it arises because of tariffs. There is evidence to suggest that American imports of labor-intensive products are restricted. These restrictions reduce the tendency towards the expected result, and may be part of the explanation.[2]

Summary

The preceding discussion shows that the basic Heckscher-Ohlin model does not explain the trade of individual countries, or the structure of world trade. As the explanations of the Leontief paradox show, factor endowments are not the only influence on trade. We now turn to the examination of theories that have offered other explanations of trade.

THE PREFERENCE SIMILARITY HYPOTHESIS: TASTES AND PRODUCT DEVELOPMENT   `3.3`

Tastes and Trade

Linder (1961) explains the pattern of trade by the effect of tastes on the type of goods produced and traded. He argues that for a country to export a commodity it is necessary that there also be a domestic demand for the product. Linder gives three reasons to support his argument. First, producers have a greater awareness of profit opportunities in their domestic market; the profits from exporting will only be obvious after a considerable period of producing for the home market. Second, research efforts are aimed at satisfying the most obvious needs, which, he suggests, are the needs of the domestic market. Third, even if entrepreneurs recognize the need for a product in a foreign market, it is expensive to develop and adapt a product to fit an unfamiliar market.

This reasoning leads Linder to the view that the range of products a country might export is a subset of the range of products it consumes. The potential range of imported products includes all the products the country consumes. Whether a particular product is actually imported depends on the price of the import in relation to the price of domestic goods. Thus, Linder argues, the range of goods that are potential exports is equal to, or is a subset of, the range of goods that may be imported. Linder's argument would lead us to

---

[2] See Baldwin (1971).

look for similarities between countries' tastes rather than differences between countries' factor endowments. The greater the overlap between countries' consumption patterns, the greater the potential for trade. This result is very different from that of the Heckscher-Ohlin theorem.

Linder offers a different explanation of trade in what are known as *primary products* (agricultural products, metals, minerals, and fuels). The basic nature of primary products implies that the potential for their export is easily recognized, and little adaptation of the product is needed. However, it is often foreign entrepreneurs who begin to export primary products, perhaps because they are more aware of the demand for the primary products in their home countries.

Linder explains the high degree of trade between countries with similar income levels by pointing to the correlation between income and tastes. Countries with similar income levels consume similar goods, and, since countries trade goods that they consume, we should expect trade between countries with similar levels of income to be high.

Limitations of the Preference Similarity Hypothesis

Although Linder's model explains the pattern of trade shown in Table 3.1, supply conditions are virtually ignored, just as demand is ignored in the Heckscher-Ohlin model. In the long run, the assumption that foreign demand is not recognized and that a country's natural advantages in some types of manufactured goods remain unexploited because of a limited domestic market seems unrealistic.

We have only to consider the case of Hong Kong to see the limitations of Linder's argument. Hong Kong produces a vast range of products quickly and cheaply using an educated mobile pool of labor. Many of these products are exported even though they are not consumed in significant amounts in Hong Kong itself (artificial Christmas trees are an example). Even if Hong Kong producers are not fully aware of all the marketing possibilities in the West, Western importers and retailers looking for low-cost sources of supply may seek out efficient foreign producers.

Linder recognizes that foreign entrepreneurs can exploit natural resources, but does not develop the same argument for manufactured goods. Where manufacturing is undertaken by foreign entrepreneurs, Linder says that the reason is often to increase exports to countries with similar demand structures. However, demand is not always the reason for developing manufacturing production in another country. For example, American automobile producers have transferred production of some parts to other countries where the costs of production are lower.

The preceding qualifications do not imply that Linder's model is wrong; like all models, it is not a complete explanation of trade. Another factor that determines the goods a country exports and imports is the availability of technology in the country.

The Product Cycle Model   3.4

Some countries have access to better technology than other countries, and this gives them a comparative advantage in the production of certain goods. The goods may be technologically advanced, or the production technology may be advanced. For example, it is clear that Japan has a comparative advantage in the production of some types of electronic equipment. Countries that do not possess the same technology cannot compete effectively.[3]

The *product cycle model*, which was put forward by Vernon (1966), suggests that trade in manufactured products may be the result of the development and application of new technology. Vernon's work was an extension of earlier work by Linder, focusing on domestic demand as a necessary condition for a good to be exported. Although Vernon accepts the commonly held view that access to technological developments is similar in advanced countries, he argues that producers are more aware of the possibilities of using the technology in their home markets. For example, he suggests that the characteristics of the United States market (higher labor costs and greater availability of capital than in most countries) have led American producers to specialize in products that allow capital to be substituted for labor.

Stages in the Product Cycle

Vernon divides the development and marketing of a product into three stages: new product, maturing product, and standardized product. He suggests that initially a product will be produced and marketed mainly in the domestic market. This enables the producer to test the product and perfect production techniques.

During the maturing product stage, the product becomes standardized and mass production becomes possible. Product standardization does not mean that product differentiation ends: variety may increase as producers recognize the characteristics that appeal to consumers. At this stage the product is marketed internationally. Producers look for similar markets in other advanced countries as potential export markets. Also, as foreign consumption of the product increases, producers begin to consider other countries as possible locations for production.

The third stage occurs when the product is at an advanced stage of standardization. Production and transport costs are the most important factors influencing the location of production at this stage. It becomes possible for exports to third countries to be made from foreign facilities rather than from the United States, and for the American market to be supplied with imports. Production and exports by the United States tail off as foreign competition develops. At this stage, production may shift to developing countries.

---

[3] Japan is now second only to the United States in the export of high-tech products.

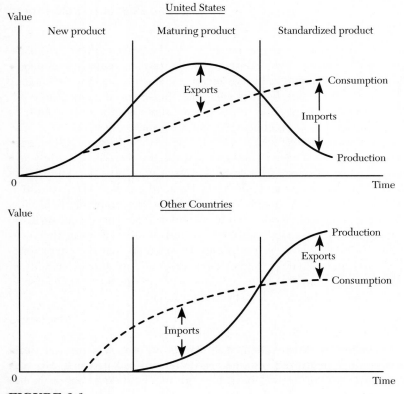

FIGURE 3.1

Stages in the Product Cycle Hypothesis

During the first stage the product is developed and sold mainly in the United States. In the second stage, the product becomes more standardized, the United States dominates the export market, and foreign production begins. In the final stage, foreign competition increases, the United States begins importing the product, and American production declines. (Adapted from Vernon, 1966.)

Figure 3.1 shows the stages of development and marketing of a good. The division of the cycle into stages is for expositional convenience; the stages will vary with different products.

The Product Cycle and the Heckscher-Ohlin Theorem

Vernon's model leads us to expect that a country will export products that are at a certain stage of the product cycle. Through time, a country will export different goods and different countries may export the same good as the good moves through its product cycle. This view of trade is very different from the Heckscher-Ohlin model in which the assumptions of constant technology, standardized products, and complete knowledge ensure that technology, marketing, and product development have no role.

If the term *factor endowment* is interpreted loosely enough, and is taken to include the ability to develop or produce new goods, then Vernon's model has similarities to the Heckscher-Ohlin model. However, such an interpretation does not seem consistent with the static nature of the Heckscher-Ohlin model.

Vernon used his model to explain the Leontief paradox. As we have seen, the model suggests that the United States exports products that are in the early part of the product cycle. Because the degree of standardization of these products is low, mass production using capital-intensive methods is not possible. However, the United States imports products that are at an advanced stage of standardization, and thus can be produced using capital-intensive methods.

Examples of the Product Cycle

The product cycle theory is often used to explain early Japanese-American trade. The United States had a technological advantage that gave it a comparative advantage in the early stages of production, whereas Japan was able to produce goods more efficiently than the United States after the initial development had been completed. More recently, it is less clear that American technology and product development are superior, and many new products are being developed by Japan. While Japan has been moving towards the development stage, other countries such as Korea and Taiwan have been able to compete in the production of goods using standardized technology.

The market for color television receivers is an example of the product cycle. Color broadcasting began in 1954 in the United States. In the early years, domestic producers dominated the market for receivers. In 1967, imports were equal to 6 percent of the market. By 1970, imports had grown to 19 percent and over 90 percent of the imports came from Japan. However, Japan did not simply copy American producers. Japanese firms adopted all-solid-state components before American firms, thus improving the quality of their sets, and they concentrated on smaller sets. (American producers were less interested in producing small sets because of the lower profit margin.) Also, Japanese firms benefited from lower costs of production. As the technology spread and the product became standardized, production spread to other countries. The share of Japan in American imports decreased to 80 percent in 1977 and 50 percent in 1978, as imports from Taiwan and Korea increased.[4]

---

[4] A more detailed description of the market for color television receivers, and the protection given to American producers, is contained in Organization for Economic Co-Operation and Development (1985).

The Product Cycle Theory's Relevance Today

Vernon (1979) himself has questioned the usefulness of the product cycle theory in helping to explain modern trade. The theory was based on the view that national markets were separate and that producers responded to domestic market conditions. The importance of the product cycle theory has been reduced by the growth of multinational companies that cater to a global market by producing in more than one country and marketing goods internationally.

Although its importance has diminished, the theory still has some relevance. The international trade of small firms that engage in research and development may conform to the product cycle theory. Such firms may begin by developing goods for the domestic market because they do not have the network of foreign subsidiaries needed to produce and market goods internationally. Also, the trade of developing countries may follow the predictions of the theory because domestic market conditions give some countries technological advantages in certain areas. However, the model no longer provides as convincing an explanation of American trade with the rest of the world as it did when it was first put forward.

Policy Relevance

An important conclusion for economic policy that emerges from this analysis, and which continues to be relevant, is that it may be unwise or impossible for countries to attempt to stay competitive in particular products. The notion that a country was, and should remain, a world leader in the production of one product is the antithesis of the product cycle approach. If a country wants to maintain or increase its exports, the answer may be for it to accept its natural role, either as a producer or developer of some types of goods, and not try to maintain a degree of competitive power in particular goods.

One of the key elements determining a country's degree of success in international trade may be the ease with which resources can be moved from one sector to another. The greater the degree of flexibility, the easier it is for an advanced country to produce new products continuously, or a less advanced country to take over the production of standardized products.

3.5   INTRA-INDUSTRY TRADE: OTHER INFLUENCES ON TRADE

So far we have assumed that countries import and export different goods, but in fact countries often export and import the same products, or, to be more precise, products that are classified as the output of the same type of industry. This phenomenon is called *intra-industry trade*. An examination of intra-industry trade is an interesting exercise for its own sake, and is useful because it serves as a background against which other influences on trade can be considered.

The existence of intra-industry trade seems to contradict the Heckscher-

Ohlin model. Firms in an industry produce similar products, and might be expected to use similar factors of production. On the basis of the Heckscher-Ohlin model, we would expect the firms in an industry to have the same comparative advantage or disadvantage because of the similarity between their use of factors of production. We shall examine explanations of intra-industry trade in order to enhance our understanding of the causes of international trade.

The Classification of Goods and Industries

Industries are classified according to the goods produced, not the factors of production used. Although firms producing the "same" goods might use the same factors of production, we cannot guarantee that this will be the case. For example, furniture may be made with many different materials, such as wood, plastic, and metal. Another example where the same product may be produced using different factors of production is the textile industry: the methods used to make nylon cloth have little similarity to the methods used to make cotton cloth. Manufacturers using different factors of production cannot be expected to face the same costs or the same competitive pressures.

In part, the simultaneous import and export of goods produced by one industry, and the use of different factors of production by firms in the same industry, reflects too high a degree of aggregation. If we were to specify the goods more carefully, different industries might be distinguished.

Industries are classified using the *Standard Industrial Trade Classification (SITC)*. The more digits used to classify an industry, the more specific the classification. For example, SITC code 7 represents machinery and transport equipment; 78 represents road vehicles (including air cushion vehicles); 782 represents motor vehicles for the transport of goods and special purpose motor vehicles; and 782.21 represents crane lorries.[5]

Grubel and Lloyd (1971) examined Australia's trade and found that the degree of intra-industry trade diminishes as the criteria for defining an industry become more stringent. To be specific, they found that intra-industry trade fell from 20 percent of total trade at the three-digit SITC level to 6 percent of trade at the seven-digit SITC level. Since intra-industry trade is found even at the lowest level of aggregation used in compiling trade statistics, the seven-digit level, this suggests that the level of aggregation is not an adequate explanation of intra-industry trade. In theory, more stringent criteria could be used, but there are other explanations of intra-industry trade that lead us to expect that such trade will be found even at very low levels of aggregation.

Entrepôt Trade

The problem of defining products is illustrated by the trade of countries that are engaged in entrepôt trade. These countries provide services, such as storage, blending, and packaging, that do not alter the goods sufficiently for

---

[5] *Standard International Trade Classification, Revision 3*. New York: United Nations, 1986.

the classification of the goods to be changed; it appears that the same goods are being imported and exported. Hong Kong and Singapore are examples of countries engaged in entrepôt trade.

Transport Costs

Intra-industry trade can be explained by the existence of transport costs. Because of transport costs, it may be cheaper to import a product from a firm just over a national border than it is to purchase the product from a firm located on the other side of the home country. To put it another way, national boundaries have not usually been drawn for economic reasons, and we would not expect potential market areas determined by transport costs to be confined neatly within national boundaries. Grubel and Lloyd suggest that border trade can probably only explain intra-industry trade in a limited range of products, for example, perishable foods, building materials, and electricity.

Temporary Differences between Demand and Supply

Fluctuations in production or consumption can give rise to intra-industry trade. For example, the growing season for agricultural products often differs between different countries. Although agricultural products can sometimes be stored, it may be cheaper to import agricultural products than to store domestic output. Electricity can also be stored, but some European countries find that, because peaks in demand do not coincide, it is cheaper to satisfy peak demand partly by importing electricity than it is to have the production and/or storage capacity needed to meet the demand for electricity at all times of the day.

Economies of Scale and Product Differentiation

Finally, intra-industry trade can be explained by *economies of scale* and by *product differentiation.* If firms concentrate on the domestic market and attempt to produce a broad range of products, they may not be able to benefit from economies of scale. International trade allows firms to specialize in a narrower range of products and produce more than can be sold domestically. In this way they may achieve economies of scale by using larger plants and longer production runs. One reason why producers in different countries choose to produce slightly different versions of the same good is because their domestic markets differ. For example, if there is a high concentration in one area of people with incomes of a certain level, producers in that area may specialize in goods consumed by this group. Although the same good may be produced in different areas, differences in average per-capita incomes could give rise to different qualities of the same good being produced.

The automobile industry is an example of an industry where the minimum-sized efficient plant is quite large, and producers specialize in different versions of the same product. In this case intra-industry trade is substantial. Intra-industry trade is also found in the aircraft and weapons industries, where long production runs are needed to recoup research and development costs, and international orders are very important.

Summary of Main Points

The Heckscher-Ohlin theorem does not explain all trade. In particular, the high degree of trade between developed countries that appear to have similar factor endowments and the emergence of Southeast Asian countries as important exporting countries cannot be easily explained using a model focusing on differences in factor endowments.

Empirical testing of the Heckscher-Ohlin model also casts doubt on the general validity of the model. Leontief tested the Heckscher-Ohlin model using data for the United States and found that more capital was needed to produce imports than was required to produce exports. This contradicted the presumption that the United States is capital-intensive and would export capital-intensive products.

Various explanations of this paradox have been offered. These include differences of labor productivity, labor skills, research and development expenditures, endowments of natural resources, production functions, and tastes, and the roles of barriers to trade and factor intensity reversals. These explanations helped stimulate work to identify other causes of international trade.

Linder's model predicts that trade will take place between countries that have similar tastes. The reasons Linder offers are that producers are more aware of profit and marketing possibilities in the home market, and adapting a product to sell in another market is expensive. Thus, goods are normally designed for the domestic market and then exported to similar markets. Linder's model explains the high degree of trade between developed countries because countries with similar incomes appear to have similar tastes.

Vernon too assumes that domestic demand influences the products produced. He suggests that the goods in which a country has a comparative advantage are influenced by the technology the country possesses. In particular, he suggested that the United States has access to higher technology than other countries and has a comparative advantage in products during the early stages of a product's development when research and development play an important role. Production later moves to lower-cost countries after the product and technology have been standardized. This model is interesting because it predicts that the products in which a country has a comparative advantage will change as the products mature. The development of multinational firms that produce and market goods internationally casts doubt on the importance of demand and supply conditions in the home market.

In practice, countries often import and export the same good. This may occur for a number of reasons, including use of too broad a classification of goods, transport costs, temporary differences between demand and supply, economies of scale, and product differentiation.

Study Questions

1. Discuss the view that the different theories of international trade presented in this chapter highlight different aspects of trade, and that one theory is no more true than another.

2. The Heckscher-Ohlin theorem is plausible but cannot explain trade in all types of goods or the pattern of trade between all countries. Discuss.

3. What is the Leontief paradox? Discuss three explanations of the paradox.

4. How can the product cycle hypothesis be used to explain the Leontief paradox and the structure of world trade shown in Table 3.1 and Table 3.2?

5. How can transport costs act both as a barrier to trade and a cause of trade?

6. How can tastes and economies of scale be used to explain the existence of intra-industry trade?

7. How can Linder's model be used to explain the fact that developed countries trade more with each other than with less developed countries?

8. Economies of scale lead to a production possibility frontier that is concave from below (it bends inwards rather than outwards as shown in the Heckscher-Ohlin diagrams). Show that in this case international trade results in complete specialization. Explain this result with reference to reasons for the difference between the degrees of specialization in the Ricardian and Heckscher-Ohlin models.

Selected References

Baldwin, R. E. "Determinants of the Commodity Structure of U.S. Trade." *American Economic Review* 61 (March 1971): 126–46. Reprinted in Baldwin and Richardson (1981).

Baldwin, R. E. "Determinants of Foreign Trade and Investment: Further Evidence." *Review of Economics and Statistics* 61 (February 1979): 40–48.

Baldwin, R. E., and Richardson, J. D. *International Trade and Finance,* Second Edition. Boston: Little Brown and Co., 1981. Third Edition, 1986.

Bharadwaj, J. "Factor Proportions and the Structure of Indo-U.S. Trade." *Indian Economic Journal* 10 (October 1962): 105–16.

Chacholiades, M. *International Trade Theory and Policy.* New York: McGraw-Hill, 1978.

Grubel, H. G. "The Theory of Intra-Industry Trade." In *Studies in International Economics,* edited by I. D. McDougall and R. H. Snape. Amsterdam: North Holland, 1970. Reprinted in Baldwin and Richardson (1981).

Grubel, H. G., and Lloyd, P. J. "The Empirical Measurement of Intra-Industry Trade." *Economic Record* 47 (December 1971): 494–517.

Krugman, P. "New Theories of Trade among Industrial Countries." *American Economic Review* 73 (May 1983): 338–42. Reprinted in *The Contemporary International Economy,* Second Edition, edited by J. Adams. New York: St. Martin's Press, 1985.

Leontief, W. W. "Domestic Production and Foreign Trade: The American Position Re-examined." *Proceedings of the American Philosophical Society* 97 (September 1953): 332–49. Reprinted in *Readings in International Economics,* edited by H. G. Johnson and R. E. Caves. Homewood, Ill.: Richard D. Irwin, 1968.

Leontief, W. W. "Factor Proportions and the Structure of American Trade: Further

Theoretical and Empirical Analysis." *Review of Economics and Statistics* 38 (November 1956): 386–407.

Linder, S. B. *An Essay on Trade and Transformation.* New York: John Wiley and Sons, 1961. An excerpt is reprinted in Baldwin and Richardson (1981).

Maskus, K. E. "A Test of the Heckscher-Ohlin Vanek Theorem: The Leontief Commonplace." *Journal of International Economics* 19 (1985): 201–12.

Organization for Economic Co-Operation and Development. *Costs and Benefits of Protection.* Paris: OECD, 1985.

Posner, M. V. "International Trade and Technical Change." *Oxford Economic Papers* 13 (October 1961): 323–41.

Stern, R. M. "Testing Trade Theories." In *International Trade and Finance,* edited by P. B. Kenen. Cambridge: Cambridge University Press, 1975.

Tatemoto, M., and Ichimura, S. "Factor Proportions and Foreign Trade: The Case of Japan." *Review of Economics and Statistics* 41 (November 1959): 442–46.

Vernon, R. "International Investment and International Trade in the Product Cycle." *Quarterly Journal of Economics* 80 (May 1966): 190–207. Reprinted in Baldwin and Richardson (1981).

Vernon, R. "The Product Cycle Hypothesis in a New International Environment." *Oxford Bulletin of Economics and Statistics* 41 (November 1979): 255–67.

Wahl, D. F. "Capital and Labor Requirements for Canada's Foreign Trade." *Canadian Journal of Economics and Political Science* 27 (August 1961): 349–58.

4

BARRIERS TO
TRADE

4.1 INTRODUCTION

In this chapter we shall examine the economic effects of barriers to trade. We begin by examining the economic effects of a tariff, and then we examine other types of trade barriers. Our discussion leads to the conclusion that, in general, barriers to trade are economically inefficient. When government intervention is justified to achieve an objective, there is usually an alternative policy that is more efficient and does not require restricting trade.

4.2 THE ECONOMIC EFFECTS OF TARIFFS

What Are Tariffs?

Taxes on traded goods are known as *tariffs*. They are one of the most common forms of trade barrier. When tariffs are applied, evasion must be prevented, that is, action must be taken to prevent smuggling. This is one reason why countries maintain guarded borders, and why people traveling between countries are occasionally searched. Most goods enter a country through a small number of ports, and usually it is not difficult or expensive for taxes to be levied as a good moves from one country to another. Tariffs can be imposed on an *ad valorem* basis (as a percentage of the value of the good), on a *specific* basis (a certain amount of money per unit of the good imported), or on a *compound* basis (a combination of *ad valorem* and specific). Tariffs can be applied narrowly, to one or two goods, or generally, to all imports or imports of certain types of goods (for example, agricultural goods).

The method of fixing the tariff need not concern us because the basic effects are the same.[1]

The effects of a tariff can be classified as follows:

1. Consumption Effect
2. Production Effect
3. Import Effect
4. Revenue Effect
5. Redistribution Effect
6. Terms of Trade Effect
7. Balance of Trade Effect
8. Income and Employment Effects

Each of these effects is discussed below. We examine them in more detail as part of our discussion of arguments for protection in the next chapter.

Consumption Effect

The effect of a tariff on consumption is clear: tariffs increase import prices, which tends to reduce the consumption of imports and increase the consumption of domestic substitutes. As consumers switch from imports to domestic substitutes, they bid up the prices of these substitutes until the prices of domestic and imported goods are equal. Since the prices of both imported goods and domestic substitutes rise, total consumption of these goods declines.

Production Effect

Domestic production of import-competing goods increases when tariffs are imposed because the reduction in the quantity of imports demanded increases the demand for domestic goods. This is one reason why domestic producers sometimes lobby for tariff protection. The extent of the production effect is determined by the initial size of the import-competing sector, and the response of domestic supply to the increase in demand caused by the tariff. Some sectors are more able to expand their output than others, and the potential for increased production is often used as an argument for protection. We return to this question when we discuss the infant-industry argument for tariff protection (in the next chapter).

Import Effect

Tariffs reduce the quantity of imports because as imports become more expensive relative to domestically produced goods fewer imports are bought. The size of the import effect is determined by the consumption and produc-

---

[1] One difference between *ad valorem* and specific tariffs is that when the price of a good rises because of inflation, a specific tariff falls as a percentage of the value of the good whereas an *ad valorem* tariff is unaffected.

tion effects. For example, if the quantity demanded of a good does not change very much as its price rises, and domestic production of the good does not increase, imports will not change greatly. However, if there is a significant fall in the quantity demanded and a large increase in the quantity supplied of domestic substitutes, there will be a large fall in the quantity of imports.

Revenue Effect

Tariffs generate revenue for the government. Tariffs levied primarily to raise revenue are called *revenue tariffs*. For *ad valorem* tariffs, the amount of tariff revenue equals the percentage tariff rate multiplied by the post-tariff value of imports (at free trade prices). For specific tariffs, the revenue equals the per unit tariff multiplied by the post-tariff quantity of imports. Obviously, if a tariff on a good is so high that no imports enter the country, there will be no revenue; in this case the tariff is said to be *prohibitive*. Clearly, when generating revenue is one of the main reasons for imposing a tariff, the government must consider the change in the quantity of imports (the import effect) as well as the revenue per unit. A high tariff may generate a lot of revenue per unit, but if very few imports enter the country little revenue will be collected.

Redistribution Effect

The discussion so far has shown that tariffs redistribute money: consumers pay more, domestic producers of import substitutes receive higher prices, and the government receives tariff revenue. This redistribution of income can be considered itself as an effect of tariff. We shall examine the overall welfare effects of a tariff in a moment, but, when reference is made to the overall welfare effects of a tariff, it must be remembered that tariffs lead to gains and losses for different groups.

Terms of Trade Effect

The *terms of trade* may be defined as the ratio of the price of exports to the price of imports. A favorable change in the terms of trade occurs if the price of exports rises in relation to the price of imports. Tariffs can lead to a favorable change in the terms of trade. When a country imposes a tariff on a good, the country's demand for imports of the good normally falls. The world price of the good may fall in response to the fall in the country's demand if the country accounts for a significant percentage of the total demand for the good.[2] To the extent that the world price of an imported good falls while the price of exports remains the same, there is a favorable change in the terms of trade.

---

[2] Recall that a fall in the demand for imports moves a country's offer curve inwards. If the country is large, the terms of trade increase. See Section 2.5.

Balance of Trade Effect

The *balance of trade* is the difference between the values of exports and imports. The balance of trade tends to increase when tariffs are imposed because of the import effect, and this increase is sometimes used as an argument in favor of tariffs. For example, countries experiencing unemployment may find an increase in the balance of trade desirable because the demand for domestic goods increases. (The conditions under which tariffs increase domestic employment are discussed below.) Countries that have fixed exchange rates sometimes use tariffs because an increase in the balance of trade reduces the demand for foreign exchange, which may help a country maintain its chosen exchange rate.

Although the balance of trade effect seems simple, there are many factors that may reduce the overall effect of tariffs on the balance of trade: although imports of the goods that bear tariffs normally decrease, consumption of other imported goods may increase and export production may be adversely affected by an increase in the cost of imported goods that are used by the export sector. The balance of trade effects of a tariff are discussed in more detail in Section 5.5. For the present it is sufficient to note that the overall effect of tariffs on the balance of trade may be much smaller than might appear at first sight.

Income and Employment Effects

Finally, to the extent that there is an increase in the balance of trade, the demand for domestic goods *(aggregate demand)* increases. An increase in aggregate demand caused by tariffs will affect national income and employment in basically the same way as an increase in government spending. The income and employment effects of an increase in aggregate demand depend on the condition of the economy when the tariff is imposed. If there is full employment, an increase in aggregate demand will not lead to an increase in output because the economy cannot produce any more; inflation will be the only result. In this case, although the monetary value of national income will go up, output will not, and therefore real income will stay the same. Unemployment is a necessary condition for tariffs to increase real income and employment.[3] If there is unemployment and aggregate demand increases, output, employment, and prices may rise together.[4]

A Diagrammatic Approach

The first five effects of a tariff are shown in Figure 4.1. Assuming that the importing country cannot affect the world price (the supply of imports is perfectly elastic), the country will be able to consume all it wants at the world

---

[3] This condition is similar to the condition for a devaluation to be effective. See Chapter 9.
[4] Economists who believe that the economy tends naturally towards full employment often doubt the usefulness of tariffs to reduce unemployment.

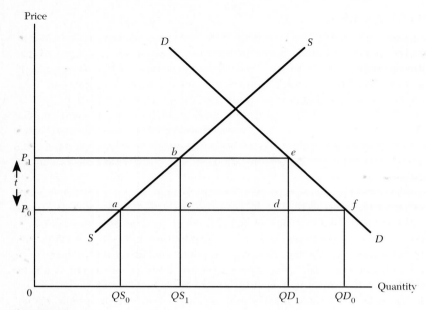

FIGURE 4.1

The Effects of a Tariff Levied by a Small Country

Domestic demand and supply are shown by DD and SS, respectively. At the world price of imports P_0, QD_0 is demanded, QS_0 is supplied domestically, and imports equal $OD_0 - QS_0$. A tariff (t) raises the domestic price of imports to P_1. Demand falls to QD_1, domestic supply rises to QS_1, and imports fall to $QD_1 - QS_1$. Consumer surplus falls by P_0P_1ef, producer surplus increases by P_0P_1ba, and tariff revenue of *cbed* is collected. The net loss from the tariff equals *abc* + *def*.

price P_0. The domestic supply of the good is shown by the supply curve SS and the domestic demand for the good is shown by the demand curve DD. The initial equilibrium price is at P_0, domestic producers supply QS_0, and domestic consumption is QD_0. The difference between domestic consumption and domestic production, QD_0-QS_0, is made up by imports.

When a tariff is imposed, the price of imports rises from P_0 to P_1. The consumption effect is the fall in consumption from QD_0 to QD_1 caused by the increase in price. The production effect is the increase in the quantity supplied domestically from QS_0 to QS_1. As consumption falls and domestic production rises, less is imported. The import effect is the fall in imports from QD_0-QS_0 to QD_1-QS_1. The difference between P_0 and P_1 is the amount of the tariff the government collects on each unit of the good. The area of the rectangle *cbed* is thus equal to the total revenue collected because the area equals the amount of the tariff per unit multiplied by the quantity imported, that is, $(P_1$-$P_0)$ × $(QD_1$-$QS_1)$. This is the revenue effect. Finally, the diagram shows that consumers pay higher prices and consume less, while producers receive higher prices and produce more. Thus, tariffs reduce the welfare of consumers and increase the welfare of producers of import substitutes. This is the redistribution effect.

THE WELFARE EFFECTS OF A TARIFF   ■ 4.3

The welfare effects of a tariff can be shown using *consumer surplus* and *producer surplus*.[5] Consumers experience a loss of consumer surplus when the price rises, which is represented in Figure 4.1 by the area of the trapezoid P_0P_1ef. There is an increase in producer surplus, which is represented by the area of the trapezoid P_0P_1ba. The tariff revenue gained by the government is represented by the area of the rectangle *cbed*. If the gains to producers and the government are deducted from the loss to consumers, we are left with two triangles: *abc* and *def*. These triangles represent the net loss to society resulting from the tariff.

This result was derived using the implicit assumption that one dollar yields the same amount of welfare whether it accrues to consumers, producers, or the government. Clearly, this is a strong assumption. However, the undesirability of tariffs can be shown without this assumption.

The Allocation of Resources

We saw in Chapter 1 that there are gains from trade. If trade is reduced we would expect those gains to be reduced. This is what happens when a tariff is imposed. A tariff leads to economic inefficiency because a tariff-levying country produces more of a good instead of buying from countries that can produce the good at a lower cost. In other words, inefficiency is shown by the increase in domestic production that results from the higher market price that a tariff generates.

Domestic producers of import substitutes gain (because they are able to sell more at the higher price), so why do we say tariffs are inefficient? An example will illustrate the answer. Britain or Canada could become self-sufficient in peaches by imposing a tariff that raises the price of peaches so that domestic production becomes profitable and imported peaches become so expensive no one buys them. Most people would agree that such a policy would be ridiculous because of the climates of the two countries. However, this

---

[5] Consumer surplus is shown by the area above the price line and below the demand curve. It represents the difference between consumers' valuation of successive units of the good, and the price paid. Producer surplus is shown by the area below the price line and above the supply curve. It represents the difference between the marginal cost of successive units of the good and the price received.

example is simply a more extreme case of the general argument that countries should import from other countries if other countries can produce at lower cost.[6]

The Tariff Viewed as a Consumption Tax and a Producer Subsidy

A tariff is in effect a tax on consumers that finances a subsidy to producers: it is a tax because consumers pay more for the goods they buy, and it is a subsidy because domestic producers receive more for the goods they sell. If the tariff is not prohibitive, tariff revenue is collected. This revenue shows that the amount paid by consumers is greater than the amount received by producers.[7] When tariff support is given to an industry, consumers are in effect taxed to support the industry. This may not be obvious because the tax on consumers and the subsidy to producers occur in the form of a higher market price, and do not result from an explicit tax-subsidy program. But this way of viewing a tariff highlights the gains and losses imposed by a tariff.

4.4 TARIFFS VERSUS SUBSIDIES FOR SUPPORT OF DOMESTIC PRODUCTION

If a country decided that it wanted to support domestic production of a good, perhaps to increase employment in a particular sector, a tariff is rarely if ever the best way to do it. A tariff supports producers of a particular good by taxing consumers of the same good. An alternative policy with the same effect on output and employment is for governments to subsidize domestic producers by the amount that the market price of the good would have risen with a tariff.

This policy of *subsidies* may be preferred to tariff support for four reasons. First, a subsidy may be financed from general taxation in a manner consistent with income distribution objectives. It does not need to be financed by taxing only consumers of the good. Thus, a subsidy can typically be financed more equitably than a tariff. Second, because consumers do not have to pay a higher price for the imported good, they will consume more of the good than if a tariff were imposed. To the extent that consumption of the good from a low cost source (other countries) is maintained, the subsidy will be less inefficient than the tariff. Third, subsidies are less likely to induce foreign retaliation. Fourth, whereas tariffs redistribute income from consumers to producers in an implicit way, subsidies are explicit redistributions. The amount of support

---

[6]This example is similar to that used by Adam Smith in his argument in favor of free trade. See Section 1.3.

[7]Producers do not benefit from the higher prices consumers pay for imports; the government receives tariff revenue instead.

given to domestic producers by subsidies is subject to public scrutiny, whereas subsidies given through tariffs are not so clear, although no less real. For people who favor an open society, subsidies are therefore preferable to tariffs.

In Figure 4.2 the effects of a subsidy are shown: a subsidy of s per unit gives producers the same revenue as they receive from the tariff shown in Figure 4.1, that is, P_0 and P_1 are the same in both diagrams and $P_0 + s = P_1$. The domestic quantity supplied (QS_1) is the same under the subsidy as it is under the tariff because producers receive the same revenue per unit. The financial cost of the subsidy is the amount of the subsidy (s) multiplied by the number of units subsidized (QS_1), the area of the rectangle P_0P_1bc. Producers

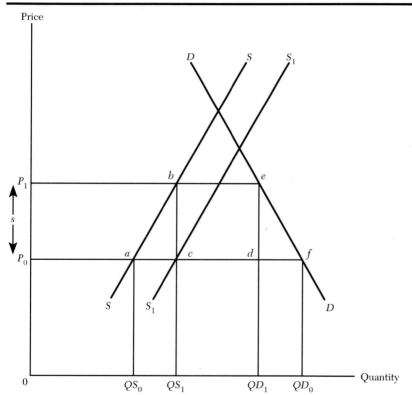

FIGURE 4.2

Subsidies versus Tariffs

The initial position is the same as in Figure 4.1. A subsidy shifts the domestic supply line from SS to S_1S_1 and raises output from QS_0 to QS_1. The monetary cost of the subsidy is P_0P_1bc and producer surplus rises by P_0P_1ba, thus the net cost of the subsidy is abc. The subsidy is preferable to a tariff that raises domestic output by the same amount, because a tariff would cause an additional welfare loss equal to def.

experience an increase in producer surplus equal to P_0P_1ba. Thus, there is a net welfare loss to society equal to the area of the triangle *abc*. There is no change in consumer surplus because the market price does not change. The subsidy is therefore a less costly way of increasing domestic production than a tariff.

Why then would tariffs ever be adopted rather than subsidies? One reason is that producers may prefer tariffs to subsidies, precisely because the support is less obvious. Who wants to be seen to be dependent on government handouts? Another reason is that tariffs generate government revenue, whereas subsidies must be financed, thus tariffs appear to cost less. However, once it is recognized that tariffs are in effect producer subsidies financed by consumption taxes, the fact that the government must levy taxes to finance subsidies is not a valid argument in favor of tariff support.

Problems of Financing Subsidies

In discussing the relative merits of tariffs and subsidies as alternative ways of providing support to an industry, we implicitly assumed that the country has a developed tax system. However, in some developing countries, tariffs may be necessary to raise revenue for government activities because other forms of taxation are not available. This does not mean that tariff support of industries is justified. Even if tariffs are needed to raise money, supporting industries through the use of subsidies is still preferable to tariff support.

In the absence of a developed tax system, the fundamental problem is how to finance the subsidies. General tariffs, covering a wide range of goods, are more efficient revenue raising devices than tariffs levied solely on the goods that the industries produce. Therefore, if financing subsidies from general taxation is not possible, subsidies financed from general tariffs should be used. In general, tariff support of industries is neither necessary nor desirable, even in developing countries.

Although revenue raising is best achieved by general tariffs, other considerations may lead developing countries to apply higher tariffs to some goods than to others. For example, it can be argued that tractors are more important for economic development than luxury motor cars. Even if the resulting tariff structure is economically inefficient, developing countries face many problems, and economic efficiency may be of less importance to them than other objectives (such as a higher rate of growth). However, it is interesting that the countries attempting to increase economic growth by restricting trade have usually grown more slowly than the countries pursuing policies that have encouraged greater international trade.[8] We shall examine some of the special problems of developing countries in Chapter 18.

---

[8] See the World Bank's *"World Development Report 1987,"* New York: Oxford University Press, 1987.

NON-TARIFF BARRIERS   4.5

Tariffs have decreased in importance over the last three decades, in part because of international agreements within the General Agreements on Tariffs and Trade.[9] However, in recent years there has been an increase in the importance of non-tariff barriers. Non-tariff barriers have been used for some time in the textile, clothing, and steel industries, but recently the coverage has also included industries such as automobiles, machine tools, and consumer electronics.[10]

Non-tariff barriers to trade can be classified into four types:

1. Restrictions on the quantity of traded goods
2. Government procurement biases
3. Taxes or subsidies to particular industries
4. Administrative obstructions that make international trade unnecessarily difficult or expensive

Quotas

A restriction on the quantity of imports or exports is known as a *quota*. Quotas may be applied as a limit on the absolute amount of goods that can be imported, or defined in terms of a share of the domestic market. The quota can be divided among a number of countries, or a global quota may be applied in which case the origin of the goods is not taken into consideration.

If a global quota is applied, the producers who are first in line will supply the market, but they will not necessarily be the producers that the government or consumers would prefer. Rather than allow supply to be determined on a first-come, first-served basis, governments typically issue licenses to importers or foreign suppliers. The division of the quota between potential suppliers is inevitably somewhat arbitrary. For example, if the division is made using historical market shares, new or growing firms will be penalized. Assessing firms according to criteria such as product quality, efficiency, price, and so on, is likely to be expensive, and the allocation will still be arbitrary because officials must interpret the different criteria and reach an overall conclusion. In some countries the discretionary power wielded by officials leads to corrupt practices.

The Economic Effects of Quotas

Quotas reduce the supply of imports of a good and cause prices to rise (because of the decrease in supply). Higher prices cause a fall in consumption, but domestic production increases. Quotas are therefore similar to tariffs in

---

[9] The history of commercial policy, including the formation and principles of GATT, is discussed in Chapter 15.

[10] These developments are discussed in Organization for Economic Co-Operation and Development (1985), in the International Monetary Fund's annual report: *Exchange Arrangements and Exchange Restrictions*, and in Kelly (1988).

their effects on consumption, production, and trade. However, quotas do not typically generate as much revenue as tariffs. Whether revenue is collected or not depends on how the quotas are imposed. Fees may be charged for the quota license, in which case the government receives some of the increase in the price of the good that occurs because of the decrease in supply caused by the import restriction.

Quota licenses may be auctioned competitively. In this case it does not matter who holds the quota license, tariffs and quotas are very much alike. Producers bidding against each other bid away any large profits that possession of a license might have yielded, and the government receives license revenue instead of tariff revenue. However, in practice, competitive auctions are not held, and quotas do not generate as much revenue for the government as tariffs. Instead, quotas generate profits for holders of licenses. If the quota licenses are held domestically, quotas generate profits for domestic firms rather than revenue for the government. Charging for the licenses merely redistributes income from quota holders to the government. In this case tariffs and quotas have the same overall effect on welfare, although they have different effects on the distribution of income. If the quota licenses are held by foreign firms, quotas reduce national welfare more than tariffs because quotas generate profits for foreign firms rather than government revenue.

The economic effects of a quota are shown in Figure 4.3. The quota equals the amount that is imported under the tariff shown in Figure 4.1, that is, $QD_1 - QS_1$. The market supply curve (S_1S_1) is obtained by adding the quota to the domestic supply curve (SS). The equilibrium price (P_1), the domestic quantity supplied (QS_1), and the amount of trade ($QD_1 - QS_1$) are the same as in the tariff case. Also, the effects on domestic producer surplus (P_0P_1ba) and consumer surplus (P_0P_1ef) are the same. The difference is that the area *cbed*, showing the money earned by quota holders buying at world prices and selling at domestic prices, does not automatically accrue to the government as revenue. Whether this area represents a further welfare loss beyond that caused by a tariff depends on whether fees are charged for quota licenses and on whether licenses are held by domestic or foreign firms, as discussed above.

Tariffs versus Quotas

Although in many respects tariffs and quotas are similar, tariffs may be preferable to quotas because tariffs generate government revenue rather than profits for quota holders. A second reason for preferring tariffs to quotas arises from the way in which quotas are applied: discrimination among suppliers is inevitable, so some are favored with licenses and some are not. This discrimination is a source of inefficiency and possible corruption. However, if a stable domestic price is desired for a good, and the world price is unstable, a quota may be preferable to a tariff. In the case of a tariff, the domestic price changes when the world price changes. A quota breaks the link between the domestic price and the world price: the domestic price is determined by domestic demand and domestic supply augmented by the quota. One reason why domes-

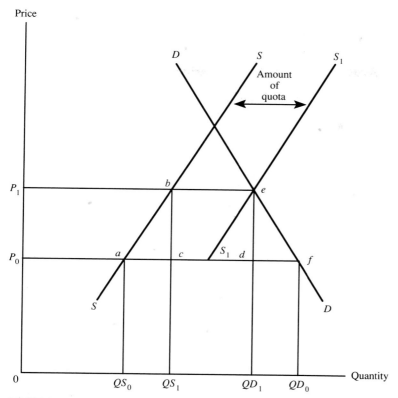

FIGURE 4.3

The Effects of a Quota

The initial position is the same as in Figure 4.1. A quota is imposed that limits imports to $QD_1 - QS_1$, the post-tariff quantity shown in Figure 4.1. The total supply (S_1S_1) equals SS plus the quota. (The country cannot consume imports at less than P_0, thus S_1S_1 does not extend below P_0.) The price effect (P_0P_1), the loss of consumer surplus (P_0P_1ef), and the gain to producers (P_0P_1ba) are the same as in the tariff case. The rectangle *cbed* is the quota holders' profit. If the quota licenses are held domestically, the net loss is the same as in the tariff case: *abc* + *def*.

tic producers may prefer quota protection to tariff protection is that an appreciation of domestic currency or escalating domestic costs may offset the protective effects of a tariff, but quotas will continue to provide protection from foreign competition.[11]

---

[11] This may be why some domestic manufacturers have argued for protection in the form of voluntary export restraints.

Voluntary Export Restraints

Recently, quotas have been adopted by foreign exporters. These are known as *voluntary export restraints (VERs)* or *orderly marketing arrangements (OMAs)*.[12] It would be more correct to say that VERs have been imposed by importing countries because, despite their name, VERs were not voluntarily adopted by exporters. Rather, foreign producers were induced to restrict exports by the danger that, if they did not do so, importing countries would impose tariffs or quotas. An obvious example of a VER is the agreement by Japanese automobile producers to limit exports to the United States. Another example is the agreement by the EEC to limit steel exports to the United States. The Multifiber Agreement, which restricts trade in textiles, is an example of an OMA. During the recession in world trade of the early 1980s, such agreements were popular with exporters worried about maintaining access to markets, and with governments concerned that imports might increase already high rates of unemployment.

Some people may find this type of policy undesirable in a democratic society, because VERs impose losses on one group (consumers) in order for another group (producers) to gain, without the VER necessarily being discussed or approved by the legislature. There is no doubt that one of the attractive features of VERs for politicians is that they can claim they support free trade while at the same time negotiating VERs to benefit important groups. Not only are VERs politically undesirable but they are also economically nonsensical, as we see below.

The Economic Effects of VERs

VERs have almost the same effects as quotas, and Figure 4.3 could represent either a quota or a VER. However, in the case of VERs, the government cannot share in the profits arising from the increase in the value of the good caused by the fall in supply (shown in the diagram by *cbed*). The foreign supplier or domestic importer benefits from the higher price. To the extent that VERs benefit mainly foreign suppliers, they are inferior to tariffs (which raise government revenue) or quotas (which may raise government revenue or generate profits for domestic license holders).[13] However, it is not surprising that foreign suppliers would rather restrict their exports voluntarily than be subject to tariffs or quotas.

---

[12]VERs are negotiated informally and bilaterally, whereas OMAs are formal agreements with all the major suppliers of a product.

[13]A VER for one product may also lead to increased imports of other products, because foreign producers can use the profits generated by the VER to finance moves into other areas not subject to controls. See Organization for Economic Co-Operation and Development (1985).

Government Procurement

Government purchases are a significant percentage of spending in most countries. Although some of this spending finances purchases of services that are not traded internationally, government spending on goods is significant. *Government procurement biases* are a form of discrimination against foreign producers. Most governments appear to have a policy of favoring domestically produced goods, although it is not usually stated explicitly. In the United States, the Buy American Act of 1933 required government agencies to buy American goods provided that imports were not more than 12 percent cheaper (50 percent in the case of defense).

Taxes and Subsidies

If domestic producers pay lower taxes or receive higher subsidies than foreign producers, domestic producers will have a competitive advantage. Export production, or the production of goods that compete with imports, can be encouraged through the tax system. Policies that help domestic producers engaged in international trade make it more difficult for foreign firms to compete, and are therefore another form of trade barrier.[14]

Administrative Regulatory Obstructions

Administrative obstructions may be imposed to discourage trade or make trading unnecessarily difficult or expensive. An example is the decision by the French government in 1982 to require all imports of videocassette recorders to enter France through a single customs post (Poitiers). This type of regulation increases the cost of goods by creating delays at customs posts. The British government was able to exclude French turkeys from Britain for the Christmas market in 1982 by insisting on excessive inspection of imported poultry, thus making imported turkeys more expensive.

Regulations may be introduced for legitimate reasons, such as health, safety, environmental considerations, or labeling information. If such regulations were uniform across countries, they would have little effect on trade. There are, however, many differences among countries' regulations regarding the production, nature, and marketing of goods, and such regulations can be used to reduce imports.[15] For example, in December 1988 there was a minor trade dispute when an EEC ban on the sale of meat containing artificial hormones was extended to cover imported meat. The United States complained that this was a restriction of trade because most American beef contains artificial hor-

---

[14] The plans of the European Economic Community (EEC) illustrate the problem: the EEC Commission has proposed that tax harmonization should be undertaken to strengthen the customs union. Little progress has been made. See Chapter 15.

[15] This is why the EEC Commission has introduced legislation to harmonize regulations between member states.

mones and there was no proven health hazard. The Commission of the European Community took the position that the ban on hormones was not a trade restriction because it covered all meat sold in the EEC and was a response to widespread public concern. The European view was that the hormone ban resembled the United States' regulation prohibiting imports of cheese made with unpasteurized milk (a product that France could export to the United States). Such disputes are bound to occur occasionally between countries that have different regulations.

Some regulations adversely affect the competitive position of domestic producers. For example, domestic producers may face higher production costs because they are required to maintain higher standards for health and safety in factories or because they face tighter pollution controls. Administrative trade barriers are probably as important as other types of trade barriers, but their importance is much more difficult to assess. Also, like VERs, they are not subject to close scrutiny by the democratic process.

Compliance Costs

In addition to the enforcement costs described above, costs are born by private individuals who must comply with the regulations. Initially, a firm must identify the tariffs and regulations its product is subject to, and this can be expensive in itself. Changing a product or its packaging to meet the regulations is also expensive, as is the preparation of the documentation necessary for a good to enter a country. These costs may be significant, and should not be ignored when discussing any actual policy.[16]

Summary of Main Points

Tariffs are taxes on traded goods. Tariffs reduce the welfare of a country by reducing the gains from trade. Although tariffs raise revenue for the government and producers of import substitutes benefit from tariff protection, the overall level of welfare falls because the loss to consumers is greater than the sum of the gain to producers and the revenue generated. When support of an industry is justified, tariff support is less desirable than support from *subsidies* that can be financed from general taxation, do not reduce the gains from trade, do not invite foreign retaliation, and provide support in a manner that allows public scrutiny. A tariff has similar effects to a consumption tax on a particular good, which is used to generate revenue and finance a subsidy to producers of the same good. It would be surprising if the best way to raise revenue to finance a subsidy to an industry were to tax consumers of the good that the industry produces.

---

[16]The Organization for Economic Co-Operation and Development (1985) cites studies showing that the average international transaction may require 35 documents and 360 copies, and cost in excess of 1 percent of the value of shipments. This cost is large when compared with the profit margins arising from foreign trade.

A *quota* limits the quantity of a good that can be imported. Quotas and tariffs have similar effects on consumers and producers, but quotas do not normally raise as much revenue as tariffs because license fees do not usually reflect the value of the license. Instead, quotas generate profits for holders of quota licenses. If the license holders are domestic residents, tariffs and quotas are similar except that they have different effects on the distribution of income. If the license holders are foreign, quotas reduce national welfare more than tariffs.

Non-tariff barriers include: quotas, *voluntary export restraints* (VERs), and *government procurement biases*. Also, policies that are not explicitly directed at international trade may affect the competitiveness of firms, for example, differences between *taxes* and *subsidies*, or *regulations* setting standards for such things as labeling, packaging, and health and safety in factories.

Study Questions

1. Briefly explain what is meant by:
   a. tariffs
   b. quotas
   c. voluntary export restraints
2. In what ways are a tariff and a quota similar and in what ways do they differ?
3. Evaluate the desirability of voluntary export restraints with reference to alternative policies to support domestic industries.
4. Using a diagram, show the welfare effects resulting from the imposition of a tariff.
5. Using diagrams, compare the welfare effects of tariffs and subsidies as alternative policies to achieve an increase in domestic production.
6. If a tariff were placed on imported steel, who would gain and who would lose? Would you expect the efficiency of the steel industry to improve in the long-run if it were given more protection?
7. Why do economists say that barriers to trade cause economic inefficiency?

Selected References

Baldwin, R. E. *Non-Tariff Distortions of International Trade.* Washington, D.C.: Brookings Institution, 1970.

Corden, W. M. *Trade Policy and Economic Welfare.* Oxford: Oxford University Press, 1974.

Johnson, H. G. "The Standard Theory of Tariffs." *Canadian Journal of Economics and Political Science* 2 (August 1969): 333–52.

Kelly, M., et al. *Issues and Developments in International Trade Policy,* International Monetary Fund Occasional Paper No. 63. Washington, D.C.: IMF, December 1988.

Michaely, M. *Theory of Commercial Policy*. Oxford: Phillip Allan, 1977.

Organization for Economic Co-Operation and Development. *Cost and Benefits of Protection*. Paris: OECD, 1985.

Stern, R. M. "Tariffs and Other Measures of Trade Control: A Survey of Recent Developments." *Journal of Economic Literature* 11 (September 1973): 857–88.

5

COMMERCIAL

POLICY

INTRODUCTION 5.1

In this chapter we critically examine the arguments for protection. We shall see that most of the arguments do not stand up to close scrutiny. Although the discussion focuses on tariffs, it applies equally to non-tariff barriers. We also consider the effects of customs unions and effective protection.

SUPPORT FOR DOMESTIC INDUSTRIES 5.2

The Infant Industry Argument

The oldest argument for tariff protection is the *infant industry argument.* It was first advanced by Alexander Hamilton in 1791, writing about the need to protect early American industries from established industries in Europe. List writing in Germany in 1841 expanded on Hamilton's work. The argument is that young industries should be protected from international competition and be allowed to grow and become efficient through experience, in other words, by learning through doing. Without protection, it is argued, output will be lower than it could be, or a new industry will not be able to become established.

The first problem that arises with infant industry tariffs is how to decide which industries should be protected. Since almost any industry will grow if it is protected, the potential for growth is not in itself sufficient justification for protection. A more stringent criterion is called the *Bastable test:* in order to merit protection, an industry must grow and become so efficient that it will be able to compensate society for the losses to society incurred by protecting it through its infancy. (By way of analogy, an infant must be able to grow and earn enough to repay the costs of his/her education.) The benefits arising from the growth of an infant industry may go totally to firms within the industry, in which case they are said to be internal, or to people and firms outside the industry, in which case the benefits are said to be external. These cases must be examined separately.

Internal Benefits

If the benefits are internal, and the industry is expected to become so much more efficient that protection is called for by the Bastable test, protection is unnecessary: the industry's expected growth and future profitability will induce private investors to support it through its infancy. If private funds are not forthcoming, even though there is a good investment opportunity, the first step in evaluating a request for government intervention should be to decide why the private market is not willing to support the infant through the learning period. Having done this, steps can be taken to ensure that funds become available.

The reason private funds are not forthcoming may be that investors do not believe that the firm will grow. In this case, if the government has superior information it could choose to make the information available, and allow private investors to finance the growth of the industry and reap the rewards. Another possibility is for the government to make the investment more attractive to private investors by providing subsidized loans or by a preferential tax treatment of investors. There are many policies that can be used to increase investment in an industry and that are preferable to protection. If attempts to encourage private investment were to fail, this would still not be a justification for tariff protection: the government could make the investment and reap the reward on behalf of society.

It is worth remembering that the fact that the government believes an industry will grow is not a sufficient reason for government intervention. There is little reason to assume that the government is any better at picking winners than the private market. But even if it is, this would not imply that supporting infant industries by tariffs is justified. It has been shown that tariffs are unnecessary and undesirable because policies can be chosen that do not distort trade.

External Benefits

In the case of external benefits, the size of an industry may be suboptimal because investors in one firm do not take account of the benefits gained by other people. For example, the development of a new production technique may be of benefit to society, but private investors will not provide funds to pay for the development of new techniques if the profits accrue to all firms. Patent law, which seeks to give producers sole rights over the use of an idea for a certain period, is one answer to this. Alternatively, research and development may be subsidized. Tariff protection is not justified under such circumstances. Protection would increase the returns to investors in the industry and the industry would grow, but there is no guarantee that increased research and development would be undertaken. The reason is that the fundamental problem would remain: knowledge has characteristics that make it difficult for firms to maintain ownership of it.

Another argument based on the existence of external benefits is that when an infant industry grows, other industries benefit as well because workers and firms in the protected industry are customers of firms in other industries. There are two reasons why this is not a valid argument for tariff protection. First, the argument ignores the costs borne by consumers of the protected product. The growth of an industry can be encouraged more efficiently without the use of tariffs. Second, it is likely that the growth of any industry will have some positive effects on other industries. Thus, the potential for external benefits is not by itself sufficient to justify protection.

The reply to the infant industry argument can be summarized as follows. Infant industry arguments may be valid arguments for government intervention. However, tariffs are not justified in such cases because industries can be supported more efficiently through policies that do not distort trade.

Other Arguments for Protection to Support Particular Industries

The infant industry argument is only one example of many arguments used to justify protection to support domestic industries. For example, it is argued that barriers to trade are justified to support industries needed for national security. Other examples of industries that are put forward as deserving cases include traditional industries that are facing increased competition from imports or industries that are important employers in particular areas. It is said that protection would help these industries continue producing when they would otherwise produce "too little" or go bankrupt.

Although tariff protection certainly does help industries, it does so at an unnecessarily high cost to the rest of society. The same degree of support can be provided openly, and at lower cost to society, through a subsidy. Tariffs are neither necessary nor desirable as a means of supporting domestic production. (This was shown in the previous chapter when a tariff was likened to a consumption tax that finances a production subsidy.) The reasons for supporting an industry do not affect the general validity of the argument against the use of tariffs as a means of giving support.

THE TERMS OF TRADE ARGUMENT   5.3

An argument for the use of tariffs by large countries rests on a favorable change in the terms of trade. A rise in the terms of trade is an improvement because the country gets more imports for a given amount of exports. Tariffs may cause a beneficial movement in the terms of trade of sufficient size to outweigh the net cost arising from a less efficient allocation of resources. On the supply side, a similar case arises when a large country, or group of countries, restricts its exports to force up the price as OPEC did in 1973. Curtailing exports does not make economic sense unless the price of exports can be affected.

When a tariff is imposed, the fall in the country's demand for the import leads to a reduced world demand for the product. If the country is large, the world price falls in response to the restricted demand, and the decline in the price of the import improves the country's terms of trade. In theory, it is possible for a country to receive an overall net gain when it imposes a tariff. To show this, assume that the terms of trade improves by so great an amount when a tariff is imposed that domestic prices do not change. Consumers and producers are unaffected if prices do not change, yet the country gains tariff revenue, so the country must have gained. If domestic prices rise by a small amount, the loss to consumers from the price increase will exceed the gain to producers, but provided that the price rise is not too big the country may still gain because of the revenue effect.

The possibility of a large country gaining from a tariff is shown in Figure 5.1. When a tariff is imposed the domestic price of imports rises from P_0 to P_1, the quantity imported falls from $QD_0 - QS_0$ to $QD_1 - QS_1$, and the world price falls from P_0 to P_2. Consumer surplus falls by $P_0 P_1 ef$, and producer surplus rises by $P_0 P_1 ba$. The area $abef$ represents the loss arising from the effects of the higher price on consumers and producers. In order to obtain the overall welfare effect we must take the tariff revenue into account. The country gains tariff revenue equal to $gbeh$. Deducting $cbed$ from $abef$ and $gbeh$ leaves a gain of $gcdh$ and losses of abc and def.[1] It is possible that the sum of abc and def is less than $gcdh$, and that a large country will gain from a tariff. (If the domestic price does not change when a tariff is imposed, as in the example above, abc and def are zero, thus the country clearly gains from a tariff.) The more elastic the country's demand for imports, and the less elastic the foreign supply, the more likely a gain from the tariff is.

The terms of trade argument is only relevant for large countries because small countries cannot affect world prices. However, even large countries cannot always expect to gain because if other countries retaliate, a country may end up worse off than it was initially. Most economists believe that although the terms of trade argument for protection is theoretically interesting, it is irrelevant for international economic policy because no country has the necessary market power. Similarly, export quotas are only feasible if a significant proportion of supply can be controlled. Although exporters may be able to influence prices in the short run by collusive agreements, experience casts doubt on their ability to do so in the long run.[2]

---

[1] In effect, $cbed$ is a transfer of money from consumers to the government because the tariff forces consumers to pay a higher price for the good.

[2] Most collusive agreements between exporters of primary products have collapsed or become ineffective. The experience of the early eighties showed that even the power of the Organization of Petroleum Exporting Countries (OPEC) to fix prices is not unlimited. See Section 14.5.

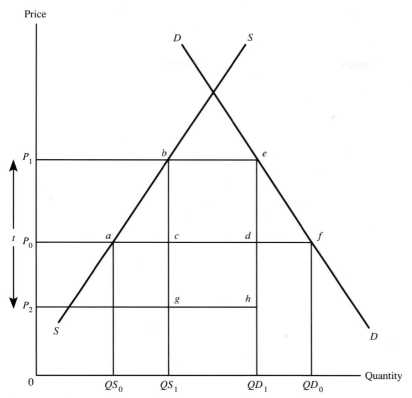

FIGURE 5.1

The Effects of a Tariff Levied by a Large Country

The large country's domestic demand and supply are shown by DD and SS, respectively. The initial price is P_0. When a tariff (t) is imposed, the domestic price rises from P_0 to P_1, the world price falls from P_0 to P_2, and the quantity of imports demanded falls from $QD_0 - QS_0$ to $QD_1 - QS_1$. Consumer surplus falls by $P_0 P_1 ef$ and producer surplus rises by $P_0 P_1 ba$, giving a net loss of $abef$ from the effects on producers and consumers. Tariff revenue of $gbeh$ is gained. Deducting $cbed$ from $abef$ and $gbeh$, the overall effect of the tariff is seen to depend on the relative sizes of $gcdh$ and the triangles abc and def.

UNFAIR COMPETITION   5.4

Dumping

Allegations of unfair competition are often made by groups who stand to gain from protection. One example of this type of argument for tariffs arises when goods are sold in foreign markets at a price below cost, a procedure known as *dumping*. Dumping may take various forms, but allegations of two kinds are common: 1) the price of the good may be low because of a government subsidy, or 2) an exporting firm may attempt to establish a market, or take over a market completely, by charging a price below the cost of producing the good *(predatory dumping)*. In both cases the problem arises because the low price is not permanent. Firms in the affected market may go bankrupt, and then, when the foreign government subsidy is withdrawn, or the foreign firm's market share has increased, consumers are faced with higher prices.[3] Clearly, bankrupting domestic firms for a short period of cheap imports is undesirable.

The difficulty in evaluating dumping complaints lies in distinguishing between dumping and normal international competition. In the case of what appears to be predatory dumping, the foreign firm may simply be more efficient, and able to sell at a lower price permanently. No one likes to admit that foreign producers are more efficient, so allegations are often made that foreign producers receive an unfairly high degree of government support. Since the treatment afforded by governments to exporting firms inevitably differs, these allegations are usually difficult to prove (or refute). However, cases do arise where the price of imports appears to be artificially low and cannot be expected to remain so. In these cases, since the problem arises from a temporarily low price for imports, the best solution may be to raise the price of imports by a temporary tariff. Permanent protection is not justified. Unfortunately, temporary protection has a way of becoming permanent.[4]

Cheap Labor

It is sometimes argued that foreign producers rely on cheap labor, hence tariffs should be used to prevent competition from these producers. There are two fundamental errors in this argument. First, the reasons why a good is produced at lower cost abroad are irrelevant unless a possible case of dumping is being examined. If the labor is cheap because of coercion there may be a moral argument for protection, but we should try to keep moral arguments separate from economic arguments.[5] Provided that the supply of low-cost imports is likely to continue, there is no economic argument for protection. However, labor may be cheap because of a government subsidy, and in this case, if there is a danger that the subsidy will be removed and the price of imports will rise, there is an argument for protection because this is an example of dumping (see the discussion above).

The second error arises because it is forgotten that labor is only one of

---

[3] Note that foreign subsidies are not a problem if they are permanent: if foreign governments are kind enough to subsidize our imports, why should we not accept?

[4] There is another answer to the dumping argument: firms that fear short-run price volatility may be able to protect themselves through the use of futures markets for their products.

[5] This does not mean that moral arguments should be ignored when commercial policy is formulated.

the inputs in the production process: we do not hear the argument that tariffs should be applied because land is cheaper in one country than in another. If we used tariffs to make all goods cost the same, by applying tariffs to offset all differences in input prices, there would be no point in trade. (Tariffs imposed to equalize costs are sometimes called *scientific tariffs*.) International trade flourishes because of differences in the prices of goods, which are often caused by differences in input prices. Differences in input prices should be welcomed and not used as an excuse for protectionist measures.

Foreign Trade Practices

Foreign barriers to trade impede exports and result in lower domestic welfare. Such barriers are often cited as a justification for domestic barriers to imports. There are two weaknesses in the argument that tariffs should be imposed on imports from countries that have high trade barriers. First, there is a gain to the domestic economy from free trade even if foreign countries maintain trade barriers. Foreign barriers that reduce exports do reduce domestic welfare, but retaliating to foreign trade barriers by imposing domestic trade barriers reduces domestic welfare still further. Second, the argument ignores the possible effects on world trade. All countries restrict trade, but they do so in different ways. If each country were to increase barriers whenever foreign barriers exceeded domestic barriers, there would be a global increase in barriers and welfare would fall. There may be a case for threatening to impose tariffs unless foreign markets are opened up, but if negotiations fail and domestic tariffs are used, the result is undesirable. Therefore, foreign trade practices are seldom likely to be a justification for domestic trade barriers.

A related argument is that trade barriers should be imposed when imports from one country exceed exports to that country. Each country trades with many other countries and there is no need for trade between two countries to balance: a country may import more from one country than it exports to it, but it will often export more to other countries than it imports from them. Tariffs that sought to balance trade between areas would lead to retaliation and lower world trade, and the welfare of all countries would fall.

THE BALANCE OF TRADE, INCOME, AND UNEMPLOYMENT   `5.5`

The balance of trade is the difference between the values of exports and imports. The balance of trade effect tends to be positive because of the import effect, that is, imports of the good bearing the tariff will decrease. However, there are five reasons why we might expect the overall effect on the balance of trade to be less than the import effect. First, if the United States were to impose tariffs, other countries might retaliate by imposing tariffs on American exports. Second, under flexible exchange rates, a reduction in the demand for imports will tend to increase the value of the dollar, and reduce the competitiveness of exports.[6] Third, unless there are unemployed resources, an increase in domestic production in the import-competing sector will attract resources away from the production of exports. Fourth, as the import-competing sector expands it will use more inputs. Some of these inputs may be imported or incorporate imported materials. Fifth, if tariffs are applied to a limited range of goods, or imports from particular countries, consumers may switch from one imported good to another imported good rather than to a domestically produced good.

Even if the balance of trade effect is significant, tariffs are not usually a suitable policy for increasing the balance of trade. Selective policies, such as barriers to trade, inevitably single out some groups of people for special treatment. This may be viewed as an advantage, for example, imports can be reduced by penalizing consumers of imported luxuries. However, this attribute can also be viewed as a disadvantage in that some people are discriminated against because their economic freedom is reduced. Many considerations are relevant to whether it is ever justifiable to single out particular groups for special treatment. These might include one's own political views, the economic problems of the country, which groups gain and lose, the nature of the good, and so on. However, one generalization is valid: selective policies are likely to be less effective than general policies—for instance, devaluation, lower government spending, or tighter monetary control—simply because selective polices affect fewer people than general policies.

Recessions and Retaliation

To the extent that there is a favorable balance of trade effect, tariffs tend to switch domestic demand from imports to domestic goods and increase the demand for domestic goods. Therefore, tariffs are likely to be popular when there is domestic unemployment. Unfortunately, tariffs do not cure unemployment so much as export it, because unemployment is created in the foreign country's export sector. The foreign country will face increased pressure from some of its own producers to impose tariffs, and it may well do so. This may create unemployment in the export sector of the country that initially imposed the tariff.

During world recessions there is a very real danger that countries will attempt to solve their domestic unemployment problems at the expense of other countries. If this happens, the level of world trade will fall and everyone will be worse off. Although some economists feel that tariffs are useful in certain special circumstances, there is general agreement that an escalation of trade barriers should be avoided. Also, once tariffs are in place their removal will probably be opposed by the people they benefit: introducing tariffs may be easier than removing them.

---

[6]The relationship between trade and the exchange rate is discussed in Chapter 6.

Tariffs are not the only type of policy that influences unemployment. If unemployment is common throughout all the sectors of an economy, there is normally a better policy available, at least for developed countries. General policies, such as reducing taxes or increasing government spending, have more widespread effects, do not disrupt trade, and do not invite retaliation. If unemployment is a problem in particular sectors, policies such as investment subsidies or retraining grants may be helpful. The argument against tariffs to increase employment in particular sectors was given in Section 5.2: barriers to trade reduce welfare and are unnecessary because the same employment effects can be obtained by a more efficient policy, for example, by production subsidies.

CUSTOMS UNIONS   5.6

In a *customs union* there is free trade between the members and a common tariff barrier is maintained for imports from nonmember countries.[7] The formation of a customs union may seem to be a step towards free trade, and as such, something that should be welcomed because it will increase welfare. Unfortunately, the truth is a little more complicated. Although trade between members is liberalized, the common tariff adopted may be the highest of the members' pre-union tariffs because each country resists a lowering of its own tariffs when a customs union is formed. This would not be a step towards freer trade. Even if the average level of union tariffs is not significantly higher than the pre-union rates of the members, the discrimination against nonmembers entailed in a customs union agreement may be a source of inefficiency.

The economic effects of the formation of a customs union are shown in Figure 5.2. There are three countries—A, B, and C. Countries B and C sell a good (X) for \$30 and \$20, respectively. Initially, country A has a nondiscriminatory tariff of 75 percent, and imports $QD_0 - QS_0$ from country C at a cost of \$35. If country A forms a customs union with country B, imports from country B can enter freely but imports from country C still bear a tariff of 75 percent. Country A will import $QD_1 - QS_1$ from country B at a cost of \$30.

Trade Creation and Trade Diversion

Country B is a higher cost producer than country C, and the only reason country A imports from country B is because there is unequal tariff treatment of countries B and C. The shift of import production from a low-cost source to a high-cost source is called *trade diversion*, and it leads to economic inefficiency. The displacement of imports from country C by imports from

---

[7]The policies of the European Economic Community (EEC) include a customs union agreement. This and other policies of the EEC are discussed in Chapter 17.

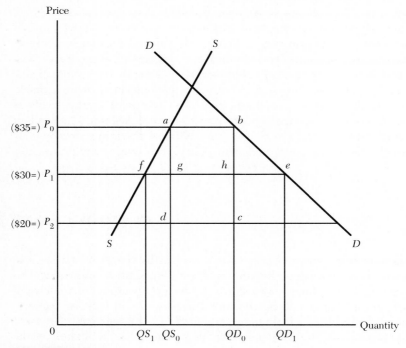

FIGURE 5.2

The Effects of a Customs Union

Initially country A has a nondiscriminatory tariff and imports $QD_0 - QS_0$ from C at $35. When A and B form a customs union, A imports $QD_1 - QS_1$ from B at $30. Consumer surplus increases by P_1P_0be, and producer surplus falls by P_1P_0af, thus the gain from the combined effect on producers and consumers equals the area *fabe*. Tariff revenue of *dabc* is lost. Therefore, the net effect of the formation of the customs union is determined by the relative sizes of *fabe* and *dabc*. Deducting *gabh* from both areas, the effect of the formation of a customs union is seen to depend on the relative sizes of the rectangle *dghc* and the triangles *fag* and *hbe*.

country B is an example of trade diversion. The shift of production from a high-cost source to a low-cost source is called *trade creation*, and it leads to an increase in economic efficiency. The displacement of domestic production by lower-cost imports, shown in the diagram by $QS_0 - QS_1$, is an example of trade creation. The abolition of all tariffs would increase welfare because there would be trade creation and no trade diversion.

The Welfare Effects of Customs Unions

The effect of a customs union on welfare can be derived by adding the effects on consumers, producers, and tariff revenue. The fall in price P_0P_1 leads to an increase in consumer surplus of P_0P_1be and a (smaller) fall in producer surplus of P_0P_1af. Before the union, country A received tariff revenue on imports from country C; but after the union, country A's imports from country B do not generate revenue. The loss of tariff revenue is shown in the diagram by the area of the rectangle *dabc*. A customs union between countries A and B will lead to an increase in welfare if the area of the trapezoid *fabe* is greater than the area of the rectangle *dabc*, that is, if the gain to consumers minus the loss to producers is greater than the loss of tariff revenue. The more elastic are demand and supply, and the smaller is the price difference between the partner country and the most efficient producer, the more likely is it that a customs union will increase welfare.

What the overall effect on country A will be we cannot say. Even if country A gains, whether world welfare is increased depends on the effects of the union on countries B and C. The ambiguity arises because a trade agreement that leads to free trade between some countries but excludes other countries is not a clear step towards free trade. The effect on nonmembers is generally negative because they face a common external tariff and cannot compete on equal terms within the customs union.

So far, we have only considered the short-run effects of customs unions. The long-run effects are more difficult to quantify but are potentially much more important. As a result of the removal of tariffs between members, competition between firms within the union will increase as firms look beyond their home markets to markets in other member countries. This competition between firms within the union may lead to significant gains in efficiency. Also, as firms expand and produce for a larger market, economies of scale may be enjoyed. Finally, there may be an inflow of foreign investment from foreign firms wishing to avoid the common external trade barrier by producing within the customs union. These long-run effects will increase the welfare of the members of the customs union.

EFFECTIVE PROTECTION   5.7

Tariffs may be applied to goods that are used as inputs by domestic producers. If domestic producers have to pay more than world prices for imported inputs because of these tariffs, they will be at a competitive disadvantage relative to foreign producers. However, domestic producers benefit if tariffs are levied on the goods they produce. For example, a tariff on imported steel will worsen the competitive position of domestic auto producers relative to foreign auto producers who can use lower-cost steel, but a tariff on imported cars will benefit domestic auto producers.

The *effective rate of protection* is a measure of the overall degree of protection given to domestic producers, taking into account the tariffs levied on inputs and the tariff on the final good. The formula for calculating the effective rate of protection (e_t) when there is one input is:

$$e_t = \frac{T - at}{1 - a}$$

where T is the tariff on the final good, t is the tariff on the input, and a is the cost of the input as a fraction of the cost of the final good. If T is equal to t, the effective rate of protection is equal to the *nominal rate of protection*. If T is larger than t, the effective rate of protection is greater than the nominal rate of protection. If T is smaller than t, the effective rate of protection is less than the nominal rate of protection. It is quite possible for the effective rate of protection to be negative if T is small and t is large. (The example given above of auto producers being adversely affected by a tariff on steel is an example where e_t is negative, because $T = 0$ and $t > 0$.)

Value Added and Effective Protection

An understanding of what is meant by *value added* is necessary for us to understand the concept of effective protection more fully. Value added is the difference between the value of a final product and the cost of the inputs used in its production. When the price of the final good rises relative to the cost of the inputs, value added rises. Domestic producers benefit from tariffs on final products because their value added rises when the price of the final product rises. However, because producers are only responsible for part of the value of the good, their value added increases by a larger percentage than the tariff. For example, if a producer is responsible for half the value of a good, and the good rises in price by 10 percent, the value added of the producer rises by 20 percent providing the quantity and prices of inputs used remain the same.[8] The effective rate of protection is a measure of the increase in value added per unit caused by a tariff structure. This is the reason that the effective and nominal rates of protection can differ.

Let us assume that a domestic producer of bicycles uses imported steel tubing, the bicycles retail for $400, and the tubing used costs $300. The producer's value added is $100 before the tariff. If a 30 percent tariff is imposed on bicycles and no tariff is imposed on tubing, the effective rate of protection is:

$$e_t = \frac{30\% - 0.75 \times 0}{1 - 0.75} = 120\%$$

The price of bicycles is $520 after the tariff, thus the producer's value added is $220. The effective rate of protection is 120 percent because value added rises by 120 percent. If a 30 percent tariff is imposed on imported tubing, the effective rate of protection is equal to 30 percent. However, if the tariff on

---

[8] Assume a good costs $100 and the cost of inputs is $50. If the price increases by $10, value added increases by $10, that is, the value added increases by 20 percent (from $50 to $60).

tubing is 40 percent, the effective rate of protection is zero. If the tariff on tubing exceeds 40 percent, the effective rate of protection will be negative. In the last case, the producer would be better off under free trade.

The Importance of Effective Protection

The concept of effective protection is useful when analyzing commercial policy. For example, in tariff negotiations, by reducing tariffs on inputs more than tariffs on final goods countries can claim to be liberalizing trade, while actually increasing effective protection. It is difficult to compare levels of protection in different countries because ideally we would want to examine effective rates of protection, not just nominal rates. In practice, tariffs often increase as a percentage of the value of goods, the nearer the goods are to the final stage of production. This is not surprising if, as seems likely, domestic producers bargain for positive effective protection. Tariff escalation is seen by some less-developed countries as a barrier to their development. They argue that the growth of their manufacturing sectors (which have the potential to export to developed countries) is prevented because developed countries' manufacturing sectors are protected by "high" rates of effective protection.

Table 5.1 shows the average nominal and effective rates of protection for the U.S., Japan, and the EEC. The effective rate of protection is generally greater than the nominal rate. Table 5.2 shows how the nominal and effective rates of protection vary across stages of production. The nominal rate of protection increases, and as a result the effective rate of protection increases at each stage of production.[9]

Summary of Main Points

The *infant industry argument* is one of the oldest arguments for tariff support of industries. The argument is that protection allows industries to grow and become efficient. Arguments have also been made for protection of industries that are major employers or industries that are needed for national security. These arguments are not valid arguments for tariff protection, because, even though government support of some industries may be justified, tariffs are less efficient than subsidies as a way of providing this support.

The *terms of trade argument* for tariffs is that if a large country imposes a tariff, the fall in the country's demand for the import may cause the world price of the good to fall. If so, it is possible that there will be an overall increase in the welfare of the country when the gain from an improvement in the terms of trade is taken into consideration. This argument is theoretically valid but has little practical significance because single countries do not usually dominate the world market for particular products.

---

[9]More recent figures showing nominal and effective rates of protection for the United States, the European Economic Community, Japan, and Canada are given in Table 15.2.

TABLE 5.1 Estimated Nominal and Effective Rates of Protection in the EEC, Japan, and the United States

Commodity Group	EEC		Japan		United States		Free Trade Share of Value Added
	Tariff Rate		Tariff Rate		Tariff Rate		
	Nominal	Effective	Nominal	Effective	Nominal	Effective	
Foods and feeds							
Meat and meat products	19.5	36.6	17.9	69.1	5.9	10.3	0.250
Preserved sea foods	21.5	52.6	13.6	34.7	6.0	15.6	0.300
Preserved fruits and vegetables	20.5	44.9	18.5	49.3	14.8	36.8	0.270
Milk, cheese, and butter	22.0	59.9	37.3	248.8	10.8	36.9	0.143
Manufactured and processed foods[a]	14.6	17.7	24.0	59.3	5.0	1.0	0.228
Flour, cereal, and bakery products	16.1	24.9	22.4	46.4	6.9	15.6	0.320
Cocoa products and chocolate	12.8	34.6	22.8	80.7	4.2	16.2	0.210
Soft drinks	14.9	−19.8	35.0	41.0	1.0	−9.5	0.400
Mill products and prepared feeds	11.4	31.6	13.8	32.2	23.4	111.0	0.270
Wood, paper, and rubber products							
Wood products	8.2	9.5	12.4	22.0	10.4	18.3	0.445
Paper products and wood pulp	7.4	20.1	6.6	12.1	2.7	5.5	0.415
Rubber products	8.3	19.0	9.3	20.2	6.1	12.5	0.360
Yarn, fabrics, and clothing							
Yarns and threads	6.2	19.4	9.9	24.2	19.5	37.1	0.280
Fabrics and clothing	14.3	29.1	13.0	22.0	27.3	40.4	0.340
Jute sacks, bags, and woven fabrics	18.2	42.9	27.1	65.0	1.4	3.2	0.330

TABLE 5.1 (con't.)

Commodity Group	EEC Tariff Rate Nominal	EEC Tariff Rate Effective	Japan Tariff Rate Nominal	Japan Tariff Rate Effective	United States Tariff Rate Nominal	United States Tariff Rate Effective	Free Trade Share of Value Added
Vegetable and animal oils							
Plant and vegetable oils[b]	11.1	138.0	10.1	64.9	9.4	17.7	0.055
Cottonseed oil	11.0	79.0	25.8	200.3	59.6	465.9	0.120
Rapeseed oil	9.0	57.2	15.1	22.3	20.8	60.9	0.150
Soya bean oil	11.0	148.1	25.4	286.3	22.5	252.9	0.070
Animal and marine fats and oils	5.2	−26.8	5.1	−1.9	4.2	10.7	0.200
Leather, tobacco, and soap							
Leather and leather products	7.8	14.6	14.8	22.6	7.0	12.8	0.397
Cigars and cigarettes	87.1	147.3	339.5	405.6	68.0	113.2	0.530
Soaps and detergents	7.5	14.4	16.6	44.4	7.9	19.3	0.230
Median tariff rate[c]	12.2	33.1	16.5	45.4	8.6	18.0	

[a]Includes roasted coffee.
[b]Consists of both crude and refined palm kernel oil, groundnut oil, and coconut oil.
[c]Median rates for the 123 individual products on product groupings.

Source: A. J. Yeats, "Effective Tariff Protection in the United States, the European Economic Community, and Japan," *Quarterly Review of Economics and Business* 14 (Summer 1974), p. 45. Reproduced with permission of the publisher: Bureau of Economic and Business Research, College of Commerce and Business Administration, University of Illinois.

TABLE 5.2 Escalation of Tariff Protection by Stage of Processing in the EEC, Japan, and the United States

Production Process	EEC		Japan		United States	
	Nominal	Effective	Nominal	Effective	Nominal	Effective
Groundnut oil						
Groundnuts, green	0.0	—	0.0	—	18.2	—
Groundnut oil, crude and cake	7.5	92.9	7.6	93.7	18.4	24.6
Groundnut oil, refined	15.0	186.4	10.1	324.8	22.0	64.9
Paper and paper products						
Logs, rough	0.0	—	0.0	—	0.0	—
Wood pulp	1.6	2.5	5.0	10.7	0.0	-0.5
Paper and paper articles	13.1	30.2	5.9	17.6	5.3	12.8
Wood products						
Logs, rough	0.0	—	0.0	—	0.0	—
Sawn wood	1.9	4.9	0.7	2.0	0.0	0.0
Wood manufactures	7.4	10.7	9.8	15.3	7.4	8.4
Dairy products						
Fresh milk and cream	16.0	—	0.0	—	6.5	—
Condensed and evaporated milk	21.3	44.3	31.7	154.8	10.7	30.1
Cheese	23.0	58.8	35.3	175.6	11.5	34.5
Butter	21.0	76.6	45.0	418.5	10.3	46.7
Wool fabrics						
Raw wool	0.0	—	0.0	—	21.1	—
Wool yarn	5.4	16.0	5.0	9.3	30.7	62.2
Wool fabrics	14.0	32.9	14.7	35.1	46.9	90.8
Cotton fabrics						
Raw cotton	0.0	—	0.0	—	6.1	—
Cotton yarn	7.0	22.8	8.1	25.8	8.3	12.0
Cotton fabrics	13.6	29.7	7.2	34.9	15.6	30.7

TABLE 5.2 (con't.)

Production Process	EEC		Japan		United States	
	Nominal	Effective	Nominal	Effective	Nominal	Effective
Leather products						
Bovine hides	0.0	—	0.0	—	0.0	—
Leather	7.0	21.4	6.2	20.2	17.8	57.4
Leather goods excluding shoes	7.1	10.3	10.5	15.8	22.4	32.5
Jute products						
Raw jute	0.0	—	0.0	—	0.1	—
Jute fabrics	21.1	57.8	20.0	54.8	0.0	-0.9
Jute sacks and bags	15.3	9.8	34.3	75.2	2.8	7.3
Palm kernel oil						
Palm nuts, kernels	0.0	—	0.0	—	0.0	—
Palm kernel oil, crude and cake	7.0	87.1	6.4	79.1	4.2	52.3
Palm kernel oil, refined	14.0	195.9	8.0	79.2	3.4	6.1
Chocolate						
Cocoa beans	5.4	—	0.0	—	0.0	—
Cocoa powder and butter	13.6	76.0	15.0	125.0	2.6	22.0
Chocolate products	12.0	-6.8	30.6	36.3	5.7	10.3

Source: A. J. Yeats, "Effective Tariff Protection in the United States, the European Economic Community, and Japan," *Quarterly Review of Economics and Business* 14 (Summer 1974), p. 47. Reproduced with permission of the publisher: Bureau of Economic and Business Research, College of Commerce and Business Administration, University of Illinois.

Allegations of unfair competition are often made by groups that will benefit from protection. In general, such arguments do not justify the use of tariffs because the economic benefits from access to cheap imports do not depend on the reason why the goods are cheap. A possible exception arises in cases of *dumping*, where firms are charging a price that is artificially low and cannot be expected to remain low. In cases of dumping, the problem is that the supply of low-cost imports is not permanent. In such cases, temporary protection may be justified. However, in assessing cases of alleged dumping, it is often difficult to ensure that allegations of dumping are not attempts to restrict normal international competition.

Tariffs raise the domestic price of imports and lead to a fall in the consumption of imported goods. This effect leads some economists to suggest that tariffs can be used to switch domestic demand from imports to domestic goods, increasing the balance of trade, domestic income, and employment. This argument is often overstated because it does not take account of the effects of tariffs on other sectors of the economy, in particular the export sector. More importantly, there is the danger that other countries will retaliate and that the country will end up worse off.

Countries forming a *customs union* agree to the elimination of tariffs on trade between members of the group and the establishment of a common external tariff on imports from nonmember countries. The effect on the welfare of the members may be positive or negative. To the extent that trade between members replaces imports from nonmembers with lower costs, the welfare of members is reduced. To the extent that trade between members increases and production moves from member countries with high costs to member countries with low costs, the welfare of members will increase.

The *effective rate of protection* measures the protection given to an industry taking into account tariffs levied on products that it uses. It is possible for the effective rate of protection to be positive or negative. In practice, the tariffs of developed countries give domestic industries positive rates of effective protection, but this may act as a barrier to exports of manufactured products from developing countries.

Study Questions

1. Explain the assertion that the infant industry argument may justify government intervention but does not justify tariff support.
2. If the United States were to impose a tariff on imported oil, why might the fall in welfare per head of population be smaller than if the same policy were enacted by a small country like Luxembourg? (Assume that the only significant difference between the two countries is their size.)
3. What is dumping? What problems are there in identifying cases of dumping that merit the use of tariffs?

4. Distinguish between the nominal and effective rates of protection. Comment on the importance of the concept of effective protection.

5. The composition of free trade value added in American bicycle manufacturing is shown below:

Cost of imported steel tubing	$100
American value added	100
Total price	$200

   a. What is the effective rate of protection given by a 10% tariff on imported steel tubing when there is no tariff on bicycles?
   b. What is the effective rate of protection given by a 10% tariff on both imported steel tubing and imported bicycles?
   c. What is the effective rate of protection given by a 10% tariff on imported bicycles when there is no tariff on steel tubing?

6. Draw a diagram showing the welfare effects from the imposition of a tariff by a large country. Using the diagram, explain why a large country may gain when it imposes a tariff.

7. Define trade creation and trade diversion. Draw a diagram showing the welfare effects from the formation of a customs union. Using the diagram, explain how a customs union will reduce members' welfare if trade diversion exceeds trade creation.

8. The cost of producing butter in Britain is as follows:

Quantity (millions of pounds)	Cost (pence per pound)
1	50
2	100
3	150
4	200
5	250
6	300

   Butter is available in unlimited amounts from New Zealand at 100 pence per pound and from France at 150 pence per pound. Initially, Britain has a nondiscriminatory tariff of 100%, and consumes 5 million pounds.
   a. Where is the butter that Britain consumes produced?
   b. Britain forms a customs union with France, retains a 100% tariff on imports from New Zealand, and continues to consume 5 million pounds. What is the new pattern of trade?
   c. How are trade creation and trade diversion illustrated by this example?

9. In the long run, tariffs are more likely to increase than decrease unemployment. Discuss.
10. If a country faces unfair foreign trade practices, should it retaliate by using tariffs itself?

Selected References

Adams, J., ed. *Tariffs, Quotas, and Trade: The Politics of Protectionism*. San Francisco: Institute for Contemporary Studies, 1979.

Baldwin, R. E., and Krueger, A. O., *The Structure and Evolution of Recent U.S. Trade Policy*. Chicago: University of Chicago Press, 1984.

Bhagwati, J. N. "The Generalized Theory of Distortions and Welfare." In *Trade, Balance of Payments and Growth*, edited by J. N. Bhagwati et al., 69–90. Amsterdam: North Holland, 1971.

Corden, W. M. *The Theory of Protection*. Oxford: Oxford University Press, 1971.

Corden, W. M. *Trade Policy and Economic Welfare*. Oxford: Oxford University Press, 1974.

Grubel, H. G. "Effective Tariff Protection: A Non-specialist Guide to the Theory, Policy, and Controversies." In *International Trade and Finance*, edited by R. E. Baldwin and J. D. Richardson. Boston: Little Brown and Co., 1974.

Johnson, H. G. "Optimal Trade Intervention in the Presence of Domestic Distortions." In *Trade Growth and the Balance of Payments*, edited by R. E. Baldwin et al., 3–34. Amsterdam: North Holland, 1965.

Johnson, H. G. "A New View of the Infant Industry Argument." In *Studies in International Economics*, edited by I. A. MacDougall and R. H. Snape. Amsterdam: North Holland, 1970.

Krauss, M. B. "Recent Developments in Customs Union Theory: An Interpretive Survey." *Journal of Economic Literature* 10 (June 1972): 413–36.

Yeager, L., and Tuerck, D. G. *Foreign Trade and U.S. Policy: The Case for Free International Trade*. New York: Praeger, 1976.

6

FOREIGN

EXCHANGE

MARKETS

INTRODUCTION 6.1

An *exchange rate* defines the value of one currency relative to another and allows us to convert prices expressed in one currency into prices in another. Exchange rates are important because they determine the relationship between the domestic and foreign prices of goods, services, and assets. Changes in the exchange rate can affect the flows of goods, services, and capital between countries.

In this chapter we examine the foreign exchange market and the determination of exchange rates. Two exchange rates are considered: the spot rate and the forward rate. Both can be thought of as prices of foreign exchange and both are determined by demand and supply. In order to understand the determination of exchange rates and why exchange rates change, we examine why people buy and sell foreign currency.

EXCHANGE RATES AND THE FOREIGN 6.2
EXCHANGE MARKET

The foreign exchange market is the largest market in the world, trading many times the value of transactions on the New York Stock Exchange. We refer to a single market, even though the market is based in many centers around the world, because the centers are so closely linked that at any time there is a single world price for a currency. The three most important international financial centers are London, New York, and Tokyo, with average daily turnovers in 1986 of $90 billion, $50 billion, and $48 billion, respectively. Other centers include: Hong Kong, Singapore, Bahrain, Frankfurt, Chicago, and San Francisco. As the sun travels west, markets in the east close and markets in the west open, so there is nearly always a market open.

Spot and Forward Defined

Foreign exchange may be purchased *spot* or *forward*. When a *spot transaction* is made, the delivery of the currency is taken at the time of purchase. Spot transactions are the type of foreign exchange transaction most people are familiar with. For example, the purchase of foreign exchange at an airport or a bank is a spot transaction. Spot transactions account for about three quarters of the turnover in the London market, and almost two thirds of the turnover in the New York market.

When a *forward transaction* is made, a price is fixed for a delivery date some time in the future. Once a forward contract is agreed, the price of foreign currency in that contract remains the same regardless of what happens to the spot exchange rate. (Penalty clauses ensure that the contract is honored.) Forward contracts may be negotiated for various dates in the future. Most forward contracts are for periods up to one year, although contracts are available for much longer periods.[1]

Published Exchange Rates

Table 6.1 is a facsimile of the table of exchange rates published by the *Wall Street Journal*. Although nearly every independent country has its own currency, only the rates of the currencies of the most important trading nations are usually quoted.[2] Note that the rates of exchange quoted are for amounts of $1 million or more. The exchange rates quoted are similar to wholesale prices; the price for purchases of foreign exchange is higher for smaller amounts.

The spot and forward exchange rates are shown in two forms: as the number of dollars per unit of foreign currency, and as the number of units of foreign currency per dollar. The two forms give the same information, one is simply the reciprocal of the other. For example, if the dollar-sterling exchange rate is 1.5, the sterling-dollar rate is 1/1.5 or 66 cents.

---

[1] There are also futures and options markets in foreign currencies, but together they account for a small percentage of transactions (well under 1% in London and 2.3% in New York). Futures contracts are traded on futures markets, for example, the International Money Market in Chicago. In order to facilitate trading in the Chicago market, futures contracts are for standardized amounts and expire on particular dates, for example, the third Wednesday of March, June, September, or December. Speculators are major users of the futures market. In a sense, forward contracts are "tailor made" and futures contracts are "off the peg." Options in foreign currencies resemble other financial options.

[2] Not all independent countries have their own currency. For example, Belgium and Luxembourg use the same currency, the franc, while retaining separate governments.

TABLE 6.1   Spot and Forward Exchange Rates

EXCHANGE RATES

Thursday, July 6, 1989

The New York foreign exchange selling rates below apply to trading among banks in amounts of $1 million and more, as quoted at 3 p.m. Eastern time by Bankers Trust Co. Retail transactions provide fewer units of foreign currency per dollar.

Country	U.S. $ equiv. Thur.	Wed.	Currency per U.S. $ Thur.	Wed.
Argentina (Austral) ...	.004000	.004000	250.00	250.00
Australia (Dollar)	.7647	.7735	1.3077	1.2928
Austria (Schilling)	.07527	.07540	13.28	13.26
Bahrain (Dinar)	2.6532	2.6532	.3769	.3769
Belgium (Franc)				
Commercial rate	.025313	.02537	39.50	39.41
Financial rate	.025318	.02529	39.49	39.52
Brazil (Cruzado)	.66304	.66304	1.5082	1.5082
Britain (Pound)	1.6285	1.6240	.6140	.6157
30-Day Forward	1.6224	1.6190	.6163	.6176
90-Day Forward	1.6100	1.6052	.6211	.6229
180-Day Forward	1.5908	1.5861	.6286	.6304
Canada (Dollar)	.8393	.8396	1.1914	1.1910
30-Day Forward	.8372	.8375	1.1944	1.1939
90-Day Forward	.8331	.8338	1.2003	1.1993
180-Day Forward	.8277	.8282	1.2081	1.2073
Chile (Official rate) ...	.0038856	.0038856	257.36	257.36
China (Yuan)	.268456	.268456	372.50	372.50
Colombia (Peso)	.002649	.002649	377.50	377.50
Denmark (Krone)	.1362	.1364	7.3415	7.3300
Ecuador (Sucre)				
Floating rate	.001837	.001837	544.25	544.25
Finland (Markka)	.2346	.2344	4.2625	4.2650
France (Franc)	.1563	.15634	6.3945	6.3960
30-Day Forward	.1563	.15633	6.3945	6.3965
90-Day Forward	.15631	.1562	6.3975	6.4010
180-Day Forward	.1561	.1559	6.4060	6.4120
Greece (Drachma)	.006146	.006150	162.70	162.60
Hong Kong (Dollar) ...	.128246	.128287	7.7975	7.7950
India (Rupee)	.061012	.061012	16.39	16.39
Indonesia (Rupiah) ...	.0005678	.0005678	1761.00	1761.00
Ireland (Punt)	1.4179	1.4125	.7052	.7079
Israel (Shekel)	.4972	.4972	2.0110	2.0110
Italy (Lira)	.0007307	.0007327	1368.50	1364.75
Japan (Yen)	.007194	.0072072	139.00	138.75
30-Day Forward	.007219	.0072332	138.52	138.25
90-Day Forward	.007262	.0072796	137.69	137.37
180-Day Forward	.007319	.0073335	136.63	136.36

Country	U.S. $ equiv. Thur.	Wed.	Currency per U.S. $ Thur.	Wed.
Jordan (Dinar)	1.8066	1.8066	.5535	.5535
Kuwait (Dinar)	3.3760	3.3760	.2962	.2962
Lebanon (Pound)	.001958	.001958	510.50	510.50
Malaysia (Ringgit)	.3725	.3717	2.6845	2.6900
Malta (Lira)	2.7972	2.7972	.3575	.3575
Mexico (Peso)				
Floating rate	.0004003	.0004003	2498.00	2498.00
Netherland(Guilder) .	.4702	.4712	2.1265	2.1220
New Zealand (Dollar) .	.5785	.5805	1.7286	1.7226
Norway (Krone)	.1443	.1444	6.9260	6.9225
Pakistan (Rupee)	.04807	.04807	20.80	20.80
Peru (Inti)	.0003441	.0003441	2906.00	2906.00
Philippines (Peso)	.047393	.047393	21.10	21.10
Portugal (Escudo)	.006332	.006337	157.91	157.78
Saudi Arabia (Riyal) ..	.2666	.2666	3.7500	3.7500
Singapore (Dollar)	.5099	.5096	1.9610	1.9620
South Africa (Rand)				
Commercial rate	.3716	.3676	2.6910	2.7203
Financial rate	.2513	.2484	3.9800	4.0250
South Korea (Won) ...	.001504	.001504	664.60	664.60
Spain (Peseta)	.008410	.008410	118.90	118.90
Sweden (Krona)	.1550	.1551	6.4475	6.4460
Switzerland (Franc) ..	.6178	.6190	1.6185	1.6155
30-Day Forward	.6190	.6201	1.6155	1.6126
90-Day Forward	.6208	.6221	1.6106	1.6074
180-Day Forward	.6237	.6248	1.6032	1.6004
Taiwan (Dollar)	.038955	.038955	25.67	25.67
Thailand (Baht)	.038714	.038714	25.83	25.83
Turkey (Lira)	.0004714	.0004714	2121.02	2121.02
United Arab(Dirham) .	.2722	.2722	3.6725	3.6725
Uruguay (New Peso)				
Financial	.001707	.001707	585.50	585.50
Venezuela (Bolivar)				
Floating rate	.02590	.02590	38.60	38.60
W. Germany (Mark) ..	.5305	.5302	1.8850	1.8860
30-Day Forward	.5316	.5313	1.8810	1.8820
90-Day Forward	.5330	.5332	1.8761	1.8752
180-Day Forward	.5355	.5353	1.8672	1.8680
SDR	1.27473	1.26584	0.784479	0.789989
ECU	1.09565	1.08411	....	....

Special Drawing Rights (SDR) are based on exchange rates for the U.S., West German, British, French and Japanese currencies. Source: International Monetary Fund.

European Currency Unit (ECU) is based on a basket of community currencies. Source: European Community Com-

Defining the Rate

In order to avoid confusion, unless stated otherwise, when reference is made to the exchange rate in this book we are referring to the number of dollars per unit of foreign currency.[3] This form of presentation allows us to think of the exchange rate as the price of foreign currency. For example, if the dollar-franc rate of exchange is 0.15, the price of 1 franc is 15 cents.

Thinking of the foreign exchange rate as the price of foreign currency helps us understand the determination of the exchange rate, and the causes of exchange rate changes. The exchange rate responds to changes in demand

---

[3]The reader should note that current practice in the foreign exchange market is normally to refer to the number of units of foreign currency per dollar.

and supply in the same way as any market price. If the demand for foreign exchange rises, or the supply falls, the exchange rate increases. If the demand for foreign exchange falls, or the supply rises, the exchange rate decreases.

Appreciation and Depreciation

When the exchange rate rises, this indicates that the value of foreign currency has increased in relation to the dollar, and may be referred to as an *appreciation* of foreign currency or as a *depreciation* of the dollar. Similarly, a decrease in the exchange rate indicates a fall in the value of foreign currency relative to the dollar, and may be referred to as a depreciation of foreign currency or as an appreciation of the dollar.

Devaluation and Revaluation

Monetary authorities sometimes maintain a "fixed" exchange rate, that is, they declare a value for their currency and buy or sell foreign currency in order to maintain that value. The terms *devaluation* and *revaluation* can be reserved to describe the decrease or increase, respectively, in the value of a currency resulting from a change in an officially declared and maintained exchange rate. However, in the present international monetary system the distinction between official and market-induced exchange rate changes is not very useful, because even though fixed rates have been abandoned by many countries most governments have unofficial target rates and intervene in the foreign exchange market. The present system is known as *dirty floating.* (A *clean float* is a system in which currencies are completely free from intervention.) Current exchange rate arrangements are summarized in Table 6.2.

Arbitrage in the Spot Market

Communication between financial centers throughout the world is virtually instantaneous, and at any given time the exchange rates in financial centers around the world are equal. If they were not equal, *arbitrage* would be profitable. Arbitrage is the act of buying in one market and selling in another in order to profit from a difference in market prices. For example, if the dollar-sterling rate in London is 1.2 and the rate in New York is 1.5, it is possible to make 30 cents profit on each pound bought in London and sold in New York. However, as people buy sterling in London and sell it in New York, the London price tends to rise and the New York price tends to fall. Thus, the opportunity for profit is removed by the arbitrage it stimulates. In practice, minute discrepancies between exchange rates would be sufficient to trigger large flows of funds because transaction costs are very low and the profit from arbitrage would be realized almost immediately.

Table 6.1 does not show all possible exchange rates; only the value of currencies against the dollar is shown. This is partly to save space: with fifty currencies there are 2450 exchange rates that might be quoted.[4] Also, quoting the rates between other currencies is unnecessary because the rate of exchange between two currencies can be calculated from the value of the two currencies against the dollar.[5] For example, if the dollar-sterling rate is 1.5, and the dollar-mark rate is 0.5, the sterling-mark rate is 0.5 divided by 1.5, that is, 0.33.

Cross Rates and Triangular Arbitrage

The rate of exchange between two currencies, calculated from the values of two currencies against a third currency, is called the *cross rate*. How can we be sure that the market rate will correspond to the cross rate? The answer is that excellent communication links between centers and the potential for *triangular arbitrage* ensure that cross rates and market rates are always equal.

Triangular arbitrage is the process of switching funds between three currencies in order to profit from differences between market rates and cross rates. For example, assume that the dollar-sterling rate is 1.5, the dollar-mark rate is 0.5, and the sterling-mark rate is 0.25. A person could convert $15 to £10, convert the £10 to 40DM, convert the 40DM to $20, and make $5 profit. In our example, triangular arbitrage would lead to one or more of the following effects: 1) as people buy sterling with dollars, the dollar-sterling rate increases; 2) as people buy marks with pounds, the sterling-mark rate increases; or 3) as people buy dollars with marks, the mark-dollar rate increases. The inequality between cross rates and market rates could be removed by any of these effects.

We cannot predict which exchange rates would change, or by how much. However, one thing is certain: disparities between market rates and cross rates do not last.[6] There are three characteristics of the foreign exchange market that allow us to be confident that triangular arbitrage would take place if cross rates were not equal to market rates:

1. the potential number of market participants is very large,
2. transaction costs are insignificant for large sums, and
3. information can be obtained quickly and inexpensively.

---

[4] If there are n currencies, there are $n-1$ possible exchange rates for each currency, thus $n(n-1)$ exchange rates can be quoted. In fact, there are well over one hundred currencies, therefore, the table of all possible exchange rates would be large.

[5] If there are n currencies, there are only $n-1$ "independent" exchange rates, in the sense that if the $n-1$ possible exchange rates for one currency are known, the values of all other possible exchange rates can be calculated.

[6] The cross rate between two currencies, calculated from their values against the dollar, reflects how transactions are made in practice, because most transactions involve the purchase or sale of dollars. For example, if a person wants to exchange francs for marks, dollars are purchased with francs, and then the dollars are sold for marks. This is possible because transaction costs are so low.

TABLE 6.2 Exchange Rate Arrangements

(As of September 30, 1988)[a]

| | | Currency Pegged to | | |
U.S. Dollar	French Franc	Other Currency	SDR	Other Composite[b]
Afghanistan	Benin	Bhutan	Burma	Algeria
Antigua & Barbuda	Burkina Faso	(Indian	Burundi	Austria
Bahamas, The	Cameroon	Rupee)	Iran, I. R. of	Bangladesh
Barbados	C. African Rep.	Kiribati	Jordan	Botswana
Belize	Chad	(Australian	Libya	Cape Verde
Djibouti	Comoros	Dollar)	Rwanda	Cyprus
Dominica	Congo	Lesotho	Seychelles	Fiji
Ecuador	Côte d'Ivoire	(South		Finland
El Salvador	Equatorial	African		Hungary
Ethiopia	Guinea	Rand)		Iceland
Grenada	Gabon	Swaziland		Israel
Guatemala	Mali	(South		Kenya
Guyana	Niger	African		Kuwait
Haiti	Senegal	Rand)		Malawi
Honduras	Togo	Tonga		Malaysia
Iraq		(Australian		Malta
Lao P.D. Rep.		Dollar)		Mauritius
Liberia				Nepal
Mozambique				Norway
Nicaragua				Papua New
Oman				Guinea
Panama				Poland
Paraguay				Romania
Peru				Sao Tome &
St. Kitts & Nevis				Principe
St. Lucia				Solomon Islands
St. Vincent				Somalia
Sierra Leone				Sweden
Sudan				Tanzania
Suriname				Thailand
Syrian Arab Rep.				Vanuatu
Trinidad and				Western Samoa
Tobago				Zimbabwe
Uganda				
Venezuela				
Viet-Nam				
Yemen Arab Rep.				
Yemen, P.D. Rep.				
Zambia				

[a] Excluding the currency of Democratic Kampuchea, for which no current information is available. For members with dual or multiple exchange markets, the arrangement shown is that in the major market.

[b] Comprises currencies which are pegged to various "baskets" of currencies of the members' own choice, as distinct from the SDR basket.

Flexibility Limited in Terms of a Single Currency or Group of Currencies		More Flexible		
Single Currency[c]	Cooperative Arrangements[d]	Adjusted According to a Set of Indicators[e]	Other Managed Floating	Independently Floating
Bahrain	Belgium	Brazil	Argentina	Australia
Qatar	Denmark	Chile	China, P.R.	Bolivia
Saudi Arabia	France	Colombia	Costa Rica	Canada
United Arab Emirates	Germany	Madagascar	Dominican Rep.	Gambia, The
	Ireland	Portugal	Egypt	Ghana
	Italy		Greece	Japan
	Luxembourg		Guinea	Lebanon
	Netherlands		Guinea-Bissau	Maldives
			India	New Zealand
			Indonesia	Nigeria
			Jamaica	Philippines
			Korea	South Africa
			Mauritania	Spain
			Mexico	United Kingdom
			Morocco	United States
			Pakistan	Uruguay
			Singapore	Zaire
			Sri Lanka	
			Tunisia	
			Turkey	
			Yugoslavia	

[c] Exchange rates of all currencies have shown limited flexibility in terms of the U.S. dollar.
[d] Refers to the cooperative arrangement maintained under the European Monetary System.
[e] Includes exchange arrangements under which the exchange rate is adjusted at relatively frequent intervals, on the basis of indicators determined by the respective member countries.
Source: IMF International Financial Statistics, January 1989.

Real Exchange Rates

When the value of a currency rises or falls, this tends to change a country's competitive position. The effect of exchange rate changes may be offset by changes in the prices of goods. For example, a 10 percent appreciation tends to make exports less competitive, but if domestic prices are stable and foreign prices are rising by 15 percent, exports are actually becoming more competitive. *Real exchange rate indices* show the change in the value of one currency relative to other currencies taking into account differences between countries' inflation rates. Such indices are useful when we want to assess the possible effects of exchange rate changes on international trade flows.

Effective Exchange Rate Indices

A currency may rise against some currencies while falling against others. If we wanted to assess the likely effects of a change in a currency's value, we might calculate the average change in value against all other currencies. However, this average is not very helpful because countries trade more with some countries than with others. Changes in a currency's value against the currencies of major trading partners are more significant than changes in relation to the currencies of less important partners. For this reason, *effective exchange rate indices* are sometimes calculated.

Effective exchange rate indices are weighted averages of exchange rates, the weights being chosen to reflect the importance of countries' trade. There are many types of effective exchange rate index. *Bilateral exchange rate indices* take into account the importance to one country of trade with other countries. The rationale is that the importance of changes in the value of domestic currency against another country's currency is higher the greater the amount of trade with the country is.

A *multilateral trade-weighted effective exchange rate index*, as published in the *Federal Reserve Bulletin*, uses the importance of countries in world markets. The rationale in this case is that a country faces competition from major trading countries in world markets, even if it does not trade directly with those countries to a significant extent. The *multilateral exchange rate model index (MERM)* published by the IMF goes one step further by taking into account the sensitivity of trade flows in response to changes in exchange rates. This index is designed to show the impact of exchange rate movements rather than merely describe the movements themselves.

6.3 THE DETERMINATION OF THE SPOT RATE

The spot rate is determined by the demand and supply of foreign currency. The demand and supply of foreign currency result mainly from international trade and capital flows. In the following discussion, we begin with a model that excludes capital flows, showing how the demand and supply of foreign exchange resulting from international trade determine the exchange rate. Then capital flows are discussed. This order of presentation is adopted for ease of exposition, and not because international trade is a more important influence on the exchange rate than capital flows. The relative importance of trade and investment varies, and we cannot say which will be more important at any given time.

Exports and the Supply of Foreign Exchange

Let us consider the case of an American exporter selling to a French importer. When the French importer sells American goods in France, the sales revenue is in French francs. Assuming that the American exporter wants to be paid in dollars, French francs must be converted into dollars. Therefore, American exports lead to sales of foreign exchange, in other words, a supply of foreign exchange. Sometimes, we find references to the foreign exchange earned by exporting firms. This is another way of saying that exports lead to a supply of foreign exchange.

The quantity of foreign exchange supplied changes with the exchange rate. Assume for simplicity that the prices of American exports are fixed in dollars. As the exchange rate rises, the value of the dollar falls in relation to the franc, the foreign currency prices of exports decrease, and the quantity of American exports demanded increases. If the demand for exports is elastic, the foreign currency value of exports increases when the foreign currency prices of exports fall. Thus, the quantity of French francs to be converted into dollars, the quantity of foreign currency supplied, increases when the exchange rate rises. This is why the supply curve for foreign currency shown in Figure 6.1 slopes upward from left to right.

Imports and the Demand for Foreign Exchange

Imports lead to a demand for foreign exchange. The revenue from selling French goods in the United States is in dollars, but French exporters want payment in francs, therefore dollars must be converted into francs. In other words, American imports lead to a demand for foreign exchange.

The quantity of foreign exchange demanded varies with the exchange rate. As the exchange rate rises, if the prices of American imports from France are fixed in French francs, the dollar prices of the goods rise (as the dollar becomes less valuable). When the prices of imports rise in domestic currency we would expect the quantity of imports demanded to fall. Thus, the quantity of foreign exchange demanded falls when the exchange rate rises, as shown in Figure 6.1.

If we think of foreign exchange as a good, Figure 6.1 is simply a standard demand and supply diagram. As the price of foreign exchange rises, the quantity of foreign exchange demanded decreases, and the quantity of foreign exchange supplied increases. The equilibrium exchange rate is determined by the intersection of the demand and supply curves. If the exchange rate is above the equilibrium rate, the excess supply of foreign exchange leads to a

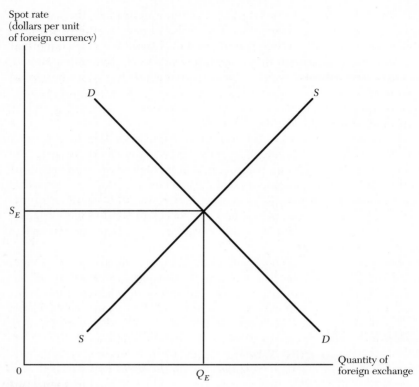

FIGURE 6.1

The Demand and Supply of Foreign Exchange
The demand for foreign exchange is shown by *DD* and the supply of exchange is shown by *SS*. The equilibrium exchange rate is S_E, the rate at which the demand and supply of foreign currency are equal.

decrease in the exchange rate. The excess supply is removed in two ways. First, as the exchange rate falls, the quantity of foreign exchange demanded rises (because the prices of imports in domestic currency fall and more imports are demanded). Second, the quantity of foreign exchange supplied decreases (because the quantity of American exports demanded decreases as export prices rise in foreign currency). Similarly, an excess demand for foreign exchange is removed by an increase in the exchange rate.

People buying foreign exchange offer domestic currency in exchange, thus the demand for foreign exchange is equal to the supply of domestic currency. Similarly, the supply of foreign exchange can be thought of as a demand for domestic currency. The basic analysis is the same regardless of whether the determination of the exchange rate is described in terms of the demand and supply of domestic currency in the foreign exchange market, or the demand and supply of foreign currency.

Asset Markets and the Exchange Rate

Consideration of the return from international investment provides another reason for the downward slope of the demand for foreign exchange.[7] The expected return (r) to an investor from a foreign investment is made up of two parts: the expected rate of return on the foreign asset (i_f) and the expected gain (or loss) from an increase (or decrease) in the value of foreign currency relative to domestic currency during the life of the investment. The total expected return can be expressed as:

$$r = i_f + \frac{(ES - S)}{S}$$

where S is the current spot rate and ES is the spot rate that is expected to exist when the investment matures.[8] For example, if an investment in France pays 10 percent, and the franc is expected to appreciate by 5 percent ($ES = 0.21$ and $S = 0.20$), the total expected return from an investment in France would be 15 percent. This is the return expected; the actual return may be more or less than the expected return, depending on how accurate investors' predictions are.

Let us consider how the quantity of foreign exchange demanded responds to a change in the exchange rate. As the spot rate falls, other things equal, the return from a foreign investment increases. The reason is that a fall in the spot rate leads to a higher expected appreciation or lower depreciation of foreign currency. (As S falls, the value of $(ES - S)/S$ rises if ES remains unchanged.) Therefore, a fall in the spot rate tends to increase the quantity of foreign assets demanded by domestic residents. Foreign investment leads to a demand for foreign exchange, thus, the quantity of foreign exchange demanded increases as the exchange rate falls. Therefore, the demand for foreign exchange slopes downward as shown in Figure 6.1.

The same approach can be used to explain why the quantity of foreign exchange supplied increases as the exchange rate rises. The total return (r') to a foreigner investing in the domestic market is:

$$r' = i_d - \frac{(ES - S)}{S}$$

where i_d is the domestic interest rate.[9] As the spot rate rises, the foreigner's expected return increases and the quantity of domestic assets demanded tends to increase. As a result, the quantity of foreign exchange supplied increases. Thus, the supply curve slopes upward.

---

[7] We assume in this section that the investment is not covered in the forward market. Covered investments are described in Section 6.7.

[8] This equation is an approximation. The exact return is: $i_f(ES/S) + (ES - S)/S$.

[9] This equation is an approximation. The exact return is: $(S/ES)(i_d - (ES - S)/S)$.

Which Is More Important, Trade or Capital Flows?

It has been shown that exchange rate determination can be explained using the demand and supply of foreign exchange resulting from international trade or capital flows. The relationship between trade flows and the exchange rate is often useful for explaining long-term exchange rate fluctuations, but it cannot explain the dramatic short-term exchange rate changes that have been observed since the move away from fixed exchange rates in 1973. Flows of goods do not change so quickly. Models that focus on asset markets and capital flows are often more useful for explaining short-term exchange rate changes.

6.4   CHANGES IN THE DEMAND AND SUPPLY OF FOREIGN EXCHANGE

Changes in the Demand or Supply of Traded Goods

Imports lead to purchases of foreign exchange and exports lead to sales of foreign exchange. Thus, changes in the demand for imports or exports can lead to changes in the exchange rate. For example, an increase in the American demand for imports from Japan will increase the demand for yen, and the dollar value of the yen will rise. This is illustrated in Figure 6.2. Similarly, an increase in the supply of exports will lead to an increase in the supply of foreign exchange and an appreciation of domestic currency.[10]

Inflation and Relative Price Changes

We would normally expect that a country with above-average inflation will have a currency that is declining in value. The reason is that when a country experiences inflation in excess of that in other countries, its exports become less attractive and imports become more attractive. Therefore, the demand for foreign exchange increases and the supply of foreign exchange decreases. This is shown in Figure 6.3 by the shift of the demand curve for foreign exchange to the right, and the shift of the supply curve of foreign exchange to the left. As a result, the exchange rate rises (domestic currency depreciates). The relationship between inflation and exchange rates is called *purchasing power parity* and is examined in more detail in Section 6.6.

Assets and the Exchange Rate

The demand for assets depends on many factors, for example, the rate of return paid to holders of the asset, the default risk on the asset, and the possibility of capital gain (either through an increase in the value of the asset

---

[10]We assume that the country is not large enough to affect world prices. If the country is large enough to affect world prices, export prices will fall as the supply increases. In this case, the quantity of foreign exchange supplied will only increase if the demand for exports is elastic (because the percentage increase in quantity of exports must be greater than the percentage fall in the price of exports.)

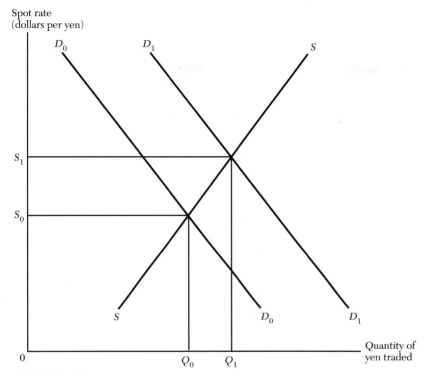

FIGURE 6.2.

An Increase in the Demand for Foreign Exchange
When the demand for Japanese imports increases, the demand for yen shifts from D_0D_0 to D_1D_1 and the dollar-yen exchange rate rises from S_0 to S_1. Such a change might also be caused by an increase in the American demand for Japanese assets.

or an increase in the value of the currency in which the asset is valued). Changes in the demand for assets are thought to be one of the major reasons for short-term fluctuations of the exchange rate.

As an example, assume that an increase in American interest rates leads to an increase in the demand for American assets by foreigners. There will be an increase in the supply of foreign exchange as foreigners buy the dollars needed to make investments in the United States. This is shown in Figure 6.4. When the supply of foreign exchange increases, the equilibrium exchange rate falls. Thus, an increase in the demand for American assets erodes the competitive position of American producers because it leads to an appreciation of the dollar. This example resembles what happened in the early eighties when the dollar increased in value because of an inflow of foreign capital.

It should be remembered that the demand and supply of foreign ex-

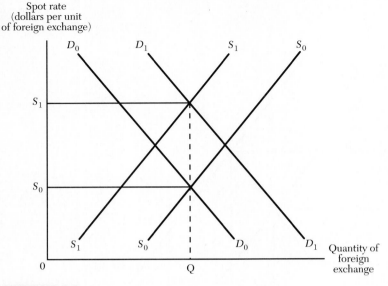

FIGURE 6.3

The Effect of Inflation on the Exchange Rate
If domestic inflation exceeds world inflation, the demand for foreign exchange increases from D_0D_0 to D_1D_1, and the supply of foreign exchange decreases from S_0S_0 to S_1S_1. As a result, the exchange rate increases from S_0 to S_1 (domestic currency depreciates).

change must be equal. Therefore, if there is a net supply of foreign exchange from investors, there must be a net demand from other market participants. Another way of describing this is to say that the net purchase of American assets is financed by a net transfer of goods to the United States. We shall see in the next chapter that in the balance of payments this would be recorded as a capital account surplus accompanied by a current account deficit.

Government Intervention in the Foreign Exchange Market

When a government fixes the exchange rate, it intervenes in the foreign exchange market to ensure that the demand and supply of foreign exchange are equal at the chosen exchange rate. For example, if the demand for foreign exchange exceeds the supply of foreign exchange, the government can increase the supply of foreign exchange and prevent the exchange rate from rising, as shown in Figure 6.5. Similarly, the government can prevent an exchange rate from falling by increasing the demand for foreign exchange. Governments can also intervene to change an exchange rate. If the govern-

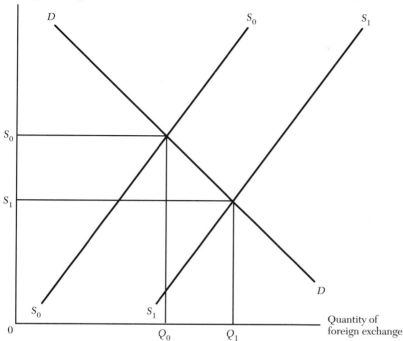

Spot rate
(dollars per unit
of foreign exchange)

FIGURE 6.4

An Increase in the Supply of Foreign Exchange

When the supply of foreign exchange increases from S_0S_0 to S_1S_1, the exchange rate decreases from S_0 to S_1. Such a change might be caused by an increase in the foreign demand for American assets or an increase in the demand for American exports.

ment thinks that the current exchange rate is too low (or too high), it can buy (or sell) foreign exchange to push the exchange rate in the desired direction.

The stocks of foreign currency that governments hold for intervention in the foreign exchange market are called *international reserves*. These stocks are limited, so a government cannot continue selling foreign currency to maintain an exchange rate below the market equilibrium rate. In contrast, if the market equilibrium rate is above the official value, a government can intervene to reduce the value of its currency for a longer period because the country can add the foreign currency to its international reserves. The domestic currency needed for purchases of foreign currency can be printed, or domestic currency can be obtained by sales of Treasury bills. (Which method is used depends on the objectives of the monetary authorities.)

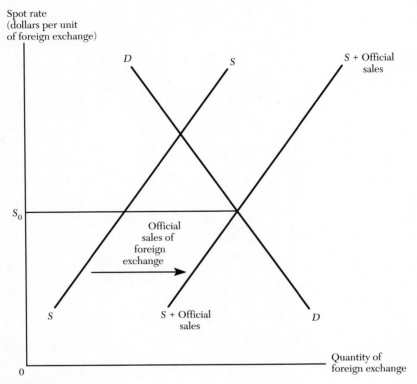

FIGURE 6.5

Official Intervention

There is an excess demand for foreign exchange at the chosen exchange rate (S_0). Sales of foreign exchange by the monetary authorities increase the supply of foreign exchange and prevent the exchange rate from rising.

Speculation in the Spot Market

We can *speculate* in the spot market by buying currencies that we expect to go up in value, and selling currencies we expect to go down in value.[11] Let us assume that the speculator's time horizon is short, so that differences between the interest rates that can be earned on assets in different currencies

---

[11] It is important to note that the term *speculation* is a technical term referring to the activity pursued. To be precise, if a person has an open position in foreign currency, that is, if the person's assets and liabilities in foreign currency are not equal, that person is speculating. The term does not imply that the person's actions are harmful or wrong in any sense. In fact, as the discussion that follows shows, speculation may have beneficial effects.

are not important. In this case, the rules for speculation in the spot market are:

$S > ES$	sell foreign currency
$S = ES$	do nothing
$S < ES$	buy foreign currency

where S and ES denote the current spot rate and the expected spot rate, respectively. For example, if a speculator expects the dollar-sterling exchange rate to rise from 1.2 to 1.5, it is profitable to buy pounds now and sell them after the exchange rate has risen. If the speculator's prediction is correct, a profit of 30 cents is earned on each pound bought and sold. (Transaction costs must be deducted, but these are trivial for large amounts.) Of course, if the prediction is wrong there may be no profit or even a loss. Therefore, speculators in the foreign exchange market attempt to make profits in the same way as speculators in other markets: by buying low and selling high.

Speculators' actions tend to move the exchange rate towards the expected exchange rate. If speculators expect a fall in the exchange rate, their sales of foreign currency make a fall in the exchange rate more likely. Similarly, purchases of foreign exchange by speculators anticipating a rise of the exchange rate make a rise more likely. Therefore, if speculators predict the future equilibrium exchange rate accurately, their actions will tend to move the exchange rate towards the equilibrium rate. The corollary is that incorrect predictions move the exchange rate away from the equilibrium long-run exchange rate.

Stabilizing and Destabilizing Speculation

Whether speculation is normally stabilizing or destabilizing, in the sense of moving the exchange rate towards or away from the long-run equilibrium rate, has been a topic for continuous debate. One view is that under flexible exchange rates, destabilizing speculation is not likely to be the norm because speculators would make losses in the long run. However, destabilizing speculation is clearly possible at times, even if it is not the norm.

Destabilizing speculation may be more likely under fixed exchange rates or dirty floating, because speculators may speculate with little chance of incurring significant losses that an officially supported exchange rate will be abandoned. For example, assume that an excess demand for foreign exchange is being offset by official intervention (sales of foreign exchange by the monetary authorities). Some speculators might believe that government intervention will not last, and speculate by buying foreign exchange. If the government does stop intervening, and the exchange rate rises, they will be rewarded with a capital gain. If the exchange rate does not change, the foreign exchange can be sold at the original exchange rate. Speculators only lose the transaction costs incurred, which are minute in comparison with the possible gain. (A fall in the exchange rate is unlikely if initially there is an excess demand for foreign exchange.)

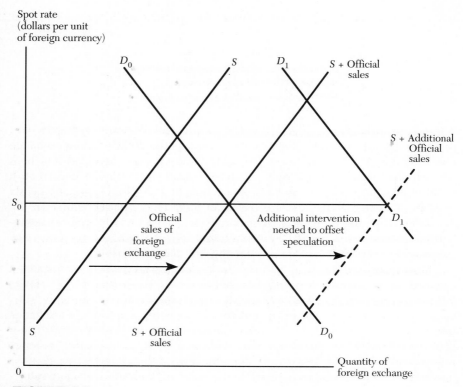

FIGURE 6.6

Official Intervention and Speculation

There is an excess demand for foreign exchange at the chosen exchange rate (S_0). Sales of foreign exchange by the monetary authorities increase the supply and prevent the exchange rate from rising. However, speculators buy foreign exchange because they expect it to appreciate. Their purchases of foreign exchange increase the demand and the demand curve shifts from D_0D_0 to D_1D_1. The result is that the amount of intervention needed to maintain the chosen exchange rate increases.

Speculators make the expected rise in the value of foreign currency more likely because their purchases add to the excess demand for foreign exchange. This is shown in Figure 6.6. The monetary authorities intervene to maintain the chosen exchange rate by running down reserves. Speculators anticipate that official intervention will not last and that foreign exchange will appreciate. Purchases of foreign exchange by speculators increase the demand for foreign exchange and shift the demand curve to the right. The monetary authorities must either increase their sales of reserves or abandon the exchange rate.

EXCHANGE MARKET STABILITY AND THE ROLE OF ELASTICITIES   6.5

The discussion in the previous sections leads to the conclusion that exchange rate changes will bring about equality between the demand and supply of foreign exchange. However, if the supply of foreign exchange is downward sloping and flatter than the demand curve, exchange rate changes will not lead to equilibrium in the foreign exchange market. Under such conditions, exchange rate changes will increase (rather than reduce) differences between the demand and supply of foreign exchange. This section explores the possibility of the foreign exchange market being unstable.

In Section 6.3 it was shown that the demand and supply of foreign exchange are related to flows of imports and exports, respectively. Depreciation may remove an excess demand for foreign exchange through the effect on imports and exports. The changes in the quantities of foreign exchange demanded and supplied depend on the elasticities of demand and supply of imports and exports with respect to changes in their prices.

The Demand for Foreign Exchange

Assuming for simplicity that import prices are fixed in foreign currency, the prices of imports in domestic currency rise when the exchange rate rises. If the demand for imports is not perfectly inelastic, which seems a reasonable assumption, the quantity of imports demanded falls, and the quantity of foreign exchange demanded declines.

Incidentally, although the demand for some products may be inelastic, this does not imply that the demand for imports in general is inelastic. The demand for imports in general is more elastic than the average of the elasticities of demand for individual commodities. The reason is that an increase in the prices of imports in general reduces consumers' real incomes, whereas the effect of an increase in the price of a single good on consumers' real incomes is comparatively small. Therefore, the consumption of an imported good declines more when its price rises as part of a general increase in import prices caused by depreciation than when an increase in its price is not part of a general increase in import prices.

The Supply of Foreign Exchange

Although we can be confident that depreciation will reduce the quantity of foreign exchange demanded, it is less certain that the quantity of foreign exchange supplied will rise. Assuming that export prices are fixed in domestic currency, depreciation lowers the foreign currency prices of exports. If the demand for exports is not perfectly inelastic, the quantity of exports demanded increases. The quantity of foreign exchange supplied tends to increase because more exports are sold, but the lower price means that each unit of exports generates less foreign currency. Which effect will dominate?

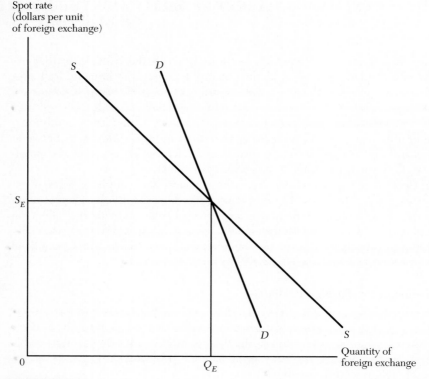

Spot rate
(dollars per unit
of foreign exchange)

FIGURE 6.7

An Unstable Foreign Exchange Market

The demand for foreign exchange is shown by *DD* and the supply of foreign exchange is shown by *SS*. In this case, the foreign exchange market is unstable because the supply curve is downward sloping and flatter than the demand curve. If the exchange rate is above S_E, it rises because there is an excess demand for foreign exchange. If the exchange rate is below S_E, it falls because there is an excess supply of foreign exchange.

In the short term, it is quite conceivable that the quantity of exports demanded will not increase significantly, and that the quantity of foreign exchange supplied will decrease when a currency depreciates. This would be shown by a supply curve of foreign currency that slopes downward from left to right. This can lead to instability in the foreign exchange market. Assume that initially there is an excess demand for foreign exchange. Foreign currency will tend to increase in value relative to domestic currency, in other words, domestic currency will depreciate. If the supply curve is downward sloping and flatter than the demand curve, depreciation increases the excess demand for foreign exchange. This possibility, shown in Figure 6.7, is the opposite of what we might normally expect.

Many international economists doubt the importance of this theoretical possibility for three reasons. First, the result requires the supply of exports to be both downward sloping and flatter than the demand for foreign exchange. Although it is possible that the quantity of foreign exchange supplied may not increase or may even decrease with a depreciation, it is less likely that the quantity of foreign exchange supplied will decrease more than the quantity of foreign exchange demanded.

Second, even if the foreign exchange market is unstable in the short run, it is more likely to be stable in the long run because the elasticities of demand for imports and exports will normally be greater in the long run than in the short run.

Third, the effects of capital flows must be considered. It has been shown above that the demand and supply of foreign exchange resulting from capital flows leads to demand and supply curves with the normal slopes. Also, we have seen that if the exchange rate departs from its equilibrium value, and speculators predict the equilibrium value correctly, stabilizing capital flows will tend to restore the exchange rate to its equilibrium value. These effects may offset the short-run inelasticity of demand for traded goods.

Exchange Rate Overshooting

The possibility that elasticities will be smaller in the short run than in the long run implies that the exchange rate change needed to remove an excess demand or supply of foreign currency may be larger in the short run than in the long run.[12] This possibility is shown in Figure 6.8. In the short run, when the demand for foreign exchange increases from D_0D_0 to D_1D_1, the exchange rate rises from S_0 to S_1. The long-run equilibrium exchange rate (S_2) is lower because the long-run supply of foreign exchange is more elastic than the short-run supply. Therefore, because of inelasticity, the exchange rate temporarily rises above the long-run rate, that is, it overshoots the long-run equilibrium rate. Some economists have suggested that this model helps explain why exchange rates have been so volatile since fixed exchange rates were abandoned in 1973.

PURCHASING POWER PARITY   6.6

The *purchasing power parity* theorem suggests that exchange rate changes reflect differences between countries' rates of inflation. The theorem can be expressed in the form of an equation:

$$\dot{P}_{US} = \dot{P}_W + \dot{S}$$

---

[12] The relationship between the balance of payments and the exchange rate is discussed in Chapter 9.

Spot rate
(dollars per unit
of foreign exchange)

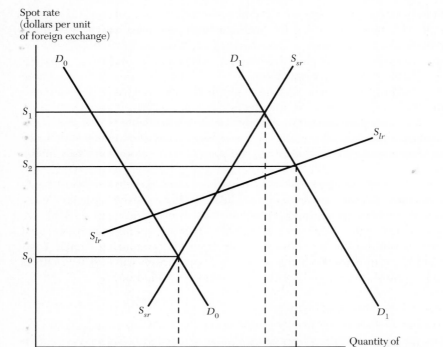

FIGURE 6.8

Exchange Rate Overshooting
The short-run supply of foreign exchange ($S_{sr}S_{sr}$) is less elastic than the long-run supply
of foreign exchange ($S_{lr}S_{lr}$). Assume that the demand for foreign currency increases, as
shown by the shift of the demand curve from D_0D_0 to D_1D_1. The exchange rate rises
from S_0 to a short-run equilibrium of S_1. In the long run, the supply of foreign exchange is more elastic and the equilibrium exchange rate is lower, at S_2.

where $\dot{P}_{US}$, $\dot{P}_W$, and $\dot{S}$ represent the rate of inflation in the United States, the
world rate of inflation, and the change in the exchange rate, respectively. If
the $\dot{P}_{US}$ is greater than $\dot{P}_W$, the theorem predicts that $\dot{S}$ will be positive (indicating an increase in the dollar price of foreign currency, that is, a depreciation of the dollar). If $\dot{P}_{US}$ is less than the world rate, the theorem predicts
that $\dot{S}$ will be negative (indicating an appreciation of the dollar). The purchasing power parity theorem suggests that inflation rates must be similar if exchange rates are to remain stable.

Purchasing power parity may be brought about by the effects of inflation
on the demand and supply of foreign exchange. If a country experiences inflation above that of the rest of the world, domestic consumers will switch from
domestic goods to imported goods as domestic goods become relatively more

expensive. Also, export sales will decrease as the prices of exports rise. As a result, the demand for foreign exchange will increase, the supply of foreign exchange will decrease, and the exchange rate will increase.

Does Purchasing Power Parity Hold?

There are three reasons why we might not expect exchange rate changes to conform exactly with purchasing power parity. First, transport costs and barriers to trade reduce the free movement of goods. The prices of goods in other countries are unimportant if imports are prevented by official controls or high transport costs. Second, not all goods and services are traded internationally. For example, we would not expect the prices of houses or haircuts to be equalized by trade.[13] Third, trade is not the only influence on the exchange rate. For example, investment and speculation lead to capital flows, which may cause the exchange rate to depart from purchasing power parity.

Although we might not expect exchange rate changes to equal inflation rate differentials exactly, it is equally unlikely that prices in different countries will diverge continuously. If inflation rate differences are not reflected in the exchange rate, the incentive to trade will increase as prices diverge. The greater the divergence between inflation rates or the longer the period we consider, the more likely it is that exchange rate changes will be related to inflation rates. Not surprisingly, empirical studies have shown that purchasing power parity helps explain long-run changes in exchange rates and exchange rate changes between countries with very different inflation rates. However, purchasing power parity is not useful for predicting short-run exchange rate changes between countries with broadly similar rates of inflation.[14]

Table 6.3 shows the average rates of inflation and exchange rate changes of a number of countries over the period 1960–82. It is clear that the nations with the highest rates of inflation experienced the greatest decline in the value of their currencies. Table 6.4 shows that rapidly increasing prices in Argentina and Brazil over the period 1983–86 were accompanied by similar increases in the amount of national currency needed to pay for a dollar.

FORWARD EXCHANGE RATES   6.7

The forward exchange rate is determined in the same way as the spot rate, by demand and supply. However, the reasons for buying and selling foreign exchange in the spot market differ from the reasons for buying and

---

[13] In addition, because countries' patterns of consumption and production differ, price indices include different goods or different weights are attached to the same good. Therefore, inflation rates are not strictly comparable.

[14] Officer (1976) reviews the theory of purchasing power parity and empirical studies of the relationship between exchange rates and purchasing power parity.

TABLE 6.3   Inflation and Exchange Rate Changes, 1960–1982

	Average Annual Inflation (%)	Total Percentage Appreciation (+) or Depreciation (−)
Germany	4.4	+42
Japan	5.9	+31
Canada	6.3	−27
France	7.4	−33
United Kingdom	9.0	−60
Italy	10.3	−1168

Note: Inflation is the average rate of change of the GDP implicit price index. The average inflation rate for the United States was 5.2. The exchange rate against the U.S. dollar was used to calculate the exchange rate changes.
Source: Data were taken from *OECD Historical Statistics: 1960–1982.* Paris: OECD, 1984.

selling foreign exchange in the forward market. One of the major reasons for buying and selling forward is to remove exchange risk arising from international trade and investment.

Exchange Risk and International Trade

Exchange risk is the risk that the value in domestic currency of an asset or liability that is held in foreign currency will change as a result of a change in the exchange rate. For example, an American importer who has contracted

TABLE 6.4   Inflation and Exchange Rates for Argentina and Brazil

	Consumer Price Index (1980 = 100)	Exchange Rate Index: National Currency Per U.S. Dollar (1980 = 100)
Argentina		
1983	2403	5850
1986	256300	523906
Brazil		
1983	984	1160
1986	23436	27320
United States		
1983	127	
1986	146	

Source: IMF International Financial Statistics, 1988 Yearbook. Exchange rate index calculated by the author.

to pay £1 million in three months time faces the risk that an increase in the dollar-sterling exchange rate will increase the dollar value of the liability. The risk can be removed by "covering forward": by buying sterling in the forward market, the importer fixes the exchange rate to be paid for the currency when it is needed.

When goods are traded, there is normally a delay between a price being agreed upon and payment being made. In general, companies that have to make future payments in foreign currency buy the currency forward, and companies that expect to receive foreign currency in the future sell the currency forward. It might be that a company that uses the forward market would have been better off if it had not covered. This does not mean that the decision to cover was wrong. We can never be absolutely certain what the future spot exchange rate will be, and if forward cover is not taken the company is speculating. The company might win or lose. Many importers and exporters choose to avoid exchange risk by using the forward market.[15]

Exchange Risk and International Investment

International investors are important forward exchange market participants. Through a process called *covered interest arbitrage,* they are largely responsible for the determination of the forward exchange rate. When comparing the rates of return between assets within a country, investors do not need to worry about exchange rates. International investment is not so simple, however, because forward cover must be taken if the investor wants to ensure that the values of international investments are not affected by exchange rate movements.

Covered Interest Arbitrage

Assume that a person is considering investing in New York or London in an asset that has virtually no risk of default, for example, Treasury bills. At maturity, the value (V_n) of an investment of X dollars in New York is:

$$\$V_n = X(1 + NR)$$

where NR is the rate of interest in New York expressed as a decimal. For example, if the rate of interest is 10 percent, the investor will receive $1.10 for each dollar invested because $1.10 = $1(1 + 0.1)$.

Calculating the yield from an investment in London is slightly more complicated because we must consider exchange rates. X dollars converted into pounds gives $X(1/S)$ pounds, where S is the spot exchange rate. At maturity, the sterling value (£V_l) of an investment in London is:

---

[15] American companies do not always face exchange risk because contracts are often expressed in dollars. In such cases, forward cover may be taken by foreign companies. When a contract between two non-American traders is expressed in dollars, as is often the case, both parties face exchange risk, and both may take forward cover.

$$\pounds V_l = X\left(\frac{1}{S}\right)(1+LR)$$

where LR is the rate of interest in London (again expressed as a decimal).

The dollar value of the London investment is uncertain because the sterling from the investment must be converted back into dollars at whatever the spot rate happens to be at the end of the period. This uncertainty can be removed by covering forward. In this case, the investor would sell sterling for dollars in the forward market. If a forward contract is taken, the dollar value of the investment is not affected by changes in the spot rate.

Assuming that forward cover is taken, each pound sold in the forward market yields F dollars, where F is the forward rate. Therefore, the dollar value ($\$V_l$) of an investment of $\$X$ in London is:

$$\$V_l = X\left(\frac{F}{S}\right)(1+LR)$$

The investments in London and New York are now comparable because both the returns are expressed in dollars and the investment in London is not subject to exchange risk. We can compare the return per dollar invested by dropping the X from each equation, thus we compare $(1 + NR)$ with $(F/S)(1 + LR)$. If V_n is greater than V_l, we would expect Americans to invest in New York; if V_l is greater than V_n, Americans will invest in London.

The problem can also be described in terms of the returns to a British investor. The sterling value to a British investor ($\pounds V_l'$) of an investment of Y pounds in London is:

$$\pounds V_l' = Y(1+LR)$$

A covered investment in New York has a value of:

$$\$V_n' = Y\left(\frac{S}{F}\right)(1+NR)$$

Comparing the returns per pound invested, the problem is whether $(1 + LR)$ is greater than or less than $(S/F)(1 + NR)$, which is the same as comparing $(F/S)(1 + LR)$ with $(1 + NR)$. Therefore, British and American investors face the same decision, and, other things being equal, will invest in the same place.

Interest Parity

Suppose that V_l is greater than V_n. When making an investment in London, American investors buy spot sterling and sell sterling forward. Therefore, the spot rate tends to rise and the forward rate tends to fall. As the forward rate falls relative to the spot rate, the rate of return on an investment in London falls, and the incentive to engage in covered interest arbitrage is removed. Similarly, if V_n is greater than V_l, British investors investing in New York sell sterling in the spot market and buy sterling in the forward market.

Therefore, the forward rate tends to rise relative to the spot rate, and the incentive to invest in New York is reduced. When the covered rates of return are equal in the two centers, that is, when

$$(1+NR)=\left(\frac{F}{S}\right)(1+LR)$$

the forward rate is said to be at *interest parity*.

The *forward premium* (p) is equal to the difference between the spot rate and the forward rate divided by the spot rate:

$$p=\frac{(F-S)}{S}$$

If a currency is worth more in the forward market than it is in the spot market, it is said to be "at a premium" in the forward market. Conversely, if a currency is worth less in the forward market than it is in the spot market, it is said to be "at a discount." If the forward rate is at interest parity, it can be shown that the forward premium is approximately equal to the interest rate differential:[16]

$$p=\frac{(F-S)}{S}=NR-LR$$

In practice, the forward premium is normally approximately equal to the interest rate differential when we compare the rate of return on similar assets. The reason is that covered interest arbitrage is free of exchange risk, thus the potential flows of short-term capital that divergences from interest parity generate are very significant. Large investors, banks, and corporations engage in this type of activity. However, there are a number of reasons why interest parity does not always hold.

Departures from Interest Parity

Investors face transaction costs when buying and selling securities or foreign exchange. The costs of purchasing domestic or foreign securities may be similar, in which case interest parity will not be affected. However, the cost

---

[16]The definition of the forward premium ($p=[F-S]/S$) yields:

$$p=\frac{F}{S}-\frac{S}{S}=\frac{F}{S}-1,$$

$$\Rightarrow \frac{F}{S}=p+1$$

The definition of interest parity is:

$$(1+NR)=\left(\frac{F}{S}\right)(1+LR)$$

Substituting (p + 1) for F/S, yields:

$$(1+NR)=(p+1)(1+LR)$$

Solving for p we obtain:

$$p=NR-LR-pLR$$

Since pLR is small, $p = NR - LR$ is a useful approximation.

of buying and selling foreign exchange only affects foreign investments and can be responsible for small departures from interest parity. The shorter the period of the investment, the more significant transaction costs are likely to be in relation to the yield on the investment.[17]

Government policies can lead to departures from interest parity. For example, foreign governments may impose controls that prevent the repatriation of funds held abroad, or the funds may even be confiscated. The risk that government policies will prevent an investment yielding the expected return is called *political risk*.

Another reason for departures from interest parity is that the rate of return on an investment reflects the degree of default risk of the investment: we would not expect the rate of return on investments with different degrees of default risk to be the same. Conformity to covered interest parity is strong on investments in government securities in the Eurodollar market because there are no capital controls in this market, and the investments are similar in the sense that the degree of default risk is negligible.

Finally, under certain circumstances speculators may influence the forward exchange rate. Flows of arbitrage funds are potentially large, therefore, for speculators to exert an influence on the forward rate there has to be a substantial degree of certainty about what the future value of the spot rate will be relative to the current forward rate. Because speculators cannot usually be sure about the future spot rate, the effects of speculators will usually be offset by flows of arbitrage funds.[18] Let us examine how speculation takes place in the forward market.

Speculation and Forward Intervention

We can speculate in the forward market by buying foreign currency forward when we expect the future spot rate to be higher than the present forward rate. If the expectations prove to be correct, the foreign currency bought at the forward rate can be sold at the higher spot rate. Similarly, if we expect the future spot rate to be lower than the present forward rate, we can sell forward. If correct, foreign currency purchased in the spot market can be sold at a higher price to meet the forward contract. The rules for speculation in the forward market are:

[17]Levi (1983) examines departures from interest parity. He finds: "When transaction costs are introduced into the management of liquid funds, there is a band or region within which it does not pay to move surplus funds temporarily abroad. The total range of this band is about a full percentage point for realistic values of transaction costs on 3-month-maturity investments." (p. 180)
[18]To be more precise, if the supply of arbitrage funds is perfectly elastic, any tendency for the forward rate to diverge from the forward rate consistent with interest parity induces a flow of arbitrage funds that ensures that interest parity is maintained.

$F > ES$	sell foreign currency in the forward market
$F = ES$	do nothing
$F < ES$	buy foreign currency in the forward market

where F and ES denote the current forward rate and the expected spot rate, respectively.

Speculation in the forward market can lead to capital flows. Assume that initially the forward rate is equal to the spot rate because interest rates in New York and London are identical. If speculators begin selling sterling forward because they expect a fall in the dollar-sterling exchange rate ($F > ES$), the dollar-sterling forward rate will fall. A fall in the forward rate reduces the return on a London investment relative to an investment in New York, therefore we would expect capital to flow out of Britain.

Government Intervention in the Forward Market

The return on investments in London can be increased, and the capital outflow prevented, by raising interest rates in London. However, the British monetary authorities may be reluctant to tighten monetary policy to raise interest rates. Such a policy tends to reduce the level of national income, and, if the authorities feel that the speculative pressure is temporary, this would be unnecessary. An alternative policy is for the British monetary authorities to intervene directly in the forward market, buying sterling forward. This policy would reduce the capital outflow by maintaining the forward rate.

At the time of intervention in the forward exchange market, the government does not need any international reserves. This is one of the advantages of intervening in the forward market rather than the spot market. However, forward intervention may lead to increased speculation that sterling will fall in value, and eventually the authorities must meet their forward commitments.

The cost of meeting forward commitments, the monetary cost of forward intervention, depends on whether sterling falls in value as speculators predicted. Recall that we assumed that the forward rate and the spot rate were equal initially. When the forward contracts mature, if sterling does not fall in value, the British authorities can honor their obligations to buy sterling without any loss of reserves. Using dollars, they buy sterling from contract holders for the same price at which sterling can be sold for dollars in the spot market. However, if sterling does fall in value, the British authorities must pay more dollars to buy sterling from contract holders than they receive when they sell sterling in the spot market, therefore the authorities lose reserves. If intervention in the forward market is large, forward exchange market intervention can be very costly.

Summary of Main Points

Exchange rates specify the value of one currency relative to another. Exchange rates are important because they determine the relationship between the domestic and foreign prices of goods, services, and assets. The *spot exchange rate* may be thought of as the dollar price of foreign currency. The *forward exchange rate* is the price used for foreign currency to be delivered in the future.

The spot rate is determined by the demand and supply of foreign exchange. Payments to foreigners for imports or American purchases of foreign assets lead to a demand for foreign exchange. Receipts from foreigners for exports or foreign purchases of domestic assets lead to a supply of foreign exchange.

An increase in the exchange rate is a *depreciation* of the dollar and a decrease in the exchange rate is an *appreciation* of the dollar. Exchange rate changes are caused by changes in the demand or supply of foreign exchange. A depreciation of the dollar may be caused by an increase in the demand for foreign exchange or a fall in the supply of foreign exchange. Similarly, an appreciation of the dollar may be caused by a decrease in the demand for foreign exchange or an increase in the supply of foreign exchange. The government can also influence the exchange rate by adding to the demand or supply of foreign exchange.

Speculators attempt to profit from differences between the current spot rate and the expected future spot rate. Speculators buy currencies that they expect to increase in value and sell currencies that they expect to fall in value. In doing this they tend to push the value of the currency in the expected direction. Speculation may be stabilizing or destabilizing, depending on whether the expected rate is an accurate prediction of the future spot exchange rate.

The effect of exchange rate changes on the demand and supply of foreign exchange is likely to be greater in the long run than in the short run, because the demand for traded goods is more elastic in the long run. In the short run, it is possible that depreciation will lead to a lower value of exports being sold (if the percentage decrease in the foreign currency price of exports is greater than the percentage increase in the quantity of exports). This possibility is less likely in the long run, when demand is more elastic. Also, the exchange market may be stabilized by capital flows.

Purchasing power parity theory suggests that exchange rate changes will reflect differences between inflation rates. If domestic inflation exceeds foreign inflation, the demand for imports tends to increase, the foreign demand for exports tends to decrease, and the dollar tends to fall in value. Small inflation differentials may be offset by other influences on the exchange rate, such as capital flows. Purchasing power is most likely to be a useful guide to long-run exchange rate changes or to short-run changes when inflation differentials are large.

The forward exchange rate is largely determined by *covered interest ar-*

bitrage. An American investing in the London market can avoid *exchange risk* by selling sterling in the forward market. Using the forward market, investors can compare the rates of return on domestic and foreign investments. *Covered interest parity* is established when the forward premium is equal to the interest differential:

$$\frac{(F-S)}{S} = NR - LR$$

When covered interest parity is established, the returns from domestic and foreign investments are equal:

$$(1 + NR) = \left(\frac{F}{S}\right)(1 + LR)$$

The forward rate is usually close to the rate that establishes covered interest parity, but divergences from interest parity can be caused by transactions costs, political risk, and speculation. Speculators in the forward market profit from differences between the forward rate and the expected future spot rate.

Study Questions

1. Why does the demand for foreign currency slope downward and the supply of foreign currency slope upward? What factors determine the slopes of the curves?

2. Under what conditions will the supply of foreign currency slope downward from left to right?

3. Using the exchange rates given below, calculate the return on $30 from triangular arbitrage assuming that the arbitrager begins and ends with dollars.

sterling-franc rate	= 0.1
franc-dollar rate	= 6.0
dollar-sterling rate	= 1.5

Why will this opportunity for profit disappear?

4. What is the likely effect on the dollar-sterling exchange rate of:
   a. an increase in American investment abroad?
   b. an increase in American imports?
   c. the British discovery of North Sea oil reserves?
   d. a fall in the world price of wheat?
   e. an across-the-board tariff on British imports?
   f. an expected fall in the value of sterling (and consequent fall in the dollar value of British assets held by Americans)?

5. Show how the Bank of England can intervene in the foreign exchange

market to maintain the sterling-dollar exchange rate when there is an excess demand for dollars. (*Hint:* the demand for foreign exchange in this
case is a demand for dollars.) Show how speculators may help or hinder
the effort to maintain the exchange rate depending on the exchange rate
they expect.

6. Assuming that there is no speculation in the forward market, show how
the forward rate is determined by covered interest arbitrage. What factors
may cause a departure from covered interest parity?

7. The dollar-sterling spot rate is 1.50. The interest rates in New York and
London are 8% and 4%, respectively. What is the dollar-sterling forward
rate? What is the forward premium? Is sterling at a premium or a discount?

8. If the rate of inflation in Argentina is 200% and the rate of inflation in the
United States is 5%, is it possible for the Argentinian monetary authorities
to maintain a constant austral-dollar exchange rate? Explain using diagrams
showing the effects of the inflation differential on Argentina's demand and
supply of foreign currency. (Use the demand and supply of dollars as functions of the austral-dollar exchange rate).

Selected References

Bank of England. "The Market in Foreign Exchange in London." Press Notice, 20
August 1986.

Bergstrand, J. H. "Selected Views of Exchange Rate Determination After a Decade of
Floating." *New England Economic Review*, May/June 1983: 14–29.

Crystal, K. A. "A Guide to Foreign Exchange Markets." *Federal Reserve Bank of St.
Louis Review* 66 (March 1984): 5–18.

Federal Reserve Bank of New York. "Summary of Results of U.S. Foreign Exchange
Market Turnover Survey." New York: Federal Reserve Bank of New York,
August 1986.

Fieleke, N. S. "The Rise of the Foreign Currency Futures Market." *New England
Economic Review*, March/April 1985: 38–47.

Fleming, J. M., and Mundell, R. A. "Official Intervention in the Forward Exchange
Market: A Simplified Analysis." *IMF Staff Papers* 11 (March 1964): 1–19.

Gaillot, H. J. "Purchasing Power Parity as an Explanation of Long-term Changes in
Exchange Rates." *Journal of Money, Credit, and Banking* 2 (August 1970):
348–57.

Kubarych, R. M. "Foreign Exchange Markets in the United States," Revised Edition.
New York: Federal Reserve Bank of New York, 1983.

Levi, M. *International Finance*. New York: McGraw-Hill, 1983.

Officer, L. H. "The Purchasing Power Parity Theory of Exchange Rates: A Review
Article." *IMF Staff Papers* 23 (March 1976): 1–59.

Organization for Economic Co-Operation and Development. *Exchange Rate Determination and the Conduct of Monetary Policy*. Paris: OECD, 1985.

Rhomberg, R. R. "Indices of Effective Exchange Rates." *IMF Staff Papers* 23 (March
1976): 88–112.

7

THE BALANCE OF

PAYMENTS

This chapter describes what the balance of payments is, and examines the principles used in compiling the balance of payments: the concept of double-entry bookkeeping and the classification of transactions into credits and debits. The meaning and significance of balance of payments deficits and surpluses, the relationship of the balance of payments to national income, and the level of international indebtedness are also considered. The focus is on the balance of payments of the United States, but most of the discussion is equally applicable to other countries.

BALANCE OF PAYMENTS ACCOUNTING 7.2

The *balance of payments* is a systematic record of the transactions by the residents of one country with the residents of other countries over a period of time (usually a quarter or a year). The data for the United States are compiled by the Department of Commerce and published in the *Survey of Current Business*. Data for other countries may be found in *International Financial Statistics* or the *Balance of Payments Yearbook;* both are published by the International Monetary Fund.

Credits and Debits

Table 7.1 shows a summary of the balance of payments of the United States using broad groupings of transactions. Some of the entries are positive in value and some are negative. The principle used when the balance of payments is compiled is that *credit* entries, those that are positive in value, record transactions that normally lead to receipts from foreigners and thus a supply of foreign exchange. For example, exports appear as a credit because

TABLE 7.1   The Balance of Payments of the United States in 1987

		Millions of dollars
1	Exports of goods and services	424,823
2	Merchandise excluding military	249,570
3	Other goods and services	175,253
4	Imports of goods and services	−565,342
5	Merchandise excluding military	−409,850
6	Other goods and services	−155,492
7	Unilateral transfers	−13,445
8	U.S. assets abroad (net increase (−))	−75,987
9	U.S. official reserve assets	9,149
10	Other U.S. government assets	1,162
11	U.S. private assets	−86,297
12	Foreign assets in the U.S. (net increase (+))	211,490
13	Foreign official assets	44,968
14	Other foreign assets	166,522
15	Allocations of SDRs	0
16	Statistical discrepancy	18,461
17	Merchandise trade balance (lines 2 and 5)	−160,280
18	Balance on goods and services (lines 1 and 4)	−140,519
19	Current account balance (lines 18 and 7)	−153,964

Source: Survey of Current Business, June 1988.

they lead to receipts from foreigners and a supply of foreign exchange. In cases where exports are donated to other countries or are bartered for imports, they are still classified as credits. The reason is that if the decision to export were not related to other transactions or considerations, exports would lead to receipts from foreigners. *Debit* items, those that are negative, record transactions that normally lead to payments to foreigners and thus a demand for foreign exchange. For example, imports appear as a debit because they lead to payments to foreigners and a demand for foreign exchange.

Merchandise Trade and Services

The first two sections of the balance of payments, showing exports and imports of goods and services (lines 1 and 4), are the largest in size. Merchandise trade is trade in goods. The most important types of service are: travel and transportation, receipts from U.S. assets abroad, and payments on foreign assets in the United States. Receipts from U.S. assets abroad are classified as a service because the countries where the assets are located benefit from the use (services) of American capital. Similarly, payments made for the use of foreign capital are classified as a service.

Unilateral Transfers

The entry for unilateral transfers (line 7) records transfers of funds (such as pensions) that are not related to sales of goods or assets and net gifts of goods and services to foreigners by Americans. The entry is needed to comply with the principles of double-entry bookkeeping (described below).

Capital Flows

Capital flows are shown by the change in the stock of U.S. assets abroad (line 8), and the change in the stock of foreign assets in the United States (line 12). These entries are jointly known as the *capital account*. An increase in U.S. assets abroad, a *capital outflow*, is recorded as a debit item because the acquisition of foreign assets involves a payment to foreigners. For example, an increase in U.S. assets abroad takes place when an American company buys a German factory.[1] An increase in foreign assets in the United States, a *capital inflow*, is recorded as a credit item because foreigners make payments to Americans when they invest in the United States. For example, an increase in foreign assets in the United States takes place when a Japanese firm buys an American factory.

Official Reserves

Changes in international reserves (line 9) are included as a capital flow. The accumulation of international reserves is analogous to the accumulation of foreign capital assets. When the United States buys foreign exchange (or gold) it makes payments to foreigners and adds to the demand for foreign exchange, thus the accumulation of international reserves is a debit entry. Similarly, an increase in foreign governments' reserves of American dollars is recorded as a credit because foreign monetary authorities increase the supply of foreign currency when they purchase dollars.

Special Drawing Rights

Special drawing rights (SDRs) are an asset issued by the International Monetary Fund.[2] When special drawing rights are allocated they are added to the stock of international reserves and the increase in reserves is shown as a debit. A credit item of an equal amount (line 15), recording the allocation of special drawing rights, is added to the balance of payments to comply with the principles of double-entry bookkeeping. SDRs were not allocated in 1987 (the last allocation was in 1981).

The Statistical Discrepancy

Finally, the statistical discrepancy is calculated and added to the balance of payments (line 16). Since the balance of payments is based on the principle of double-entry bookkeeping, it should always sum to zero. In practice, the

---

[1] It may help to think of a capital outflow as the import of a piece of paper, the paper being a claim to a foreign asset.
[2] Special drawing rights are described in Chapter 13.

data collected only refer to one side of a transaction. For example, import data are collected separately from data showing how imports are financed. It is hoped that by trying to identify all transactions the balance of payments will be accurate. The statistical discrepancy is a reflection of omitted transactions and imperfect valuation. For instance, unrecorded capital flows are thought to be one of the main reasons for the statistical discrepancy. The discrepancy can be large—in 1982 the statistical discrepancy was $36 billion.

The last three entries in Table 7.1 show measures of net trade with the rest of the world. The significance of measures such as these is discussed in the following sections.

Measurement Problems

The data on trade flows are obtained from customs declarations. The data are quite reliable in the sense that most goods are recorded. However, the value of the goods may not always be accurate because companies sometimes have an incentive to overcharge or undercharge for goods, perhaps to avoid taxes or as a way of transferring capital between countries.[3] Another problem is that goods are not necessarily paid for at the time they are shipped. Thus, in an accounting period, there can be a difference between the value of merchandise trade and the value of payments associated with the trade. Under certain circumstances, such as when a currency is expected to increase or decrease in value, transactions may be brought forward or delayed. Leads and lags in payments may be another major factor responsible for the statistical discrepancy.

Data relating to international transactions by the government are reasonably complete, with the exception of the data on military and security operations. Most of the remaining data making up the balance of payments are obtained from surveys. Data on services are obtained from surveys of banks and financial corporations. Tourist expenditures are calculated from surveys of a small number of passengers, and total spending by tourists is estimated using the total number of tourists. Data on fees and royalties are obtained from surveys of trade organizations. Data on capital flows are obtained from surveys of the major institutions dealing in international investment. Although efforts are made to ensure that the surveys are accurate, some degree of error is inevitable. Imperfect measurement of capital flows is thought to be another major reason for the statistical discrepancy.

Double-Entry Bookkeeping

The balance of payments is drawn up using *double-entry bookkeeping*. This method uses the principle that every transaction has two sides: the transfer of whatever is sold (goods, services, or assets), and the payment. One side of the transaction leads to a credit, and the other side leads to a debit. There-

---

[3]Transfer pricing is discussed in Chapter 19.

fore, when one side of an international transaction is recorded as a credit or debit item, there is always an accompanying debit or credit, respectively, of an equal amount showing the other side of the transaction. The concept of double-entry bookkeeping is perhaps best illustrated by examples.

1. An American company exports a machine and is paid with a check drawn on the New York bank account of a French company.

The export of the machine is recorded as a credit because exports normally lead to receipts from foreigners. The reduction in the size of the French company's American bank account is recorded as a debit showing a reduction in foreign assets in the U.S. The reason is that if the reduction in the French company's account had taken place independently (instead of being a payment for American goods), the American bank would have made a payment to the French company.

2. An American firm imports champagne from France and pays with a check drawn on its bank account in France.

The imported champagne appears as a debit under merchandise imports because imports normally lead to payments to foreigners. The reduction in the size of the American firm's bank account in France is recorded as a credit showing a decline in U.S. assets abroad. The reason is that if the reduction in the American firm's account had been undertaken independently (instead of being a payment for French goods), the French bank would have made a payment to the American company.

3. An American company uses a check drawn on a New York bank to pay for a factory in Britain, and the check is deposited in the New York account of a British firm.

The purchase of the British factory is recorded as a debit, showing an increase in U.S. assets abroad, because the purchase entails a payment to foreigners. The increase in the British firm's New York bank account is recorded as a credit, showing an increase in foreign assets in the U.S. The reason is that if the increase in the British firm's bank account had taken place independently, the British firm would have made a payment to an American bank.

4. An American company reduces the size of its foreign bank account and repatriates the funds.

The decline in the American company's foreign bank account is recorded as a credit showing a reduction in U.S. assets abroad. The amount of dollars held by foreigners declines when the American firm repatriates its funds. This is recorded as a debit, showing a decline in foreign assets in the United States, because buying dollars from foreigners entails making payments to foreigners.

5. The American government gives $100 million cash to a less developed country which holds the money in a New York bank account.

The gift is shown as a debit under unilateral transfers because it is a payment to foreigners. A credit records an increase in foreign official assets in the United States because if the increase in the foreign government's bank account had taken place independently, the foreign government would have made a payment to the American bank.

7.3 DEFICITS AND SURPLUSES

An understanding of the principles of balance of payments accounting is important as a background to the concepts of surplus and deficit in the balance of payments. There are two important conclusions. First, since the balance of payments must sum to zero, it follows that there can only be a surplus or deficit on part of the balance of payments. In other words, there is no such thing as an overall surplus or deficit. When reference is made to a balance of payments surplus or deficit, it is the structure of the balance of payments that is being referred to, not the overall value. Second, we should not assume that a balance of payments surplus is necessarily good and a deficit is bad. A surplus on part of the accounts is always matched by a deficit on the rest of the accounts.

Balance of Payments Equilibrium

It is inevitable that, at any given time, some parts of the accounts will be positive in total and some will be negative. Economically, the terms *surplus* and *deficit* imply more than just that the total of some parts of the balance of payments is positive or negative. Surpluses and deficits are balance of payments positions that are not sustainable: in other words, the terms indicate the existence of disequilibrium balance of payments positions. For example, large net borrowing from abroad may indicate a long-run disequilibrium position because a country cannot borrow or run down its holdings of foreign assets continuously. (This is true under fixed or flexible exchange rates.)

Under fixed exchange rates, balance of payments equilibrium often takes on a more specific meaning, that is, surpluses and deficits are positions that are not consistent with the maintenance of a stable exchange rate. For example, assume that international reserves are being depleted (because the monetary authorities are intervening in the foreign exchange market to prevent domestic currency from falling in value). This is not an equilibrium because the stock of reserves is limited. Eventually the monetary authorities will be forced to stop selling foreign currency, and domestic currency will fall in value.[4]

The Balance of Payments and the Foreign Exchange Market

The foreign exchange market and the balance of payments are closely related. In the foreign exchange market, the amount of foreign exchange sold must obviously be equal to the amount of foreign exchange bought. Foreign exchange is not created or destroyed in the market, it is transferred from one holder to another. The balance of payments can be thought of as a record of possible reasons for purchases and sales of foreign currency. Therefore, it

---

[4]In Chapter 9 and Chapter 10 the expression *balance of payments equilibrium* denotes positions where the demand and supply of foreign currency are equal at the existing exchange rate without intervention by the monetary authorities.

would seem that the balance of payments must sum to zero because the supply and demand for foreign currency must be equal. Unfortunately, it is not quite so simple.

The correspondence between the balance of payments and the foreign exchange market is not perfect because the balance of payments also includes records of transactions that do not lead to foreign exchange transactions. Gifts of goods and barter trade are obvious examples. Another example of a transaction that does not lead to a foreign exchange transaction is an export by a Japanese company to the United States that is paid for by transferring ownership of a dollar deposit in New York. The balance of payments would record the acquisition of U.S. assets by foreigners and the sale of exports to foreigners, but in this case neither would be accompanied by a foreign exchange transaction. Also, recall that the balance of payments is not a completely accurate record of international transactions (hence the need for the statistical discrepancy).

Another problem when using balance of payments statistics as a guide to the motives underlying foreign exchange transactions is that the balance of payments does not distinguish between transactions that are undertaken independently (for their own sake) and transactions that result from the financing of independent transactions. For example, an increase in foreign assets in the U.S. may occur because Japanese investors want to invest in the United States, or it may reflect a temporary use of funds received by Japanese firms for goods they have sold to the United States (as in the example above).

ACCOUNTING BALANCES   7.4

Various accounting balances have been used to measure balance of payments surpluses and deficits. As countries have moved towards more flexible exchange rates and exchange rate policy has become less important, the importance of these accounting balances for current policy has decreased. Therefore we shall only discuss the concepts briefly. The purposes of this discussion are: to illustrate the principles of balance of payments accounting, to set the background for the analysis of balance of payments adjustment in the following chapters, and to facilitate the historical analysis in Part Two.

Definitions of accounting balances within the balance of payments reflect three distinctions: 1) between real and financial transactions, that is, between trade in goods and services, and capital flows; 2) between short-term capital flows and long-term capital flows; and 3) between official transactions carried out by the monetary authorities and other international transactions.

The Current Account Balance

The *current account* records trade in goods and services, and unilateral transfers. In a sense, the current account measures the extent to which a country lives within its means. Ignoring unilateral transfers, a deficit in the current account indicates that an economy is spending more on imports of goods and services than it is earning from exports of goods and services. Why is this unsustainable?

The current account shows an economy's net foreign investment. If a country spends more than it earns on goods and services, it must be running down its stock of foreign assets, and/or increasing its debts to foreigners. This cannot go on forever because the country's stock of foreign assets is limited, and there is probably a limit to how much foreigners will be willing to lend to one country.[5] Therefore, a current account deficit may be an indication of balance of payments disequilibrium.

The current account balance is also of interest because it is part of a nation's national income accounts. As such, it represents the contribution to aggregate demand resulting from trade. For example, a current account surplus implies that foreign trade adds to aggregate demand because foreigners are purchasing more of a country's output than domestic residents are buying abroad. However, the effects of capital flows on economic activity are not shown by the current account. (In the absence of official intervention, a current account surplus is accompanied by a capital account deficit, implying that more capital is flowing out of the country than is flowing into the country.)

The Basic Balance

The *basic balance* adds long-term capital movements to the current account balance. The basic balance is supposed to show the underlying long-term balance of payments position of a country. The proposition is that trade and long-term capital flows do not fluctuate in response to temporary economic disturbances but reflect long-term forces.

How does the basic balance relate to the concept of balance of payments equilibrium? The reasoning behind the basic balance is that the amount of short-term capital that a country can attract is limited, and the stock of reserves is limited, therefore a country cannot finance a deficit on the rest of the balance of payments by incurring short-term debt or running down reserves.

As a theoretical concept this measure of the balance of payments may have some appeal, but in practice the measure is much less attractive because capital flows cannot be classified unambiguously into short-term and long-term flows. For example, some holders of American companies' stocks, which are classified as long-term investments, may be prepared to liquidate those investments at short notice, whereas many supposedly short-term investments often follow long-term trends. Whether an investment is short-term or long-term depends as much on the investor's intentions as on the nature of

---

[5] How much a country may borrow probably depends on what the borrowing is used for. We return to this topic when we discuss the sectoral balance later in this chapter.

the asset. Thus, the distinction between short- and long-term investments is not particularly useful. The basic balance cannot be calculated for the United States after 1977 because the distinction between short- and long-term capital flows is no longer made in published figures.[6]

The Liquidity Balance

The *liquidity balance* was designed to show the possible pressure on American reserve assets (in particular gold). The balance distinguishes between liquid and nonliquid short-term capital flows, and is defined as the sum of changes in U.S. reserves and changes in U.S. liquid liabilities to foreigners (private and official).[7] The distinction between liquid and nonliquid liabilities is that liquid liabilities are easily transferable whereas nonliquid liabilities are not. For example, trade financing loans with a duration of less than three months made by foreign banks to U.S. corporations are not transferable and are recorded as short-term nonliquid liabilities.

The justification for this balance of payments definition is that a liquidity balance deficit is not an equilibrium position—either the stock of reserves is falling or the stock of U.S. liquid liabilities is increasing. A deficit cannot be permanently financed by reserves because the stock of reserves is limited, and increasing U.S. liquid liabilities to foreigners are inconsistent with the maintenance of a fixed exchange rate. If foreigners suddenly chose to sell the American assets they held, the American monetary authorities would be obliged to intervene in the foreign exchange market, and American reserves would fall.

The liquidity balance suffers from serious flaws. Although liquid liabilities to foreigners are considered, American holdings of foreign liquid assets are not considered. This asymmetrical treatment means that the balance is of dubious significance. For example, if an American bank and a British bank agreed to increase their deposits with each other, the liquidity balance of payments deficit would increase because U.S. liabilities are part of the deficit but U.S. claims are ignored. Also, the liquidity balance does not show what it is supposed to show, the vulnerability of American reserves, because the balance of payments records changes in the stock of assets, not the size of the stock. The size of the stock of liquid assets, not changes in the stock, is an indicator of the vulnerability of the American reserves. Finally, as shown in the discussion of the basic balance, in practice it is impossible to distinguish clearly between short-term and long-term capital flows.

---

[6]The reasons for changing the presentation of balance of payments data are discussed in: "Report of the Advisory Committee on the Presentation of Balance of Payments Statistics," *Survey of Current Business*, June 1976, pp. 18–27.
[7]The liquidity balance should not be confused with another balance the reader may encounter, the *net liquidity balance*. This equals the change in reserve assets plus the difference between liquid private claims on foreigners and liabilities to foreigners.

The Official Settlements Balance

The *official settlements balance* is a modified version of the liquidity balance. A distinction is drawn between official and private U.S. liquid liabilities, and the balance is defined as the sum of official liquid liabilities to official foreigners (central banks) and changes in reserves. The official settlements balance has similar flaws to the liquidity balance: it measures changes in stocks not the stocks themselves, and U.S. liquid assets are ignored.

Under the Bretton Woods system (see Chapter 13), the official settlements balance was supposed to show the vulnerability of American gold reserves because dollars held by foreign central banks (liquid liabilities to official foreigners) could be used to buy gold from America. When the option to buy gold ended in August 1971, the official settlements balance ceased to be significant.

Summary

It is clear from this brief discussion of balance of payments accounting that because there are many possible ways of defining balance of payments deficits or surpluses, unqualified references to "the" balance of payments surplus or deficit are meaningless. We must specify which balance of payments we are referring to.

7.5 NATIONAL INCOME AND THE BALANCE OF PAYMENTS[8]

Gross national product is equal to the value of goods and services produced in an economy over a period of time. The increase in gross national product is often used as an indicator of improvements in economic welfare. In an economy without trade, the *value of output* is equal to the sum of three different types of spending in an economy: consumption (C), investment (I), and government spending (G).[9] The value of output is usually called *national income (Y)* because the value of goods and services produced is equal to the sum of incomes earned in the production process.[10] Thus:

$$Y = C + I + G \tag{1}$$

This is an identity because any output not sold to consumers or the government is by definition part of investment, that is, the accumulation of inventories is classified as investment.

---

[8] The following discussion assumes that students are familiar with the basic concepts of national income accounting in a closed economy. The discussion focuses on the effects of trade on national income.

[9] In this chapter, I refers to actual investment. In the following chapter, a distinction is made between planned and actual investment.

[10] The value of goods and services is equal to spending on goods and services. Since every cent spent on goods and services accrues to someone as income in some form, if all sources of income are identified, income equals the value of output.

Net Exports Add to the Demand for Goods and Services

If we want to calculate the gross national product of an economy that trades, there are two additional considerations. First, because output may be sold abroad as well as at home, the value of exports (X) must be added to domestic spending. Second, the value of imports (M) must be deducted because some domestic spending may be on imported goods and services rather than domestic goods and services. Therefore the expression for national income in an open economy is:

$$Y = C + I + G + X - M^{11} \tag{2}$$

Alternatively, we can express national income as the total value of spending or *absorption* (consumption, investment, and government spending) plus the current account (net exports of goods and services):[12]

$$Y = A + X - M \text{ (where } A = C + I + G) \tag{3}$$

In this form the relationship between net exports $(X - M)$ and national income is clear. If national income exceeds absorption $(Y > A)$, net exports will be positive. If absorption exceeds national income $(A > Y)$, net exports will be negative. This presentation leads to an important conclusion: net exports can only increase if income rises relative to absorption. If income does not rise, absorption must fall if net exports are to increase. We shall return to the role of absorption in the following chapters.

Sectoral Balance

Income can be spent, saved (S), or taken as taxes (T). Therefore,

$$Y = C + S + T \tag{4}$$

The allocation of income must be equal to the level of income earned, thus, equations 2 and 4 must be equal. Combining these equations, subtracting C from both sides, and moving M to the right, yields:

$$I + G + X = S + T + M \tag{5}$$

Equation 5 is derived from national income accounting, and must hold because of the way in which the variables are defined in the national income accounts. Although it has no behavioral implications, this equation can be used to yield insights into the relationship between components of national income by sector. For example, equation 5 can be rewritten:

$$(I - S) + (G - T) + (X - M) = 0 \tag{6}$$

In this form it shows that the difference between private sector investment and saving $(I - S)$, the government deficit $(G - T)$, and the current account

---

[11] This expression gives gross national product. If the country receives gifts (transfers) from other countries, these must be added to gross national product to give national income.

[12] For simplicity we assume net unilateral transfers are zero.

balance $(X - M)$, must add up to zero. The difference between investment and saving shows net borrowing by the private sector. The difference between government spending and taxation is government borrowing. Also, recall that the current account balance is equal to net foreign investment, that is, net lending by the country to foreigners. Thus, equation 6 shows that net borrowing by one sector must be matched by net lending in other sectors.

Sectoral Balance and the Current Account

In the discussion of balance of payments equilibrium, it was suggested that a current account deficit is an indication of disequilibrium, because foreigners would not be willing to increase investments in a country continuously and the stock of foreign assets is limited.[13] Let us examine this issue a little more carefully.

The willingness of foreigners to invest in an economy may be influenced by the possibility of long-term real growth. Using the sectoral balance equation (6), it is clear that a current account deficit must be accompanied by an excess of private investment over saving, or an excess of government spending over taxes. Since government spending (in the form of public investment) or private investment may increase the long-run income of an economy, under some circumstances an inflow of foreign investment can continue. We might expect the inflow of capital to dry up most quickly if the trade balance is reflected in government spending that finances current consumption rather than public investment.

The Balance of Payments of the United States

An illustration of the sectoral balance is shown in Table 7.2. During the seventies changes in the government deficit were mainly reflected in the disparity between saving and investment. This relationship held during the first years of the eighties: net foreign investment was not significantly affected even when the federal deficit caused the overall government deficit to explode in 1982. Significant American borrowing from abroad began in 1983, and by 1984 the government deficit was reflected mainly in large net borrowing from abroad. When, as in 1984, a government deficit is accompanied by a trade deficit of roughly the same amount, borrowing from abroad is approximately equal to the government deficit. However, the temptation to say that foreign countries lend to the government and finance government spending should be avoided. Foreign funds may be invested in the private sector, and domestic funds loaned to the government.

Some economists have suggested that the growth of the federal budget deficit was responsible for these changes. The argument is that government

---

[13] If international reserves finance the current account deficit, the fall in reserves is recorded as a fall in U.S. assets abroad. International reserves cannot finance a current account deficit continuously because the stock of reserves is finite.

TABLE 7.2   The United States Sectoral Balance

Year	$I-S$	$G-T$	Net foreign investment	Other factors[a]
1970	−15.7	10.6	4.8	−0.3
1971	−18.1	19.5	1.3	2.7
1972	−1.4	3.4	−2.9	−0.9
1973	−5.2	−7.9	8.8	−4.3
1974	−13.5	4.3	5.4	−3.8
1975	−84.0	64.9	21.6	2.5
1976	−43.7	38.4	9.0	3.7
1977	−10.4	19.1	−8.7	0.0
1978	7.8	0.4	−10.1	−1.9
1979	9.0	−11.5	2.6	0.1
1980	−41.4	34.5	13.0	6.1
1981	−35.0	29.7	10.6	5.3
1982	−109.8	110.8	−1.0	0.0
1983	−89.9	128.6	−33.5	5.2
1984	−8.7	105.0	−90.9	5.4
1985	−22.2	131.8	−114.4	−4.8
1986	−15.7	144.4	−142.4	−13.7
1987	47.6	104.9	−160.6	−8.1

[a] Includes the statistical discrepancy and allocations of SDRs.
Source: Economic Report of the President, 1989, p. 340.

sales of debt combined with a tight money policy led to a high real interest rate in the United States. Investors were attracted by American investments, and the demand for dollars by foreign investors, as well as a reduced demand for foreign currency by American investors, pushed up the value of the dollar. The result was that net exports were crowded out as the dollar increased in value.

The Balance of International Indebtedness

The net capital inflow into the United States in the early eighties is reflected in the international investment position of the United States shown in Table 7.3. The decline in the net investment position of the United States after 1983 occurred because American investment abroad (shown by the increase of U.S. private assets) was smaller than foreign investment in the United States (shown by the increase of foreign assets in the U.S.).

The Net Credit Position of the United States

A word of caution is appropriate at this point. The data showing assets are not accurate enough to make precise statements about the size of a country's net external assets. In particular, U.S. investments abroad made many years

TABLE 7.3   The International Investment Position of the United States

	1979	1980	1981	1982	1983	1984	1985	1986	1987
U.S. assets abroad	510.6	607.1	719.8	824.9	873.9	896.1	950.3	1071.4	1167.8
U.S. reserves	19.0	26.8	30.1	34.0	33.7	34.9	43.2	48.5	45.8
Other official assets	58.4	63.8	68.7	74.6	79.5	84.8	87.6	89.5	88.4
U.S. private assets	433.2	516.6	621.2	716.4	760.7	776.3	819.5	933.4	1033.6
Foreign assets in the U.S.	416.1	500.8	578.7	688.1	784.5	892.6	1061.0	1340.7	1536.0
Official assets	159.9	176.1	180.4	189.1	194.5	199.3	202.6	241.7	283.1
Other foreign assets	256.3	324.8	398.3	498.9	590.0	693.3	858.4	1098.9	1252.9
Net investment position	94.5	106.3	141.1	136.9	89.4	3.5	−110.7	−269.2	−368.2

Source: Economic Report of the President, 1988, p. 369; 1989, p. 429.

TABLE 7.4   U.S. Saving and Investment Percentage of GNP, 1949–87

	1949–81	1982–86	1987
Gross private investment	16.0	15.7	16.0
Gross national saving	16.3	13.7	12.6
Net foreign saving	−0.3	1.9	3.3

Source: *Economic Report of the President*, 1988, p. 100.

ago are undervalued because they are recorded at historical cost.[14] Recent foreign investment in the United States may be more accurately measured. However, there seems little doubt that the United States is now a net debtor. An indication of this net debt position is that in the third quarter of 1987 payments on foreign-owned assets in the United States exceeded receipts from assets abroad for the first time in recent U.S. history.[15]

The significance of being a net debtor is that servicing debt to foreigners is a drain on national income. Therefore, the rate at which the United States is accumulating foreign debt may lead us to be concerned about the effects on future U.S. prosperity. The effects on future income depend on how the funds are used. If borrowing from abroad finances productive investment, it will lead to higher future real income. Under these conditions, the accumulation of net debt may not be a source of concern if the debt declines in relation to real income. However, Table 7.4 shows that the capital inflow of the mid-eighties merely allowed the United States to continue investing at a rate close to the postwar average at a time when national saving fell relative to postwar averages.

International comparisons between countries' rates of investment are imperfect because of differences between the ways countries measure investment. However, the data in Table 7.5 suggest that the United States is investing less than other major industrial countries, even with the benefit of an inflow of foreign capital.

Net External Asset Positions of Other Countries

A question that readily springs to mind is: If the United States has been borrowing so heavily, which countries have been lending? Table 7.6 shows that while the net assets of Canada and the United States decreased, the net assets of three of the five other major industrial countries (Germany, Japan, and the United Kingdom) increased substantially over the period.

---

[14] We might also note that some of the assets that the United States holds are unlikely ever to be repaid, for example, loans made to some developing countries. Therefore, some assets may be overvalued.

[15] See *Economic Report of the President*, 1988, p. 99.

TABLE 7.5   Comparative Rates of Investment

	1975–85	1987
Canada	19.7	21.2
France	18.8	16.7
Germany	16.4	17.7
Italy	15.9	18.2
Japan	24.7	28.9
United Kingdom	17.6	17.3
United States	16.3	16.0

Source: IMF *World Economic Outlook*, April 1988, p. 21.

TABLE 7.6   Net External Assets of Major Industrial Countries

	1980	1987
Canada	−106.5	−149.3
France	−11.8	−3.4
Germany	27.2	150.5
Italy	−14.7	−34.0
Japan	23.7	266.0
United Kingdom	56.0	159.5
United States	125.9	−435.4

Source: IMF *World Economic Outlook*, April 1988, p. 89.

Summary of Main Points

The *balance of payments* is a record of the transactions of the residents of one country with residents in other countries. *Debit* items reflect transactions that would normally lead to payments to foreigners, for example, purchases of imports or American investment abroad. *Credit* items reflect transactions that would normally give rise to receipts from foreigners, for example, exports or foreign investment in the United States.

The major parts of the balance of payments show: imports and exports of goods and services, American purchases of foreign assets, and foreign purchases of American assets. The final entry is the statistical discrepancy, which reflects valuation errors and transactions that are not recorded.

The balance of payments must sum to zero because it is drawn up using the principles of *double-entry bookkeeping*. Since the balance of payments must sum to zero, a surplus or deficit can only exist on part of the accounts.

The balance of payments shows why people buy and sell foreign currency. Credit items might be expected to lead to a supply of foreign exchange and debit items a demand for foreign exchange. The demand and supply of foreign exchange must balance, and the balance of payments must sum to zero. Thus, the relationship between the balance of payments and the foreign exchange market appears close. However, some balance of payments entries reflect transactions where there were no corresponding transactions in the foreign exchange market. Also, some international transactions (particularly capital flows) are not recorded.

Balance of payments equilibrium refers to the structure of the balance of payments, that is, to the relative value of different types of international transaction. A disequilibrium balance of payments position is one that is not sustainable, for example, a country may not be able to continue borrowing large amounts. When the exchange is fixed, a disequilibrium balance of payments position is one that is not consistent with maintaining the chosen exchange rate, for example, a country cannot support a fixed exchange rate by running down its holding of foreign exchange reserves continuously.

Various measures of the balance of payments have been used. One of the objectives historically has been to indicate whether the position was likely to make exchange rate changes more likely. The concept of balance of payments equilibrium was more important under fixed exchange rates than it is now.

One balance of payments measure that is still published is the *current account* balance showing the balance of exports and imports and of goods and services, and unilateral transfers. It is of interest because the current account is a measure of the extent to which international trade affects domestic aggregate demand. Also, this balance measures the extent to which a country is spending more than it earns: the current account balance is equal to the net change in foreign assets. A country with a current account deficit must have falling net foreign assets.

The United States has had large current account deficits during the eighties, which have been reflected in a fall in America's net foreign assets. At the present time America is the world's largest debtor.

The sectoral balance equation

$$(I-S)+(G-T)+(X-M)=0$$

can help us analyze the American experience. During the seventies, the government deficit was reflected mainly in the balance between saving and investment. From 1984 on the government deficit was reflected mainly in current account deficits, that is, net American borrowing from abroad.

Study Questions

1. Explain what is recorded in the current account and the capital account. Using examples for each account, explain the principles used to determine whether a transaction is recorded as a debit or a credit.
2. How are the following transactions shown in the balance of payments?
   a. An American company exports a good and is paid with a deposit into a bank account it holds in a foreign country.

  b. An American company exports a good and allows three months before payment must be made.
  c. An American import is financed by a payment into the New York account of a foreign exporter.
  d. An American factory is purchased by a Japanese company using a check drawn on the Japanese company's account in New York.
  e. An American tourist pays a British hotel bill with dollars.
3. Explain what is meant by *double-entry bookkeeping*. If this method is used, why is there a statistical discrepancy? How can there be a balance of payments deficit or surplus if double-entry bookkeeping is used?
4. How do the accounting balances discussed in the text reflect the proposition that a deficit is a disequilibrium position? Why does no one seem to worry about surpluses?
5. If saving is greater than investment, and government spending equals taxation, explain how we can deduce whether the current account or capital account is in surplus or deficit.
6. Using the sectoral balance equation, discuss reasons for the decline of the American trade balance from 1980 onward.
7. Why might we be concerned about the long-term effects of a prolonged American trade deficit?

Selected References

Cooper, R. N. "The Balance of Payments in Review," *Journal of Political Economy* 74 (August 1966): 379–95.
International Monetary Fund. *Balance of Payments Manual*, 4th Ed. Washington, D.C.: IMF, 1977.
Kemp, D. S. "Balance of Payments Concepts—What Do They Really Mean?" *Federal Reserve Bank of St. Louis Review*, July 1975: 14–23.
Kindelberger, C. P. "Measuring Equilibrium in the Balance of Payments." *Journal of Political Economy* 77 (December 1969): 873–91.
Stern, R. M., et al. "The Presentation of the U.S. Balance of Payments: A Symposium." In *Essays in International Finance*, No. 123. Princeton, N.J.: Princeton University Press, 1977.
Yeager, L. B. *International Monetary Relations*, 2d Ed. New York: Harper and Row, 1976.

8

THE DETERMINATION OF INCOME IN AN OPEN ECONOMY

In this chapter we examine the factors that determine the level of national income in an open economy. We begin with a simple model of a closed economy (no foreign trade) with fixed prices and without a government sector. Using the assumption that the exchange rate is fixed, the model then is extended to include a government sector and international trade. Finally, the assumptions of the model are relaxed and the effects of inflation and exchange rate changes are considered. At first the model may seem unrealistic, but it is developed to incorporate the elements needed to show the role of international trade in the determination of income and to identify reasons why income may change. The model also shows how the incomes of different countries are linked through trade.

THE DETERMINATION OF INCOME 8.2
IN A CLOSED ECONOMY WITH NO GOVERNMENT

Gross national product (GNP) is the value of goods and services produced in an economy over a period of time. GNP is often referred to as *national income* because the value of goods and services produced is equal to the sum of incomes earned in the production process. (The value of goods and services produced is equal to expenditure on the goods and services. Every dollar spent ends up as income to someone if all sources of income are identified. Thus, income is equal to output.)

The value of national income (Y) in a closed economy with no government is equal to the value of consumption (C) plus investment (I):

$$Y = C + I \tag{1}$$

Because income is the value of goods and services produced, it is also called *aggregate supply*.

The Equilibrium Level of Income

The *equilibrium level of income* is the income level at which aggregate demand is equal to aggregate supply. In an economy with no government or foreign trade, *aggregate demand (D)* is composed of the demand for consumption goods and services (C) and the demand for investment goods or planned investment (I_p):

$$D = C + I_p \tag{2}$$

Initially we shall assume that there are unemployed resources in the economy and that the level of income (aggregate supply) can increase without the price level increasing. It will be shown that in this case the equilibrium level of income is determined solely by aggregate demand. We begin by examining the determination of consumption because it plays an important role in the process of income determination.

The Consumption Function

We would normally expect consumption to increase with the level of income. We assume that the relationship between consumption (C) and income (Y) is

$$C = C_a + cY \tag{3}$$

where C_a represents a particular level of consumption that does not change with income *(autonomous consumption)*, and c is the amount of each extra dollar of income that is consumed (the *marginal propensity to consume*). Autonomous consumption can be thought of as a level of consumption determined by habits, wealth, and past income levels. If income increases, autonomous consumption does not change. Total consumption does increase with income though, the amount of the increase being determined by the marginal propensity to consume. For simplicity we assume that the marginal propensity to consume is constant.

The marginal propensity to consume is less than 1 because people use increases in income to finance saving as well as consumption. The amount of each extra dollar that is saved is the *marginal propensity to save (s)*. Since each extra dollar is allocated between consumption and saving, the sum of the marginal propensity to consume and the marginal propensity to save equals 1, that is, $c + s = 1$.

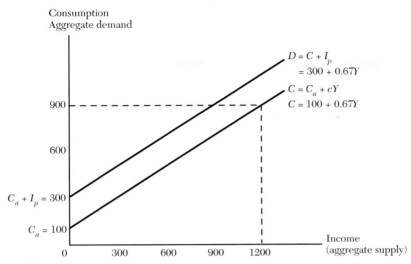

FIGURE 8.1

The Consumption Function and the Level of Aggregate Demand
The consumption function $(C = C_a + cY = 100 + 0.67Y)$ shows how consumption increases with the level of income. For example, at an income level of 1200, consumption equals about 900. Aggregate demand (D) is obtained by adding planned investment $(I_p = 200)$ to consumption.

For example, if the consumption function is

$$C = \$100 + 0.67Y$$

autonomous consumption equals $100, the marginal propensity to consume is 0.67, and the marginal propensity to save is 0.33. If income equals $1,200, consumption equals about $900 ($100 + 0.67 × $1,200).

The consumption function is shown in Figure 8.1. The vertical intercept represents autonomous consumption, and the function slopes upward showing that consumption increases as income increases. The slope is the increase in consumption per dollar increase in income, that is, the slope of the consumption function is the marginal propensity to consume (0.67).

Investment
We assume that investment demand, or planned investment, is determined *exogenously*, in other words, by factors that are outside of the model. This assumption does not imply that the potential effects of changes in planned investment on the level of income are ignored. These effects are examined after the determination of the level of income has been discussed. The main

purpose of the assumption is to simplify the analysis: we treat the level of planned investment as constant while the basic model of the determination of the equilibrium level of income is developed.

Aggregate Demand

Recall that aggregate demand equals consumption plus planned investment. If planned investment equals 200, in Figure 8.1 the line representing aggregate demand $(D = C + I_p)$ is a line 200 above the consumption function. The intercept of 300 on the vertical axis shows the total amount of autonomous expenditure, the level of demand that is independent of the level of income. The intercept represents the sum of planned investment (200) and autonomous consumption (100). The level of aggregate demand increases with income because consumption increases with income.

The Equilibrium Level of Income

The determination of the equilibrium level of income is shown in Figure 8.2. The horizontal axis shows income, or aggregate supply, and the vertical axis shows aggregate demand. Points at which aggregate demand and aggregate supply are equal are shown by the 45-degree line. The equilibrium level of income $(Y_E = 900)$, where aggregate demand and supply are equal, is the income level at which the aggregate demand line crosses the 45-degree line.

If the level of income differs from the equilibrium level, the excess aggregate demand or supply is reflected in firms' inventories of goods, and a process is initiated that eventually leads to the establishment of equilibrium. For example, below the equilibrium level of income, aggregate demand is greater than aggregate supply. Firms find that their inventories are falling (because demand exceeds supply), they respond by increasing production, and the level of income rises. Similarly, above the equilibrium level of income, aggregate demand is less than supply. Firms find that their inventories are rising, they decrease production, and the level of income falls.

Saving and Investment

The equilibrium level of income was defined as the income at which aggregate demand and aggregate supply are equal. The equilibrium level of income can also be defined as the level of income at which saving and planned investment are equal. To show this, consider how people can use their income.

People can use their income to finance consumption or saving:

$$Y = C + S \tag{4}$$

Setting aggregate demand equal to income, we obtain

$$C + I_p = C + S$$

or more simply

$$I_p = S \tag{5}$$

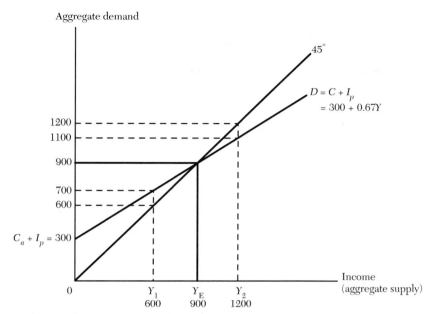

FIGURE 8.2

The Determination of the Equilibrium Level of Income

Aggregate demand and aggregate supply are equal at the equilibrium level of income $Y_E = 900$. At income levels below Y_E, aggregate demand exceeds aggregate supply, inventories are falling, firms respond by increasing output, and income rises. For example, when the level of income (aggregate supply) is at $Y_1 = 600$, aggregate demand equals 700. At income levels above Y_E, aggregate supply exceeds aggregate demand, inventories are rising, firms respond by decreasing output, and the level of income falls. For example, at $Y_2 = 1200$, aggregate demand equals 1100.

If income is greater than aggregate demand, saving is greater than planned investment. ($Y > D$ implies that $C + S > C + I_p$, thus $S > I_p$.) If income is less than aggregate demand, saving is less than planned investment. ($Y < D$ implies that $C + S < C + I_p$, thus $S < I_p$.)

In Figure 8.3, the level of saving is shown by the vertical distance between the consumption line and the 45-degree line. The level of planned investment is shown by the vertical distance between the aggregate demand line and the consumption function. At the equilibrium level of income (Y_E), saving and planned investment are equal. Below Y_E, saving is less than planned investment, and above Y_E saving is greater than planned investment.

To investigate the relationship between planned investment and saving in more detail we must introduce the *saving function*.

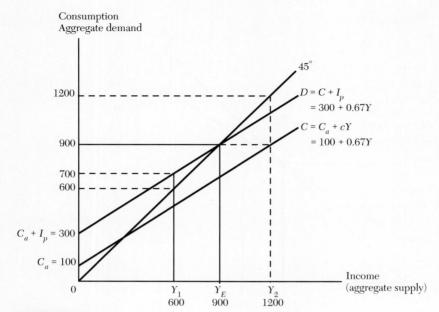

FIGURE 8.3

The Equality of Saving and Planned Investment at the Equilibrium Level of Income

Saving and planned investment are equal at the equilibrium level of income. At income levels below the equilibrium level, planned saving is less than planned investment. For example, at $Y_1 = 600$, saving equals 100 ($Y - C = 700 - 600$) and planned investment equals 200. At income levels above the equilibrium level, planned investment is greater than saving. For example, at $Y_2 = 1200$, saving is 300 ($Y - C = 1200 - 900$) and planned investment is 200.

The Saving Function

The difference between income and consumption equals saving:

$$S = Y - C \tag{6}$$

Substituting equation 3 (the consumption function) into equation 6 we obtain

$$S = Y - C_a - cY \tag{7}$$

which can be written as

$$S = -C_a + (1-c)Y \tag{8}$$

or more simply

$$S = -C_a + sY \tag{9}$$

where s is the marginal propensity to save ($s = 1 - c$).

For example, if the consumption function is

$$C = 100 + 0.67Y$$

the saving function is

$$S = -100 + 0.33Y$$

The saving function is shown in Figure 8.4. The slope of the saving function is the marginal propensity to save: in this case the vertical change per unit change in the horizontal is the change in saving per dollar increase in income.

When planned investment is added to the diagram, the level of income (Y_E) at which saving and planned investment are equal can be determined. Below Y_E, planned investment exceeds saving, thus aggregate demand is greater than aggregate supply. Above Y_E, saving exceeds planned investment, thus aggregate demand is less than aggregate supply. Figures 8.2 and 8.4 are different ways of showing the same relationship.

Although planned investment and saving may differ, it should be noted that in this model, with no government or international trade, actual investment and saving are always equal. Recall that income is the value of goods and services produced, the sum of consumption and actual investment (equation 1), and that income can be used for consumption or saving (equation 4). Putting equations 1 and 4 together it is clear that

$$S = I \qquad\qquad (10)$$

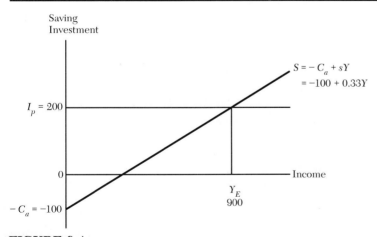

FIGURE 8.4

Saving and Planned Investment

Saving is negative at zero income because savings are used to finance autonomous consumption. As income rises, the level of saving rises. The equilibrium level of income $Y_E = 900$ is the level at which planned investment and saving are equal.

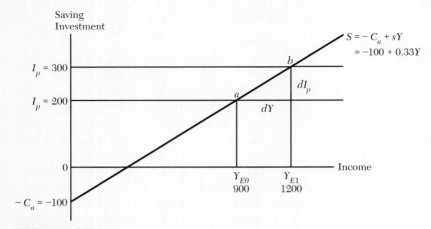

FIGURE 8.5

The Effect of an Increase in Planned Investment

If planned investment increases from 200 to 300, the equilibrium level of income increases from $Y_{E0}=900$ to $Y_{E1}=1200$. The slope of the saving function between points a and b is the marginal propensity to save ($s=0.33$), and is equal to the change in investment divided by the change in income (dI_p/dY). The multiplier (k) is the change in income divided by the change in investment (dY/dI_p), thus the multiplier is the reciprocal of the slope ($k = 1/s = 1/0.33 = 3$).

Investment and Income

Having set up the basic model of income determination, we can use the model to examine how changes in the level of planned investment lead to changes in the level of income. If planned investment rises, at the initial level of income aggregate demand exceeds supply, and income rises. For example, in Figure 8.5, when planned investment increases from 200 to 300, the equilibrium level of income increases from 900 to 1200. The same result could be obtained by moving the aggregate demand line upward in Figure 8.2. Clearly, a fall in planned investment would lead to a fall in income.

The Multiplier

The size of the increase in income caused by an increase in planned investment is determined by the *closed-economy multiplier*. To be specific, the change in income equals the change in planned investment multiplied by the multiplier. The multiplier for a closed economy with no government is $1/(1-c)$, where c is the marginal propensity to consume. Because $1-c$ is the marginal propensity to save, the multiplier can also be defined as $1/s$. For example, if the marginal propensity to consume is 0.67, the multiplier is 3 ($= 1/(1-0.67)$). In this case, if planned investment rises by 100, the level of income rises by 300.

The multiplier can be derived from Figure 8.5. The multiplier (k) is defined so that the change in income (dY) is the multiplier times the change in planned investment (dI_p): $dY = k dI_p$. Therefore, the multiplier is equal to dY/dI_p. Figure 8.5 shows that the slope of the saving function, the marginal propensity to save (s), is equal to dI_p/dY. Therefore, the multiplier is the reciprocal of the slope of the saving funciton, that is, $k = 1/s$. In the example shown, $k = 1/0.33 = 3$.

THE DETERMINATION OF INCOME ■ 8.3 ■
IN AN OPEN ECONOMY WITH A GOVERNMENT

The determination of income in an open economy with a government sector is slightly more complicated, but the method is basically the same. In an open economy with a government sector, the level of aggregate demand (D) is made up of consumption (C), planned investment (I_p), government spending (G), and net exports $(X - M)$:

$$D = C + I_p + G + X - M \tag{11}$$

The equilibrium level of income is the income level at which aggregate demand and income (aggregate supply) are equal. The determination of the equilibrium level could be portrayed in the way shown in Figure 8.3. The aggregate demand curve for an open economy resembles that shown in Figure 8.3, and the equilibrium level of income would be the intersection of the aggregate demand line and the 45-degree line. In this section an alternative method of presentation is used because we can show the balance of trade as well as the level of income.

Equilibrium in an Open Economy with a Government Sector

Income may be used to finance consumption (C), saving (S), and taxes (T):

$$Y = C + S + T \tag{12}$$

(Equation 12 is similar to equation 3. The addition of a government sector means that some income is taken by taxes.) If aggregate demand equals aggregate supply, equations 11 and 12 are equal:

$$C + S + T = C + I_p + G + X - M \tag{13}$$

Equation 13 can be rearranged to give

$$I_p + G + X = S + M + T \tag{14}$$

This equation is the equilibrium condition for our model of the determination of income in an open economy with a government sector.

The terms on the left are called *injections* and the terms on the right are called *withdrawals*. Thus, the equilibrium level of income can be defined as the income level at which injections and withdrawals are equal. Income increases if injections increase or withdrawals decrease, and income falls if the level of injections decreases or withdrawals increase. In order to explore the determination of the equilibrium level of income, the determinants of the levels of injections and withdrawals must be considered.

Injections

Initially, we assume that injections are constant because they are determined exogenously, that is, they are not directly related to the level of domestic income. For example, the level of investment may be determined by interest rates and expectations, exports by the levels of income in other countries and by relative prices, and government spending by political considerations. Because injections are exogenously determined, injections are also sometimes called *autonomous expenditures*. The response of income to changes in injections is considered after the determination of the level of income has been examined.

Withdrawals

The relationship between saving and income is basically the same in this model as in the simple closed economy model with no government, that is, saving increases with income.[1] For simplicity, we assume that imports are a constant proportion of income, that is, $M = mY$, where M and m denote total imports and the *marginal propensity to import*, respectively. When income increases, imports increase along with the general income-induced increase in consumption. (If we were to draw the import function (with income on the horizontal axis and imports on the vertical axis), it would slope upward from the origin, the slope being the marginal propensity to import.) Finally, we assume that total tax revenue (T) is also a constant proportion (t) of income, that is, $T = tY$. Thus, total tax revenue, like total imports, rises with income.

Equilibrium

Figure 8.6 shows the determination of the equilibrium level of income, the level of income where injections and withdrawals are equal. If the level of income is above the equilibrium level, withdrawals exceed injections, and the level of income falls. If the level of income is below the equilibrium level, injections exceed withdrawals, and the level of income rises.

The Balance of Trade and the Level of Income

An alternative presentation of the determination of the level of income is useful for our purposes because the balance of trade $(X - M)$ at the equilibrium level of income can be shown.

---

[1] When there are no taxes, saving increases by $1 - c$ when income increases by 1. There is a slight difference when taxes are present because saving is financed out of disposable income. If income increases by 1, disposable income increases by $1 - t$ (where t is the tax rate), and saving increases by $(1 - c)(1 - t)$.

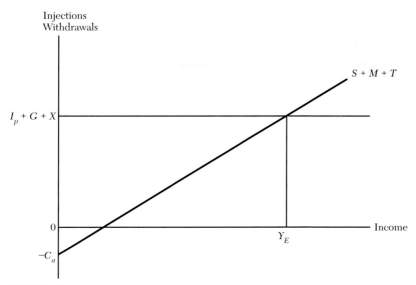

FIGURE 8.6

Injections, Withdrawals, and the Equilibrium Level of Income
The equilibrium level of income is the income level at which injections equal withdrawals. Above Y_E, injections are less than withdrawals, and the level of income falls. Below Y_E, injections are greater than withdrawals, and the level of income rises.

Equation 14 can be rearranged to give

$$X - M = S + T - I_p - G \tag{15}$$

If we plot $X - M$, as in Figure 8.7, it slopes downward because imports increase with domestic income while exports do not change (because exports are determined by incomes in other countries). The slope of the line showing $X - M$ is equal to the marginal propensity to import multiplied by -1. The line showing $S + T - I_p - G$ slopes upward because saving and taxes increase with income, while investment and government spending do not change. The slope of $S + T - I_p - G$ is equal to $1 - c(1 - t)$.[2] The equilibrium level of income is the intersection of the $X - M$ line and the $S + T - I_p - G$ line. The balance of trade (B) at this income level can be read from the vertical axis.

Absorption and Trade

Domestic *absorption* (A) is total domestic spending, that is, the value of consumption, investment, and government spending:

$$A = C + I_p + G \tag{16}$$

---

[2] The slope is given by the sum of the increases in saving and taxes when income increases by one dollar. Saving increases by $(1 - c)(1 - t)$ and taxes increase by t, thus the slope is equal to $1 - c(1 - t)$.

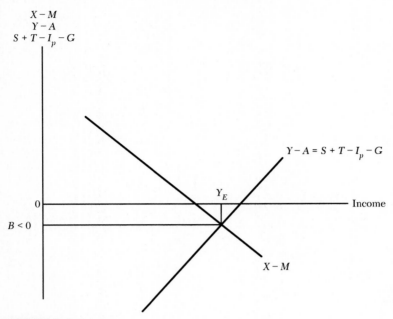

FIGURE 8.7

The Balance of Trade and the Equilibrium Level of Income

By rearranging the variables that make up withdrawals and injections, the equilibrium level of income, the level at which injections equal withdrawals, can be expressed as the income level at which $X - M = S + T - I_p - G$, or $X - M = Y - A$. This presentation allows us to read the trade balance (B) from the vertical axis. In this case, the country has a trade deficit at the equilibrium level of income Y_E.

The line showing $S + T - I_p - G$ shows the difference between income and absorption:[3]

$$S + T - I_p - G = Y - A \qquad (17)$$

Recall that $S + T - I_p - G$ also shows the trade balance (equation 15). Combining equations 15 and 17 shows that the balance of trade is equal to the difference between domestic income and absorption:

$$X - M = Y - A \qquad (18)$$

---

[3] From equation 11:
  $S + T = Y - C$
Deducting $I_p + G$ from both sides gives
  $S + T - I_p - G = Y - C - I_p - G$
    $= Y - A$

When the balance of trade is expressed in this form, it is clear that, if the level of output is fixed, the balance of trade can only increase if the level of domestic absorption falls. The three components of absorption $(C, I,$ and $G)$ generate welfare, therefore, if income is constant, lower welfare is the price that must be paid for increasing the balance of trade. This is a sobering conclusion for a country with limited growth prospects seeking to increase its balance of trade.

Having derived the equilibrium level of income, it is interesting to examine reasons why income and the balance of trade may change in our open economy model.

An Increase in Planned Investment or Government Spending

An increase in planned investment or government spending increases the demand for domestic goods and services, and leads to an increase in the equilibrium level of income. The effects are shown in Figure 8.8. The $S + T - I_p - G$

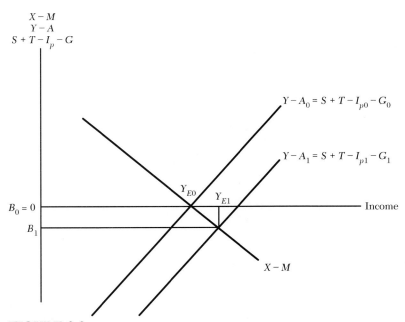

FIGURE 8.8

The Balance of Trade and Changes in Domestic Autonomous Spending

An increase in investment or government spending shifts the line showing $Y - A = S + T - I_p - G$ downward. The level of income increases from Y_{E0} to Y_{E1} because the demand for domestic goods and services increases. The balance of trade (B) deteriorates from an initial zero balance to B_1 because the level of imports increases with the increase in income.

line shifts downward and the level of income increases. It is important to note that, as income increases, the balance of trade decreases because of an income-induced increase in imports. The size of the change in the balance of trade is determined by the marginal propensity to import.

The size of the marginal propensity to import also helps determine the effect of changes in government spending and investment on the level of income. For a small, very open economy such as Luxembourg, increases in government spending have a small impact on aggregate demand, because as the level of income increases there is a large increase in the demand for imports. This reduces the overall effect on domestic demand and income. (Diagrammatically, the $X - M$ line is steeply sloped for Luxembourg, thus, when the $S + T - I_p - G$ line shifts downward, the change in income is small.) For a country such as the United States, the income-induced increase in imports is much less significant, and government spending has a greater impact on income. (The $X - M$ line is much flatter for the United States than it is for Luxembourg.)

An Increase in Exports

Figure 8.9 shows the effects of an increase in exports. An increase in exports shifts the $X - M$ line upward and leads to an increase in the equilibrium level of income. The reason is that an increase in exports, like an increase in government spending or investment, increases the demand for domestic goods and services.

The balance of trade increases when exports increase, but an income-induced increase in imports partly offsets the positive effect on the balance of trade. In Figure 8.9, if income had remained unchanged at Y_{E0}, the balance of trade would have changed from B_0 to B_2. However, because income increases from Y_{E0} to Y_{E1}, the balance of trade only increases to B_1.

The Multiplier

The amount by which income changes when autonomous spending (C_a, I_p, G, or X) increases is determined by the *open-economy multiplier*. The multiplier for an open economy with a government is slightly more complicated than the multiplier we derived for a closed economy with no government. The multiplier for an open economy with a government sector is $1/[1 - c(1 - t) + m]$. The multiplier can be derived from Figure 8.6 using the same method used to derive the closed economy multiplier from Figure 8.5.[4]

The Foreign Trade Multiplier

When income rises, imports increase. These imports are the exports of other countries, therefore other countries experience an increase in injections and their income levels increase. As other countries' incomes increase, they

---

[4]The slope of the withdrawals line showing $S + M + T$ is equal to $1 - c(1 - t) + m$. The multiplier equals the reciprocal of the slope of the withdrawals line.

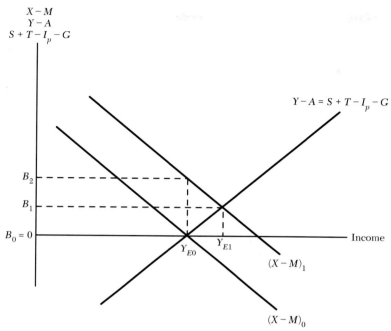

FIGURE 8.9

The Effects of an Increase in Net Exports

An increase in net exports shifts the line showing $X - M$ upward. The equilibrium level of income increases because the demand for domestic goods and services increases and the balance of trade increases. If income remained at the initial level, the balance of trade (B) would increase from B_0 to B_2 when exports increase. However, the balance of trade only increases to B_1 because imports increase as the level of income rises from Y_{E0} to Y_{E1}.

will increase their imports, and the home country's exports will increase. Therefore, we would expect growth in one country to spill over to other countries, and increasing trade and economic growth to occur together.

The international effects of an increase in income that results from a 1 percent increase in government spending in one country are shown in Table 8.1. The figures show the level of income after a number of years relative to the level of income in the base period. The impact of one country on another country is determined partly by the domestic multipliers of the countries and partly by the amount of trade between them. For example, the effect on Europe of an increase in American income is much greater than the effect of an increase in Japanese income because Europe exports far more to the United States than it does to Japan (see Table 3.2).

Further support for the idea that growth in one country spills over to other countries is provided by the similarity of the experiences of France, Germany, the United Kingdom, and the United States during the twentieth

TABLE 8.1   The Effects on Real Income of an Increase in Government Spending of 1 Percent

Effect on	Year	Country increasing government spending		
		United States	Europe	Japan
United States	1	1.5	0.1	0.1
	2	1.0	0.1	0.1
	4	0.2	—	—
Europe	1	0.2	1.2	—
	2	0.3	1.1	0.1
	4	0.3	0.5	0.1
Japan	1	0.4	0.1	1.2
	2	0.5	0.1	1.4
	4	0.3	0.1	0.8

Source: IMF "World Economic Outlook," April 1986, p. 79.

century. During the early years of this century, income and trade grew in all four countries. Experience was mixed during the twenties and thirties, but in general trade and income grew slowly or declined. There was a recovery just before World War Two, and after the war trade and incomes grew together. This is shown in Table 8.2.

8.4 INCOME, INFLATION, AND TRADE

Inflation

When the effects of changes in autonomous expenditure $(C_a, I_p, G,$ or $X)$ were discussed earlier, we assumed that domestic prices were constant. However, if the economy is at or near full employment, the rate of inflation tends to increase as aggregate demand increases. As firms attempt to increase production, their demand for labor increases, but, if the economy is already at full employment, employment cannot increase. The excess demand for labor leads to higher wages and inflation. Labor is not the only input that may increase in price. As firms increase their demand for inputs in general, the prices of inputs will increase, and costs will increase.

Inflation and Trade

If the economy is at or near full employment, an increase in autonomous expenditure may be offset by falling net exports (caused by rising domestic inflation). This is shown in Figure 8.10. Initially, the country has balanced

TABLE 8.2   The Growth of Trade and Real Income (average annual percentage growth rates)

	France		Germany		United Kingdom		United States	
	Imports	Income	Imports	Income	Imports	Income	Imports	Income
1900–13[a]	5.6	2.6	4.9	2.8	3.0	1.7	5.8	4.2
1920–30[b]	0.5	5.2	–3.6	1.0	–6.0	1.7	–4.1	2.7
1930–34	–18.6	–3.2	–19.0	1.4	–8.5	0.7	–14.4	–4.2
1934–38[c]	18.8	–0.8	9.4	10.5	5.9	3.4	6.4	5.7
1950–60	8.6	5.0	15.5	8.8	6.1	2.8	6.8	3.3
1960–70	13.7	6.1	10.2	4.5	7.2	2.9	9.3	3.8

[a] 1901–13 for France
[b] 1925–30 for Germany
[c] 1935–38 for Germany

Sources: Calculated by the author using data from *European Historical Statistics* by B. R. Mitchell (New York: Columbia University Press, 1978); the U.S. Department of Commerce, *Historical Statistics of the United States* (Washington, D.C.: U.S. Department of Commerce, 1975); and the International Monetary Fund, *International Financial Statistics Yearbook, 1987* (Washington, D.C.: IMF, 1988).

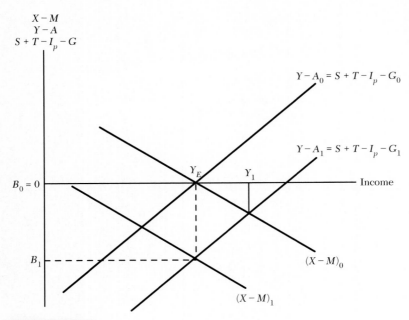

FIGURE 8.10

The Effects of Inflation on Net Exports and Income

An increase in government spending shifts the line showing $S + T - I_p - G$ downward and the level of income tends to increase. If the economy is at or near full employment, the increased demand for inputs increases input prices and the rate of inflation increases. As the country's inflation rate rises relative to the world inflation rate, the country's competitive position is eroded, and net exports decrease. The $X - M$ line shifts downward and there is a lower balance of trade (B_1 rather than B_0). In the figure, the inflation-induced fall in net exports offsets the effect on income of increased government spending, and the equilibrium level of income (Y_E) stays the same.

trade and stable prices, and income is at the full employment level. An increase in autonomous expenditure shifts the $S + T - I_p - G$ line downward, and the level of income rises to Y_1. However, inflationary pressures build up and erode the country's competitive position, shifting the $X - M$ curve downward, reducing the balance of trade and reducing the level of real income to its initial level. In other words, as the economy approaches full employment, increases in government spending crowd out net exports.

Exchange Rates, Trade, and Income

Exchange rate changes can also change a country's competitive position. If a country's currency rises in value, its exports become more expensive in foreign markets and imports become more attractive to domestic consumers. The change in relative prices brought about by appreciation is similar to the change in relative prices that would be caused by domestic inflation above the world rate. Diagrammatically, the effects of inflation and currency appreciation are the same: the $X-M$ line shifts downward.

Devaluation has the effect of shifting the $X-M$ line upward because net exports increase. The level of income increases because an increase in net exports increases aggregate demand. However, if devaluation takes place in a country that is at or near full employment, as the level of income tends to rise, prices rise. The result may be that inflation offsets the effect of devaluation on the country's competitive position: the $X-M$ line shifts downward because of inflation. This suggests that devaluation alone may not be sufficient to improve a country's competitive position. Deflationary policies may be needed to make a devaluation "work," that is, to prevent domestic inflation eroding the gain in competitiveness brought about by devaluation. We return to the price effects of devaluation in Chapter 9.

The American Economy in the Eighties

It is interesting to use this model to explain the behavior of the American economy during the early eighties. During this period the size of the budget deficit increased dramatically. In the model, this would be shown by a downward shift of the $S+T-I_p-G$ line. However, at the same time the dollar increased in value, which would be shown by a downward shift of the $X-M$ line. Our model would lead us to expect that the trade balance would decline. This is exactly what happened. (The model does not predict whether income will rise or fall. This depends on the relative strengths of the two effects.)

As always, we must be careful in using any model not to claim that this is all that happened. One factor that is omitted is an explanation of why the dollar rose in value. However, the model does provide important insights into the recent behavior of the American economy. Also, the model highlights the choices facing American policymakers. The most pleasant way to achieve an increase in the balance of trade would be for real income to grow. But, if the growth of real income is insufficient, an improvement in the trade balance can only occur if domestic absorption falls. Which components of absorption should the American government encourage to fall if it wants to reduce the trade deficit?

Summary of Main Points

Gross national product or *national income* is the value of goods and services produced in a country over a period of time. In a fixed-price model, the level of national income *(aggregate supply)* is determined by the level of aggregate demand. In a closed-economy model with no government sector, *aggregate demand* is made up of consumption plus planned investment.

The *equilibrium level of income* can be defined as the level of income at which aggregate demand equals aggregate supply, or the level at which saving and planned investment are equal. An increase in investment leads to a multiple increase in income, the *closed-economy multiplier* being $1/(1-c)$.

In an open economy with a government sector, aggregate demand is made up of consumption, planned investment, government spending, and the balance of trade. The equilibrium level of income is where aggregate demand and supply are equal. This equilibrium can also be defined as the income level at which *injections* $(I_p + G + X)$ equal *withdrawals* $(S + M + T)$.

The equilibrium level of income can be shown as the point at which the trade balance $(X - M)$ is equal to the difference between income and *absorption* $(Y - A)$. This form of presentation shows that an increase in the balance of trade can only be achieved by an increase in income relative to absorption. If income cannot grow, absorption must be reduced if the balance of trade is to increase.

The equilibrium level of income can also be defined as the level at which the difference between income and absorption is equal to $S + T - I_p - G$. This form of presentation is useful because we can examine the effects on income and the balance of trade of changes in injections and withdrawals.

The effect on income of changes in injections is shown by the *open-economy multiplier* $(1/[1 - c(1 - t) + m])$. Increases in government spending or investment lead to higher income, but a lower balance of trade because imports increase as income increases. An increase in exports increases both the level of income and the trade balance, however, the trade balance increases by less than the increase in exports because imports increase as the level of income rises.

Inflation tends to reduce net exports because the prices of domestic goods rise relative to foreign goods, and this leads to a lower level of income (as the $X - M$ line moves downward). Appreciation of domestic currency has a similar effect to inflation: domestic goods become relatively more expensive. Depreciation increases net exports and leads to an increase in income (as the $X - M$ line moves upward).

As the level of income approaches the full employment level, increases in injections (which tend to increase income) may be offset by inflation. For example, if a country devalues when income is at the full employment level, inflation may offset the effect of devaluation. Thus, policies to reduce absorption may be needed if the balance of trade is to increase at the full employment level of income.

Study Questions

1. If the marginal propensity to import is 0.25, how large a change in income is needed to remove a deficit of $300? If the marginal propensity to consume is 0.66, and the tax rate is 0.25, how large a change in government spending would be needed to produce the desired change in income?

2. Calculate the level of income and the balance of trade in each of the cases shown below.

	c	C_a	I_p	t	G	m	X
a.	0.660	50	100	0.25	50	0.25	100
b.	0.660	100	300	0.25	100	0.25	100
c.	0.750	200	100	0.20	100	0.10	200
d.	0.800	100	100	0.25	100	0.10	100
e.	0.875	100	100	0.20	100	0.50	100

3. Using the information given in the table above, show the composition of the equilibrium condition $(S + M + T = I + G + X)$ at each of the equilibrium levels of income.

4. What is the value of the multiplier in a closed economy with no government sector when the marginal propensity to consume is 0.75? If a foreign sector is introduced, but there is still no government sector, what is the value of the multiplier if the marginal propensity to import is 0.25? Why is the multiplier for an open economy less than the multiplier for a closed economy?

5. Discuss the effects of a cut in government spending on the level of income and the balance of trade. What are the factors that determine how large a cut in government spending is needed to remove a given trade deficit?

6. Discuss why the level of income in one country may fall if the level of income in other countries falls. What are the implications for international economic policy?

7. If an economy has above-average inflation, why might we expect the level of real income to fall if the exchange rate is stable? How can exchange rate changes alter the situation?

8. Describe the conditions under which the effectiveness of a devaluation may be reduced by (a) increasing income, (b) inflation.

Selected References

Alexander, S. S. "Effects of a Devaluation on a Trade Balance." *IMF Staff Papers* 2 (April 1952): 263–78.

Dornbusch, R. *Open Economy Macroeconomics.* New York: Basic Books, 1980.

Rivera-Batiz, F. L., and Rivera-Batiz, L. *International Finance and Open Economy Macroeconomics.* New York: Macmillan, 1985.

Stern, R. M. *The Balance of Payments: Theory and Economic Policy.* Chicago: Aldine, 1973.

9

BALANCE OF
PAYMENTS
ADJUSTMENT

9.1 INTRODUCTION

In this chapter we examine balance of payments adjustment under fixed and flexible exchange rates. Two themes run throughout the discussion. First, balance of payments adjustment imposes costs on an economy, no matter how it takes place. Second, although balance of payments adjustment processes may appear to be based on different variables, there are strong similarities between the adjustment processes.

Given that fixed exchange rates have been abandoned by many developed countries, it may seem strange to begin a chapter on balance of payments adjustment as we do here, by examining adjustment under fixed exchange rates. However, exchange rates are not fully flexible. To the extent that exchange rate flexibility is constrained, balance of payments adjustment under the present system of limited exchange rate flexibility (dirty floating) resembles adjustment under fixed exchange rates. Also, the assumption of fixed exchange rates is useful because it allows us to focus on particular aspects of the adjustment process that are relevant to adjustment in both fixed and flexible exchange rate systems.

Our discussion concentrates on the removal of a balance of payments deficit because the pressure on surplus countries to adjust is much less than the pressure on deficit countries. In Chapter 7, it was shown that there are various ways of measuring deficits and surpluses in the balance of payments. Throughout this chapter the terms *deficit* and *surplus* imply an excess demand for foreign exchange and an excess supply of foreign exchange, respectively. A balance of payments deficit is shown in Figure 9.1.

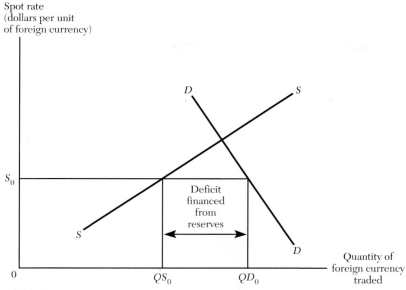

FIGURE 9.1

A Balance of Payments Deficit

A balance of payments deficit exists at the initial exchange rate S_0 because there is an excess demand for foreign currency. If the monetary authorities want to maintain S_0, they must sell foreign currency (equal to $QD_0 - QS_0$) from the stock of international reserves. In the long run, financing a deficit from reserves is not possible because the stock of reserves is limited. Thus, in the long run, the choice is between an exchange rate increase, or the adoption of policies that increase the demand for foreign currency or reduce the supply of foreign currency.

MONETARY ADJUSTMENT UNDER FIXED EXCHANGE RATES 9.2

Intervention and the Money Supply

When the monetary authorities intervene in the foreign exchange market to maintain a chosen exchange rate, they buy or sell foreign currency. When they buy foreign currency, they sell domestic currency, and when they sell foreign currency, they buy domestic currency. Thus, intervention in the foreign exchange market affects the money supply. Let us examine the monetary effects of foreign exchange market intervention in more detail.

If a country has a balance of payments deficit, the excess demand for foreign exchange at the maintained exchange rate is met by sales of foreign currency from the stock of international reserves held by the monetary authorities. Sales of foreign exchange reduce the money supply because the central bank receives domestic currency in return for its sales of foreign currency. Similarly, if a country has a balance of payments surplus, the monetary authorities buy foreign exchange to maintain the exchange rate. Since foreign exchange is purchased with domestic currency, the money supply increases. Essentially the monetary effect of sales (or purchases) of foreign exchange is identical to the effect of sales (or purchases) of Treasury bills by the monetary authorities.

If the monetary authorities do not offset the effects of foreign exchange market intervention on the money supply, an adjustment process will begin that will eventually restore balance of payments equilibrium.[1] The monetary adjustment process includes changes in domestic prices, the interest rate, and national income. Let us examine each in turn.

The Price Effect

A deficit reduces the supply of money and domestic prices tend to fall as a result. In the domestic market, imports become less attractive relative to domestic goods as the price of domestic goods falls, and the demand for foreign exchange falls as people switch from imports to domestic goods. Similarly, the home country's exports become more attractive to foreign consumers, and the supply of foreign exchange increases as exports increase. Therefore, the excess demand for foreign exchange tends to be removed by changes in both the demand and supply of foreign exchange.

The relationship between the price level, the money supply, and the balance of payments was recognized by David Hume more than two hundred years ago. He suggested that an increase in the money supply would lead to an increase in the domestic price level and a balance of payments deficit. Over a longer period, the balance of payments deficit reduces the money supply, the domestic price level falls to its initial level, and balance of payments equilibrium is restored. Hume's argument is interesting because it suggests that persistent balance of payments deficits are caused by persistent monetary growth—a view many economists still hold.

The Interest Rate Effect

The price effect of monetary adjustment was discussed first for historical reasons. In fact, when the money supply falls because of a balance of payments deficit, the most important initial effect may be a rise in the rate of interest. A higher domestic interest rate encourages foreign investors to invest in the home country, and also encourages domestic investors to invest at home rather than abroad. Therefore, an increase in the interest rate tends to

---

[1] It is often said that monetary adjustment is automatic in the sense that adjustment does not require an explicit policy decision. In practice, the adjustment process is not automatic because the monetary authorities can prevent or alter the speed of adjustment.

remove an excess demand for foreign exchange in two ways: first, by increasing the quantity of foreign exchange supplied by foreign investors, and second, by decreasing the quantity of foreign exchange demanded by domestic investors.[2]

The size of the capital flow depends on the degree of capital mobility, that is, the responsiveness of capital flows to the difference between the interest rate in one country and another. If there is a high degree of capital mobility, an interest rate differential will induce a large change in capital flows. If there is a low degree of capital mobility, the effect on capital flows will be small. Clearly, when considering using interest rates to influence the demand/supply of foreign exchange, the degree of capital mobility is important. In passing, it is worth noting that the degree of capital mobility is also an important determinant of the degree of domestic monetary autonomy, because capital flows tend to remove differences between interest rates.[3]

The Income Effect

A higher interest rate leads to a fall in aggregate demand because some expenditures fall as the interest rate rises. For example, an increase in the interest rate may lead to lower investment or a fall in purchases of consumer durables. The level of aggregate demand may also fall because of the cash balance effect. When there is a balance of payments deficit, people find that the amount of cash they have available falls because they are transferring cash to the monetary authorities. They may respond by reducing expenditure in order to replenish their cash balances. As aggregate demand falls, the level of National income tends to fall. The balance of payments deficit decreases as the level of income falls, because the demand for imports declines with income.

Foreign Adjustment

A domestic balance of payments deficit must be accompanied by a surplus in other countries. Whereas a balance of payments deficit reduces the money supply, a surplus increases the money supply. Therefore, monetary adjustment tends to be two-sided because the monetary effects experienced domestically are felt in reverse in foreign countries.

The Costs of Monetary Adjustment

It has been shown that monetary adjustment leads to the removal of balance of payments deficits (and surpluses). However, like other forms of adjustment, monetary adjustment entails real adjustment costs. To be specific,

---

[2] When a country raises its interest rate to reduce an excess demand for foreign exchange, it does so by reducing the money supply. Interest rate policy and monetary policy are the same thing. It is interesting that people often refer to using the interest rate to influence the balance of payments (or the exchange rate); this shows how strong the interest rate effect is.

[3] See Section 10.2.

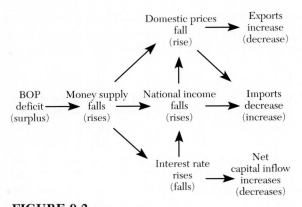

FIGURE 9.2

Monetary Adjustment

in the short run, removal of a balance of payments deficit through a contraction of the money supply leads to a higher interest rate, lower real income, and lower employment. In the long run, as people revise their expectations of inflation, we might expect lower monetary growth to be reflected in a lower interest rate and lower wage demands, and the level of real income to return to its natural rate. However, at least in the short run, there are real adjustment costs.

Lags in the Adjustment Process

The effect of the money supply on the balance of payments is not immediate. There are two important lags in the monetary adjustment mechanism. First, the effect of changes in the money supply on domestic income and prices is subject to long and variable lags. Second, the response of the balance of trade to changes in relative prices, whether caused by devaluation or monetary contraction, is not immediate.[4] The interest effect of monetary contraction may not be subject to significant lags, provided that capital flows are sensitive to interest rate changes. However, if capital does not flow freely between countries, or is prevented from doing so, this mechanism cannot be relied on. For some countries, for example, where the risks to investors are high because the countries are heavily in debt, capital inflows may not take place. In these cases, other policies are needed, at least in the short run.[5]

---

[4] See the discussion of the J-curve effect below.

[5] The delay in balance of payments adjustment may mean that the monetary authorities run out of reserves before the balance of payments deficit is removed. If so, waiting for automatic monetary adjustment is clearly not possible if the authorities want to maintain a fixed exchange rate. This, Johnson (1958) suggests, is an argument for increased international reserves.

The Monetary Approach to the Balance of Payments

Proponents of the *monetary approach* to the balance of payments hold the view that the balance of payments is essentially a monetary phenomenon. They argue that balance of payments deficits and surpluses reflect an excess supply and an excess demand for money, respectively. Two assumptions are common: first, that purchasing power parity holds; second, that interest rates are equalized by capital flows. Under these conditions, monetary growth above that in other countries leads to higher inflation and lower interest rates than in other countries, and a balance of payments deficit develops.

The balance of payments is seen as a mirror of domestic monetary conditions. If the supply of money exceeds the demand for money, a balance of payments deficit develops, and the money supply falls. If the supply of money is less than the demand for money, a balance of payments surplus develops, and the money supply rises. Thus, the balance of payments not only reflects differences between the demand and supply of money, the demand and supply of money are equalized by the monetary effects of the balance of payments. The implication is that a balance of payments deficit cannot persist unless the money supply is being continuously increased.

Sterilization

A country may decide that monetary adjustment is undesirable, perhaps because of the adjustment costs. In this case, the effect on the money supply of sales of foreign exchange can be offset by an increase in the money supply through open market operations. The central bank buys Treasury bills from the public, increasing the public's holding of domestic currency to offset the fall in the money supply that would otherwise result from official sales of foreign exchange. When offsetting open market operations take place, the monetary effects of the balance of payments deficit are said to be *sterilized*. However, if the exchange rate is to be maintained, sterilization alone is not a long-term option because eventually the monetary authorities will run out of international reserves. Sterilization merely stops the monetary adjustment mechanism from working. Having prevented monetary adjustment, other policies must be adopted to bring about balance of payments equilibrium. Let us examine how fiscal policy affects the balance of payments.

FISCAL POLICY AND THE BALANCE OF PAYMENTS   9.3

Fiscal Policy

A balance of payments deficit can be reduced by an increase in the balance of trade. This may be induced by a deflationary fiscal policy, that is, a reduction in government spending or an increase in taxes.[6] A reduction in

---

[6]The effects of changes in the levels of government spending and taxation on income and the balance of trade were discussed in the previous chapter.

government spending or an increase in taxes are referred to as deflationary policies because they lead to lower income and prices.

The Income Effect

Lower government spending leads to lower income because cuts in government spending reduce the level of aggregate demand. Assuming that the level of exports is exogenously determined, by relative prices and the levels of income in other countries, a reduction in the level of income increases the balance of trade by lowering the demand for imports. If the *marginal propensity to import* is denoted by m, the demand for imports (M) is

$$M = mY \tag{1}$$

where Y represents the level of income. The balance of trade (B) is

$$B = X - mY \tag{2}$$

where X represents the exogenous level of exports.

It is clear that a reduction in income increases the balance of trade. The larger the proportion of income spent on imports, the smaller the change in income that is needed for a given change in the balance of trade. For example, an increase of $10b in the balance of trade can be achieved by a cut in income of $50b if the marginal propensity to import equals 0.2, but if the marginal propensity to import equals 0.1, income must fall by $100b. This approach to balance of payments adjustment is called the *income approach,* for obvious reasons.

The effects of a fall in the level of income brought about by a cut in government spending are shown in Figure 9.3. The line showing $S + T - I_p - G$ shifts upward when G falls, and the equilibrium level of income decreases. The change in the balance of trade is shown on the vertical axis. The larger the marginal propensity to import, the steeper the $X - M$ line, and the greater are the effects of fiscal policy on the balance of payments.

The Price Effect

When aggregate demand falls, the price level tends to fall. The (short-run) price effect resulting from a deflationary fiscal policy is similar to that which might result from a deflationary monetary policy: the demand for domestic goods decreases and the price level falls. Balance of payments adjustment takes place because domestic goods become more attractive relative to foreign goods. Diagrammatically, the price effect of deflationary fiscal policy on the balance of trade could be shown by an upward movement of the $X - M$ line. The price and income effects of deflationary fiscal policy are summarized in the chart in Figure 9.4.

The Costs of Adjustment

The main cost of adjustment incurred when reducing a balance of payments deficit by lowering income is the reduction in expenditure that does not fall on imports. The larger the proportion spent on imports, the smaller

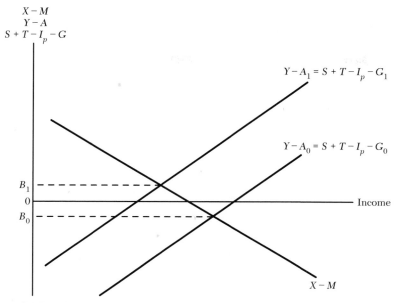

FIGURE 9.3

Fiscal Policy and the Balance of Payments

If government spending is cut from G_0 to G_1, the line showing $Y - A = S + T - I_p - G$ moves upward. The equilibrium level of income falls and the balance of trade increases (because imports fall as the level of income falls). The greater the marginal propensity to import, the steeper the $X - M$ line, and the greater is the increase in the balance of trade for a given reduction in government spending.

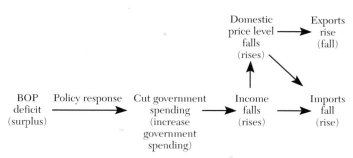

FIGURE 9.4

Fiscal Policy and the Balance of Payments

TABLE 9.1   The Costs of Adjustment (1980 data, billions of dollars)

Country	Income	Imports	Imports Income
Belgium-Luxembourg	89.4	71.7	80.2
Canada	285.4	59.0	20.7
Denmark	52.6	19.3	36.7
France	534.4	134.9	25.2
Germany	664.1	185.9	28.0
Greece	38.3	10.6	27.7
Ireland	16.6	11.1	66.9
Italy	346.3	99.7	28.8
Japan	989.5	141.1	14.3
Netherlands	140.5	76.9	54.7
Portugal	21.6	9.3	43.1
Spain	174.0	34.2	19.7
United Kingdom	479.1	120.2	25.9
United States	3052.0	241.2	7.9

Source: U.S. Bureau of the Census, Statistical Abstract of the United States: 1984, Washington, D.C.: 1983, pp. 868–9.

the cost of adjustment, because the smaller the change in income needed to achieve a given change in imports. An indication of the difference in adjustment costs is given by Table 9.1.[7]

The income approach leads to the conclusion that a balance of payments deficit can be removed by a fall in the level of income. It is not surprising that this policy is not always popular, especially in poor countries where the level of income per head is not high to begin with. Such a policy is sometimes referred to as an *austerity program*. The International Monetary Fund is often criticized for recommending this policy. However, there is more to IMF recommendations than austerity. In practice, when a government adopts an austerity program it is usually part of a package of policies to achieve economic stability and correct a balance of payments deficit. For example, we shall see in the next section that if devaluation and deflationary fiscal policy are combined, the fall in income need not be so great as when the only policy instrument used is a cut in government spending.

Foreign Repercussions

One country's imports are another country's exports. If one country reduces its income level in order to reduce imports, the level of income will fall in other countries as their exports fall. If a number of countries pursue defla-

---

[7] Ideally, we should use the marginal propensity to import. We assume that the average propensity to import is equal to the marginal propensity to import. If the marginal propensity is larger than the average propensity, the table overestimates the costs of adjustment.

tionary fiscal policies to reduce their imports, incomes will fall generally as trade decreases. This is partly what happened during the thirties. In the post–World War Two period, the opposite happened: income growth in developed countries was accompanied by an expansion of world trade. These events are discussed in Part Two.[8]

BALANCE OF PAYMENTS ADJUSTMENT AND EXCHANGE RATES   9.4

Flexible Exchange Rates

Assuming that the demand and supply curves of foreign currency have the "normal" shape, if the exchange rate is flexible, the demand and supply of foreign currency are equalized by exchange rate movements. Flexible exchange rates are a form of automatic adjustment in the sense that adjustment takes place without any explicit policy decision being made by the government. An excess demand for foreign exchange is removed by an increase in the exchange rate. An excess supply of foreign exchange is removed by a fall in the exchange rate. Therefore, because the exchange rate adjusts continuously to equate the demand and supply of foreign exchange, balance of payments deficits and surpluses do not occur under flexible exchange rates.

Devaluation

The process by which *devaluation* removes an excess demand for foreign exchange under fixed exchange rates resembles the process by which depreciation equates the demand and supply of foreign exchange under flexible exchange rates. Devaluation increases the price of imports in domestic currency, and reduces the price of exports in foreign currency. Domestic consumers are induced to switch from imports to domestic goods, and foreign consumers are induced to switch from foreign goods to buying the home country's exports. This is why devaluation is sometimes called an *expenditure switching policy*. The adjustment mechanism is summarized in the chart in Figure 9.5.

Elasticities and Devaluation

Under fixed exchange rates, the size of an exchange rate change is determined by the government. The size of the exchange rate change needed to remove an excess demand or excess supply of foreign exchange depends on the *elasticities* of demand and supply of foreign exchange. The smaller the elasticities are, the greater the exchange rate change that is needed. However, a problem for policymakers is that elasticities are not constant. To be specific, the elasticities of demand for imports and exports will normally be

---

[8]Also, see Table 8.2.

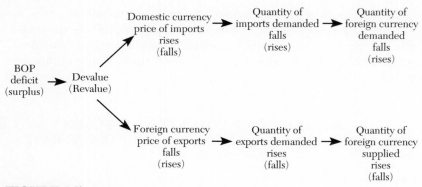

FIGURE 9.5

Devaluation and the Balance of Payments

greater in the long run than in the short run, therefore the effects of a devaluation will be larger in the long run than in the short run.

For simplicity, as in Chapter 6, let us assume that the elasticities of supply of traded goods are infinite, that is, that the prices of traded goods are
constant in the exporter's currency.[9] In this case, the elasticities of demand
and supply of foreign exchange are determined by the elasticities of demand
for imports and exports. Following an increase in the price of imports caused
by a devaluation, we would expect a fall in the quantity of imports demanded,
and a fall in the quantity of foreign exchange demanded. However, it takes
time for people to adjust to the price change and switch from imported goods
to domestically produced goods. The longer the time period, the more likely
it is that consumers will find suitable domestic substitutes for imported goods.
Therefore, the elasticity of demand for imports is likely to be greater in the
long run than in the short run. As a result, the effect of devaluation on the
demand for foreign exchange will be greater in the long run than the short
run.

Similarly, following a fall in the foreign currency price of exports we would
expect an increase in the quantity of exports demanded, and thus an increase
in the quantity of foreign exchange supplied. The longer the time period, the
greater the increase in the quantity of exports demanded is likely to be, and
the greater the increase in the quantity of foreign exchange supplied will be.[10]

---

[9] Branson (1983) examines the importance of supply conditions for a successful devaluation.

[10] Assuming infinite supply elasticities, the condition for a devaluation to improve the balance of
trade is that the absolute value of the sum of the elasticity of demand for imports (E_{dm}) and the
elasticity of demand for exports (E_{dx}) exceeds 1, that is:

$$|Edm + Edx| > 1$$

This is called the *Marshall-Lerner condition*. It is a sufficient condition, not a necessary condition. If the supply elasticities are sufficiently small, the balance of trade may improve even if the
Marshall-Lerner condition is not met. See Stern (1973).

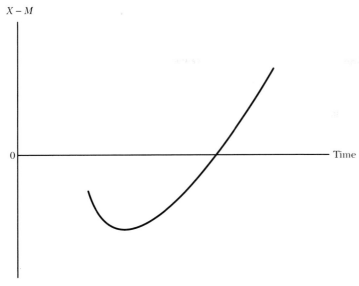

FIGURE 9.6

The J-Curve

When a country devalues, the demand and supply of traded goods does not change as much in the short run as in the long run. The balance of trade (X–M) may decrease in the short run before increasing. If so, the time path of the balance of trade following a devaluation resembles a letter *J*.

In the short run, it is possible that, because of low demand elasticities, the balance of trade will decrease following a devaluation.[11] As an extreme example assume that the demands for imports and exports are perfectly inelastic, and, for simplicity, let us continue to assume that the prices of traded goods are constant in the exporting country's currency. In this case, following a devaluation, the quantity of exports demanded does not increase. Since the foreign currency price of exports falls when a country devalues, the supply of foreign currency falls. And, because the quantity of imports and the foreign currency price of imports are assumed constant, the demand for foreign exchange does not change. Therefore, in this case devaluation leads to a decrease in the balance of trade.[12]

As time passes, and the elasticities of demand for imports and exports increase, the balance of trade is more likely to increase. When we plot the time path of the balance of trade following a depreciation, as in Figure 9.6,

---

[11] The possibility that low demand elasticities will lead to a fall in the balance of trade following a devaluation is also discussed in Section 6.5.

[12] Normally it is assumed that devaluation increases aggregate demand by increasing net exports. However, it has been shown that devaluation may reduce net exports at least in the short run. Therefore, devaluation may initially reduce aggregate demand.

in practice it often seems to resemble a letter *J*. Hence, the delayed response of the balance of trade to a depreciation is known as the *J-curve effect*.

For example, as Figure 9.7 shows, the British balance of trade increased slowly after the devaluation of sterling in November 1967. Figure 9.8 shows that the American balance of trade decreased following the 1971 devaluation of the dollar, and then increased.

The general conclusion that results from the preceding discussion is that the response of the balance of trade to changes in the exchange rate is not immediate. Figure 9.9 shows the value of real net exports and the value of the dollar six quarters before. (The value of the dollar is shown on an inverted scale, that is, an increase in the value of the dollar is shown by a downward movement.) The correspondence between changes in the value of the dollar and changes in the real trade balance is remarkable. For example, the value of the dollar rose from 1980 until the beginning of 1985. When this increase in the value of the dollar is plotted six quarters later, as in Figure 9.9, it is

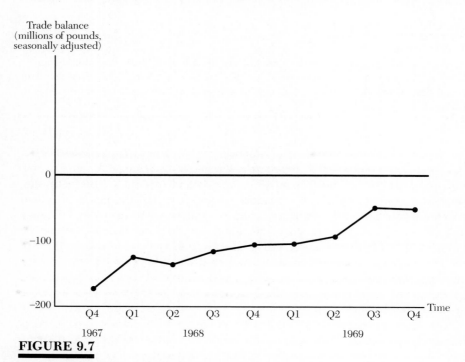

FIGURE 9.7

The British Balance of Trade 1967–69

The British pound was devalued in November 1967. As the figure shows, the trade balance increased gradually over the following two years.

Source: Organization for Economic Cooperation and Development, *Main Economic Indicators: Historical Statistics 1964–83*, Paris, 1984, p. 639.

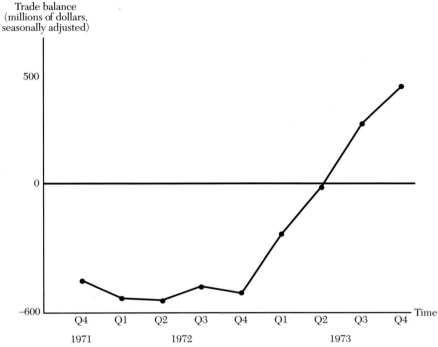

FIGURE 9.8

The American Balance of Trade 1971–73
The American dollar was devalued in December 1971 as part of the Smithsonian
Agreement, under which exchange rates were realigned (some increased in value and
some decreased). The figure shows that the American trade balance followed a J-curve,
that is, the trade balance decreased before increasing gradually.
Source: Organization for Economic Cooperation and Development, *Main Economic
Indicators: Historical Statistics 1964–83,* Paris, 1984, p. 85.

clear that the rise in the value of the dollar preceded a similar fall in the value
of real net exports. The dollar subsequently fell in value, and real net exports
increased.

Policy Responses to the J-Curve
One solution to the J-curve effect following a devaluation is for the government to adopt temporary policies to reduce the excess demand for foreign
exchange. For example, a temporary general tariff may be used to decrease
the demand for foreign exchange. Other policies such as deflationary monetary and fiscal policies may also be used.

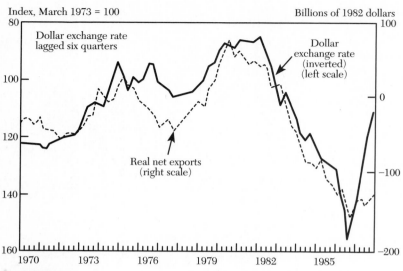

FIGURE 9.9

The Value of the Dollar and Real Net Exports

The figure shows the value of real net exports and the value of the dollar six quarters before (the value of the dollar shown for the third quarter of 1986 is actually the value of the dollar in the first quarter of 1985). The value of the dollar is shown on the vertical axis on the left using an inverted scale, thus an increase in the value of the dollar is shown by a downward movement. When presented in this form, the data strongly suggest that increases in the value of the dollar precede decreases in real net exports. Similarly, decreases in the value of the dollar precede increases in real net exports. (*Source: Economic Report of the President,* 1988, p. 27.) *Note:* The value of the dollar is the nominal multilateral trade-weighted value of the dollar against the other G10 currencies plus the Swiss franc.

Arguments against Devaluation

A common argument against devaluation is that the demand for exports is inelastic. By itself, this is not a valid argument against devaluation. The demand for exports may be inelastic in the short run and elastic in the long run. In this case other policies may be needed in the short run, but in the long run the devaluation will be effective. Moreover, even if the demand for exports is inelastic in the long run, the balance of trade will increase if the demand for imports is sufficiently elastic.

Income, Prices, and Devaluation

In discussing the effects of devaluation we have so far followed what has come to be called the *elasticities approach,* that is, we have assumed that income and prices remain unchanged and the change in the balance of payments has been described in terms of the elasticities of demand for traded goods. However, increases in income and prices following a devaluation may reduce the effectiveness of devaluation. Thus, devaluation may need to be accompanied by other policies.

As the balance of trade increases following a devaluation, the demand for domestic goods and services increases. If the economy is operating at less than full employment, real income and employment increase. However, as real income increases, we would also expect the price level to increase (because the higher level of economic activity puts upward pressure on wages and prices). When an economy is already at full employment, output cannot increase, and the effect of increased aggregate demand will be inflation without any increase in real income. The combination of increased income and inflation depends on whether there are unemployed resources when the country devalues.

Increases in domestic income and prices tend to reduce the effects of a depreciation. One reason is that an increase in imports can be expected as part of the general increase in consumption that accompanies an increase in income. Also, an increase in domestic prices makes domestic goods relatively less attractive to domestic and foreign consumers, thus imports increase and exports decrease. If devaluation takes place when the economy is already at full employment, the price level rises until the effects of the devaluation are completely offset. The price and income effects of devaluation are shown in Figure 9.10.

The Vicious Circle

The inflationary effect of devaluation is particularly important for open economies where imported goods are a large percentage of consumption. In these countries, devaluation directly increases the prices of many goods. Wage demands are likely to rise as workers seek higher wages to offset increases in the cost of imported goods, and the prices of other goods will increase as wage costs rise. It is possible that a further devaluation could be used, and that further inflationary pressure would reduce its effects. Thus, a cycle of devaluation and inflation might even be established. The scenario of repeated inflation and devaluation is known as a *vicious circle* and is shown in Figure 9.11.

Increasing the Effectiveness of Devaluation

Clearly, if balance of payments adjustment is the major objective, it would be better if the inflationary effects of a devaluation could be offset by another policy. For example, a cut in government spending could be used to decrease aggregate demand. In Figure 9.10, the effect would be to shift the $S + T - I_p - G$ line upward. By an appropriate combination of deflationary fiscal policy and devaluation, an increase in the balance of trade can be achieved at the initial price and income levels.

Alternatively, the government can prevent an increase in prices and incomes by reducing the rate of monetary growth. This policy would reduce the

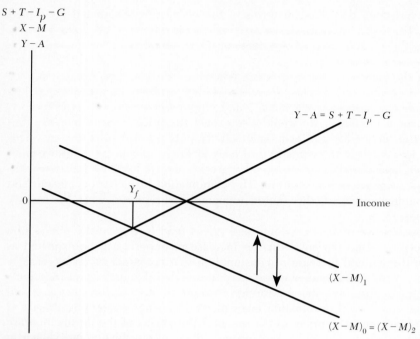

FIGURE 9.10

Devaluation, Income, and Inflation

Devaluation shifts the $X-M$ line upward. As the level of income increases, prices increase and the $X-M$ line shifts downward to some extent. If the initial level of income (Y_f) is at the full employment level, income cannot increase. The increase in aggregate demand (resulting from an increase in net exports) leads to an increase in the price level. As domestic prices rise, the $X-M$ line moves downward to its initial position, and the excess aggregate demand is eliminated. (The solution is to reduce aggregate demand by shifting the line showing $S+T-I_p-G$ upward.)

level of aggregate demand because an increase in the interest rate leads to a fall in interest-sensitive expenditures such as investment and purchases of consumer durables. Diagrammatically, a fall in consumption (a rise in saving) and a fall in planned investment lead to an upward movement of the $S+T-I_p-G$ line. In addition to removing the inflationary stimulus of the devaluation, lower monetary growth attracts foreign capital because the interest rate rises. Thus, monetary contraction removes the excess demand for foreign exchange by both current and capital account changes.

The Cost of Balance of Payments Adjustment by Devaluation

One cost of adjustment is that the prices of imports increase when a country devalues. If a country is already suffering from inflation, the inflationary stimulus of a devaluation may be undesirable. Unfortunately, even if defla-

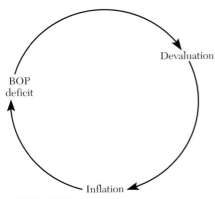

FIGURE 9.11

The Vicious Circle
Devaluation increases the price of imports and increases aggregate demand. The rate of inflation increases, and inflation results. Domestic inflation reduces competitiveness, and leads to a balance of payments deficit, another devaluation, and the cycle is repeated.

tionary policies are used to prevent inflation, there are still costs of adjustment because domestic absorption falls, the distribution of income changes, and there are costs of reallocating resources.

Recall that the current account can be expressed as the difference between income and absorption:[13]

$$X - M = Y - A$$

Assuming that the demand for traded goods is sufficiently elastic, devaluation increases the balance of trade, that is, income rises relative to absorption. The reason income rises is that an increase in net exports increases aggregate demand and thereby increases income. As income increases, absorption increases, but the net effect is an increase in the current account. However, if income is fixed, absorption must fall if the current account is to increase. One reason this may happen is that devaluation increases the prices of imported goods, which tends to reduce consumption (part of absorption). However, if domestic wages are revised upward in response, as workers seek higher wages to compensate for the increase in the cost of living, the effectiveness of de-

---

[13] In other words, the balance of trade is the difference between what a country produces (Y) and the goods purchased or absorbed by domestic residents. Goods are purchased for consumption (C), investment (I), and by the government (G). Thus, absorption (A) is defined as follows:
$$A = C + I + G$$
(It is not necessary to distinguish here between planned and actual investment because they are equal at the equilibrium level of income.)

valuation may be offset by inflation. This possibility is particularly important for open economies where imports are a significant part of consumption.

To prevent domestic inflation from offsetting the effects of devaluation, the government may reduce government spending and/or the money supply. The fall in absorption may take the form of lower consumption, government spending, or investment, depending on the deflationary policy chosen. Whichever form it takes, lower absorption implies a lower level of economic welfare for a given level of income.

Devaluation also redistributes income and alters the allocation of resources. People who consume above average quantities of imported goods suffer. Exporters, conversely, experience an increase in profits because their foreign currency earnings increase and foreign currency is worth more relative to domestic currency. Also, there is an increase in the demand for import substitutes, and people in this sector may receive higher wages and profits. To the extent that production changes entail a reallocation of resources, devaluation leads to costs of adjustment because resources do not move freely from one sector to another.

9.5   FIXED AND FLEXIBLE EXCHANGE RATES

Historically, countries have usually intervened to influence the values of their currencies in the foreign exchange market. At the present time, although there is not a general international agreement to fix exchange rates, countries continue to intervene in the foreign exchange market.[14] Some countries fix the values of their currencies formally, each in relation to the currency of an important trading partner; others fix against a group of currencies. Even when currencies are not linked formally to one or more other currencies, countries still intervene to influence the values of their currencies. If flexible exchange rates equate the demand and supply of foreign currency, why have governments traditionally limited exchange rate flexibility, and why do they continue to intervene?

There are many arguments for and against flexible exchange rates. The basic argument in favor of flexible rates is that the exchange rate, being the price of foreign currency, can and should be allowed to change to bring demand and supply into balance. An advantage claimed for such a system is that adjustment takes place continuously without the need for government intervention. Continuous adjustment, it is claimed, prevents the development of severe balance of payments problems, and thus removes the need for policies to correct such problems. Put simply, domestic economic policies do not have

---

[14] See Table 6.2.

to be sacrificed in order to maintain arbitrary exchange rate targets.[15] Flexible exchange rates also free countries from the need to hold stocks of international reserves for intervention in the foreign exchange market.

Exchange Risk as a Deterrent to Trade and Investment

Perhaps the most common and the most important argument used by proponents of fixed exchange rates is that exchange risk under flexible exchange rates deters trade and investment. For example, if an exporter has contracted for a certain price in foreign currency, as the value of foreign currency fluctuates the value of the contract in domestic currency fluctuates. Expressing a contract in domestic currency merely shifts the exchange risk to the foreign importer. If the exchange rate changes, the foreign importer may seek to renegotiate the contract or simply not renew it. Therefore, regardless of the currency of invoice, exchange rate movements can cause losses of revenue or markets.

There are three replies to this objection to flexible exchange rates. First, the argument presupposes that flexible rates will be unstable rates. Proponents of flexible exchange rates argue that this supposition is false. Although flexible rates may change in response to economic policies and conditions, they believe flexible rates are not inherently unstable. Second, as shown in Chapter 6, traders can take forward cover against exchange risk. Although long-term cover is more expensive to obtain than short-term cover, the duration of most contracts is short enough for cover to be readily available. Third, experience suggests that exchange risk does not act as a barrier to trade and investment: trade and investment grew rapidly during the seventies even though the international fixed exchange rate system had been abandoned.

Long-Term Exchange Rate Movements

Intuitively, it may seem that exchange risk must deter some firms from making long-term investments aimed at foreign markets. However, there are grounds for believing that exchange risk may not be a significant barrier even to long-term investment. If exchange rates are correlated with inflation rates through purchasing power parity, the fall in value of foreign revenue or assets that occurs when foreign currencies depreciate is accompanied by inflation-induced increases in the foreign currency values of foreign revenue or assets. Therefore, the rate of return in the long run is determined independently of the exchange rate because increases in foreign currency prices offset losses from decreases in the value of foreign currency. Although exchange rate changes do not always conform to purchasing power parity exactly, we might expect that exchange rate changes that are not related to differences in inflation rates

---

[15] A related argument in favor of flexible exchange rates is that the effectiveness of monetary policy is greater under flexible than under fixed exchange rates. The effectiveness of monetary and fiscal policy under fixed and flexible exchange rates is discussed in the next chapter.

will tend to average out in the long run. If firms take this into account, exchange risk need not be a barrier to long-term investments.

Even if long-term risk is a deterrent to trade and investment, this does not necessarily imply that fixed exchange rates are preferable to flexible rates. In the long run, if governments pursue different economic policies, we would expect inflation rates to differ, and ultimately exchange rates to change. This is true whatever the exchange rate system is. The argument that exchange risk will be lower in the long term under fixed exchange rates is based on the implicit assumption that governments will be constrained to pursue similar policies by the need to maintain the values of their currencies—in particular, that inflationary policies will not be adopted.

Exchange rate targets may have constrained government policies in the past, but it is unlikely that a return to fixed exchange rates would do so. Governments now know that exchange rates can be changed without bringing the international financial system to an end. Indeed, international trade has survived and grown under flexible exchange rates. Thus, there is little reason to believe that governments will see any need to return to a system under which domestic policies are constrained by exchange rate targets.

Finally, the argument that exchange risk deters trade and investment is based on the implicit assumption that firms have significant assets or liabilities in particular currencies. In practice, multinational firms may face very little exchange risk in relation to turnover because their operations are spread out over many countries. What they gain on one currency they lose on another. The movement towards global operations has reduced the significance of exchange risks associated with international trade.[16]

Therefore, the exchange risk argument against flexible exchange rates is much weaker than it appears at first sight.

Elasticity Pessimism

It has been suggested by opponents of flexible exchange rates that the exchange market is not stable. More specifically, they suggest that the supply of foreign exchange may be downward sloping due to an inelastic demand for exports, hence the argument is referred to as *elasticity pessimism*. Although elasticity pessimism was once common among economists, the general opinion now is that the elasticities argument is not an important objection to flexible rates.[17]

Speculation

Opponents of flexible exchange rates argue that flexible exchange rates encourage destabilizing speculation. However, advocates of flexible exchange rates argue that fixed exchange rates encourage destabilizing speculation. It is not clear which view is correct.

---

[16]The same argument does not apply to political risk because the losses in one market are not necessarily matched by gains in another.

[17]The possibility that the foreign exchange market is unstable is examined in Section 6.5.

Under flexible exchange rates, if the determination of the exchange rate is dominated by speculators who predict the exchange rate incorrectly, other market participants (such as importers and exporters) may suffer. Although destabilizing speculation may not be profitable, and is therefore unlikely to continue in the long run, periods of destabilizing speculation are possible in the short run. Destabilizing speculation is also possible under fixed exchange rates, because speculators may be encouraged to speculate against the official exchange rate, if there is some doubt about whether the rate will be maintained. Unfortunately, as is shown in Part Two, historical evidence does not clearly support one view or the other. Although the role of speculation is an important issue, it cannot help us determine which exchange rate system is preferable.

The Movement toward Flexibility

The arguments for and against flexible exchange rates are inconclusive. Thus, it is not surprising that the abandonment of the Bretton Woods system in 1973 can be traced to specific attributes of that particular system. Fixed exchange rates were definitely not abandoned because the flexible exchange rate proponents won. The experience since 1973 does not clearly support the case for fixed or flexible exchange rates. Trade and capital flows have increased, but exchange rate changes have seemed excessive at times. Also, exchange rates have not been truly flexible, and it is difficult to assess the extent to which domestic macroeconomic policy changes were responsible for exchange rate fluctuations. However, the worst fears of the opponents of flexible exchange rates have not been realized, and now discussions are often concerned with how much intervention should take place rather than whether a return to fixed exchange rates is needed. We return to this discussion in Chapter 14, which reviews the performance of the international monetary system in recent years.

Summary of Main Points

A balance of payments *deficit* may be defined as an excess demand for foreign exchange. When there is a balance of payments deficit under fixed exchange rates, the sale of foreign currency by the monetary authorities to maintain the exchange rate tends to reduce the money supply. Assuming that the monetary effects of intervention in the foreign exchange market are not offset *(sterilized)*, a process of monetary adjustment begins that eventually removes the balance of payments deficit: domestic interest rates rise and the levels of prices and income fall.

A balance of payments deficit in one country is accompanied by a *surplus* in other countries. If the monetary effects of the surplus are not sterilized, adjustment in surplus countries takes place via falling interest rates and rising levels of prices and income.

Fiscal policy may be used to remove a balance of payments deficit because lower government spending reduces aggregate demand and hence the level of income. Import consumption falls with the income-induced fall in overall consumption. The size of the reduction of income needed to reduce imports by a given amount is determined by the *marginal propensity to import*. Domestic prices may also fall if lower government spending reduces inflationary pressure in the economy. A major cost of balance of payments adjustment via a fall in the level of income is the loss of consumption of non-traded goods.

Under flexible exchange rates, the exchange rate adjusts to equate the demand and supply of foreign exchange. Therefore, a balance of payments deficit as defined in this chapter, an excess demand or supply of foreign exchange, cannot exist under flexible exchange rates. Under fixed exchange rates, *devaluation* removes an excess demand for foreign exchange by increasing the price of foreign exchange.

The response of the balance of payments to devaluation is not immediate because the demand and supply of traded goods do not adjust instantly. If the demand for traded goods is inelastic, the balance of trade may fall in the short run. In the long run, the balance of payments is more likely to increase because the demand for traded goods will be more elastic in the long run.

Devaluation must reduce *absorption* relative to income if the current account is to increase. Thus, if income is fixed, absorption must fall if the current account is to increase. Devaluation increases the prices of imported goods, which tends to reduce consumption. If domestic wages are revised upward in response, the effectiveness of devaluation may be offset by inflation. This possibility is particularly important for open economies where imports are a significant part of consumption. To prevent domestic inflation from offsetting the effects of devaluation, the government may reduce government spending and the money supply.

Proponents of flexible exchange rates argue that the exchange rate should be allowed to adjust to equate the demand and supply of foreign currency. A flexible exchange rate frees economic policy from the constraints of maintaining a fixed exchange rate.

The traditional argument against flexible exchange rates is that exchange rate stability is needed if international trade and investment are to flourish. Proponents of flexibility argue that the assumption that flexible rates will be unstable is unwarranted. Also, they point out that forward cover can be taken to reduce exchange risk. The argument that exchange risk deters international trade and investment does not seem strong in the light of the world's rapid growth of trade and investment under flexible exchange rates.

Although it seems that exchange risk must deter long-term trade and investment, there are grounds for doubting whether this is a strong argument for official exchange rate intervention. Long-term changes in exchange rates may reflect differences in inflation rates, in which case losses from depreciation are offset by increases in foreign currency prices. Also, fixed exchange rates would not prevent long-term changes, unless governments felt constrained to pursue similar policies.

The debate over fixed versus flexible exchange rates may now be over.

The performance of flexible exchange rates has probably not been so bad that governments are likely to give up independence of domestic economic policies for the sake of more stable exchange rates. Thus, fixed exchange rates are unlikely to return in the near future.

Study Questions

1. Assume that a country has a balance of payments deficit. Show how monetary adjustment removes the deficit. What are the costs associated with monetary adjustment?

2. Show diagrammatically how an increase in taxes can lead to an increase in the balance of trade. Show that the same change in the balance of trade could be produced by a devaluation. Why, in view of the other effects of these policies, might it be wise to use a combination of these policies rather than one?

3. Explain the adjustment process by which devaluation leads to the removal of a balance of payments deficit. (Assume that the demand for traded goods is elastic.)

4. Under what conditions will a devaluation lead to
   a. an increase in a balance of payments deficit?
   b. domestic inflation and no change in the balance of payments?

5. Using the information shown in Table 9.1, why might Belgium-Luxembourg be more willing to remove a balance of payments deficit by a deflationary (income-reducing) fiscal policy than the United States?

6. In an open economy where traded goods are a large percentage of consumption, why might other policies be needed to ensure that devaluation is effective?

7. In an economy with full employment, whichever adjustment mechanism is chosen, an increase in the balance of trade can only be achieved if absorption falls relative to income. Show how a fall in absorption relative to income can be achieved by (a) monetary policy, (b) fiscal policy, and (c) an exchange rate change.

8. Assume that you are an economic adviser. You are asked to recommend fixed or flexible exchange rates. Taking into account the various arguments for and against each system, which would you choose and why?

Selected References

Alexander, S. S. "Effects of a Devaluation on a Trade Balance." *IMF Staff Papers* 2 (April 1952): 263–78.

Artus, J. R., and Young, J. H. "Fixed and Flexible Exchange Rates: A Renewal of the Debate." *IMF Staff Papers* 26 (December 1979): 654–98.

Branson, W. H. "Economic Structure and Policy for External Balance." *IMF Staff Papers* 30 (March 1983): 39–66.

Frenkel, J. A., and Johnson, H. G. *The Monetary Approach to the Balance of Payments*. London: Allen and Unwin, 1975.

Friedman, M., "The Case for Flexible Exchange Rates." In *Essays in Positive Economics* by M. Friedman, Chicago: University of Chicago Press, 1953.

Hooper, P., and Kohlhagen, S. W. "The Effects of Exchange Rate Uncertainty on the Prices and Volumes of International Trade." *Journal of International Economics* 8 (November 1978): 483–511.

Hume, D. "Of the Balance of Trade." First published in 1752 in *Essays, Moral, Political, and Literary*. Reprinted in *The Gold Standard in Theory and History*, edited by G. Eichengreen, New York: Methuen, 1985.

Johnson, H. G. "Towards a General Theory of the Balance of Payments." In *International Trade and Economic Growth* by H. G. Johnson, London: Allen and Unwin, 1958.

Johnson, H. G. "The Case for Flexible Exchange Rates, 1969." *Federal Reserve Bank of St. Louis Review* 51 (June 1969): 12–24.

Kindelberger, C. P. "The Case for Fixed Exchange Rates, 1969." In *The International Adjustment Mechanism*, Federal Reserve Bank of Boston, Conference Series No. 12, 1970, 93–108.

Magee, S. P. "Currency Contracts, Pass-through and Devaluation." *Brooking Papers in Economic Activity* 1 (1973): 303–23.

Mundell, R. A. *International Economics*. New York: Macmillan, 1968.

Stern, R. M. *The Balance of Payments: Theory and Economic Policy*. Chicago: Aldine, 1973.

10

ECONOMIC
POLICY IN AN
OPEN ECONOMY

The previous chapter concentrated on balance of payments adjustment, that is, the attainment of external balance. This approach was useful for expository purposes, because it allowed us to examine the factors that influence international trade and investment. In this chapter we examine the effectiveness of monetary and fiscal policy in an open economy. We begin by assuming that the major concern of economic policy is the domestic economy (internal balance). Then the discussion is broadened to examine the policies that are appropriate for the attainment of both internal and external balance. Finally, we consider how international economic fluctuations are transmitted between countries, and the effects of such fluctuations.

MONETARY AND FISCAL POLICY UNDER FIXED **10.2** EXCHANGE RATES

Monetary Policy in a Closed Economy

In a closed economy, we would expect an increase in the money supply to lead to an increase in aggregate demand. There are two reasons. First, monetary expansion leads to a lower interest rate, and interest-sensitive expenditures such as investment and purchases of consumer durables increase. Second, monetary expansion leads to increased cash balances and higher consumption (as people increase expenditure to reduce their holding of cash to the level they desire).

The effects of an increase in aggregate demand on income, employment, and inflation depend on the initial conditions in the economy. If the economy is already at full employment, an increase in aggregate demand leads only to inflation because real income and employment cannot increase. If the economy is at less than full employment, an increase in aggregate demand leads to a higher price level, but also higher real income and employment. Therefore, consideration of the effects of monetary policy in a closed economy leads to the conclusion that in some circumstances monetary policy may be a useful tool of macroeconomic policy.

The Ineffectiveness of Monetary Policy under Fixed Exchange Rates

For a small country with a fixed exchange rate, monetary policy ceases to be a useful policy if there is a high degree of capital mobility. To illustrate the problem, assume that the country has unemployment, and that the monetary authorities attempt to stimulate the economy by increasing the money supply. Initially, the interest rate tends to fall (because at the initial interest rate the supply of money exceeds the demand for money). However, as the domestic interest rate falls below the interest rates of other countries, there is a decrease in capital inflows and an increase in capital outflows as foreign investments become more attractive than domestic investments. Thus, a balance of payments deficit (an excess demand for foreign exchange) develops.

In order to prevent a depreciation of domestic currency, the monetary authorities are obliged to sell foreign exchange (buy domestic currency), and the money supply falls as a result. The money supply continues to fall as long as the interest rate is below the international interest rate. The process ends when the money supply has fallen to the initial level, and the domestic interest rate is equal to the international interest rate once more.

When a country attempts to reduce the money supply, the adjustment process is the same, with the variables changing in the opposite directions. As the domestic interest rate rises above the international interest rate, capital inflows increase, outflows decrease, and there is a balance of payments surplus. To prevent an appreciation of domestic currency, the monetary authorities must buy foreign exchange (sell domestic currency), and the money supply rises as a result. The process ends when the money supply has expanded enough to bring the interest rate down to the world level again.

Therefore, monetary policy is ineffective under fixed exchange rates because the monetary effects of intervention in the foreign exchange market (to maintain the exchange rate) offset the initial change in the money supply. The monetary adjustment process under fixed exchange rates is shown in the chart in Figure 10.1.

In the case of perfect capital mobility, any slight tendency for the interest rate to change induces such a large change in capital flows that the change in the money supply is immediately offset. Capital flows keep the money supply at the level that is consistent with equality between the domestic rate of interest and the world rate, and monetary policy is completely ineffective. When there is a low degree of capital mobility, capital flows are not large enough to equalize interest rates immediately or completely, and monetary policy may

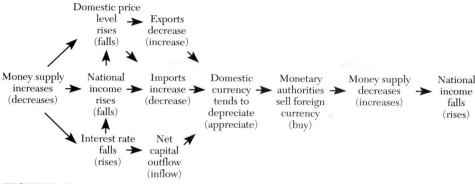

FIGURE 10.1

Monetary Policy under Fixed Exchange Rates

have an effect. However, the effectiveness of monetary policy is less than in a closed economy because, to the extent that capital does flow, the monetary authorities must intervene to maintain the fixed exchange rate, and intervention offsets the initial money supply change.

American Monetary Policy

The process is different for the United States than for most countries for two reasons. First, the American interest rate influences interest rates in other countries. Second, the value of the dollar relative to other currencies has often been maintained by intervention by the monetary authorities of other countries (rather than intervention by the American monetary authorities). By way of illustration, consider the effects of an increase in the American money supply. This leads to lower domestic interest rates and a net capital outflow from the United States. Other countries experience a capital inflow and thus balance of payments surpluses. Foreign monetary authorities buy foreign exchange (dollars) to prevent their currencies appreciating, their money supplies increase, and interest rates in other countries fall.

In this scenario, American monetary policy still has an effect on American aggregate demand because the domestic interest rate falls when the American money supply increases. However, the effectiveness of American monetary policy is offset to some extent by the capital outflow. As a result of the capital outflow, some of the increase in the American money supply is held by foreign monetary authorities (in the form of international reserves).[1] If there had been no outflow, the fall in the American interest rate would have been greater.

---

[1] Some people have argued that this is what happened in the Bretton Woods system, that is, the role of the dollar as an international reserve currency enabled the United States to finance capital outflows (purchase foreign assets) by printing dollars. This is discussed in Chapter 13.

It has been shown that the effectiveness of monetary policy is less in an open economy than in a closed economy. In the long run, the standard conclusion about the effects of monetary policy remains whether the economy is closed or open: attempts to raise the level of income above the full employment level merely lead to inflation.

The Effectiveness of Fiscal Policy under Fixed Exchange Rates

When government spending increases under fixed exchange rates, the domestic price and income levels tend to rise in response to the increase in aggregate demand. (The effects of a cut in taxes are basically the same as an increase in government spending.) The demand for money rises with the price and income levels (as the value of expenditure increases). If we assume that the money supply is not changed, the interest rate increases as the demand for money increases. Also, in the case of an increase in government spending financed by borrowing, the interest rate rises because of the government borrowing.[2]

The balance of payments is subject to two influences. First, the balance of trade tends to decrease because imports increase and exports decrease as the domestic price and income levels rise. Second, the capital account tends to increase because of the increase in the interest rate. Thus, there is a net increase in the demand for foreign exchange from the trade balance, and a net increase in the supply of foreign exchange from the capital account. A major determinant of the relative importance of these two effects is the degree of capital mobility.

If capital is highly mobile, any slight increase of the rate of interest leads to a large net inflow of capital and a balance of payments surplus. Although the balance of trade falls, the capital inflow is much larger. Under fixed exchange rates, the monetary authorities must sell domestic currency to prevent its value from increasing, and the money supply increases as a result. Therefore, a monetary stimulus is induced to accompany the fiscal stimulus, that is, the effect of fiscal policy on aggregate demand is augmented by the induced change in the money supply. As a result, fiscal policy is an effective policy instrument under fixed exchange rates. Adjustment following a change in government spending is summarized in Figure 10.2.

The result is different if capital mobility is low. In this case, domestic currency tends to depreciate because the increased net capital inflow is not large enough to offset the decrease in the balance of trade. The monetary authorities are obliged to sell foreign currency, the money supply falls, and thus the overall effect of fiscal policy on aggregate demand is reduced.

Clearly, the degree of capital mobility is important. For many developed

---

[2] At the initial interest rate, there is an excess supply of bonds due to government borrowing. Monetary equilibrium with a given money supply is achieved by a fall in the price of bonds (an increase in the interest rate).

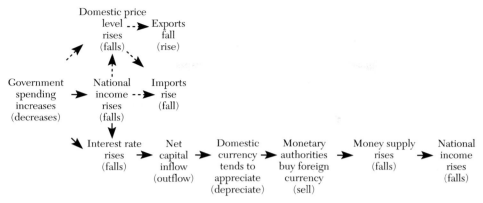

FIGURE 10.2

Fiscal Policy under Fixed Exchange Rates

In this figure we assume that capital mobility is high, thus domestic currency tends to appreciate when government spending increases (because the net capital inflow is greater than the decrease in the balance of trade). As a result, the monetary authorities must intervene to prevent domestic currency from rising in value when government spending increases.

countries, it is probably realistic to assume a high degree of capital mobility. Therefore, for these countries, we may conclude that fiscal policy will be effective. However, this does not mean that a country can increase the level of real income in the long run simply by using government spending to increase aggregate demand. In the long run, government spending has other effects that tend to offset the effect on income, for example, government spending may reduce (crowd out) private sector investment.

MONETARY AND FISCAL POLICY UNDER FLEXIBLE 10.3
EXCHANGE RATES

The Effectiveness of Monetary Policy under Flexible Exchange Rates

Flexible exchange rates free the monetary authorities from the obligation to intervene in the foreign exchange market. As a result, the money supply can be set independently of the exchange rate and the balance of payments. Let us consider the effects of monetary expansion in a small country (which cannot affect the world interest rate).

For ease of exposition, let us assume that there are no capital flows for a moment. In this case, an increase in the money supply leads to an increase in aggregate demand as it would in a closed economy. As the domestic price and income levels rise in response to the increase in aggregate demand, there

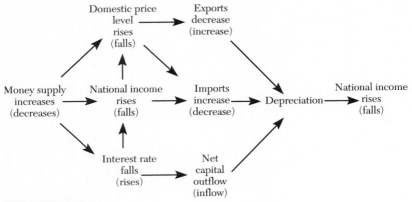

FIGURE 10.3

Monetary Policy under Flexible Exchange Rates

is an increase in the demand for imports and a fall in the quantity of exports demanded by foreigners (as the price of exports rises). The increased demand and reduced supply of foreign exchange lead to a rise in the exchange rate (the price of foreign currency), sufficient to keep the balance of trade equal to zero at the higher level of income. Therefore, an increase in the supply of money is accompanied by a depreciation of domestic currency.

Now let us make the analysis more realistic by introducing capital flows. In this case, even if the price and income levels do not rise much in the short run, the tendency for the interest rate to decline leads to a net capital outflow, depreciation, and hence an increase in net exports.[3] An increase in net exports increases aggregate demand, and the domestic price and income levels rise. The greater the degree of capital mobility, the greater the depreciation, the greater the increase in the balance of trade, and the greater is the increase in aggregate demand.

Therefore, under flexible exchange rates, monetary policy is an effective instrument for influencing aggregate demand. The effectiveness increases with the degree of capital mobility. The monetary adjustment process under flexible exchange rates is shown in Figure 10.3.

Monetary Equilibrium in the Long Run

How is equality between the domestic interest rate and the world rate restored following an increase in the money supply? We have seen that monetary expansion is followed by depreciation. The domestic price and income

---

[3]The currency depreciates by the amount needed to maintain equality between the overall demand and supply of foreign exchange. In this case, a trade surplus is accompanied by a capital outflow.

levels rise in response to the increase in aggregate demand (caused by the higher money supply and higher net exports).[4] The demand for money rises as the domestic price and income levels rise, and the domestic interest rate rises in consequence. This process of depreciation and rising domestic income and prices continues until the demand for money has increased enough to push the domestic interest rate back up to the world level once more.

As we would expect, in the long run it is not possible to achieve higher real income by printing money. Assuming that purchasing power parity is established in the long run, the interest rate equals the world rate, and the price level and the exchange rate (the price of foreign exchange) rise by the same amount. Therefore, the real exchange rate is unchanged, and net exports and real income return to their original levels. However, some economists have argued that the benefit of being able to use monetary policy for short-run stabilization is an important argument in favor of flexible exchange rates.

Exchange Rate Overshooting

Although monetary policy affects the price and income levels as well as interest rates, the price and income effects may take much longer than the interest effect. This can result in *exchange rate overshooting*. An example of exchange rate overshooting occurs when the long-run equilibrium exchange rate rises: during the process of adjustment the exchange rate rises to a point above the new equilibrium rate (in the short run), before falling to equal the new equilibrium rate (in the long run). Overshooting is shown in Figure 10.4.

Overshooting may result from the effects of monetary expansion on relative rates of return between countries and the response of capital flows. Because the domestic price and income levels respond slowly to monetary expansion, domestic monetary equilibrium is maintained in the short run by a fall in the rate of interest. Why would international investors be willing to hold investments in a country where the interest rate is lower than in other countries? They will do so if they anticipate an appreciation of the currency. For such an appreciation to take place, the value of domestic currency must fall below its new long-run equilibrium value. In other words, the exchange rate must rise above the new long-run equilibrium value, that is, it must overshoot. (If the value of domestic currency is not below the new long-run equilibrium rate, investors refuse to hold assets in the currency, and the value of domestic currency falls until it is below the long-run rate.)

Investors must expect an appreciation of the currency if they are to be willing holders of assets that bear an interest rate below the world rate. But this does not explain why the exchange rate should appreciate. One reason is that in the long run the volume of traded goods responds to the depreciation, that is, net exports increase. This causes an appreciation.

---

[4]The domestic price level also rises because import prices increase when domestic currency depreciates.

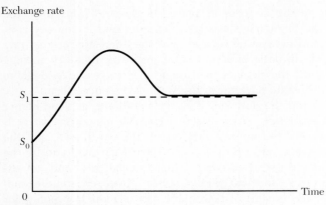

FIGURE 10.4

Overshooting Following Monetary Expansion
Following domestic monetary expansion, the long-run equilibrium exchange rate (domestic currency per unit of foreign currency) rises from S_0 to S_1. Overshooting takes place when the exchange rate rises above S_1 in the short run before falling to S_1 in the long run. In other words, the value of the currency falls below its long-run value and then appreciates to equal the long-run value.

In the long run, the level of real income is not affected by the money supply, and the equality between the domestic interest rate and the world interest rate is restored as the rising price level increases the demand for money, and the domestic interest rate rises.

A similar effect can be expected from monetary contraction. Initially, monetary contraction increases the interest rate and leads to a large fall in the exchange rate (appreciation of domestic currency). Higher interest rates attract investors and the currency appreciates until the high interest rates on domestic investments are offset by an expected depreciation of domestic currency. In the long run, the price level falls, the interest rate falls to equal the world rate once more, and the exchange rate rises to its long-run equilibrium level (domestic currency depreciates). This scenario resembles what happened to the dollar in the early eighties when many commentators suggested a fall in the value of the dollar was imminent, but foreign investors were willing holders of dollar assets because the interest rate on dollar investments was high.

Fiscal Policy under Flexible Exchange Rates

Under flexible exchange rates, an increase in government spending leads to two opposite effects on the exchange rate. First, government spending reduces net exports because, as aggregate demand increases, the domestic price and income levels increase. Thus, there is a net increase in the demand for foreign exchange from the trade effect of increased government spending. Second, government spending causes a net increase in capital inflows because

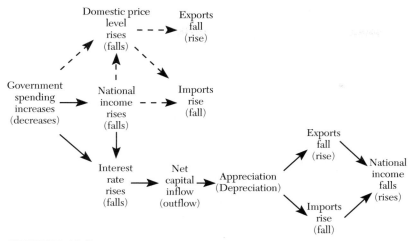

FIGURE 10.5

Fiscal Policy under Flexible Exchange Rates

In this figure we assume that capital mobility is high, thus when government spending increases the exchange rate appreciates because the decrease in the balance of trade is smaller than the increase in the net capital inflow.

increased government spending pushes up interest rates (either through the effects of government borrowing or because of the increase in the demand for money caused by higher income and prices). Thus, there is a net increase in the supply of foreign exchange from the effect on capital flows.

The effect on the exchange rate depends on the degree of capital mobility. If capital mobility is low, the net increase in the supply of foreign exchange (resulting from the effect on capital flows) is smaller than the net increase in the demand for foreign exchange (resulting from the trade effect). Thus, the currency depreciates to equate the demand and supply of foreign exchange. If capital mobility is high, the net increase in the supply of foreign exchange is larger than the net increase in the demand for foreign exchange, and the currency appreciates.

In the chart in Figure 10.5 we assume that capital mobility is high enough for increased government spending to cause an appreciation of domestic currency. As a result of the appreciation and rising domestic income and prices, net exports decrease.[5] Thus, the effect of increased government spending on aggregate demand is offset to some extent by a decrease in net exports. The higher the degree of capital mobility, the less effective fiscal policy will be. In the extreme case of perfect capital mobility, any tendency for income to

---

[5]The experience of the American economy during the early eighties is a striking example of how increased government spending may adversely affect net exports. See Section 7.5.

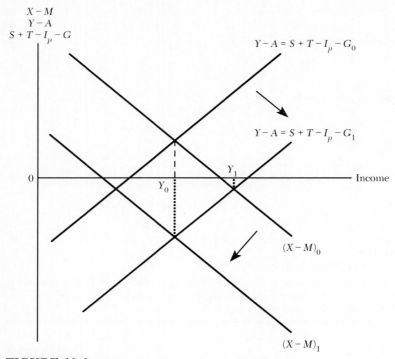

FIGURE 10.6

Government Spending Reduces Exports

An increase in government spending shifts the line showing $S + T - I_p - G$ downward, and the level of income tends to rise from Y_0 to Y_1. As the domestic price level and/or the level of income rises, the demand for money increases, the interest rate rises, and a capital inflow pushes up the value of domestic currency. In consequence, net exports decline from $(X - M)_0$ to $(X - M)_1$. In the case of perfect capital mobility shown here, the increase in government spending is completely offset by a fall in net exports.

increase leads to an increase in interest rates, currency appreciation, and a fall in net exports. The result is that government spending crowds out net exports and the level of income is unaffected. This extreme case is shown in Figure 10.6.

Table 10.1 summarizes the results of our discussion of the effectiveness of monetary and fiscal policy when there is a high degree of capital mobility.

10.4   INTERNAL AND EXTERNAL BALANCE

So far we have assumed that there is only one objective, either internal or external balance. In this section we examine the policies that should be pursued when both internal and external balance are targets. We consider

**TABLE 10.1   The Effectiveness of Monetary and Fiscal Policy
(assuming a high degree of capital mobility)**

	Fiscal Policy	*Monetary Policy*
Fixed exchange rates	Effective	Ineffective
Flexible exchange rates	Ineffective	Effective

two examples of internal imbalance: a combination of inflation and low unemployment, and a combination of low inflation and high unemployment. We
also consider two examples of external imbalance: a balance of payments deficit, and a balance of payments surplus. We assume that the exchange rate is
fixed because external balance is only an issue when the exchange rate is fixed
(since flexible exchange rates automatically adjust to equate the demand and
supply of foreign exchange).

Case 1: Unemployment and a Balance of Payments Deficit

In this case, the appropriate policy is a devaluation because devaluation
will increase the balance of trade and stimulate aggregate demand at the same
time. Because there are unemployed resources and inflation is low, the inflationary impact of a devaluation (higher import prices and increased aggregate
demand) is not a major concern. If aggregate demand is increased by an increase in the money supply, unemployment falls, but the balance of payments
deficit increases. Therefore, expansionary monetary policy is not consistent
with the objective of external balance.

Case 2: Unemployment and a Balance of Payments Surplus

In this case, expansionary monetary policy is appropriate because an increase in aggregate demand leads to an increase in income and lower unemployment. Also, because the country initially has a balance of payments surplus,
the outflow of capital caused by lower domestic interest rates and the fall in
net exports caused by income growth are not problems. Devaluation would
increase aggregate demand and increase employment, but the balance of payments surplus would increase. Thus, devaluation is not consistent with the
objective of external balance.

Case 3: Inflation and a Balance of Payments Deficit

In this case, a reduction of aggregate demand by deflationary monetary
policy is called for because a fall in aggregate demand helps reduce both the
balance of payments deficit and the rate of inflation. A revaluation would reduce inflation by reducing import prices and lowering aggregate demand
(through lower net exports), but revaluation would increase the balance of
payments deficit.

Case 4: Inflation and a Balance of Payments Surplus

The appropriate policy in this case is a revaluation because this reduces both domestic inflation and the balance of payments surplus. Deflationary monetary policy is not appropriate because the balance of payments surplus would increase.

Fiscal Policy and the Problem of Internal and External Balance

We have seen that an increase in government spending leads to an increase in the level of aggregate demand. The effect of increased government spending on the balance of payments depends on the degree of capital mobility. If capital mobility is low, an increase in government spending leads to a decrease in the balance of payments because net exports fall as the level of income rises (and the change in capital flows is relatively unimportant). Therefore, increased government spending could be used in Case 2 to increase aggregate demand and reduce the balance of payments surplus, and lower government spending could be used in Case 3 to decrease aggregate demand and reduce the balance of payments deficit.

If capital mobility is high, increased government spending leads to an increase in the balance of payments because net capital inflows increase as higher government spending pushes up domestic interest rates. (In this case, the fall in net exports is relatively unimportant.) Therefore, increased government spending can be used in Case 1 to increase aggregate demand and reduce the balance of payments deficit, and lower government spending can be used in Case 4 to reduce aggregate demand and reduce the balance of payments surplus.

In practice, one policy alone is unlikely to solve internal and external balance exactly. A combination of policies will normally be needed. However, the preceding classification shows how domestic economic conditions and the balance of payments position can be used to select the primary adjustment policy.

Inflation and Unemployment

In the four cases discussed above, one policy helps solve two problems. A more difficult problem is the appropriate policy to adopt when a country has inflation and unemployment. Here the problem is that internal balance cannot be pursued by a policy that influences aggregate demand. To reduce unemployment, an increase in aggregate demand is called for, whereas to reduce inflation, a reduction in aggregate demand is called for. The "solution" adopted by many governments during the seventies was to concentrate on the problem of inflation. The problem of unemployment was judged to be of secondary importance, in part because governments hoped that unemployment would return to normal levels after inflation had been reduced. Also, unemployment was seen as an unavoidable cost of reducing inflation. Balance of payments considerations were of secondary concern, and flexible exchange rates allowed governments to concentrate on domestic economic problems.

These policies had the desired result, inflation was reduced. Unfortunately, as expected, unemployment increased.

INTERNATIONAL INTERDEPENDENCE 10.5

The preceding discussion has shown the importance of trade and capital flows. As trade and capital flows have increased over the past few decades, the interdependence between countries has increased. This interdependence is shown by the general increase in inflation throughout the world in the seventies, and the general decline in growth in the early eighties. Also, it has become clear that changes in the price of traded goods, in particular the price of oil, can have significant effects.

In this section we examine how the economic policies of one country, the United States, influence other countries. We refer to the effects of American policies partly for ease of exposition, and partly because the United States is probably the only country that is large enough for its policies to have a significant impact on other countries. Also, we examine the effects of changes in the demand and supply of traded goods.

Monetary Expansion

It has been shown that monetary expansion in the United States leads to a lower domestic interest rate and higher prices and income. The American balance of payments tends to move into deficit as a result of a net capital outflow and a balance of trade deficit. Assume that, as in the Bretton Woods system, other countries intervene in order to maintain the values of their currencies against the dollar. In this case, as the dollar tends to fall in value, other countries buy dollars with their own currencies and their money supplies expand. Thus, monetary expansion in the United States spills over to other countries, interest rates in other countries fall, and world prices rise. It is clear that monetary expansion in the United States could lead to world inflation.

This outcome is not inevitable. If other countries allow their currencies to rise against the dollar, American monetary expansion is not transmitted to other countries. With flexible exchange rates, foreign money supplies need not change because foreign monetary authorities do not intervene in the foreign exchange market. In the long run, under flexible exchange rates, the exchange rate (dollars per unit of foreign exchange) will rise by the same amount as the American price level.[6]

---

[6]The case of monetary expansion under flexible exchange rates is examined in more detail in Section 10.3.

Monetary Contraction

American monetary contraction has the opposite effects. If other countries maintain fixed exchange rates, their money supplies fall, interest rates rise, and their price levels fall. Again, flexible exchange rates break the monetary transmission mechanism by freeing foreign monetary authorities from the obligation to intervene in the foreign exchange market.

It has been shown that American monetary policy influences other countries' money supplies when other countries fix the values of their currencies against the dollar. Although many countries no longer have a formal fixed exchange rate, they continue to intervene in the foreign exchange market to stabilize their currencies against the dollar. Therefore, to some extent, other countries continue to be influenced by American monetary policy.

Fiscal Expansion

An increase in government spending in the United States leads to an increase in the American interest rate, if the American money supply is not increased. Under fixed exchange rates, with a high degree of capital mobility, the effect is similar to that of monetary contraction: a net capital inflow into the United States leads to foreign balance of payments deficits and downward pressure on foreign money supplies. (Recall that when there is a balance of payments deficit, intervention to maintain a currency's value leads to a fall in the money supply and a higher interest rate.) If other countries choose flexible exchange rates, the dollar will rise in value relative to foreign currencies, and other countries will experience trade surpluses and capital outflows. However, the inflationary effects of depreciation, an increase in import prices and higher aggregate demand, may not be welcome in countries that already have inflation problems.[7]

The effects of American policies on other countries depend on the policies chosen by the other countries. However, a comprehensive list of all possible policies and reactions is not necessary, because the purpose of the discussion has been achieved; it has been shown that other countries can be affected by American economic policy. Let us now consider how a country can be affected by changes in the demand or supply of goods that it trades.

An Increase in World Prices (Imports and Exports)

Under fixed exchange rates, an increase in world prices can lead to domestic inflation. As world prices increase, net exports increase as the country's goods become more competitive. As a result, a balance of payments surplus

---

[7] In the early eighties, European governments were attempting to decrease inflation, and did not want their currencies to depreciate too much (because import prices would increase). They argued that the budget deficit and the low rate of monetary growth in the United States were forcing interest rates up. (Some economists have suggested that this argument should not be taken too seriously: European governments wanted to keep monetary growth down in order to reduce inflation, and were happy to be able to put the blame on the United States.)

develops, the money supply expands (as the monetary authorities intervene to stabilize the exchange rate), and aggregate demand increases. If the economy is already at or near full employment, an increase in aggregate demand leads to inflation. Again, flexible exchange rates can insulate an economy from world inflation. In this case, the difference between domestic and higher world inflation would be reflected in an appreciation of the country's currency.

An Increase in the Demand for a Country's Exports

An increase in the demand for exports raises the price of exports relative to the price of imports.[8] The macroeconomic model we have used so far is not completely appropriate in this case because it does not allow us to examine the effects of changes in relative prices. When the terms of trade improve, as in this case, trade theory and intuition lead us to expect that resources will move into the export sector from other sectors and that the level of real income will increase. The greater the ability of a country to increase export production, the greater the increase in real income will be. However, even without any increase in export production, real income increases when the value of a country's exports increases (because the revenue from a given amount of exports increases).

An Increase in the Supply of Exports

An increase in the supply of exports, resulting from an increase in a country's ability to produce, leads to an increase in real income.[9] Under fixed exchange rates, a balance of payments surplus develops as the balance of trade increases. This surplus increases the money supply. In this case, an increase in the money supply finances a higher level of economic activity, and does not necessarily cause inflation. Under flexible exchange rates, the link between the money supply and the balance of payments is broken. If the money supply is not increased in line with the increase in economic activity, domestic currency appreciates and the price level falls.

Dutch Disease

In recent years the experience of some countries has led economists to examine more closely the benefits of an expansion of exports under flexible exchange rates. We have seen that domestic currency tends to appreciate when the supply of exports increases. This appreciation leads to a reduction in the net exports of sectors that are not growing, and possibly an increase in unemployment. Although overall real income increases when the supply of exports increases, not everybody gains from the increase. For example, some

---

[8] A small country can sell as much as it likes without affecting the price of its exports. Thus, an increase in the demand for its exports is shown by an increase in the price of exports.

[9] We assume that the country is not large enough to influence the world price of its exports significantly. It is theoretically possible that a fall in the value of exports could outweigh the benefits of an increase in the supply of exports. This unlikely case is discussed in Section 2.5.

economists suggest that unemployment in the Netherlands and Britain resulted from Dutch exports of natural gas and British exports of oil. These
exports tended to increase the values of the guilder and the pound, and led
to unemployment in the manufacturing sectors of the Netherlands and Britain. In theory, if the growing sector employs a large number of people, and
labor moves easily from one sector to another, unemployment may not be a
problem. However, employment is minimal in the cases of oil and natural gas.

An Increase in the Price of Imports (An Oil Price Increase)

An increase in the price of imports can also lead to inflation. As an example, let us consider an oil price increase. In this case, the domestic price
level increases because consumers pay more for oil and oil products. However, the inflationary effect is much wider because production costs rise in
sectors that use oil as an input, and because wage demands throughout the
economy increase to reflect the increase in the cost of living. An oil price
increase has other effects. The balance of trade decreases because imported
oil costs more. Also, since more real income must be used to purchase oil,
less is spent on other goods. Thus, the levels of real income and employment fall.

As was shown at the end of the last section, there are no easy solutions
to the problem of unemployment and inflation. In deciding whether to take
measures to influence the level of aggregate demand, in the short run the
government must choose between lower inflation or lower unemployment. If
the level of employment is maintained by increasing aggregate demand, inflation increases even more. If inflation is kept low, unemployment increases.

The good news is that a fall in the price of oil has the opposite effect:
lower prices and higher employment. This is why many economists welcomed
the fall in the price of oil in the mid eighties. The doubts raised by some
economists about the benefits of the fall were mainly because they felt that
oil price instability is undesirable. Although a stable price might be better for
oil importers and exporters, the problem is, of course, what the price
should be.

Summary of Main Points

For small countries, monetary policy is ineffective under fixed exchange
rates. Following an increase in the money supply, the tendency for interest
rates to fall, and for income and prices to rise, leads to a balance of payments
deficit. The monetary authorities are obliged to sell foreign currency (buy
domestic currency) to support the exchange rate, and the money supply tends
to fall to its initial level. For the United States, monetary policy may have an
effect because the United States is probably large enough to influence world
monetary conditions.

If capital is mobile, fiscal policy is effective under fixed exchange rates
because as income rises interest rates rise, and a balance of payments surplus
results. Intervention to prevent domestic currency from rising in value leads

to an increase in the money supply. Thus, the effects of fiscal policy on aggregate demand are augmented by an induced increase in the supply of money. If capital mobility is low or capital flows are restricted, the effectiveness of fiscal policy is reduced because a balance of payments deficit results from increased government spending and the money supply falls (the monetary authorities are forced to sell foreign exchange to support the exchange rate).

Under flexible exchange rates, monetary policy is effective because the tendency to develop a balance of payments deficit (following an increase in the money supply) leads to depreciation, which increases the expansionary effect on aggregate demand. In contrast, if capital mobility is high, fiscal policy is not effective because the tendency toward surplus leads to an appreciation of domestic currency, and falling net exports offset the expansionary effect of increased government spending.

Under flexible exchange rates, when the money supply is increased, the long-run equilibrium exchange rate increases. The exchange rate may *overshoot*, because in the short run the interest rate falls and investors will be unwilling to hold assets that earn a lower interest rate than assets in other countries. Thus, the currency's value must fall in the short run until the expected appreciation (to the new long-run rate) is large enough to offset the lower interest rate. One reason why the currency may appreciate is that, following depreciation, net exports will increase more in the long run than in the short run.

One policy alone may move an economy towards internal and external balance. Devaluation increases net exports, aggregate demand, and import prices, thus it is appropriate when an economy has unemployment, low inflation, and a balance of payments deficit. Revaluation reduces net exports, aggregate demand, and import prices, thus it is appropriate when an economy has high inflation and a balance of payments surplus.

Lower monetary growth is appropriate when the economy has inflation and a balance of payments deficit. The effect of fiscal policy depends on the degree of capital mobility. Reduced government spending lowers aggregate demand and net exports increase as income falls. When capital mobility is low, lower government spending is appropriate for an economy with inflation and a balance of payments deficit. However, if capital mobility is high, reduced government spending lowers interest rates and leads to an outflow of capital, which increases the balance of payments deficit. Thus, when capital mobility is high, lower government spending is appropriate when an economy has inflation and a balance of payments surplus.

In practice, one policy alone is unlikely to solve all problems, but the government may be able to achieve balance of payments equilibrium at full employment by combining exchange rate adjustment, monetary policy, and fiscal policy. When faced by high unemployment and high inflation in the seventies, many countries chose to concentrate on reducing inflation. Flexible exchange rates allowed governments to choose economic policies without worrying about the exchange rate.

Countries are not independent; they feel the effects of international economic developments. Countries may avoid inflationary developments in other countries by allowing their currencies to rise in value. Increases in the price of important imported goods such as oil can lead to lower real income and inflation. Increases in the demand (and hence price) for a major exported good lead to higher real income. However, not all people benefit because an increase in the foreign demand or domestic supply of exports may lead to appreciation that hurts other sectors.

Study Questions

1. Why is monetary policy useful under flexible exchange rates but not under fixed exchange rates?
2. Why is fiscal policy more useful under fixed exchange rates than under flexible exchange rates?
3. Under what circumstances can an increase in government spending be expected to lead to
   a. appreciation?
   b. depreciation?
4. Under flexible exchange rates, what is the effect of monetary expansion on the long-run exchange rate? Why might the short-run exchange rate overshoot the long-run rate?
5. Under fixed exchange rates, why does the expansionary effect of fiscal policy increase with capital mobility?
6. Why does the inflationary impact of monetary policy increase with the degree of capital mobility under flexible exchange rates?
7. "Capital controls are necessary under fixed exchange rates; otherwise governments cannot manage aggregate demand." Discuss with reference to the role of capital flows in determining the effectiveness of monetary and fiscal policy under fixed exchange rates.
8. Why might we expect a fall in the American money supply to lead to a world recession?
9. "If European countries do not like American monetary policy, they should stop intervening to influence the values of their currencies against the dollar." Discuss.

Selected References

Branson, W. H. *Macroeconomic Theory and Policy*, Third Edition. New York: Harper & Row, 1989.

Corden, W. M. "Booming Sector and Dutch Disease Economics: Survey and Consolidation." *Oxford Economic Papers* 35 (1984): 359–80.

Dornbusch, R. *Open Economy Macroeconomics*. New York: Basic Books, 1980.

Dornbusch, R., and Fischer, S. *Macroeconomics*, Fourth Edition. New York: McGraw Hill, 1987.

Enders, K., and Herberg, H. "The Dutch Disease: Causes, Consequences, Cures and Calamatives." *Weltwirtschaftliches Archiv* 69 (1983); 473–97.

Fleming, J. M. "Domestic Financial Policies under Fixed and Floating Exchange Rates." *IMF Staff Papers* 9 (1962): 369–79.

Krause, L. B., and Salant, W. S. *Worldwide Inflation: Theory and Recent Experience.* Washington, D.C.: Brookings, 1977.

Kreinin, M., and Officer, L. *The Monetary Approach to the Balance of Payments,* Studies in International Finance No. 43. Princeton, N.J.: Princeton University Press, 1978.

Mundell, R. A. *International Economics.* New York: Macmillan, 1968.

Pippenger, J. E. *Fundamentals of International Finance.* Englewood Cliffs, N.J.: Prentice Hall, 1984.

Rivera-Batiz, F. L., and Rivera-Batiz, L. *International Finance and Open Economy Macroeconomics.* New York: Macmillan, 1985.

Stern, R. M. *The Balance of Payments: Theory and Economic Policy.* Chicago: Aldine, 1973.

PART TWO

HISTORICAL
EXPERIENCE

11

THE GOLD

STANDARD,

1880–1914

The gold standard was an international monetary system in which the relative values of currencies were determined by the values of the currencies relative to gold. The gold standard did not exist for a long time, thirty-five years at most, but it was an important period in international monetary history. A measure of the significance of the gold standard is that it continues to be the subject of debate, and recently the American government set up a group to consider whether a return to a gold standard was desirable. (This question is considered in the last section of this chapter.) The continued interest in the gold standard era arises from certain characteristics of the period: incomes grew, free trade flourished, exchange rates were stable, and balance of payments crises did not occur. In this chapter we shall examine the nature and operation of the gold standard and attempt to assess the degree to which the gold standard was responsible for the economic success of the period. Such a study is an interesting exercise for its own sake, but it is also useful because it helps us understand the present international monetary system.

THE EVOLUTION OF THE GOLD STANDARD 11.2

The international gold standard was not created by collective decision; it emerged as different countries adopted gold as the basis of their currencies. In this section we shall examine the evolution of the system and how the system functioned. But first, let us consider how gold served as the basis of the system.

The Role of Gold

Under the gold standard, gold did not act as the sole common currency of countries in the system; paper currency and coins circulated as they do now. Gold acted as a reserve backing for currencies. The amount of currency a government was allowed to issue was related to the quantity of gold it held; central banks were not allowed to print as much as they wished. These regulations reduced the danger of inflation arising from an increase in the money supply, and fostered confidence in paper currencies. Countries also linked the value of their currencies to gold. Each country chose a price of gold expressed in its own currency, and bought and sold gold freely at the stated price, or *par value*. Thus the value of a currency could be seen from the amount of gold a unit of the currency was worth.

Exchange Rates and the Gold Price

The system was a fixed exchange rate system because when two currencies are expressed in value relative to gold, they are linked to each other through their relationship to gold. For example, if 1 ounce of gold is worth either X dollars or Y pounds, then X dollars are worth Y pounds, and the dollar-sterling exchange rate equals X/Y. Actually, throughout the gold standard era, 1 ounce of gold was worth £4.248 in Britain and $20.67 in the United States. Therefore, the exchange rate was 4.866 dollars per pound sterling. As long as each currency remained fixed in value relative to gold, the exchange rate remained fixed.[1]

Conditions for an International Gold Standard

If two countries have established official gold prices, an international gold standard does not necessarily exist. People must be allowed to convert currency into gold (by buying gold) or gold into currency (by selling gold), and imports and exports of gold must be free from control. If all these conditions are met, then the countries are on a gold standard. The beginnings of the gold standard can thus be traced to the decisions of various countries to fix the values of their currencies relative to gold, and to allow people to trade freely in gold at the fixed price.

The Early Years

The Coinage Act of 1816 authorizing the minting of gold sovereigns marks the beginning of Britain's movement towards a gold standard. By 1821, Britain permitted free trade in gold and paper currency was convertible into gold at the official price. Other systems remained in use by other countries for many years after that. Some countries fixed the value of their currencies in

---

[1] If we think of the gold prices of currencies as being rates of exchange of currencies against gold, the rate of exchange between two currencies is given by the cross rate, calculated in the way described in Chapter 6.

relation to silver, that is, they were on *silver standards*. Some countries fixed their currencies in relation to gold and silver, that is, they were on *bimetallic standards*, and some countries' currencies were not convertible. Currencies do not have to be convertible into precious metal to be useful; modern currencies are not convertible in this sense.

The movement towards an international gold standard began in the 1850s when the world price of gold fell as a result of discoveries of gold in California and Australia. The United States was on a bimetallic standard at the time, which valued 1 unit of gold as the equivalent of 16 units of silver. As the supply of gold increased, gold tended to fall in value (to less than the 16:1 ratio). Gold therefore became overvalued in terms of silver at the official 16 to 1 ratio, and silver became undervalued in terms of gold. The result was that people were willing to sell gold to the monetary authorities, but not silver. Hence, increases in the money supplies of countries officially on bimetallic standards were determined by the supply of gold, that is, the countries were in effect on a gold standard. This illustrates a problem with bimetallic systems, namely, that both the official prices must be in line with market conditions or one of the metals will not function as a base for the system.

By 1870 the world was not yet on a gold standard: Britain was still on gold; some countries that were officially on bimetallic standards were de facto on gold, for example, France; some countries, such as Germany, were still on silver standards; and some countries had currencies that were not convertible, for example, Russia, Austria-Hungary, Italy, and the United States. Wars and revolutions had forced the last group on to inconvertible currencies.[2]

The Beginning of the International Gold Standard

In the 1870s the movement towards an international gold standard accelerated. Germany led the movement when it switched from a silver standard to a gold standard following the end of the Franco-Prussian War and the receipt of gold from France as reparations. Germany took this action for a number of reasons. Some of its trading partners had been forced to abandon their link with silver and had inconvertible currencies. A large part of German trade was conducted through London, and since Britain was on a gold standard it made sense for Germany to adopt the same policy. It was also felt that the wealth and importance of Britain at the time was partly due to Britain's link with gold.[3] When it changed to a gold standard, Germany began selling off its silver holdings. These sales added to a world silver glut that already existed because of new discoveries of silver, and led to a fall in the price of silver. Initially, countries on silver or bimetallic standards bought the silver, but they began to abandon silver because their money supplies were increas-

---

[2] Suspending convertibility allows a government to finance a war by printing money.

[3] It was said at the time: "Gold is the currency of rich countries, and silver is the currency of poor ones."

ing as they gave out paper currency and accumulated silver. The dates at which some countries adopted gold as the basis of their monetary systems are shown in Table 11.1. The international gold standard emerged as more and more countries adopted gold and relative currency values came to be determined by the values of currencies relative to gold (as shown by gold prices).

The United States adopted a gold standard in 1879. However, silver mining interests opposed the change, which removed the guaranteed market for their output. The minting of silver coins had been restricted in 1873 while the country was using inconvertible greenbacks, and over the next two decades there was pressure on the government to buy silver. This pressure resulted in the passage of acts requiring the Treasury to buy specified amounts of silver: the Bland-Allison Act of 1878, and the Sherman Silver Purchase Act of 1890. The monetary role of silver was an issue in the 1896 election, but Bryan, who supported unlimited coinage of silver, was beaten by McKinley. It was not until 1900, when the Gold Standard Act was passed, that the system that already existed in the United States was embodied in law. This is one reason why some people date the gold standard from 1900. Another is that in 1900 there were more countries on the gold standard because some countries that had been on silver in 1880 had switched to gold.

TABLE 11.1   Dates of Adopting Gold Standards

1816	Great Britain
1871	Germany
1873	Sweden, Norway, Denmark
1874	France, Belgium, Switzerland, Italy, Greece
1875	Holland
1876	Uruguay
1879	United States
1892	Austria
1895	Chile
1897	Japan
1898	Russia
1901	Dominican Republic
1904	Panama
1905	Mexico

Note: The dates are approximate only, for some of the countries made the change from bimetallism or silver monometallism to gold in several steps.
Source: Adapted from *The Economics of Money and Banking,* 4th Edition, by Lester V. Chandler, table on p. 472. Copyright 1948, 1953 by Harper & Row, Publishers, Inc. Copyright 1959, 1964 by Lester V. Chandler. Reprinted by permission of the publisher.

THE GOLD STANDARD IN THEORY AND PRACTICE   11.3

Gold Flows and Exchange Rate Stability

It was thought that under the gold standard exchange rates were stabilized by gold flows. To see how this mechanism was supposed to have worked, we can use the dollar-sterling exchange rate as an illustration. From the discussion above we know that the exchange rate was 4.866, when calculated from the British and American gold prices. (This was called the *mint parity* because it was calculated from the prices used by governments when they minted coins.) Assume the dollar-sterling exchange rate in the New York foreign exchange market tends to rise slightly above 4.866, because of an increase in the demand for sterling. People could get sterling by trading dollars for sterling in the normal way in the foreign exchange market, or they could buy gold with dollars, ship it to Britain and sell the gold for sterling in London. This activity involves a cost: the cost of shipping and insuring the gold. However, if the exchange rate were to exceed the mint parity by more than the cost of shipping and insurance, it would be cheaper to obtain sterling by buying gold in New York and selling gold in London than from the foreign exchange market.

The Gold Points

The cost of transporting gold worth 1 pound was only 2 or 3 cents, so the exchange rate could not diverge very far from the mint parity of 4.866. As the rate rose towards 4.89, people wanting to buy pounds would do so by shipping gold from the United States to Britain; no one would be willing to buy pounds in the foreign exchange market at an exchange rate above 4.89. Similarly, if there was an excess supply of pounds, no one would sell pounds for less than 4.84 because at that price it was possible to convert pounds into dollars by buying gold with pounds in Britain and selling gold for dollars in the United States. The upper and lower limits within which the exchange rate could fluctuate were known as the *gold points* and are shown in Figure 11.1.[4] The importance of convertibility at a guaranteed price and free trade in gold are obvious from this example.

Gold Flows and Payments Adjustment

Gold flows were believed to have maintained fixed exchange rates. Gold flows were also credited with acting as part of an adjustment process that maintained balance of payments equilibrium at the fixed exchange rates. Gold

---

[4] Speculators selling gold as the exchange rate approaches the upper gold point, and buying gold as the exchange rate approaches the lower gold point, could make the supply and demand curves perfectly elastic (horizontal) at the upper and lower gold points, respectively. The actions of speculators are described below.

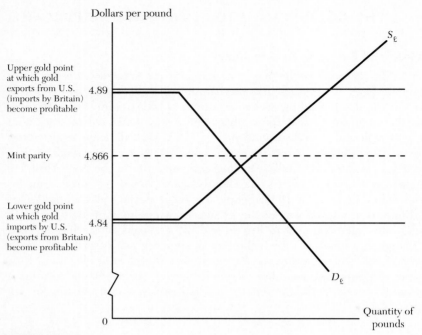

Dollars per pound

Upper gold point at which gold exports from U.S. (imports by Britain) become profitable   4.89

Mint parity   4.866

Lower gold point at which gold imports by U.S. (exports from Britain) become profitable   4.84

$S_{\pounds}$

$D_{\pounds}$

0   Quantity of pounds

FIGURE 11.1

The Limits of the Dollar-Sterling Exchange Rate

The official prices of gold in dollars and sterling determined the mint parity (4.866). The dollar-sterling exchange rate could not depart substantially from the mint parity: No one would pay more than \$4.89 per pound because at that price it was possible to convert dollars into sterling by buying gold with dollars, shipping the gold to Britain, and selling it for pounds. (Thus, the demand for pounds becomes perfectly elastic at an exchange rate of 4.89.) Similarly, no one would sell sterling for less than \$4.84 because at that price sterling could be converted into dollars by shipping gold from Britain to the United States. (Thus, the supply of sterling becomes perfectly elastic at 4.84.) The limits of the exchange rate, the gold points, were thus determined by the cost of shipping and insurance.

fulfilled this role, it was suggested, because money supplies were linked to gold and gold flows led to money supply changes. To see how, assume a country is becoming less competitive. The country will tend to develop a balance of payments deficit. This will be reflected in the foreign exchange market by an upward movement of the exchange rate (the price of foreign currency): at the initial exchange rate there is an excess demand for foreign exchange. As the rate approaches the upper gold point, gold exports become profitable. The export of gold reduces the amount of gold in the country, and because the money supply is linked to gold, the money supply is reduced. This causes domestic prices to fall, competitiveness is increased, and the balance of payments deficit is removed. Similarly, in a surplus country where there is an excess supply of foreign exchange, as the exchange rate falls, gold begins to flow into the country, the money supply goes up, and the surplus is removed. This is the monetary adjustment mechanism described in Section 9.2.

In theory, this adjustment mechanism would include a beneficial flow of resources to countries experiencing natural disasters. For example, if a very bad harvest reduces the supply of food, domestic prices rise, and imports of food increase. At the initial exchange rate there is an excess demand for foreign exchange equal to the cost of the extra imports. This puts upward pressure on the exchange rate and a gold outflow takes place, as described above. Initially the gold outflow pays for the excess imports. Gold outflows decrease the domestic money supply, and adjustment of the balance of payments takes place as domestic prices fall relative to world prices. Although after adjustment the country consumes the value of what it produces, that is, exports equal imports, during the adjustment period it consumes more.[5] When the harvest returns to normal, prices fall, there is an inflow of gold in exchange for exports, and for a period the country consumes less than it produces. Therefore, the gold standard included a mechanism whereby a country that had a poor harvest could consume more food than it produced, and consume less food later.

Gold Did Not Flow

What we have described so far in this section is how people believed the gold standard worked, but that is not what appears to have actually happened. At the heart of the myth of the gold standard was the belief that gold flowed between countries. In practice, gold flows were not substantial, and economists therefore tried to explain how balance of payments adjustment took place without gold flows. We shall examine this question in a moment, but first we shall show how exchange rates remained constant without gold flows.

Stabilizing Capital Flows

During the period of the gold standard, people had confidence that the declared prices of gold would be maintained, and thus that exchange rates would not change. This confidence gave rise to stabilizing capital flows. As a country moved towards balance of payments deficit, the exchange rate moved towards the gold export point. Since this was the upper limit of the exchange rate (because gold flows would prevent the rate from rising further), it was believed that the rate would fall sooner or later. An exchange rate might not fall immediately, but the exchange rate could not rise above the upper gold

---

[5] Even if the adjustment process is fast, the country must consume more than it produces. It is the excess consumption that gives rise to the balance of payments deficit needed for the gold outflow and the fall in the money supply.

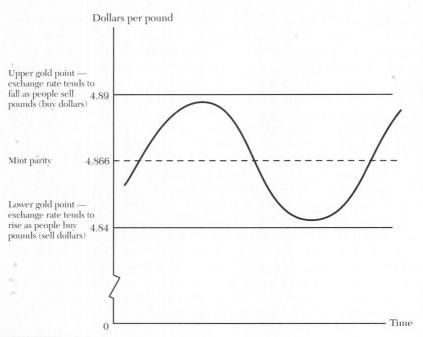

Dollars per pound

Upper gold point —
exchange rate tends to
fall as people sell   4.89
pounds (buy dollars)

Mint parity   4.866

Lower gold point —
exchange rate tends to
rise as people buy   4.84
pounds (sell dollars)

0   Time

FIGURE 11.2

The Role of Capital Flows

The actions of speculators helped stabilize the exchange rate. At the upper gold point, the dollar was at its lowest possible value. Speculators bought dollars (sold pounds) knowing that the dollar could only rise in value. This tended to push the value of the dollar up, that is, the exchange rate tended to fall. At the lower gold point, the pound was at its lowest possible value. Speculators bought pounds knowing that the pound could only rise in value. This tended to push the value of sterling up, that is, the exchange rate tended to rise. If speculators' actions were insufficient, the monetary authorities could use the interest rate to induce capital flows. Gold flows were not necessary to keep the exchange rate within the gold points.

point while the official gold prices remained unchanged (see Figure 11.2). Speculators holding a currency acquired at the higher limit of the exchange rate would be rewarded with a capital gain if the currency were sold after a fall in the exchange rate. For example, in the case of an American deficit, British speculators buying dollars at 4.9 to the pound, might be able to sell the dollars at 4.866 dollars per pound and make a profit of 2.4 cents for each pound traded.[6] Therefore, as the dollar-sterling exchange rate moved toward

---

[6]The gain may not seem large, but if it can be repeated a number of times a year the return is significant. In addition, investors received a rate of return on the assets they invested their money in.

the upper gold point, a capital inflow into the United States took place. Exchange risk was virtually zero. Governments were committed to maintaining the gold prices, and while they did so exchange rates were fixed (within the limits set by the cost of shipping and insurance).

Bank Rate

In the discussion so far we have assumed that the central banks were passive, that is, that they allowed adjustment to take place through market forces. In fact, it was also possible for stabilizing capital flows to be encouraged by a central bank changing the interest rate that investors received. In Britain, the *bank rate* was a rate of interest set by the Bank of England, and it acted as the basis for other British interest rates: a rise in the bank rate led to a rise in other interest rates in Britain. (It was similar to the discount rate of the American Federal Reserve.) As the value of sterling began to depreciate, and the dollar-sterling exchange rate moved towards the lower gold point of 4.84 (the point at which gold exports from Britain were profitable), the Bank of England raised the bank rate. This attracted foreign capital and reduced the pressure on the exchange rate. Even if a capital inflow did not occur, there was a reduction in the size of the outflow, which had a similar effect. Belief in the effectiveness of the bank rate in attracting foreign currency or gold is reflected in the famous saying that if the bank rate were raised as high as 7 percent it would bring gold from the North Pole. Other central banks also manipulated interest rates. Thus, it is clear that the view that equilibrium under the gold standard was maintained automatically, that is, without government intervention, is mistaken.

Movements in the bank rate were believed to be more than just short-run palliatives. According to this view, higher interest rates reduced investment, lowered income and employment, and, as economic activity declined, caused prices to fall. An excess demand for foreign exchange was removed when the bank rate increased because a lower level of prices and incomes led to an improved current account balance. However, Lindert (1969) argues that

> in the short run, bank rate increases worked on the balance of payments primarily through the capital account. Their impact on the balance of trade via contractions in aggregate demand was probably too delayed to account for the speed and smoothness with which the Bank of England improved the exchanges and attracted gold. (p. 77; reprinted by permission)

Britain was able to attract funds easily because it was at the center of the international monetary system. For other countries the mechanism may not have been so smooth.

Fractional Reserve Banking

We have seen that, under a gold standard system, when there is a deficit the money supply goes down and gold reserves go down as people buy gold and send it abroad. Essentially, the government finances the deficit from gold reserves while downward adjustment of domestic prices is brought about by a falling money supply. Adjustment will be completed before the money supply reaches zero, and therefore if paper money is backed by gold holdings of an equal value reserves will not be exhausted. However, in practice, the backing for money was less than 100 percent. This meant that gold reserves might fall by a large proportion before adjustment. For example, if paper money is backed by gold equal to 10 percent of its value, a 10 percent fall in the money supply, brought about by people buying gold and exporting it, would exhaust the gold stock. Therefore, governments took action to speed the adjustment mechanism by ensuring that the money supply changed in proportion to the change in gold. This may be part of the explanation of how exchange rates remained stable and adjustment took place when gold flows were not large: gold flows were of greater significance than they appear in retrospect, because falling reserves prompted governments to adopt adjustment measures. This is another example of how, in contrast to the theoretical model, the system was not completely automatic.

Balance of Payments Adjustment

We have not considered how fundamental disequilibria in the balance of payments were removed. The reason is that fundamental disequilibria were not a problem for the important trading countries at the center of the system. During the period of the gold standard, prices and wages moved in harmony, so divergent trends in international competitiveness did not occur. This harmony can be attributed to the absence of government restrictions on trade or capital flows that allowed disturbances to be transmitted between countries. Tariffs existed, but the prevailing philosophy was that of *laissez-faire capitalism.* In this environment, countries experienced similar inflationary/deflationary trends as their money supplies changed with the supply of gold.

Exchange rate stability was not universal. For the countries at the center of the system (Britain, France, Germany, and the United States) exchange rates were stable, but Latin American countries frequently devalued. Downward revision of wages and prices was not necessary. Triffin (1968) states: "Wherever substantial inflation had been allowed to develop, international cost competitiveness was nearly invariably restored through devaluation rather than through downward price and wage adjustments" (pp. 6–7). The monetary price adjustment mechanism described in Section 9.2 (wherein deficits lead to monetary contraction, lower prices, and increased competitiveness) was not a significant feature of the gold standard.

Britain's Role

Finally, the position of Britain during the gold standard deserves special mention. Britain's commitment to free trade and a fixed gold value of sterling meant that sterling could act as an international money: it was as good as gold. The London money market led the world in the provision of banking and insurance services. Britain dominated international investment. Yeager (1976) reports: "British foreign investments shortly before World War I amounted to roughly twice the French, more than three times the German, and many times as large as the foreign investments of any other country" (p. 300). Britain consistently ran a merchandise trade deficit, which was financed by interest earned on foreign investments; interest earnings were large enough to enable Britain to add to its foreign investments.

Nurkse (1954) reports that as much as 7 percent of British national income was devoted to foreign investment, this often taking the form of investment in public utilities. (Forty percent was in railways, 5 percent was in other utilities, and 30 percent in loans to governments.) Nurkse states that roughly two-thirds "went to the so-called 'regions of recent settlement': the spacious, fertile and virtually empty plains of Canada, the United States, Argentina, Australia, and other 'new' countries in the world's temperate latitudes" (p. 745).

A RETURN TO GOLD?   **11.4**

Recently the gold standard became a topic for debate when the possibility of restoring a monetary role for gold was considered by the *Commission on the Role of Gold in the Domestic and International Monetary Systems*. The idea of returning to gold was rejected, but it is interesting to consider the types of arguments that have been put forward. This adds to our understanding of the gold standard, and it helps us to understand the way in which the international monetary system operates now.

The Myth of the Gold Standard

The arguments for a return relate more to the myth of the gold standard than to what actually happened. It is said that during the gold standard the level of income rose in participating countries, and inflation was not a problem. A return to a gold standard would yield these desirable benefits, proponents suggest. Incomes did grow, but it does not seem appropriate to attribute the growth solely to the international monetary system because many factors could have influenced incomes, for example, the trend towards industrialization, or improvements in transport and communication. Moreover, even if we believe that the monetary system helped, a gold standard is clearly not necessary because real incomes often grew faster under the Bretton Woods system (see Chapter 13).

As for price stability, prices in 1910 were about the same as they were in 1850. But Triffin (1968) shows that wholesale prices declined over the years 1872–1896 by 36 percent in Germany and 50 percent in the United States, and between the years 1896 and 1913 prices increased by 32 percent in the United Kingdom and 49 percent in the United States. Prices were not stable: they fell, then rose. This can be seen from the figures in Table 11.2.

TABLE 11.2   Wholesale Price Indexes, 1849–1913

			(1913 = 100)		
	U.S.	U.K.	Germany	France	Italy
1849	80	90	71	96	—
1872	133	125	111	124	—
1896	67	76	71	71	74
1913	100	100	100	100	100

Source: From *Our International Monetary System: Yesterday, Today and Tomorrow* by Robert Triffin, p. 18. Copyright 1968 by Random House, Inc. Reprinted by permission of the publisher.

Inflation and the Supply of Money

There is a striking similarity between the movements in price levels of the major countries, suggesting that they were affected in similar ways by changes in the supply of gold. The explanation of the general fall and rise in prices is that the supply of gold, and thus money supplies (because they were linked to gold holdings), did not increase as fast as real incomes in the earlier period, and in the later period the supply of gold increased more rapidly than real incomes.[7]

An argument used in favor of returning to gold is that linking money supplies to gold would take control of money out of the hands of government. It is said that governments have used their control over money to achieve political objectives at the expense of economic stability. However, under a gold standard the stability of the money supply is determined by the stability of the supply of gold, and it is unlikely that the supply of gold will grow in line with real incomes. Therefore, a gold standard is not a guarantee of price stability.

Government Intervention

A gold standard is attractive to economists who favor minimal government intervention. The theoretical model does not require discretionary government action: the system adjusts automatically. (Deficits are removed by a falling money supply and surpluses by a rising money supply.) In practice, governments did intervene during the gold standard as we have seen (for example, interest rates were used to influence gold flows). However, at the turn of the century government intervention in domestic economic affairs was

---

[7]The average annual growth in monetary gold stocks was 6.2% between 1849 and 1872, 1.4% between 1873 and 1892, and 3.6% between 1893 and 1913. Over the same periods, the total money supply increased by 4.2%, 3.3%, and 4.3%, while uncovered money, that is, money in excess of gold and silver reserves, increased by 6.5%, 4.0%, and 5.4%, respectively. (Triffin, 1968, p. 28)

less than now because during the gold standard period governments had limited economic objectives. It is unrealistic to suppose that modern governments would sacrifice domestic economic objectives if they conflicted with maintaining a fixed gold price. A more likely scenario is that direct controls would be introduced, or the fixed price of gold would be abandoned.

Fixing the Gold Price

The initial problem that would be faced if a gold standard were to be restored is: What would the price of gold be? At $100 per ounce people would rush to buy gold and official gold reserves would be depleted quickly. At $2,000 per ounce people would sell gold for paper currency. Assuming that the United States could choose a price so that demand and supply would be in approximate balance, changes in demand and supply might make it difficult to maintain the price, especially if speculators expected a change in the gold price.

Is an International Gold Standard Likely?

An international gold standard would only exist if other countries linked their currencies to gold, and why should they? One reason other countries might be reluctant to adopt a gold standard is that the working of the last fixed exchange rate system, the Bretton Woods system, was not entirely satisfactory (see Chapter 13). Fixed exchange rates could not be sustained because governments were unwilling to pursue domestic economic policies that were consistent with exchange rate stability. Governments now know that exchange rates can be changed: they are not given by God. This means that they can, if they wish, allow domestic economic objectives to take precedence over the need to maintain balance of payments equilibrium. They are unlikely to give up this right and agree to have domestic policies determined by international forces. Even if they say they will, they could always change their minds later and abandon convertibility at a fixed gold price. As Hawtrey (1927) said:

> The gold standard can only be established in a country by legislation. In an emergency it can be swept away at a moment's notice by new legislation. (p. 88)

Therefore, even in the unlikely event of a gold standard being reestablished, people would not have the confidence in the system that they had before, and hence stabilizing capital flows would be less likely. The world has changed during the last sixty years, and duplication of the gold standard is impossible.

Conclusion

The gold standard shows how an international monetary system can function when there is confidence. The gold standard worked in large part because people expected it to continue. Some people favor a return to a gold standard, but it is unlikely that a return is feasible in the foreseeable future. Even if official gold prices were established, it would be virtually impossible to establish confidence that the system would be maintained.

Summary of Main Points

An international gold standard exists when countries fix gold prices, the monetary authorities buy or sell gold in order to maintain the prices, and free trade in gold is permitted. The gold standard emerged in the last quarter of the nineteenth century as countries adopted these requirements.

A gold standard is a fixed exchange rate system because the relative value of two currencies (the *mint parity*) can be calculated from the official prices of gold in the currencies. At the time, more importance was given to the role of gold flows than appears to be warranted. In particular, the role of gold in maintaining fixed exchange rates and balance of payments equilibrium was overemphasized. This misplaced emphasis has come to be known as the *myth of the gold standard.*

It was thought that gold flows maintained fixed exchange rates. As the demand for foreign currency increased, the price of foreign currency increased. However, under the gold standard, it was possible to buy gold, ship it abroad, and sell it for foreign currency. Thus, the value of foreign currency could not exceed the mint parity by more than the cost of shipping and insurance. Similarly, the value of foreign currency could not fall below the gold import point, the price at which gold could be purchased, shipped, and sold for domestic currency.

Gold flows were credited with maintaining balance of payments equilibrium through their influence on money supplies. Gold flows from deficit to surplus countries led to monetary contraction in deficit countries and monetary expansion in surplus countries (because money supplies were linked to gold). In deficit countries, balance of payments adjustment then took place by an increase in interest rates, and downward pressure on the price and income levels. Surplus countries experienced changes in the opposite direction.

Later observers pointed out that gold flows were too small to have maintained fixed exchange rates and balance of payments equilibrium. They looked for other explanations. In the short run, capital flows played an important role. Speculators believed that gold prices would be maintained. An exchange rate might depart from the mint parity, but the size of the departure was limited by the cost of shipping and insurance. Therefore, currencies acquired at the lower limit of their value could be sold later after they had risen in value. Although governments were not supposed to manipulate monetary conditions, in fact they often used interest rates to induce stabilizing capital flows.

In the long run, balance of payments crises did not occur; countries were subject to similar influences because their money supplies were linked to gold and their inflation rates tended to move together. Also, countries were closely linked by trade and governments did not attempt to exert a major influence on economic conditions.

Some people advocate a return to a gold standard, claiming that prices and exchange rates would be stable, and government intervention would be constrained. Such a view is often based on a misrepresentation of the experience of the gold standard period: some proponents of a new gold standard claim that prices were constant during the gold standard when in fact they were not. Also, proponents of a gold standard appear to confuse the characteristics of the period with the results of the gold standard.

It is almost certain that the proposal to return to gold will not succeed in the near future. Even if the United States were to favor such a return, other countries would not follow. However, the debate over a possible return to gold is interesting in that it helps us focus on particular aspects of international adjustment that are still relevant today.

Study Questions

1. What were the gold points? Describe why gold flows would take place, and in what direction, for the case of a country with a payments surplus, and for the case of a country with a payments deficit.
2. Automatic adjustment takes place without government action being needed to bring it about. Describe the automatic adjustment mechanism by which adjustment was believed to take place during the gold standard.
3. How were exchange rates fixed under the gold standard? Why were convertibility and the absence of restrictions on trade in gold important?
4. How and why did stabilizing capital flows take place? What actions could the monetary authorities take to encourage them?
5. Explain why, under the myth of the gold standard, we would expect prices in deficit and surplus countries to move in opposite directions. In fact, countries' prices followed similar long-run trends. Why?
6. Using the demand and supply curves for foreign exchange show how an American balance of payments deficit might be removed by a gold outflow. Now show how the corresponding British surplus is removed. What factors are likely to influence the speed of adjustment?
7. Write a report arguing for a return to a fixed exchange rate system based on gold. What are the weak points in the argument?

Selected References

Bloomfield, A. I. *Monetary Policy under the International Gold Standard: 1880–1914.* New York: Federal Reserve Bank of New York, 1959.

Eichengreen, B. *The Gold Standard in Theory and History.* New York: Methuen, 1985.

Gold Commission. *Report to the Congress of the Commission on the Role of Gold in the Domestic and International Monetary Systems*. Washington, D.C.: U.S. Government Printing Office, 1982.

Hawtrey, R. G. *The Gold Standard in Theory and Practice*. London: Longmans Green, 1927.

Lindert, P. H. *Key Currencies and Gold 1900–1913*. Princeton Studies in International Finance No. 24. Princeton, N.J.: International Finance Section, Princeton University, 1969.

Nurkse, R. "International Investment Today in the Light of Nineteenth Century Experience." *Economic Journal* 64 (1954): 134–50.

Triffin, R. *Our International Monetary System*. New York: Random House, 1968.

Yeager, L. B. *International Monetary Relations*, Second Edition. New York: Harper & Row, 1976.

12

THE INTERWAR
YEARS: THE ROAD
TO BRETTON
WOODS

The interwar years represent an important part of international monetary history. The lessons of this period had a strong influence on the international monetary system that was adopted after World War Two, and they continue to influence international economic policy even now. References to these years are common, and analogies are often drawn between current events and the experience of that period. In this chapter we do not attempt to give a detailed description of the events of these years. Our objective is to identify the major trends, policies, and lessons of the period.

After World War One, the reestablishment of a gold standard was seen as part of the process of postwar recovery, and by the mid twenties a gold standard had been reestablished. The success was short-lived; by 1932 the interwar gold standard had collapsed. We shall examine the return to a gold standard and the reasons for its collapse. This study in interesting for its own sake and because it illustrates the general problems of establishing and maintaining fixed exchange rates.

The collapse of the interwar gold standard was followed by a period of economic nationalism during which countries took little account of the effects of their policies on other countries. For example, there were many devaluations and protectionist policies were adopted with little concern for international monetary stability or international trade. Countries soon realized that such policies were harmful, and economic nationalism began to give way to policies that acknowledged the interdependence between countries. World

War Two stopped this process, but also gave the world the chance to design a new international monetary system, the Bretton Woods system. As is shown in the next chapter, the Bretton Woods system was an attempt to avoid the problems of the interwar period: exchange rate instability and economic nationalism.

Let us begin our examination of the interwar gold standard by considering how the prewar gold standard collapsed. This approach is useful as an introduction to the problems countries faced in their attempt to reestablish a gold standard.

12.2 THE EFFECTS OF THE WAR

World War One led to the breakup of the gold standard. The first signs of the end of the system began to show as war became likely towards the end of July 1914.[1] London was the major center of the international monetary system at that time. A strong demand for sterling developed as British investments were repatriated, British banks stopped lending abroad, and other countries repatriated their investments through London. As a result, the value of sterling began to increase.

Under the prewar gold standard the value of a currency could not rise significantly above the mint parity because the currency could be obtained by shipping gold. However, at this time shipping was not safe so the option of obtaining sterling by shipping gold to London was removed. Thus, outside of Britain the value of sterling could rise substantially above the mint parity. For example, the pound rose to $6.35 in New York in the last week of July 1914. (Recall that the mint parity was 4.866). This incident is interesting because what happened was that the exchange rate diverged from the mint parity as the gold points widened because of an increase in the cost of shipping and insurance. On August 12, the Bank of England agreed to accept gold in Canada in exchange for sterling, and the price of sterling fell. Faced with the prospect of a loss of gold, American bankers reached an agreement to limit gold shipments. However, gold shipments were small because the excess demand for sterling was quickly reduced by the effects of the war. By December 1914, the British demand for imported materials for the war had pushed the value of the pound below the mint parity.[2]

Inflation and Government Policy during the War

In the warring countries, the need to finance the war naturally took precedence over the desire for monetary stability and concern for the gold standard. Financing the war effort led to inflation: taxes were not sufficient to

---

[1] Britain declared war on August 4 following the German invasion of Belgium.
[2] These events are described in more detail in the first chapter of Brown (1940).

TABLE 12.1   Postwar Wholesale Prices

	(1913 = 100)		
	1918	*1919*	*1920*
Canada (Bureau of Statistics)	199	209	244
France (Official)	344	356	506
Germany (Official)	217	415	1,486
Italy (Bachi)	409	366	624
Netherlands (Official)	373	304	292
United Kingdom (Economist)	225	235	283
United States (Bureau of Labor)	194	206	226

Source: League of Nations, *Memorandum on Currency and Central Banks: 1913–1924*, Geneva, 1925, pp. 206–16.

finance the increase in government spending and budget deficits were met by borrowing or creating new money. Even neutral countries experienced inflation as the war increased the prices of traded goods and balance of payments surpluses led to monetary growth.[3]

The conditions for a gold standard are the freedom to buy and sell gold at a fixed price from the central bank (convertibility between currency and gold) and free trade in gold. Convertibility and trade in gold were suspended by most countries, central banks took measures to acquire all the gold they could, and capital exports were restricted.[4]

These measures allowed countries to maintain their prewar exchange rates during the war. Even though rates of inflation varied from country to country, exchange rates did not reflect these differences because trade and financial links between countries were disrupted. (One of the reasons why divergent price trends did not develop in the prewar gold standard was that economies were closely linked by trade and capital flows.) An indication of wartime inflation is given in Table 12.1, which shows the postwar value of the wholesale price index relative to its 1913 value.

---

[3] The effects of an increase in world prices on domestic prices are described in Section 10.5.
[4] Some neutral countries restricted gold imports in an attempt to avoid the inflationary effects of payments surpluses.

Economic Conditions after the War

When the war ended, wartime restrictions began to be relaxed. Trade and foreign investment began to return to normal, and it became impossible for countries to continue with the pretense of prewar exchange rates. The divergences between the purchasing powers of currencies were too great. As a result, most currencies were floated. Inflation did not end when the war ended. In some countries, such as Britain, Canada, and the United States, inflation was brought under control by 1920. In others, such as France and Germany, budget deficits financed by monetary expansion caused inflation to continue longer.

The changes that had taken place in the purchasing powers of currencies were not the only reason why an immediate return to the prewar gold standard was impossible. The war had changed countries' international economic and financial positions. For example, European countries found that their prewar dominance of international trade had diminished. Trade with Russia virtually ceased after the revolution in 1917. In the postwar climate of increasing protectionism, it was difficult for countries to redevelop trading relationships. The war had disrupted international trade and encouraged the spread of industrialization. After the war, protectionist policies were often used to support the industries that had developed and international competition was more intense.

The war also changed the structure of international indebtedness. The United States was transformed from being a net debtor to a net creditor by loans made during the war and later to finance postwar reconstruction. (However, many loans made in the war were never collected.) Britain's dominant prewar position as an international creditor was eroded by the sale of foreign assets to pay for materials for the war. Germany was transformed from being an important creditor to a debtor: like Britain, it had depleted its foreign assets, and after the war Germany was faced with demands for reparations payments from the Allies. Also, Britain, France, and Germany lost assets in Russia when, following the revolution, the government refused to acknowledge debts incurred under the czar. Belgium, France, and Italy owed money to each other and to Britain, and they all owed money to the United States.

12.3   THE RETURN TO A GOLD STANDARD

The United States left the gold standard in 1917 (when licenses were introduced for the export of gold) and returned to it in June 1919 at the prewar price of $20.67 per ounce. This was possible because American inflation had been lower than that of other countries, the export capacity of the United States was great, it had become a net creditor during the war, and when the war ended it held almost 40 percent of the world's official gold reserves.

In other countries, a return to the gold standard was seen as part of the overall rebuilding that was needed. The prewar gold standard appeared to have worked well, and the sooner it was restored, the better. The link of the dollar to gold and the importance of the American economy meant that the purchasing power of the dollar set the pace for countries wanting to return to gold. Wholesale prices in the United States rose until 1920 and then fell. In 1924, American prices were equal to 150 percent of their 1913 level. Thus, in 1924 an ounce of gold could buy two thirds of the goods that could have been bought in 1913. Countries that had experienced higher inflation than the United States could either devalue their currencies by adopting higher gold prices or deflate their economies in order to bring their price levels down to American levels.

Germany after the War

Germany experienced the worst postwar inflation. The cause of the inflation was the economic policy of the government. It spent more than it received in taxes and financed the difference by new money. The German wholesale price index rose to well over 100 trillion, from a base of 100 in 1913. As German inflation soared above inflation in other countries, the value of the mark fell, as Table 12.2 shows. This period in German history is a classic example of hyperinflation and the working of purchasing power parity.

Inflation reached its climax at the end of 1923 when the government replaced the old mark with a new one worth 1 trillion old marks. The old currency had virtually ceased to be useful as money and the new currency was welcomed by the public. The government brought spending under control, increased taxes, and monetary stability was restored. In 1924, with the help of foreign loans, Germany linked the new mark to gold. The new mark was worth about 24 cents. The monetary reform was a success: inflation did not return and the gold price was maintained. The lessons of this period continue to influence German economic policy. Germany has avoided inflationary monetary policy more diligently than most countries.

TABLE 12.2   The Decline in the Value of the Mark

Average Number of Cents per Mark	
December 1914	22.32
December 1918	12.09
December 1919	2.10
December 1920	1.37
December 1921	0.53
December 1922	0.01
June 1923	0.001
December 1923	0.000 000 000 022 7

Source: Young (1925), pp. 531–32.

The Reparations Issue

Germany was forced to agree to pay reparations to the Allies by the terms of the peace treaty signed at Versailles in 1919. Early demands for reparations were unrealistic and Germany responded by claiming that it was unable to meet the payments. In 1921, the Reparations Commission assessed the damage at over $30 billion.

In order to meet reparations payments, large amounts of German currency would have had to be converted into foreign currency. Germany was incapable of earning enough foreign currency to make the reparations payments. German production had not recovered from the war, the economy was experiencing massive inflation in the early twenties, and Germany did not have the necessary export capacity. In any case, other countries would have been unable or unwilling to absorb enough goods for Germany to earn the foreign currency needed. In 1924, Germany received foreign loans under the Dawes Plan. These loans helped Germany return to the gold standard and meet reduced demands for reparations. For the first time since the war, reparations payments began to proceed smoothly. In fact, German borrowing from other countries after 1924 was greater than reparations payments, thus Germany did not need to run a trade surplus. When these loans ceased, German payments ceased.[5]

British Economic Policy after the War

After the war the objective of the British government was to return to the prewar parity as soon as economic conditions allowed. The return was seen as a matter of national pride and honor. For example, it was argued that holders of sterling assets acquired before the war should be able to sell the assets for the same amount of gold as when they were acquired. Also, it was felt that a link between sterling and gold was needed to prevent monetary expansion, to remove uncertainty, and to maintain and strengthen London's position as an international financial center.

In order to return to the prewar parity, Britain had to restore its competitive position that had been eroded by wartime inflation. One of the first steps was to bring government spending under control. During the war, a budget deficit had been financed by printing new money. After the war, it was felt that a budget deficit was no longer justifiable, and certainly should not be financed by money creation if Britain was to return to gold. A large budget deficit in 1918–19 was turned into a budget surplus in 1920–21 by cuts in government spending and increased taxes. The money supply was brought under control and reduced, and prices began to fall. While the battle to reduce prices was taking place, the pound was allowed to float.[6] This was seen

---

[5] German payments ended in 1931 when, as part of the breakdown of the interwar gold standard, there was a capital flight from Germany and payments on war debts were suspended. See Yeager (1976), p. 340.

[6] Britain abandoned the gold standard officially after the war; wartime measures and conditions made it irrelevant during the war.

Dollars per pound

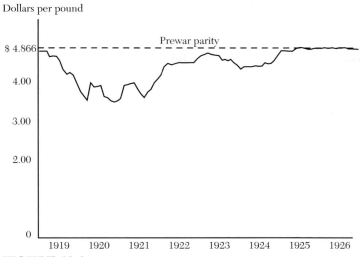

FIGURE 12.1

The Dollar-Sterling Exchange Rate, 1919–1926
Source: Data from Brown (1940), p. 231.

as a temporary measure pending the return to an official gold price and fixed exchange rates.

The pound gradually rose in value over the following years, as Figure 12.1 shows. The deflationary policy, and the rise in the pound, meant that British exports were less competitive and some traditional markets were lost (which added to unemployment problems). Britain also lost markets because other countries were growing. For example, cotton textile exports by Britain suffered as Japan entered the export market and domestic production in India displaced imports from Britain.

In April 1925, Britain returned to the prewar gold price after negotiating loans to help support sterling and raising the bank rate to attract short-term capital to Britain. Even at the time, the logic of restoring the prewar gold price was questioned by some people, notably the economist J. M. Keynes. He argued that the gold standard was a "barbarous relic" and that the world had moved to a paper system:

> Advocates of the ancient standard do not observe how remote it now is from the spirit and the requirements of the age. A regulated non-metallic standard has slipped in unnoticed. *It exists.*[7]

Unfortunately for the British, Keynes's argument against the restoration of the prewar gold price was not heeded, and the economy suffered as a

---

[7]J. M. Keynes, *Monetary Reform,* New York: Harcourt Brace and Co., 1924, p. 187.

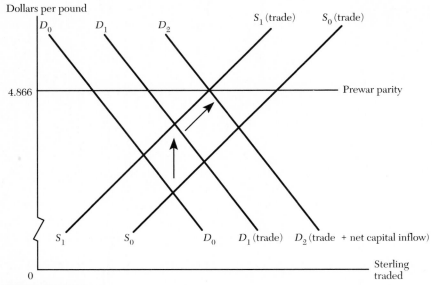

FIGURE 12.2

The Overvaluation of Sterling

Britain's policy of deflation was intended to increase the value of sterling by increasing the demand for sterling and reducing the supply of sterling. This is shown by the shift of the supply curve to the left (S_0S_0 to S_1S_1) and the shift of the demand curve to the right (D_0D_0 to D_1D_1). When Britain returned to gold at the prewar parity of \$4.866, the policy had not been completed, and the supply of sterling (shown by S_1S_1) was greater than the demand for sterling (shown by D_1D_1). The value of sterling was maintained by a capital inflow (which increased the demand for sterling to D_2D_2).

result.[8] The suffering continued after the restoration of the prewar gold price, because the task of reducing the British price level had not been fully completed. The prewar parity is thought to have overvalued sterling by about 10 percent. Thus, the government had to maintain a high interest rate and continue with a deflationary policy. Unemployment during the twenties (and thirties) was always above 10 percent; before the war, unemployment of 5 percent or less had been common.[9] The British balance of payments problem is illustrated in Figure 12.2.

Yeager (1976) concludes his discussion of the era:

---

[8] In the sixties, British economic growth was again sacrificed to maintain an exchange rate that overvalued the pound. Many economists believe that the British devaluation of 1967 was too little too late.

[9] The experience of these years helps explain the British preference for low unemployment in the Bretton Woods period.

In short, British monetary experience in the 1920s consisted of several years of deflationary struggle back to the prewar parity; temporary success in this questionable effort; and then continued business stagnation and chronic unemployment, the need for relatively high interest rates, and a precarious accumulation of mobile short-term foreign funds—all under the influence of an inappropriate exchange rate. (p. 324)

French Economic Policy after the War

France had similar problems to Germany, but not on quite the same scale. When the franc was allowed to float following the war, as so often happens when a currency is floated, it sank. The government was committed to reconstruction, and although government spending exceeded taxes, it was felt that there was no need for concern because reparation payments from Germany would finance reconstruction. The French government financed its excessive spending by printing money, which led to inflation, and the franc fell further.

The value of the franc was also influenced by speculation. Speculators feared that the franc might collapse as the mark had. They saw the franc fall, anticipated further decreases, and sold francs. This flight of capital pushed the value of the franc lower. Thus, speculators' expectations were self-fulfilling. The monetary authorities did not attempt to support the franc at this time and French gold reserves were not affected. The flight of capital, shown by a capital account deficit, was financed by a current account surplus.

French Stabilization

The stabilization of the French economy began in 1926. After a succession of governments, a new government (headed by Poincaré) raised taxes and removed the budget deficit. The franc, which had been weakened by speculation, began to recover; from just over 2 cents in July it rose to over 3.9 cents in December. The government stabilized the rate in December 1926 and France was back on a fixed rate. The return to a gold standard was made official in 1928.

Postwar inflation in France had lasted long enough to make the prewar parity of 19.3 cents irrelevant, and the new rate of 3.9 cents undervalued the franc slightly. As a result, from 1926 onward France ran balance of payments surpluses (which added to Britain's problems of maintaining an overvalued exchange rate). Another factor adding to France's surpluses was the repatriation of capital that had fled France prior to stabilization. As the French monetary authorities intervened to maintain the value of the franc, they accumulated international reserves.[10] The domestic monetary effects of the balance of payments surpluses were sterilized to prevent inflation. The undervaluation of the franc is illustrated in Figure 12.3.

---

[10] French international reserves increased from less than $1 billion to about $2.5 billion from the end of 1925 to the end of 1928.

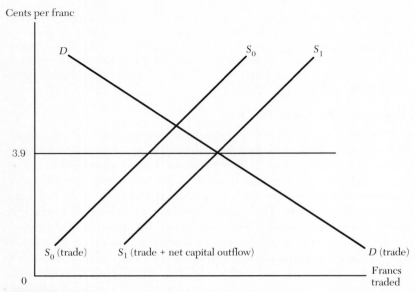

Cents per franc

FIGURE 12.3

The Undervaluation of the French Franc

When France returned to gold, a current account surplus financed a capital account deficit. The current account surplus is shown by the difference between supply and demand for francs resulting from international trade, S_0S_0 and DD, respectively. The overall supply and demand of francs, DD and S_1S_1, respectively, were equal because the excess demand for francs from trade was met by a supply of francs from the French capital outflow. When the capital outflow ceased, the franc was undervalued, and the French monetary authorities had to sell francs (purchase foreign currency) to prevent the franc from rising in value.

The movement towards a gold standard was not confined to Europe. Over the period 1924–28 a large number of countries moved back to gold (see Figure 12.4). Many people expected that the restoration of a gold standard would lead to the restoration of prewar economic conditions. However, the interwar gold standard was different from the prewar gold standard.

Comparing the Prewar and Interwar Gold Standards

Before the war, London had been the undisputed center of international finance. Britain was the most important investing and trading nation, and there was confidence in sterling and the British banking system. Imbalances between other countries could be settled by the transfer of ownership of sterling balances. British monetary policy was conducted with reference to the balance of payments. Small imbalances between Britain and the rest of the world were reflected in changes in the bank rate, which increased or reduced

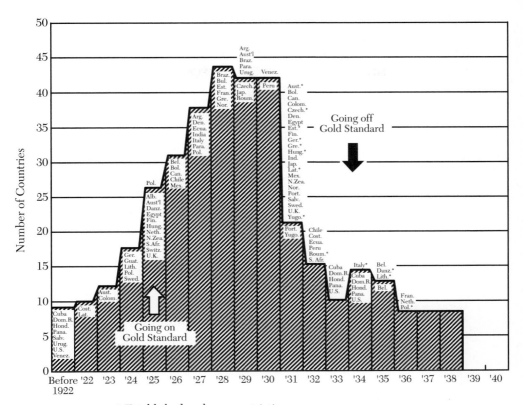

° Established exchange restrictions

FIGURE 12.4

The Rise and Fall of the Interwar Gold Standard
Reproduced from *The Economics of Money and Banking*, Third Edition, by Lester V.
  Chandler. Copyright 1959, Harper & Row Publishers, Inc.

British lending abroad without disrupting international markets to any great
extent. This system worked because people had confidence that exchange rates
would remain unchanged, because money supplies were linked to gold, and
because countries in general (Britain in particular) did not pursue independent monetary policies.

Economic Policies

    After the war, New York rivaled London as the most important financial
center. However, the United States is large and trade was relatively unimportant to it. Thus, American monetary policy was not sensitive to the balance
of payments. For example, during the early twenties, the American balance
of payments surplus was sterilized to prevent inflation resulting from a rising

money supply. In fact, American prices fell during the interwar gold standard. This added to the adjustment problems of other countries, notably Britain. Without sterilization, the American money supply and price level would have risen and the amount of British deflation needed would have been smaller.

During this period, governments began to accept that they bore some responsibility for domestic economic problems such as inflation and unemployment. They became reluctant to allow balance of payments considerations to dictate economic policy. Although declining reserves forced deficit countries to adjust or devalue, surplus countries, such as the United States and France, faced no such pressure. Lack of adjustment by surplus countries increased the adjustment problems of deficit countries. This problem plagued the Bretton Woods system, and continues as a problem even now.

Capital Flows and Protectionism

When there is more than one international monetary center, people can shift funds between the centers. If there is confidence in the stability of exchange rates, this possibility may not be important. But, as confidence in the parities of the interwar gold standard declined (at the beginning of the thirties), large capital flows made the maintenance of fixed exchange rates impossible. Countries responded by abandoning fixed exchange rates and introducing capital controls.

Another difference between the interwar and prewar periods is that protectionist policies were more common during the interwar period. Protectionism began to take hold before World War One, but after the war protectionist pressures increased as countries concentrated on national economic interests. This issue is examined in Chapter 15.

Exchange Rates

Turning to the monetary system itself, the exchange rates were not chosen to ensure international consistency: each country fixed its gold price independently at what was thought to be appropriate for its own economic conditions and interests. This meant that some countries had payments surpluses and others had deficits. Adjustment might have taken place eventually (if countries had maintained gold prices and allowed their money supplies to be determined by their balances of payments), but domestic economic problems were often of greater concern than external balance, so automatic adjustment was not permitted.

The Role of Gold

Gold played a smaller role in the interwar gold standard than it had before the war. Wartime measures had reduced the value of gold in private hands, gold coin had been replaced by paper currency, and people had become accustomed to paper currency. The role of gold as a base for the monetary system also changed. Official gold stocks had not increased in line with real income.[11] In order to economize on limited amounts of gold, countries adopted *gold exchange standards*.[12] Under a gold exchange standard, countries count as part of their gold reserves currencies of other countries that are convertible into gold. This meant, for example, that gold held in the Bank of England supported the issue of sterling, and some of the sterling supported paper currency issued by other countries. Therefore, two or more countries could increase "gold reserves" simply by holding each other's paper currency.

Confidence in the System

The interwar system only worked as long as confidence existed that the currencies were as good as gold. If lack of confidence caused people to demand the limited gold on which the pyramid of paper money was built, the system could collapse. Two currencies that were particularly vulnerable were sterling and the dollar. Both currencies were held in significant amounts by foreign central banks as international reserves. Thus, Britain and the United States could be faced with demands for conversion of large amounts of their currencies into gold. As the interwar system moved towards collapse, this is exactly what happened.[13]

THE COLLAPSE OF THE INTERWAR GOLD STANDARD   12.4

Background

When France legally returned to gold in 1928, the central bank was prevented from accepting convertible currencies. The French monetary authorities demanded gold for the foreign exchange obtained from foreign exchange market intervention. (Recall that the French balance of payments was in surplus.) This put pressure on the gold reserves of Britain and the United States, and undermined confidence in the link of sterling and the dollar to gold.[14] According to Nurkse: "The fate of the gold exchange standard was sealed when France decided in 1928 to take nothing but gold in settlement of the enormous surplus accruing to her from the repatriation of capital and the current balance of payments."[15]

---

[11] When nominal gold prices are fixed, as under a gold standard, inflation reduces the real gold price (because the amount of goods that can be purchased with an ounce of gold declines). As the real gold price declined during and after World War One, the supply of newly mined gold declined.

[12] The gold exchange standard was recommended by the Genoa Conference of 1922, and central bank statutes were amended to allow them to hold foreign exchange rather than gold against issues of money.

[13] See League of Nations (1944), pp. 39–41.

[14] French gold reserves increased from $1.3 billion at the end of 1928 to $3.3 billion at the end of 1932.

[15] League of Nations, p. 39. (Most of this report was written by Ragnar Nurkse.) Chapter 11 of Eichengreen (1985) is an extract of this publication.

The collapse of the international monetary system can also be traced to the Wall Street crash of 1929 and the beginnings of the Great Depression (1930–33). The Wall Street crash followed a period of record investment in the United States and the bubble burst when opportunities for profitable investment were exhausted. As investment fell, the American economy moved into recession. Another very important factor contributing to the depression in the United States was a decline in the money supply. Lack of confidence led to runs on banks, the Federal Reserve failed to fulfill its duty to act as lender of last resort, banks failed, and the money supply declined.

Some countries moved into recession before the United States. During the twenties, the supply of primary products and agricultural products increased more rapidly than the demand for these products (because of technological progress and the development of new sources of supply). The consequent collapse in prices led to lower export earnings for the less-developed countries, which relied on exports of these commodities. The collapse of American foreign investment at this time added to the international recession.

A decline in the American demand for imports, partly because of the recession and partly because of protectionism, was another factor contributing to the spread of the recession. The Smoot-Hawley tariff of 1930 drastically curtailed American imports and other countries responded with their own protectionist policies. World trade fell dramatically, and this added to recessionary forces. This is an example of the foreign trade multiplier at work. The imports of one country are the exports of other countries. Protectionist policies that reduce imports, reduce other countries' exports, and hence the incomes of other countries.[16]

The Collapse

The interwar gold standard was inherently weak and could not survive major financial crises. The collapse of the interwar gold standard began in Austria. In May 1931, a revaluation of the assets of the Austrian Credit-Anstalt revealed that it was insolvent and a run began on it and on other Austrian banks. Austria was forced to abandon convertibility. Attention then began to focus on Germany. The German Danat (Damstadter und National Bank) faced a run when the fall of a major textile company it had made loans to was announced. The German government responded to the ensuing flight of capital by raising the discount rate and introducing exchange controls in August 1931. In effect, this marked the departure of Germany from the gold standard because free trade in gold was severely curtailed.[17]

---

[16] Commercial policy during this period is examined in more detail in Section 15.4.
[17] Devaluation was rejected because, as a result of the German experience of the early twenties, devaluation was associated with inflation.

Britain Abandons Gold

Against this background of bank failures and flights of capital, the weak British balance of payments position did not help maintain confidence in the value of sterling. Confidence was further undermined by the report of the Macmillan Committee in July 1931, which showed that London's short-term claims on foreigners were far smaller than London's liabilities to foreigners: London had a net short-term liability of over $1 billion. Britain used reserves, borrowed, and raised the bank rate to maintain the sterling's value. However, when some Royal Navy sailors protested against their pay on September 15, it was reported as a mutiny, and a serious run began on sterling. The new coalition government was not in the mood for further deflation because there was already massive unemployment, so Britain abandoned the gold standard on September 21, 1931.[18]

Incidentally, other countries suffered losses when Britain devalued and the value of their sterling assets fell. In view of these losses, it is not surprising that some countries showed a preference for holding their international reserves in the form of gold rather than foreign exchange during the years preceding the collapse of the Bretton Woods system. It is also interesting to note in passing that by April 1934 the pound had risen to a value of over $5, that is, its value was more than the $4.866 value Britain had been unable to maintain in 1931.

Other Countries Follow Britain's Departure

Other countries followed Britain's abandonment of the gold standard, in part because they wanted to avoid being put at a competitive disadvantage by a rise in the value of their currencies relative to other currencies. Also, speculators believed that countries would be unable to maintain gold prices and their activities made the maintenance of gold prices difficult. The desire of international investors to avoid loss was probably as strong a motive for capital transfers as the desire for profit.

Meanwhile, in the United States, the domestic monetary system was under strain. People increased their holdings of currency and gold as they lost confidence in the American monetary system, and gold left the United States. Over one third of American banks collapsed in the years from 1930 to 1933. Following a rush of gold and currency hoarding, President Roosevelt declared a "bank holiday" on March 6, 1933, to prevent further gold losses. Gold exports were outlawed and the right of Americans to hold gold was suspended.[19]

---

[18] Following Britain's break with gold, a group of countries with close trade and financial links with Britain pegged their currencies to sterling and held sterling reserves. This group made up the *sterling area*.

[19] Americans were required to sell their gold to the Treasury. The ban on private gold holding remained in effect until 1974.

TABLE 12.3   Exchange Rates in the Thirties

	(December 1930 = 100) Values of Currencies against the U.S. Dollar		
December:	1932	1934	1936
Argentina	76	99	98
Brazil	80	86	91
Australia	59	88	87
Sweden	67	95	94
India	68	102	101
United Kingdom	67	102	101
Canada	87	101	100
Czechoslovakia	100	141	119
Italy	100	162	100
Belgium	100	168	121
France	100	168	119

Source: League of Nations (1944), p. 129.

The United States abandoned the gold standard officially on April 20, 1933. Devaluations of other currencies had weakened the American competitive position, but this was not the primary reason for the break of the link with gold. The recently elected Roosevelt administration felt that a rise in prices was needed to stop the recession and it was thought that by some mysterious mechanism commodity prices would rise with the gold price. The dollar was devalued by raising the gold price. A price of $35 an ounce was fixed in January 1934.

1934–39

The American departure from gold effectively marks the end of the interwar gold standard, although some currencies clung to gold for a while longer. For example, Belgium did not devalue until March 1935 and France and Switzerland devalued in September 1936. The collapse of the interwar gold standard in 1933 was the beginning of a period in which there were many devaluations.[20] Although exchange rates fluctuated as the interwar gold standard collapsed, Table 12.3 shows that by the end of 1936 exchange rates were roughly what they had been in 1930. This suggests that weaknesses in the system and speculation played a large role in determining the size of deval-

---

[20] Some economists describe the ensuing muddle as a period of "competitive devaluations" during which countries sought to reduce the relative value of their currencies in order to gain a competitive advantage over other countries. Rolfe and Burtle (1973) argue that this is not an accurate description of the policies of the most important trading nations, although some small primary-producing countries may have behaved in this way.

uations. The devaluations do not appear to have been an attempt to realign currencies with underlying competitive forces.

One characteristic of this period was the adoption of exchange controls by countries in Central Europe and Latin America.[21] These were often designed to reduce capital flows. Earnings of foreign exchange had to be sold to the monetary authorities. The authorities rationed the availability of foreign exchange, or charged different prices for foreign exchange, according to how it was to be used. Germany controlled the availability of foreign exchange for virtually all purposes, including imports of goods. Bilateral trade agreements, such as barter, were used to maintain trade. As a result, countries became concerned with bilateral trade balances, and the gains from specialization and trade were undermined. Countries without exchange controls, such as Britain, were induced to take part because they had frozen assets in the countries with exchange controls or they wanted some form of service payment on loans they had made.[22]

The value of the French franc, established in 1936, lasted only nine months. Following speculation, the franc was floated in June 1937, then pegged against sterling in April 1938. This arrangement lasted into World War Two. Meanwhile, under Hitler, Germany continued to pursue policies of economic nationalism and continued to exercise controls over international transactions.

The dollar-sterling exchange rate was reasonably stable around 4.95 until the summer of 1938. Then, a British current account deficit and rising international tensions led to speculation and a slight fall in the rate. In 1939, the dollar-sterling rate was stable at 4.68 until August, when transfers of funds increased as war seemed inevitable. Britain declared war on September 3, 1939. As in World War One, international trade and financial links were broken or tightly controlled.

Conclusion

The collapse of the interwar gold standard is not surprising in view of the inherent weaknesses in the system. It is difficult to summarize the events of the interwar period, but the lesson of the period is clear: if countries pursue their own interest without taking into account the effects of their policies on other countries, all countries can suffer. This lesson was to have a major influence on the postwar economic system, and remains relevant today.

Summary of Main Points

After World War One, countries wanted to return to a gold standard. Differences between countries' inflation rates had altered the purchasing power of currencies and made an immediate return to prewar gold prices and ex-

---

[21] See Chapter 7 in League of Nations (1944).
[22] As a result of 170 clearing agreements, barter accounted for 70%–75% of European trade in 1937. Bilateral clearing was less important for other countries, and accounted for at most 12% of world trade. (S. Pollard, *Peaceful Conquest: The Industrialization of Europe 1760–1970*, revised edition, New York: Oxford University Press, 1982, pp. 303–4.)

change rates impossible. Also, the trade and financial positions of countries had changed.

The United States was able to return to gold soon after the war, and it did so at the prewar gold price. This meant that other countries wishing to return to gold had to bring their price levels down to the American level, or devalue their currencies in terms of gold. Germany and France experienced inflation well above that of the United States. When monetary stability was eventually restored in these countries, gold prices were fixed that set the value of their currencies below the prewar levels.

Britain chose to return to gold at the prewar gold price. To bring the British price level down to the American price level, the government pursued a deflationary policy that resulted in low growth and high unemployment. When the gold price was reestablished, the deflationary policy and high interest rates had to be maintained because the British price level had not fully fallen to the American level.

Britain's difficulty in returning to gold was made worse by the decision of the Federal Reserve to sterilize the monetary effects of the American surplus. In the absence of sterilization, American prices would have been higher, and Britain's deflation need not have been so severe. Also, the French franc was undervalued and France ran balance of payments surpluses.

It was clear that the exchange rates that had been established were not equilibrium rates: some currencies were overvalued and others undervalued. Also, the willingness of governments to sacrifice domestic economic objectives to maintain fixed exchange rates was in doubt. The interwar gold standard began to come under strain with the onset of the Great Depression. These events led to a collapse of confidence and amid increasing speculation countries were forced to abandon their links with gold.

During the period following the collapse, currencies were often devalued and countries used protectionist policies in an attempt to increase domestic employment. The lesson of the interwar period is that when countries pursue their own interests without taking into account the effects of their policies on other countries, all countries can suffer.

Study Questions

1. Explain what is meant by purchasing power parity with reference to the problems of restoring a fixed exchange rate system after World War One.
2. Using the demand and supply of the currency, show how the value of a currency can be increased by deflation. (Use dollars per unit of currency as the exchange rate.)
3. Show that if the demand and supply of a currency are equal when there is a large capital outflow, the currency will be undervalued if the capital outflow ceases. (Use dollars per unit of currency as the exchange rate.)
4. Why was there a capital flow out of France in 1925? Why did it cease after 1926?

5. Why did most countries adopt flexible exchange rates after World War One?

6. Why did the decision of the Federal Reserve to sterilize the monetary effects of American payments surpluses make it difficult for Britain to return to and maintain the prewar parity of sterling?

7. Using the concept of purchasing power parity, describe how Britain returned to gold. What were the costs of Britain's return to gold?

8. What were the differences between the prewar gold standard and the interwar gold standard that contributed to the collapse of the interwar gold standard?

9. Why might capital flows have been stabilizing under the prewar gold standard and destabilizing under the interwar gold standard?

Selected References

Ashworth, W. A. *A Short History of the International Economy Since 1850.* Fourth Edition. New York: Longman, 1987.

Brown, W. A., Jr. *The International Gold Standard Reinterpreted: 1913–1934.* New York: National Bureau of Economic Research, 1940.

Chandler, L. V. *The Economics of Money and Banking.* Revised Edition. New York: Harper & Row, 1953.

Clarke, S. V. O. *The Reconstruction of the International Monetary System: The Attempts of 1922 and 1933.* Princeton Studies in International Finance No. 33. Princeton, N.J.: Princeton University Press, 1973.

Eichengreen, B., ed. *The Gold Standard in Theory and History.* New York: Methuen, 1985.

Ellsworth, P. T. *The International Economy.* Fourth Edition. Toronto: Macmillan, 1969.

Kenwood, A. G., and Lougheed, A. L. *The Growth of the International Economy: 1820–1980.* Boston: George Allen & Unwin, 1983.

League of Nations. *International Currency Experience: Lessons of the Interwar Period.* Geneva: 1944.

Rolfe, S. E., and Burtle, J. *The Great Wheel: The World Monetary System.* New York: Quadrangle/New York Times Book Co., 1973.

Schuker, S. A. *American "Reparations" to Germany, 1919–33: Implications for the Third World Debt Crisis.* Princeton Studies in International Finance No. 61. Princeton, N.J.: Princeton University Press, 1988.

Yeager, L. B. *International Monetary Relations.* Second Edition. New York: Harper & Row, 1976.

Young, J. P. *European Currency and Finance.* Commission of Gold and Silver Inquiry, United States Senate. Washington, D. C.: Government Printing Office, 1925.

13

THE BRETTON
WOODS SYSTEM

INTRODUCTION

In July 1944, while World War Two was still in progress, forty-four coun-tries met in Bretton Woods, New Hampshire, to discuss the structure of the international monetary system that would be created when peace returned. The experience of the interwar years had shown that when countries pursue their own national interests without regard to the interests of other countries, all countries suffer. In particular, the participants felt that frequent changes in exchange rates, the use of exchange controls, and protectionist policies should be avoided.

At the conference it was agreed to establish an international monetary system incorporating fixed exchange rates. A new organization, the *Inter-national Monetary Fund (IMF)*, was created to oversee the functioning of the system. It was also agreed to establish the *International Bank for Re-construction and Development* (often called the *World Bank*). The World Bank was to be concerned with postwar reconstruction and later interna-tional development.[1]

In this chapter we shall examine the objectives and early performance of the IMF and the international monetary system.

THE IMF AND THE BRETTON WOODS SYSTEM

Objectives

The objective of the IMF as described in Article I of the Articles of Agreement is to facilitate the pursuit of full employment and growth. This is to be done by creating a stable international monetary system for trade and

---

[1]Although the IMF and the World Bank often work closely together, their major concerns are different. Criticisms of the IMF often reflect a lack of understanding of the roles of the World Bank and the IMF. See Nowzad (1981).

investment, and promoting international monetary cooperation and consultation. Members are to be assisted in reducing balance of payments disequilibria, and exchange rate stability is to be increased, without members needing to resort to "measures destructive of national or international prosperity." This was a reference to the intention to avoid the problems that had plagued the thirties.

Fixed Exchange Rates

The Bretton Woods system was based on *fixed but adjustable* exchange rates. The value of the dollar was defined relative to gold, there being $35 per ounce. The United States agreed to sell gold to the monetary authorities of other countries at this price. There was no commitment to sell gold in the private market. Thus, limited convertibility of the dollar was established. The values of other currencies were defined relative to the dollar. The chosen values were called *par values*. Members agreed to maintain the value of their currencies within 1 percent of their par value. Thus, currencies were fixed in value relative to each other through their links with the dollar (the exchange rate between two currencies being equal to the cross rate).

The IMF agreement is significant because it recognized that the value of a currency was of common concern. A member country could only change the value of its currency after consultation with the IMF, and only in cases of "fundamental disequilibrium."[2] The term *fundamental disequilibrium* was not defined in the agreement, but refers to payments imbalances that reflect a country's long-term relative competitive position (rather than imbalances that are inherently short-term, such as seasonal fluctuations in trade). For example, a fundamental disequilibrium might develop from one country having an inflation rate above the world rate.

The Fund of Reserves

A fund of international reserves was established that countries could draw on for the purpose of maintaining declared parities during temporary payments difficulties. This fund of reserves is still in use. Each country was allocated a *quota*, which was based on a country's trade, national income, and international reserves. Countries paid this quota to the IMF, 25 percent in gold or dollars and 75 percent in their own currencies. Thus, a stock of currencies was created from which countries could borrow. The initial allocation of quotas in 1945 was $8.8 billion, which represented less than 20 percent of total reserves at the time. The other types of international reserve assets are gold, foreign exchange, and, after 1970, special drawing rights. Special drawing rights are described in this chapter. IMF quotas are reviewed regularly and have been increased as follows:

---

[2]The IMF could not object if the proposed change and previous changes amounted to less than 10% of the initial par value.

TABLE 13.1   IMF Quotas

	Millions of SDRs	Percentage of Total
Canada	2,941	3.27
France	4,483	4.98
Germany (Fed. Rep.)	5,404	6.00
Italy	2,909	3.23
Japan	4,223	4.69
Saudi Arabia	3,202	3.56
United Kingdom	6,194	6.88
United States	17,918	19.91

Source: IMF Survey, September 1, 1986, p. 263.

1959	50%
1965	25%
1970	25%
1976	33.6%
1978	50%
1983	47.5%

In 1987, total quotas amounted to SDR 90 billion, which was equal to about 18 percent of international reserves.[3] The countries with the largest quotas are shown in Table 13.1

Voting in the IMF

In passing, we may note that the quotas are used to determine voting rights in the IMF. Major changes in IMF policy need a majority of 85 percent, thus the larger, richer nations, which have the biggest quotas, dominate the voting. The United States is in a unique position because its quota exceeds 15 percent, thus it holds the right of veto.[4] This characteristic of the system has been criticized by smaller, poorer countries.

Borrowing from the Fund

A country borrows by depositing its own currency with the IMF and withdrawing foreign currency. The amount a country can borrow is determined by its quota. A country can borrow 25 percent of its quota by right without restriction. This 25 percent is called the *reserve tranche* and is counted

[3] At the end of October 1988, one SDR was worth $1.33. The creation of SDRs is described below.
[4] If IMF quotas are revised to reflect the growing importance of other countries, such as Japan, the United States may lose the power of veto.

as part of a country's international reserves. Further drawings can be made up to an additional 100 percent of the quota, the 100 percent being divided into four *credit tranches*. Countries may borrow additional amounts under other IMF financial facilities described below.

The IMF lays down conditions for the loans it makes. The conditions become more stringent as the amount that a country wishes to borrow increases. The conditions are intended to ensure that the loans are part of a program "aimed at establishing or maintaining the enduring stability of the member's currency at a realistic rate of exchange." The IMF charges interest on the credit advanced, and a country is expected to repay IMF loans when it has brought its balance of payments under control. The repayment is made by the member repurchasing its currency. Although many countries have moved towards more flexible exchange rates, IMF loans continue to be an important part of the international monetary system.

The financial facilities of the fund and the conditions attached to them are as follows:

Tranche policies
First credit tranche
Member demonstrates reasonable efforts to overcome balance of payments difficulties in program. Performance criteria and purchase installments not used. Repurchase are made in $3\frac{1}{4}$–5 years.
Upper credit tranches
Member must have a substantial and viable program to overcome its balance of payments difficulties. Resources normally provided in the form of standby arrangements that include performance criteria and purchases in installments. Repurchases are made in $3\frac{1}{4}$–5 years.
Extended Fund facility
Medium-term program aims at overcoming structural balance of payments maladjustments. A program is generally for three years, although it may be lengthened to four years. . . .
Resources are provided in the form of extended arrangements that include performance criteria and drawings in installments; repurchases are made in $4\frac{1}{2}$–10 years.
Enlarged access policy
Policy used to augment resources available under standby and extended arrangements, for programs that need large amounts of Fund support. Applicable policies on conditionality, phasing, and performance criteria are the same as under the credit tranches and the extended Fund facility. Repurchases are made in $3\frac{1}{2}$–7 years, and charges are based on the Fund's borrowing costs.
Compensatory financing facility
The compensatory element provides resources to a member for an export shortfall or an excess in cereal import costs that are due to factors largely beyond the member's control. . . . Repurchases in 3–5 years.
Buffer stock financing facility
Resources help finance a member's contribution to an approved international buffer stock. Repurchases in $3\frac{1}{4}$–5 years.

Structural adjustment facility
>   Resources provided on concessional terms to low-income member countries facing protracted balance of payments problems, in support of medium-term macroeconomic and structural adjustment programs. Member develops, and updates, with the assistance of the Fund and the World Bank, a medium term policy framework. . . . Detailed annual programs are formulated prior to disbursement of annual loans, and include quarterly benchmarks to assess performance. Repayments are made in 5½–10 years.

Enhanced structural facility
>   Objectives, eligibility, and basic program features of this facility parallel those of the SAF. . . .[5]

Special Drawing Rights

In response to fears that the supply of international reserves was not keeping pace with the need for reserves, the IMF created a new international reserve asset in 1967, the *Special Drawing Right (SDR)*. SDRs are bookkeeping entries that members agree to accept as they would other reserve assets. They were allocated for the first time in 1970, the allocation being made in relation to countries' IMF quotas.[6] Further allocations have brought the total to SDR 21.4 billion. In 1988 this represented approximately 4 percent of nongold international reserves. Thus, SDRs are not significant in relation to total international reserves.[7]

The Scarce Currency Clause

The IMF was designed to provide resources to countries while measures were being taken to remove their balance of payments deficits. It was recognized that surplus countries would not need to borrow from the IMF and would face little pressure to adjust. Since the deficit of one country is another country's surplus, continuing surpluses imply continuing deficits. Thus, it was desirable to find a way to encourage surplus countries to adjust. The *scarce currency clause* provided for measures (such as discriminatory exchange controls for current account transactions) to be taken against a country that continually had a surplus. Given that the participants at Bretton Woods expected American post-war surpluses to continue, the inclusion of the clause was seen as a significant concession by the United States. Things did not turn out as expected: the United States soon began running deficits. The clause was never used against the countries that did have surpluses.

---

[5] Abridged from *IMF Survey,* Supplement on the Fund, September 1988, p. 2.

[6] The method of allocating SDRs has been the subject of much debate. The proposal to use the allocation of SDRs as a form of international aid is discussed in Chapter 18.

[7] The SDR is sometimes used as a unit of account. The value of an SDR is defined in terms of a basket of five* currencies: U.S. dollar, German mark, Japanese yen, French franc, and British pound. See *IMF Survey,* Supplement on the Fund, September 1988.

Exchange Controls

The Bretton Woods agreement prohibited the use of exchange controls on current account transactions, that is, transactions in foreign currency arising from trade in goods and services were not to be restricted. Members were permitted to retain controls for a transitional period. It was until 1958 that most European countries restored convertibility to nonresidents for current account transactions. Members were permitted to use exchange controls to limit capital flows, and many countries retained capital controls throughout the Bretton Woods period. However, the effectiveness of such controls is never complete because there is an incentive to evade the controls by using foreign currency earned through trade or purchased for trade to finance capital transfers.[8]

The General Agreement on Tariffs and Trade

It is clear from the Bretton Woods agreement that the participants recognized that there are gains from trade. The Bretton Woods agreement was mainly concerned with financial stability. But, international trade cannot flourish if countries maintain trade barriers. The problem of barriers to trade was addressed in 1947 by the *General Agreement on Tariffs and Trade (GATT)*. GATT is an international organization that attempts to regulate commercial policies and reduce trade barriers. During the Bretton Woods period, GATT helped countries negotiate substantial reductions in trade barriers. GATT is examined in more detail in Chapter 15.

THE BRETTON WOODS SYSTEM 1945–60   **13.3**

Reconstruction and the Implementation of the Bretton Woods System

The physical destruction caused by World War Two was greater than that of World War One, and severely reduced the productive capability of the belligerents. The war affected all stages of the production process. To begin with, the war reduced the supply of factors of production. Millions of people were killed. Also, capital was depleted by the war. The major belligerents ran down their foreign assets, used up their inventories, and borrowed from other countries to finance their war efforts. Maintenance was not a priority during the war, and obsolete machines were not replaced. Many factories were destroyed or converted to military production. The resources that remained had to be reallocated from production for the war to peacetime production. People

---

[8] The use of capital controls and other policies restricting international transactions is summarized in IMF *Annual Report on Exchange Arrangements and Exchange Restrictions*, Washington, D.C.

as well as machines had to change activities. Finally, the distribution network of harbors, roads, and railways, which had been military targets, was badly in need of repair. Not surprisingly, the first priority when peace was restored was reconstruction.

Post-War Financial Conditions

As had happened during World War One, wartime economic policy was geared to the war effort. The rate of inflation varied between different countries, but exchange rates did not reflect inflation differentials because of wartime controls and disrupted trade. Even neutral countries experienced a measure of inflation because the prices of traded goods increased in response to wartime demand, and balance of payments surpluses led to monetary expansion.

Differential rates of inflation and varying degrees of destruction of productive capacity meant that the exchange rates at the end of the war were unrealistic. European countries ran balance of trade deficits because their currencies were overvalued relative to the dollar and their consumption was higher than their production. In 1947, Europe was consuming about 5–6 percent more than it was producing, the difference being reflected in a current account deficit of about $7 billion. Over two thirds of this deficit resulted from Europe's trade with the United States.[9] The dominance of the United States is further shown by the fact that at that time the United States accounted for a third of world exports but only a tenth of world imports. This trade imbalance gave rise to the *dollar shortage:* the demand for dollars to pay for imports of American goods was greater than the supply of dollars earned from exports to the United States (at the maintained exchange rates).

Why Not Devalue?

Devaluation of the European currencies relative to the dollar could have removed the dollar shortage, but, in the early postwar years, European countries were reluctant to rely on this strategy. Imports were needed to help postwar reconstruction. Also, even though the trade imbalances of European countries were small in relation to GNP, it was felt that the costs of adjustment were unacceptable in economies that had been weakened by the war. The weakness of European currencies was seen as a temporary phenomenon that would disappear naturally as reconstruction progressed. The experience of the thirties may also have added to the generally accepted view that devaluations were not the answer.

The Need for Aid

In the absence of devaluations, aid from the United States was needed to finance the balance of payments deficits. Initially, postwar reconstruction was financed partly through direct American loans and partly through the United

---

[9]Triffin (1957) contains useful data relating to this period.

Nations Relief and Rehabilitation Administration (UNRRA). However, it became clear by 1947 that this approach was not working. Europe remained weak and there were fears in the United States that economic weakness might lead to political instability. Also, Americans felt sympathy for their European friends.

The Marshall Plan

American support for reconstruction was organized through the Marshall Plan, which came into effect in 1948. Under this plan American grants and loans were made to Europe and Japan to help finance postwar recovery. By the end of 1951, Europe had received almost 11.5 billion, 90 percent in grants and 10 percent in loans.[10] However, there was far more to Marshall aid than American handouts. European countries were encouraged to restrict their imports from the United States, increase their trade with each other, and increase their exports to the United States. Even though many currencies had fallen in value since the end of the war, the United States insisted that recipients of aid devalue their currencies (because it did not want the aid exhausted in attempts to defend unrealistic exchange rates). The devaluations took place in 1949.[11] These policies reflected the view that the American trade surplus and strength in world markets in the immediate postwar period was likely to continue.

European Recovery

The pace of European recovery was spectacular. In 1947, production was 9 percent lower than before the war. By 1948, this gap had almost been closed, and for the following three years production increased by about 7 percent each year. This growth cannot be attributed solely to Marshall aid, which was not large in relation to the economies of the recipients. During the years 1947–50, Marshall aid accounted for between 5 and 10 percent of European GNP, or a quarter of Europe's imports of goods and services.[12] However, Marshall aid helped Europe to maintain a reasonable level of consumption while undertaking high levels of investment. Also, the devaluations of 1949 were of great importance. They helped make European countries competitive even before full recovery had been completed.

Postwar reconstruction, the 1949 devaluations, and the outbreak of the Korean War reduced the American trade surplus from \$5.5 billion in 1949 to \$1.5 billion in 1950. The overall deficit, as measured by the liquidity balance,

---

[10] Yeager (1976), p. 385.

[11] Some countries followed Britain's lead and devalued by 30.5%. For some other countries, the 1949 devaluations were only part of a process of exchange rate adjustment. The French franc fell in value by over 60% from the end of the war until 1949. The replacement of the reichsmark by the deutschmark in 1948 entailed a depreciation of over 90%. In 1949, the deutschmark was devalued by 20.7%. The postwar value of the yen (371 to the dollar) represents a devaluation of over 98% relative to the prewar value (of 4 to the dollar).

[12] Yeager (1976), p. 385.

was 4567 in 1947, 1005, in 1948, 175 in 1949, and −3580 in 1950.[13] The deficit in 1950 was the beginning of a phenomenon that was to continue throughout most of the Bretton Woods period and that would lead ultimately to the collapse of the system. However, at the time it was thought that, because of the strength of the American economy, an American deficit could only be temporary.

The American Balance of Payments

Although the trade balance declined after 1949, a deficit was not recorded on America's balance of trade until 1971. Thus we must look for other explanations of the American deficits. Military expenditure is one part of the story: typically this accounted for a debit entry of $2–$3.5 billion in the Bretton Woods years. After 1950, U.S. government grants usually added another $2 billion to the deficits. Finally, private American foreign investment, particularly long-term investment, was a major part of the deficits. For example, between 1950 and 1960, there was a net long-term private capital outflow from the United States of $19 billion.[14] This capital flow continued and grew in the sixties.

Deficits and Dollars

The method by which American balance of payments deficits were financed must be understood if we are to appreciate how the Bretton Woods system worked and why it collapsed. American deficits meant that more dollars were being supplied than were demanded (there was an excess demand for foreign exchange by Americans). Foreign central banks were obliged to intervene in the foreign exchange market to maintain the values of their currencies against the dollar. Given the excess supply of dollars, this meant that foreign central banks bought dollars and added them to their reserves. The American deficit was also financed partly by American reserves. Between the beginning of 1950 and the end of 1960, an official settlements balance deficit of $16 billion was financed by an increase in U.S. official liquid liabilities of $9.3 billion and a decline in international reserves (gold) of $6.7 billion. (See Table 13.2)

The United States was able to finance balance of payments deficits with its own currency because the dollar was an international reserve currency. The ability of the United States to buy foreign goods or assets and pay for them with dollars (or American debt) was criticized by some countries (notably France), which charged that the United States was able to accumulate "debts without tears." Charles de Gaulle called this the "exorbitant privilege"

[13] *Economic Report of the President*, 1967, p. 301.
[14] *Economic Report of the President*, 1967, p. 301.

TABLE 13.2   The Balance of Payments of the United States, 1947–60

(millions of dollars)

	Current Account Balance	Official Settlements Balance	Net Change in Liabilities to Foreign Official Holders	Reserves (−increase)
1947	8992		—	−3315
1948	1993		—	−1736
1949	580		—	−266
1950	−2125	−3312	1554	1758
1951	302	538	−505	−33
1952	−175	−822	1237	−415
1953	−1949	−2104	848	1256
1954	−321	−1523	1043	480
1955	−345	−741	559	182
1956	1722	−261	1130	−869
1957	3556	1145	20	−1165
1958	−5	−3027	735	2292
1959	−2138	−2283	1248	1035
1960	1794	−3592[a]	1449	2143

[a] Slight differences in definition of liabilities to official foreign agencies are responsible for the difference between the 1960 official settlements balances shown in Tables 12.2 and 12.4.
Sources: Economic Report of the President, 1966, p. 301; 1975, p. 351.

of the United States. However, American deficits provided the world with international reserves (see below).

Although some observers were aware of the underlying weaknesses of the Bretton Woods system, the forces for change were not great. In the period up to 1960, countries recovered from the war, trade barriers and currency restrictions were gradually removed, and trade grew quickly. The forces for change were stronger after 1960 because the underlying disequilibrium became more obvious as American deficits increased.

THE PROBLEMS OF THE BRETTON WOODS SYSTEM   13.4

Early Signs of Weakness

The first signs of weakness in the Bretton Woods system began to show in 1958 when the first of a series of large American deficits was recorded. It became clear that there was no longer a dollar shortage but a *dollar glut*. This led to speculation in 1960 that there would be a devaluation of the dollar. Because the value of the dollar was defined in terms of gold, a devaluation

TABLE 13.3   The Balance of Payments of the United States, 1960–73

	Current Account Balance	Current Account Plus Long-Term Capital	Official Settlements Balance	Net Change in Liabilities to Foreign Official Agencies	Reserves (−increase)
			(millions of dollars)		
1960	1794	−1191	−3403	1258	2145
1961	3070	2	−1348	742	606
1962	2460	−1028	−2650	1117	1533
1963	3199	−1328	−1934	1557	377
1964	5788	−75	−1534	1363	171
1965	4287	−1829	−1290	67	1222
1966	1943	−2110	219	−787	568
1967	1544	−3723	−3418	3366	52
1968	−962	−1935	1641	−761	−880
1969	−1633	−3637	2739	−1552	−1187
1970	−324	−3778	−9839	7362	2477
1971	−3817	−10559	−29753	27405	2348
1972	−9807	−11235	−10354	10322	32
1973	450	−1026	−5304	5095	209

Source: Economic Report of the President, 1975, p. 351.

would have increased the dollar gold price. People began selling dollars and buying gold, pushing the price to $40 in October 1960. The price was forced down by official American gold sales. Also, speculation slackened in response to statements made by Kennedy at the end of October 1960, in the presidential campaign, that he was committed to maintaining the dollar price of gold.

In November of the following year, the Gold Pool was formed to maintain the gold price in private markets at $35 an ounce by official intervention.[15] The members, and the United States in particular, were afraid that if the private price was allowed to rise above the official price, this might undermine confidence in the value of the dollar. For example, private investors might sell their dollar assets and official holders of dollars might be tempted to convert their dollars into gold in anticipation of an American devaluation. The Gold Pool succeeded in maintaining the gold price until 1968.

The deficit of the United States continued, as Table 13.3 shows. American capital controls failed to halt the flow of American foreign investment as the private sector found ways to evade them. American deficits were reflected in

---

[15]The members were Belgium, Britain, Germany, the Netherlands, Switzerland, and the United States. France declined to join.

surpluses in other countries. Germany in particular had a very strong position in 1960: the economy was booming and there was a trade surplus. The payments surplus led to inflationary pressure, so the Bundesbank pursued a restrictive monetary policy. This raised interest rates and attracted foreign capital. In response to market pressure, the German mark was revalued on March 6, 1961 by 5 percent. The Netherlands revalued the guilder by the same amount the following day. The German revaluation was needed but it was not sufficient to remove the German trade surplus, which, although slightly lower in 1962, rebounded in 1963 and continued throughout the sixties.

The Adjustment Problem

The continuing surpluses of Germany and the Netherlands are examples of the *adjustment problem* in the Bretton Woods system. Surpluses came to be associated with success. Surplus countries that were experiencing export-led growth had little or no incentive to reduce balance of payments surpluses. They argued that deficit countries should take measures to live within their means.[16] Surplus countries could accumulate reserves and avoid adjustment by sterilizing the monetary impact of the balance of payments. (The scarce currency clause was never used.)

In contrast, deficit countries were under pressure to adjust. Deficit countries must sell foreign exchange if they are to maintain the value of their currencies. However, in cases of fundamental disequilibrium, exchange market intervention by itself is not a long-run policy option for deficit countries because they eventually run out of reserves. (Countries can borrow additional funds from the IMF, but the resources available are limited, conditions are attached to the loans, and the IMF charges interest.)

In the long run, a deficit country must take measures to remove the deficit. The choice is between devaluation and domestic deflation of prices and income. Recall that, in the absence of real growth, an increase in the balance of trade implies a fall in domestic absorption. This is true whether devaluation or deflation is used. Naturally, adjustment was not an attractive prospect to a deficit country. Also, under the Bretton Woods system, devaluation came to be regarded as a sign of failure. Misleading analogies were drawn, and unfortunately continue to be drawn, between the strength of a country, the strength of an economy, and the value of its currency. However, although devaluations were delayed, some countries did devalue during the Bretton Woods years.[17]

A second dimension of the adjustment problem was the lack of adjustment between sterling, the dollar, and other currencies. Britain and the United States felt that they could not devalue their currencies because a devaluation of either would have resulted in capital losses for foreign central banks that

---

[16] In recent years, similar arguments have sometimes been used to counter criticisms of German and Japanese trade surpluses.

[17] For example, France devalued in 1957, 1958, and 1969. Yeager (1976) discusses the French franc during the Bretton Woods period (see his Chapter 23).

held stocks of the currencies as reserves. Also, it was felt that such action would have undermined confidence in the international monetary system. It is true that sterling was devalued in November 1967 (from \$2.80 to \$2.40), but not until strong efforts had been made to avoid this course of action.[18] The response of the British balance of payments to the devaluation is a famous example of the J-curve effect.[19]

The Liquidity Problem

Trade grew rapidly during the Bretton Woods period, and there was an increase in the demand for international reserves to offset fluctuations in trade.[20] The *liquidity problem* arose because the Bretton Woods system lacked a mechanism whereby the level of international reserves might increase in line with the need for reserves. The creation of the SDR was an attempt to overcome this problem, but the first allocation of SDRs was not until 1970. Before SDRs, there were three types of international reserve assets: gold, foreign exchange, and a country's reserve position at the IMF.

At the officially maintained price of \$35 per ounce of gold, the private market absorbed the supply of new gold, thus the stock of gold held as international reserves did not increase.[21] IMF quotas were increased, but they did not grow as fast as trade, and they have never been a significant form of international reserves. Increased stocks of foreign exchange (mainly dollars) accounted for over 50 percent of the increase in reserves from 1950 to 1960, and for over 80 percent of the increase in reserves from 1960 to 1970 (see Table 13.4). Apart from availability, there were other reasons to hold dollars. Central banks could convert their dollars into gold, and dollars could be held in the form of short-term interest-bearing assets. However, relying on dollars for increased international reserves meant that the growth of international reserves was determined by the size of American deficits rather than need.

The distribution of new international reserves was also a source of concern. Foreign exchange was accumulated by surplus countries rather than deficit countries, thus the countries that claimed to "need" reserves did not receive them. We must be skeptical of the claims made by deficit countries that they were deprived of needed reserves. It is true that inadequate reserves may force countries to take adjustment measures to offset temporary balance of payments deficits, when it might be better to finance such deficits with reserves and avoid disrupting economic policies. However, deficit coun-

---

[18] The devaluation of sterling is described in Yeager (1976) and Meier (1982).

[19] See Section 9.4.

[20] To offset a 10% fluctuation in \$100 billion of trade requires more reserves than a 10% fluctuation in \$50 billion.

[21] An increase in the price of gold would have increased the value of reserves and increased the quantity of new gold supplied to the monetary authorities. This method of increasing reserves was rejected because countries with the largest gold reserves would have received the largest capital gains. Thus, the plan would have benefited the countries that had "undermined" the system by demanding gold in exchange for dollar reserves, notably France.

TABLE 13.4   The Growth and Composition of International Reserves, 1950–73

	Gold[a]	Foreign Exchange	IMF Position	SDRs	Total
			(billions of dollars)		
1950	35.3	13.3	1.7	—	50.3
1960	37.9	18.5	3.6	—	60.0
1970	37.2	44.8	7.7	3.1	92.8
1971	35.9	75.0	6.4	5.9	123.1
1972	35.6	95.9	6.3	8.7	146.7
1973	35.6	101.8	6.2	8.8	152.4

[a]Valued at $35 per ounce.
Source: IMF *International Financial Statistics.*

tries may be tempted to use reserves in cases of fundamental disequilibria rather than incur adjustment costs. If deficit countries delay adjustment to fundamental disequilibria until reserves are exhausted, any level of reserves will be inadequate.[22]

Confidence

The nature of the *confidence problem* was that people did not have confidence that official exchange rates would be maintained. As a result, speculators shifted funds between currencies. This lack of confidence is not surprising in view of the clear imbalances that existed and the reluctance of countries to adjust. The rules of the system were partly to blame. Countries could only change the value of their currencies in cases of fundamental disequilibrium, not to prevent such disequilibria from developing. However, once a clear disequilibrium had developed, speculators knew which way an exchange rate was likely to change. Deficit countries might devalue, they would not revalue. Therefore, allowing disequilibria to develop encouraged speculation because speculators could not lose.

One factor contributing to the lack of confidence in the value of the dollar was the changes in American assets and liabilities over the Bretton Woods period. At the beginning of the postwar period, the value of American gold reserves was greater than the value of dollars held abroad. But, as foreign official holdings of dollars increased, the ratio fell. The ratio of gold to official short-term liabilities was 7:1 in 1946, 1:2 in 1970, and 1:6 in 1972 (see Table 13.5). This change in the gold backing for dollars undermined confidence in

[22]See Flanders, J., "International Liquidity Is Always Inadequate," *Kyklos* 22 (1969), 519–29.

TABLE 13.5   The Gold and Liabilities of the United States

	(billions of dollars)	
	Gold	Liabilities to Foreign Official Agencies[a]
1946	20.7	3.0
1950	22.8	3.1
1960	17.8	11.9
1970	11.1	24.4
1971	10.2	51.2
1972	10.5	61.6
1973	11.7	66.8

[a] Before 1960, data refer to "long-term and short-term U.S. government obligations."
Sources: U.S. Department of Commerce, *Historical Statistics of the United States: Colonial Times to 1970*, Part 2, p. 869; and *Economic Report of the President*, 1976, p. 281.

the system, because there was clearly not enough gold to allow all central banks to exercise their right to sell dollars for gold should they have chosen to do so.

13.5 THE COLLAPSE OF THE BRETTON WOODS SYSTEM

Speculation and Underlying Weaknesses in the System

Following the devaluation of sterling in 1967, there was speculation that the dollar would be devalued. Between September 1967 and March 1968 the Gold Pool sold about $3.5 billion of gold to meet the demand of people selling dollars for gold in anticipation of a rise in its price. Of these sales, the United States accounted for about $2.4 billion, which was nearly 20 percent of its gold reserves.[23] Faced with a substantial decline in gold stocks, the Gold Pool stopped maintaining the private gold price in March 1968. Official transactions continued at $35 per ounce, but the private market price was allowed to fluctuate; that is, there was a *two-tier* gold market.

This arrangement did not end speculation. The weaknesses in the Bretton Woods system were clear. In May 1968, shortly after the collapse of the Gold Pool, political unrest and a general strike in France led to fears that the franc would be devalued. German surpluses continued, and there was also speculation that the German mark would be revalued again. Speculation carried little risk: even if France did not devalue or Germany revalue, there was little

---

[23] Solomon (1982), p. 119.

danger of losing by selling francs and buying marks. In three days in November 1968, the Bundesbank acquired almost $1.8 billion in an effort to prevent the mark from rising.[24] Speculative sales of French francs for marks accounted for much of these purchases. (Foreign exchange market intervention is usually carried out in dollars, thus the Bundesbank acquired mainly dollars.) The pressure was resisted in 1968 (France adopted exchange controls), but eventually speculators were rewarded when France was forced to devalue (by 11.1 percent in August 1969) and Germany revalued (by 9.5 percent in October).

German Intervention

Germany's experience is a good example of how lack of adjustment led to speculation that exchange rates would change. German balance of payments surpluses were shown by an excess demand for marks. The excess demand for marks can also be described as an excess supply of foreign exchange (dollars). The Bundesbank sold marks (bought dollars) to prevent the mark from rising in value. The sales of domestic currency were sterilized to prevent inflation, thus the German surplus remained. However, as speculators bought marks in anticipation of a revaluation, their sales of foreign currency increased the intervention needed to prevent the mark from rising. International reserves increased, and offsetting the inflationary effects of the surplus by sterilization became more difficult. Eventually, the Bundesbank revalued the mark and speculators were rewarded with a capital gain (see Figure 13.1).

Balance of Payments Imbalances in the Final Years

The American official settlements balance was actually in surplus in 1968 and 1969, although the trade balance fell substantially. This fall in the trade balance can be partly explained by the effects of the Vietnam War, which increased aggregate demand and the demand for imports. The official settlements surplus was largely the result of surpluses in the short-term capital account. A tight monetary policy combined with increasing income led to an increase in interest rates in 1968 and 1969, and induced an inflow of foreign capital. In 1970, American monetary policy was relaxed and interest rates fell. The capital that had flowed into the United States began to flow out, and the United States recorded a record official settlements balance deficit of $9.8 billion, by far the largest deficit the world had seen. In 1971, capital outflows continued and a new record was set with a deficit of $29.8 billion. As part of the 1971 deficit, the United States recorded its first trade deficit of the postwar period.

The American deficit was reflected in surpluses in other countries, which experienced increasing reserves and inflationary pressure. President Nixon adopted the policy of *benign neglect:* since the United States could not devalue (because of the reserve currency role of the dollar), American deficits

---

[24]Yeager (1976), p. 507.

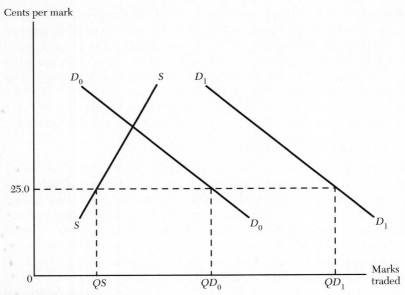

FIGURE 13.1

Germany's Balance of Payments Position in 1968–69
The balance of payments surplus of Germany is shown by the excess demand for marks
(QD_0–QS) at the official exchange rate of 25 cents. The Bundesbank sold marks (bought
dollars) to prevent the mark from rising. Speculators realized that the mark was undervalued and bought marks (sold dollars) on a large scale. Their purchases increased the
demand for marks from D_0D_0 to D_1D_1. When the mark was revalued to 27.3 cents,
speculators were rewarded with a capital gain.

were allowed to take their course in 1970 and 1971. The large capital flows
from Europe to the United States in 1968 and 1969, followed by flows from
the United States to Europe in 1970, led to complaints that European monetary policy was being destabilized by the American balance of payments.[25]

Meanwhile, the strength of the German economy and its balance of payments continued, and, in May 1971, there was speculation that the mark would
be revalued again. The Bundesbank bought $1 billion during trading on May
3 and May 4. It bought about the same amount in forty minutes on Wednesday May 5, before the market was closed.[26] When the market reopened on
May 10 the mark was floated.

---

[25] Dissatisfaction with the performance of the international monetary system was one of the factors
that led to pressure for European monetary integration. This topic is discussed in Chapter 17.
[26] Yeager (1976), p. 512.

The Collapse of Bretton Woods

During mid 1971, attention again turned to the dollar. When American balance of payments figures for the second quarter were announced showing a balance of trade deficit, pressure became stronger. The report by the Reuss Committee (August 6) that the dollar was overvalued intensified speculation. The dollar reserves of other countries were increasing rapidly as they intervened to prevent their currencies rising in value. The United States was faced with requests from foreign central banks for some of these dollars to be converted into gold. The conversion of dollars into gold could quickly have exhausted American gold reserves. Therefore, on August 15, 1971, President Nixon announced the suspension of convertibility of the dollar into gold. This action marked the end of the Bretton Woods system.

The problem of the American balance of payments remained. A 10 percent import surcharge was imposed by the United States and a domestic price and income freeze adopted. Surplus countries were faced with the choice of accumulating inconvertible dollars (if they maintained the value of their currencies against the dollar) or revaluing against the dollar. Negotiations began on a realignment of currencies and in the meantime currencies were floated.

The Smithsonian Agreement

In December, the Group of Ten met at the Smithsonian Institution in Washington and agreed on a series of exchange rate changes.[27] Under the Smithsonian agreement the dollar was devalued (7.9 percent) against gold by raising the price of gold from $35 to $38 per ounce. The yen was revalued (7.7 percent), as were the German mark (4.6 percent) and the Benelux currencies (2.8 percent).[28] The French franc and sterling remained unchanged, and the lira was devalued (1 percent).[29] In addition, exchange rates were made more flexible by increasing the permitted range of variation from ±1 percent to ±2.5 percent. As part of the package, the United States agreed to remove its import surcharge.

The Smithsonian agreement was an attempt to return to fixed exchange rates. However, the parities chosen were influenced by historical and political forces. There was no attempt to make an objective assessment of how currencies might be realigned to reflect underlying competitiveness. Stability was restored temporarily, but, with the benefit of hindsight, it is not surprising that the Smithsonian parities were not sustainable.

During 1972 the American deficit fell, but it was still the second largest ever. Speculative sentiments fluctuated, and intervention was sufficient to

---

[27] The Group of Ten was made up of Belgium, Britain, Canada, France, Germany, Italy, Japan, the Netherlands, Sweden, and the United States. Switzerland was an associate member.
[28] The Benelux is made up of Belgium, the Netherlands, and Luxembourg.
[29] These exchange rate changes refer to a currency's value against gold.

maintain exchange rates.[30] However, at the beginning of 1973, a number of factors combined to cause a crisis that led to the end of the fixed exchange rate system.

In the United States, lack of progress in ending the Vietnam War, a large budget deficit, and the relaxation of price controls led to fears that inflation would increase. The announcement that the trade deficit for 1972 ($6.4 billion) was substantially greater than the deficit for 1971 ($2.3 billion) weakened confidence in the value of the dollar. Meanwhile, German and Japanese trade surpluses continued.

Switzerland led the move to abandon fixed exchange rates, following strong speculation that the Swiss franc would rise in value. Growing uncertainty was increased further by inopportune statements from American officials that the dollar was probably overvalued again. Speculators again turned to the German mark: the Bundesbank bought about $6 billion during the first seven trading days of February 1973.[31] The dollar was devalued for the second time on Monday, February 12, when the gold price was raised to $42.22 per ounce (an 11 percent devaluation). Some countries floated immediately following the devaluation and many more followed in early March when it became clear that the devaluation of the dollar had failed to restore confidence.

Discussions about restoring the system continued for some time afterward, but essentially the Bretton Woods system collapsed in August 1971 when the convertibility of the dollar was suspended. The Smithsonian agreement merely papered over the cracks.

Conclusion: Success or Failure?

Was the Bretton Woods system a success? To some extent, it clearly was. Trade and incomes grew rapidly and there were no major recessions during this period. Also, countries recognized their mutual interdependence and cooperated in the planning and implementation of an international monetary system.

As with the gold standard, we may question whether the international monetary system played a major part in promoting trade and growth. Trade and incomes continued to grow in the seventies following the collapse of the Bretton Woods system. This suggests that fixed exchange rates are not necessary for growth. Also, there are many other explanations for postwar growth, for example, technological progress, faster and cheaper international transport, and improved communications.

---

[30] Britain was forced to abandon its Smithsonian parity in June 1972 following reports of poor economic performance.

[31] Yeager (1976), p. 515. Given that the American official settlements balance deficit for the whole of 1973 was only about $10 billion, the importance of speculation is obvious.

Summary of Main Points

International monetary instability in the thirties induced countries to co-operate in establishing the Bretton Woods system. Currencies were fixed in value relative to the dollar, and thus were fixed in value relative to each other. It was hoped that fixed exchange rates would encourage trade and economic growth.

The *International Monetary Fund (IMF)* was created to oversee the system and promote international consultation and cooperation. Each member country of the IMF has a *quota* that represents its subscription to the IMF. These quotas established a fund of resources available to countries with balance of payments difficulties. The amount a country may borrow is determined by the country's quota. The IMF attaches conditions to the loans it makes, the conditions becoming more stringent as the amount borrowed increases.

The major concern after World War Two was reconstruction. As this progressed, controls on trade were gradually relaxed and international trade grew. At first, the United States ran large surpluses, and it was assumed that this position would continue. However, the United States gradually developed an overall balance of payments deficit. This deficit was reflected in surpluses in other countries, which were forced to buy dollars in order to prevent their currencies from appreciating. Thus, American balance of payments deficits provided the world with dollars that were added to stocks of international reserves.

The Bretton Woods system was characterized by lack of adjustment. Surplus countries had no incentive to adjust, and deficit countries avoided adjustment. Devaluation was seen as a sign of failure and downward adjustment of the domestic price and income levels was resisted because it entailed a cut in welfare. At times, it became clear that existing exchange rates were not sustainable. This encouraged speculators to gamble that an official exchange rate would be changed. The direction of change was obvious from the country's balance of payments problems, thus there was little risk of loss.

The weaknesses of the Bretton Woods system became clear toward the end of the sixties: sterling was devalued in 1967, the agreement to maintain the dollar price of gold in private markets was abandoned in 1968, and in 1969 the French franc was devalued and the German mark revalued. Speculation played a major role in these events and in the collapse of the Bretton Woods system.

In 1971, the United States' deficit reached record levels. Foreign monetary authorities were accumulating large amounts of dollars, partly because of the deficit, but mainly because speculators were selling dollars in anticipation of a devaluation of the dollar. Foreign monetary authorities had the right to convert dollars into gold by buying gold from the United States at $35 per ounce. Faced with the prospect of a depletion of American gold stocks, President Nixon suspended the convertibility of the dollar on August 15, 1971. This marked the end of the Bretton Woods system.

In December 1971, the Smithsonian agreement was signed under which exchange rates were realigned. This agreement lasted a little over one year before it collapsed amid renewed speculation.

Study Questions

1. How were the lessons of the thirties reflected in the Bretton Woods agreement?
2. What was the adjustment problem in relation to
   a. deficit and surplus countries?
   b. the dollar relative to other currencies?
3. Why did confidence in the gold value of the dollar diminish?
4. What were the adjustment, confidence, and liquidity problems? How were they related?
5. How were American deficits financed during the Bretton Woods system?
6. Why did capital flows reduce divergences from official exchange rates during the pre-1914 gold standard, but sometimes force countries to abandon official exchange rates under the Bretton Woods system?
7. Under the Bretton Woods system, the world moved from a period of dollar shortage to dollar glut. Discuss the role of this development in the collapse of the system.
8. Keynes said that the Bretton Woods system was the opposite of a gold standard: "For instead of maintaining the principle that the internal value of a national currency should conform to a prescribed *de jure* external value, it provides that its external value should be altered if necessary so as to conform to whatever *de facto* internal value results from domestic policies."[32] Discuss with reference to the system in theory and practice.

Selected References

Adams, J. *The Contemporary International Economy.* Second Edition. New York: St. Martins, 1985.

Ashworth, W. A. *A Short History of the International Economy Since 1850.* Fourth Edition. New York: Longman, 1987.

Machlup, F. et al. *International Monetary Arrangements: The Problem of Choice.* Report on the Deliberations of an International Study Group of 32 Economists. Princeton, N.J.: Princeton University Press, 1964.

Meier, G. M. *Problems of a World Monetary Order.* Second Edition. New York: Oxford University Press, 1982.

[32] From Keynes' speech to the House of Lords recommending acceptance of the Bretton Woods agreement. Cited in Meier (1982), p. 49.

Nowzad, B. "The IMF and its Critics." Essays in International Finance, No. 146. Princeton, N.J.: Princeton University Press, December 1981.

Rolfe, S. E., and Burtle, J. B. *The Great Wheel: The World Monetary System.* New York: Quadrangle/New York Times Book Co., 1973.

Solomon, R. *The International Monetary System: 1945–1981.* New York: Harper & Row, 1982.

Southard, F. A. "The Evolution of the International Monetary Fund." Essays in International Finance, No. 135. Princeton, N.J.: Princeton University Press, December 1979.

Triffin, R. *Europe and the Money Muddle.* New Haven: Yale University Press, 1957.

Yeager, L. B. *International Monetary Relations.* Second Edition. New York: Harper & Row, 1976.

14

THE
INTERNATIONAL
MONETARY
SYSTEM AFTER
BRETTON WOODS

14.1 INTRODUCTION

The international monetary system that has existed since 1973 is often described as one of floating exchange rates. It is true that the majority of countries have fixed exchange rates, but it has been estimated that, because the major trading nations have floating exchange rates, between two thirds and four fifths of trade is covered by floating exchange rates. Exchange rate policies differ widely, and the rules governing the system are, to put it charitably, rather loose. Thus, some people question whether it is appropriate to refer to present arrangements as a system. We do so for want of a better term.

After examining the rules governing exchange rate policy under the present system, we look at how the system works. Dissatisfaction with the performance of the international monetary system has led to numerous reform proposals. We examine the major characteristics of these proposals, and then end the chapter by investigating the effects of oil price fluctuations.

14.2 LEGAL CHANGES IN THE SYSTEM

Following the collapse of the Smithsonian agreement in 1973, countries discussed possible reforms of the international monetary system. For a while, floating exchange rates were seen as a temporary measure until the shock waves from the collapse of the Bretton Woods system died down. Attempts to establish a reformed international monetary system failed. There were two main reasons. First, international economic conditions were not conducive to the launching of a new system. For example, during 1973–74 the world experienced the first oil crisis, rising inflation, and a dramatic fall in economic growth. Second, many countries had been unhappy with their experience under the Bretton Woods system, especially in the last few years of the system, and they were reluctant to commit themselves to a new international monetary system.

The Jamaica Agreement

The rules governing the present system, such as they are, result from a meeting of the members of the IMF in Jamaica in 1976. At this meeting, the members acknowledged that the Bretton Woods system was no more by amending Article IV of the IMF charter to allow floating exchange rates.[1] Until then, flexible exchange rates had been illegal. Following the Jamaica agreement, countries were free to choose their exchange rate system.

The IMF is required to exercise "surveillance" over members' exchange rate policies, and has adopted three principles to guide these policies:

A. A member shall avoid manipulating exchange rates or the international monetary system in order to prevent effective balance of payments adjustment or to gain an unfair competitive advantage over other members.

B. A member should intervene in the exchange market if necessary to counter disorderly conditions which may be characterized *inter alia* by disruptive short-term movements of the exchange value of its currency.

C. Members should take into account in their intervention policies the interests of other members, including those of the countries in whose currencies they intervene.[2]

Developments that might indicate a need for discussion between the IMF and a member include "protracted large-scale intervention in exchange markets in one direction; an unsustainable level of . . . borrowing or lending for balance of payments purposes; restrictions or incentives affecting current transactions, payments, or capital flows; the pursuit, for balance of payments purposes, of monetary and other domestic financial policies that provide abnormal encouragement or discouragement to capital flows; and behavior of the exchange rate that appears unrelated to underlying economic and financial conditions."[3]

The loose set of guidelines governing the present system leaves much to be desired. The adjustment mechanism is virtually ignored: members are not

---

[1] Article IV had required members to declare par values for their currencies.
[2] *IMF Survey*, Supplement on the Fund, September 1986, p. 7.
[3] *IMF Survey*, Supplement on the Fund, September 1988, p. 8.

supposed to prevent balance of payments adjustment, but no mention is made of when or how adjustment should take place. This lack of attention to adjustment issues is not surprising. Under the present system, countries do not have to maintain fixed exchange rates, therefore, the balance of payments is not as important as it was under the Bretton Woods system. Indeed, there is very little consensus about what significance should be attached to balance of payments statistics.

The agreement reflects a change in attitude: exchange rate stability is to result from economic stability, not vice versa. However, the IMF does not have the power to make countries pursue policies that will lead to exchange rate stability. The statement that a member should use its policies to foster "orderly economic growth with reasonable price stability," is merely a statement of the objectives that would be pursued for domestic economic reasons. It is significant that the IMF is required to exercise "surveillance," not control, over members' policies.

The agreement to promote exchange rate stability is not very significant. Why would countries want to promote instability? With respect to intervention, the guidelines do not specify the exact conditions under which countries should intervene, how central banks should coordinate their intervention, or how appropriate exchange rate targets might be determined. In practical terms, the Jamaica agreement did little more than legalize the status quo.[4]

14.3   EXCHANGE RATES

Many observers feel that the changes in exchange rates since 1973 have been excessive, in the sense that variability has been far greater than seems warranted by changes in economic conditions. In particular, attention has focused on the lack of relationship between inflation rates and exchange rates. Purchasing power parity theory leads us to expect that the exchange rate changes will reflect differential inflation rates. This has not been the case. For example, the inflation rate of the United Kingdom was consistently higher than the rate in the United States, as Table 14.1 shows, and cannot explain the behavior of the dollar-sterling rate shown in Figure 14.1.

The increase in the value of the dollar against the yen from 205 yen per dollar at the beginning of 1981 to over 277 yen per dollar in 1982, and its dramatic decline beginning in fall 1985, is another example (see Figure 14.2). Japan had an inflation rate below that of the United States throughout the eighties. The lack of relationship between inflation and exchange rates illus-

---

[4]One minor change was that the agreement reduced the role of gold in the international monetary system. Currencies and the SDR were no longer to be defined in terms of gold, and gold sales from official reserves were allowed.

TABLE 14.1   Inflation in Six Major Industrial Countries, 1970–87

	1970–79	1980	1981	1982	1983	1984	1985	1986	1987
Canada	7.4	10.2	12.5	10.8	5.8	4.3	4.0	4.2	4.4
France	8.9	13.3	13.4	11.8	9.6	7.4	5.8	2.5	3.3
Germany	4.9	5.4	6.3	5.3	3.3	2.4	2.2	-0.2	0.2
Italy	12.3	21.2	17.8	16.5	14.7	10.8	9.2	5.9	4.7
Japan	7.5	7.7	5.0	2.7	1.9	2.3	2.0	0.6	0.1
United Kingdom	12.5	18.0	11.9	8.6	4.6	5.0	6.1	3.4	4.2
United States	7.1	13.5	10.3	6.1	3.2	4.3	3.6	1.9	3.7

Note: Inflation is measured as the rate of change of consumer prices (IMF *World Economic Outlook*, October 1988, p. 68).
Source: IMF *World Economic Outlook*, October 1988, p. 68.

Dollars per pound

FIGURE 14.1

The Dollar-Sterling Exchange Rate, 1976–1988
Source: IMF *International Financial Statistics.*

trates the conclusion of our discussion of purchasing power parity in Section 6.6, that the theory is not particularly useful for predicting short-term exchange rate changes.

Significance of Exchange Rate Behavior

Exchange rate *volatility* may be important because of the effects on trade and investment or because of the effects of exchange rate misalignments. The effects of exchange rate variability on trade and investment were discussed in Section 8.5. Recall that the availability of forward cover reduces the significance of variability, although some long-term investments may be affected.[5] Empirical studies of the effects of exchange rate variability on trade have produced mixed results depending on the countries chosen and the methodology used. The failure of many studies to find a significant adverse effect of exchange rate variability on trade, and the substantial increase in trade that has

---

[5] Proponents of fixed exchange rates often ignore the risks of operating in a limited number of markets. Diversified international operations allow firms to reduce these risks. Exchange risk is also reduced by diversification.

Yen per dollar

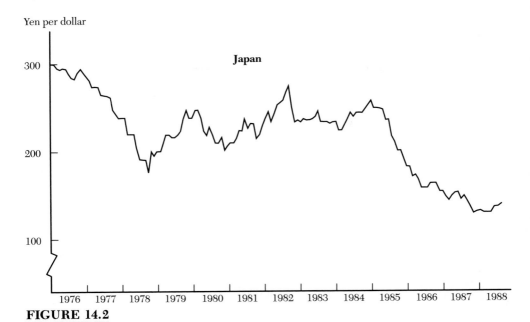

FIGURE 14.2

The Dollar-Yen Exchange Rate, 1976–1988
Source: IMF *International Financial Statistics.*

occurred since 1973, suggest that it is appropriate to conclude that exchange rate volatility does not have a significant adverse effect on trade.[6]

Williamson (1985) argues that currency *misalignments* are potentially more important than volatility and until recently have often been ignored. A currency is misaligned when it is overvalued or undervalued relative to the long-term equilibrium exchange rate. For present purposes, we may think of the long-term equilibrium exchange rate as the long-term trend of the exchange rate. It is clear from the preceding discussion that exchange rates have fluctuated above and below their long-term trends. These divergences can have significant welfare effects.

If a currency is overvalued for a long period, perhaps a year or more, employment and income tend to fall because of the effects of overvaluation on net exports. When the overvaluation ends, the economy cannot return to "normal" as though nothing had happened. There are four effects of overval-

---

[6]The trade effects of exchange rate volatility are considered in "Exchange Rate Volatility and World Trade," IMF Occasional Paper No. 28, 1984. The study failed to find significant effects of exchange rate volatility.

uation. First, markets for traded goods are disrupted. For example, an overvalued exchange rate gives the producers of imports the time and resources needed to establish a distribution network. Also, export markets are lost and must be redeveloped when the currency eventually falls in value. Second, overvaluation is likely to increase protectionist pressures from producers who compete with imported goods. (A lower level of real income can be expected if protectionism does increase.) Third, changes in the allocation of resources lead to adjustment costs. For example, when firms have closed and employment has fallen it takes time and resources to restart production. Finally, future incomes are lower because a current account deficit accompanied by a capital account surplus (net capital inflow) erodes a country's net investment position.

The effects of undervaluation may not be so bad because a current account surplus increases the country's income, and the accompanying capital account deficit (capital outflow) adds to net assets. However, when export industries are established on the basis of an undervalued domestic currency, adjustment costs are born if these industries subsequently have to contract when the currency appreciates.

Therefore, there is reason to believe that exchange rate misalignments, and to a lesser extent exchange rate volatility, are damaging to welfare. Let us review the possible causes of exchange rate misalignments and exchange rate variability.

Explanations of Exchange Rate Behavior

There are two broad explanations of exchange rate misalignments and variability: (1) exchange market inefficiency, such as exchange rate overshooting or instability resulting from capital flows, and (2) unstable or different macroeconomic policies.[7] In practice, it may be difficult to distinguish between these two explanations because capital flows are often related to economic policies.

Overshooting

The theory of *exchange rate overshooting* developed in response to the behavior of exchange rates. Overshooting is one reason why exchange rates do not always reflect contemporaneous economic conditions. For example, one model suggests that when the money supply increases, the interest rate tends to fall, and the currency falls in value. For investors to be willing holders of low interest assets in the currency, they must expect an appreciation, thus the currency depreciates by a large amount and then appreciates. In other words, overshooting leads to a period in which the currency increases

---

[7]Williamson (1985) adds a third explanation of exchange rate behavior: misguided official intervention. Although intervention may not always have been stabilizing, it seems unlikely that large swings in exchange rates can be attributed to misguided official intervention. However, intervention has taken place under floating exchange rates. See IMF (1984).

in value following an increase in the rate of monetary growth. (See the discussion of Figure 10.4.)

Exchange rate overshooting of the long run equilibrium exchange rate seems plausible to many observers. However, knowing that exchange rates may behave in this fashion does not really help policymakers or traders. The problem is to define and measure the long run equilibrium exchange rate. For example, many observers felt that the dollar was overvalued in 1984 and 1985, but there was little agreement on how much.

Exchange Market Instability

Whether markets are inherently stable in the absence of official intervention is impossible to say. Economists often argue that speculative flows of capital can play a stabilizing role, but press and television reports often suggest less desirable behavior. Two effects are: bandwagon effects and bubbles. A *bandwagon effect* is self-propelling once it has begun. Essentially, people jump on the bandwagon and hope to profit by the continuation of the effect. Quite often this behavior pays off. For example, some people profited by joining the gold bandwagon that increased the price of gold from $520 in December 1980 to $850 in January 1981. Some, those who joined the bandwagon too late, lost when it fell by over $200 in the week from January 21 to January 28.

A second effect is the *bubble*. In this case, people may expect a fall in a currency's value, but they are willing to buy and hold the currency because they do not expect the fall to occur just yet. For example, as remarked above, many people felt that the dollar was overvalued in 1984–85, but there was a net capital inflow into the United States, which shows that foreigners were willing holders of dollar assets.

Attempts to test whether these types of behavior are common have been inconclusive. One obvious explanation is that people behave differently at different times. For example, bandwagon effects may have occurred, but whether any particular bandwagon is likely to continue rolling is a very different problem.

The "Problem" of Capital Mobility

Greater capital mobility allows a more efficient allocation of capital. However, fluctuations in capital flows can lead to substantial exchange rate changes over short periods of time. Capital flows may be influenced by expectations of possible future events as much as by current events. Since expectations cannot be observed, it is often difficult to explain or predict the behavior of capital flows. This in turn makes predicting the exchange rate difficult.[8]

---

[8] Although some observers verge on claiming that capital flows are random disturbances, there are often *(ex post)* plausible explanations of capital flows. For example, expectations that real growth would lead to capital gains from higher share prices were probably partly responsible for the capital inflow into the United States in the early eighties.

One "answer" is to tax or prohibit capital flows. This approach can be likened to throwing the baby out with the bath water. The benefits of an international capital market would be lost because "there is no reliable (*ex ante*) method of separating 'productive' from 'nonproductive' capital flows by reference to such factors as maturity (short-term versus long-term) or ownership (portfolio versus direct investment)."[9] Also, capital controls are notoriously ineffective, and it would be difficult to make them effective without considerable invasion of privacy and restrictions on liberty.[10] Exchange rate variability may be the price we have to pay for an international capital market.

Economic Policy

Before examining the effect of domestic policies on exchange rates, let us briefly consider the effect of the exchange rate system on economic policy. One common argument used against floating exchange rates was that floating rates allow countries to pursue inflationary policies without worrying too much about the exchange rate. This freedom, it is alleged, contributed to the problem of international inflation during the seventies. In contrast, it is argued, fixed exchange rates entail a beneficial monetary discipline. It is clearly not true that floating exchange rates necessarily lead to inflation, because inflation has been brought down, as Tables 14.1 and 14.2 show. Also, the diversity of countries' inflationary experiences suggests that countries have a measure of control over their own destinies.[11] We return to this topic in the next section where we discuss the effects of oil price fluctuations.

Policy Instability and Diversity

If governments pursue different economic policies, exchange rates will change. The response of exchange rates to changes in macroeconomic policy changes is not simple. For example, trade responds to changes in exchange rates with a lag, and capital flows may be influenced by expectations as much as by current events. The question of how much we can attribute exchange rate changes to the pursuit of different policies is constantly debated.

Exchange Rates and Anti-Inflation Policies

It is often implicitly assumed that governments favor stable exchange rates. However, it seems that some countries have used exchange rate changes to complement their domestic economic policies. For example, the increase in the value of sterling from $2.0 at the beginning of 1979 to over $2.4 in October 1980 was welcomed, if not deliberately encouraged, by the British gov-

---

[9] IMF (1984), p. 52.

[10] For example, international communications would have to be monitored (to prevent people making private arrangements to avoid the controls).

[11] In Section 10.3 it is shown that flexible exchange rates allow countries to pursue independent monetary policies. This does not imply that inflation is more likely under flexible rates. For example, Germany and Switzerland, which experienced difficulty sterilizing the monetary effects of payments surpluses, probably found it easier to pursue low inflation policies when they abandoned fixed exchange rates.

ernment, because the decline in the prices of imported goods helped reduce inflation. In retrospect, it is clear that sterling was overvalued in 1980; the pound fell to $1.8 in September 1981.

Similarly, the value of the dollar increased as the United States began to reduce its rate of monetary growth (in October 1979). Again, appreciation helped reduce inflation by lowering the cost of imported goods.

The Role of Policy Coordination

Some of the arguments in favor of fixed exchange rates suggest that exchange rate instability is a cause of domestic economic instability. The preceding discussion suggests that the reverse can also be true, that is, exchange rate instability may be the result of domestic economic instability or differences in economic policies. Although governments often claim to be in favor of exchange rate stability, they do not show many signs of wanting to adopt similar policies to achieve this goal.

Lack of Agreement on the Need for Reform

There are two main reasons for the lack of consensus on the need for reform. First, although many people argue that the present system is imperfect, assessments of the importance of the imperfections of the present system differ greatly. (If trade and investment flourish, does it really matter if exchange rates bounce around a little?) Second, some people recognize that imperfections in the present system do not justify a return to fixed exchange rates or the abandonment of exchange market intervention completely. No system will ever be perfect. The real question is whether there is a better alternative. So far, countries have not been able to agree on one.

It is difficult to imagine a fixed exchange rate system that could have survived the economic and political disturbances the world experienced after 1973. For example, there were a number of regional conflicts, two oil crises that were accompanied by financial disruptions, discoveries of natural resources, two recessions, a period of international inflation, and large differences between countries' policies and economic conditions. These were "accommodated without either suspending the operation of exchange markets or implementing wide-scale restrictions on trade or capital flows."[12] Viewed in this way, the performance of the present system has been rather impressive.

REFORM PROPOSALS   14.4

Given the lack of agreement on the need for reform, we shall not give a detailed description of the myriad reform proposals but concentrate on the main issues.

---

[12] IMF (1984), p. 45.

Open or Secret Exchange Rate Targets

Assuming that some degree of intervention is to take place, the first issue is whether the monetary authorities should announce their exchange rate target. If they do so, this may invite speculation against the target, or, if speculators believe that the target will be successfully pursued, stabilizing speculation may result. The degree of confidence in the likelihood of the target being attained plays a crucial role.

Proponents of flexible exchange rates argue that market participants would predict the long run exchange rate and stabilizing speculation would push the market rate towards the long run rate. Proponents of open targets argue that experience under floating exchange rates shows this does not happen. Exchange rate forecasts differ widely, and without the announcement of official targets, there is little to guide exchange market participants. It is feared that secret targets will be ineffective because foreign exchange reserves are small in relation to the volume of transactions in the foreign exchange market. Also, open official targets would place some pressure on the authorities to achieve the announced rate. If targets are secret, the authorities can describe any exchange rate as the "right" rate.

The Degree of Flexibility

A second issue is the degree of flexibility that should be allowed. Governments are probably unwilling to return to a system in which domestic policy is of secondary importance to balance of payments considerations. But, in the absence of common domestic policies, exchange rates must change. If exchange rate changes are infrequent, the direction of change is likely to be predictable. Large flows of capital may take place in anticipation of exchange rate changes.

One solution is to combine wider bands with regular parity revisions. If the band around the target rate is narrow, and the market exchange rate is held down by prolonged intervention, a change in the target rate can lead to a large jump in the market rate, and large profits for speculators. This is shown in Figure 14.3A. If the band is wide, as shown in Figure 14.3B, and the target is revised regularly, the currency may continue rising in value gradually without large jumps occurring each time the target is revised. This reduces the profit from speculation. However, if exchange rate targets are revised too often, or the band width is too great, little extra stability might be gained.

The success of the European Monetary System with regular reviews of targets leads some economists to favor the adoption of such a system by other countries.[13] Analogies between the international monetary system and the European Monetary System are misleading. The European Monetary System is held together by a strong political will that it should continue. It has become a symbol of European unity, and members have shown a willing-

---

[13]The European Monetary System is discussed in Section 17.5.

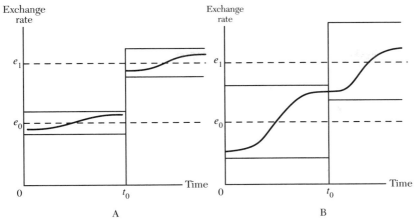

FIGURE 14.3

Intervention Rules and the Profits from Speculation

In both diagrams, there is the same underlying upward trend in the exchange rate. The target rates of exchange are shown by e_0 and e_1. In the first figure (A), the exchange rate is held within the narrow band by official intervention. When the authorities revise the target from e_0 to e_1, speculators profit because the market exchange rate changes by a large amount. In the second figure (B), the band width is wide. The authorities do not intervene on a large scale (the main purpose of the target is to provide guidance to market participants). As the currency approaches the upper limit, the band is moved upward. The market exchange rate does not jump when the target is revised, it merely continues along its trend. The revision of the band does not generate profits for speculators.

ness to sacrifice a degree of independence in policy-making in order to make the system work. Also, some of the members are so closely linked through trade that economic stability is related to exchange rate stability. Finally, because the European Economic Community is much more than an exchange rate system, compromise packages are possible: a member may agree to an exchange rate change in the expectation of gaining from another policy of the Community.

How Much Should an Exchange Rate Change?

A third issue relates to the criteria by which exchange rate changes are decided. A number of *objective indicators* have been proposed to indicate the appropriate size of changes in exchange rates, but a consensus has yet to be reached. Such a consensus is unlikely to emerge because different factors may be important to different countries at different times. Also, an "equilibrium" exchange rate may reflect expectations of future developments as well as current conditions. Therefore, no measure of current conditions will be sufficient. Finally, even if an appropriate indicator could be identified, speculation in advance of exchange rate changes based on the indicator might be a problem. Unfortunately, in the absence of such an indicator, disagreements between countries over the "correct" values of currencies are inevitable.

14.5 OIL PRICES

The use of floating exchange rates since 1973 is partly due to the ability of floating exchange rates to accommodate major disruptions. This was demonstrated shortly after their adoption. In October 1973 the "Yom Kippur" War broke out when Egypt and Syria invaded Israel. Arab oil exporters declared an oil embargo against the Netherlands and the United States because of their ties with Israel. As oil companies bid for the limited supply, the price of oil rose dramatically.

The embargo was a failure in the sense that it did not stop the flow of oil to the United States or the Netherlands, which bought oil from other oil producers and obtained OPEC oil by having it shipped through other countries. However, in a few months the price of oil quadrupled (to $11–12 a barrel) and OPEC discovered that it made sense to restrict output. Because the demand for oil is inelastic in the short run, oil revenue increases when output is cut and the price increases.

Effects of an Increase in the Price of Oil

The increase in the price of oil had two effects on the economies of the oil importers. First, the oil price increase added to the inflation that industrial countries were experiencing. Oil is used in the production and distribution of many goods, so the oil price increase led directly to higher prices for these goods. Inflation spread throughout the economies of the oil importers, as workers in other sectors sought higher wages to compensate for the higher prices. Second, the oil price increase tended to reduce real income because more real income was devoted to paying for oil. (In this respect, oil price increases are similar to increases in taxes.) The effect on world inflation and growth is shown in Table 14.2. Diagrammatically, the income effect can be derived by moving the X-M line downward, as shown in Figure 14.4.[14]

Figure 14.4 leads us to expect a fall in the balance of trade. The effect on current accounts was dramatic, as Table 14.3 shows. The current account surplus of industrial countries of $20.3 billion in 1973 was transformed into a current account deficit of $10.8 billion in 1974. Developing countries were also affected. The current account deficit of non-oil exporting developing countries rose from $11.3 billion in 1973 to $37.0 billion in 1974.

---

[14]The price and income effects can be shown using aggregate demand and aggregate supply: an oil price increase shifts the (short-run) aggregate supply upward and leads to a rise in the price level and a fall in the real level of income.

TABLE 14.2   Inflation and Growth in Industrial Countries, 1972–87

	Inflation	Growth
1973	7.7	6.1
1974	13.1	0.5
1975	11.1	−0.6
1976	8.3	5.0
1977	8.4	4.0
1978	7.2	4.1
1979	9.0	3.4
1980	11.8	1.4
1981	10.0	1.5
1982	7.4	−0.3
1983	4.9	2.8
1984	4.7	5.0
1985	4.1	3.3
1986	2.3	2.7
1987	3.0	3.3

Note: Inflation is measured by the change of consumer prices, growth by the change of real GNP.
Sources: IMF *World Economic Outlook,* 1983, p. 170 and p. 175; and October 1988, p. 60 and p. 67.

TABLE 14.3   Current Account Balances, 1973–77

	(billions of U.S. dollars)				
	1973	*1974*	*1975*	*1976*	*1977*
Industrial countries	20.3	−10.8	19.8	0.5	−2.2
Non-oil developing	−11.3	−37.0	−46.3	−32.6	−28.9
Oil exporters	6.7	68.3	35.4	40.3	30.2

Source: IMF *World Economic Outlook,* 1983, p. 185.

Financing of Oil Deficits

Current account deficits were financed largely through capital flows. The Eurodollar market played an important role in the recycling of funds from oil exporters to oil importers: oil revenue was invested in the Eurodollar market and loaned to oil importing countries.[15] Part of the debt problem of developing countries can be traced to debts incurred at this time.[16] These events

---

[15] The success of the Eurodollar market in recycling funds is discussed in Chapter 16.
[16] The debt problems of LDCs are discussed in Chapter 18.

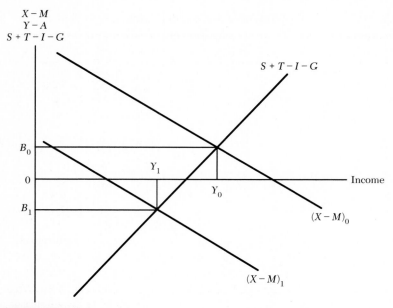

FIGURE 14.4

An Increase in the Price of Imported Goods

An increase in the price of imported oil shifts the $X - M$ line downward. This leads to a fall in the level of income from Y_0 to Y_1, and a fall in the balance of trade from B_0 to B_1.

demonstrated the resilience of flexible exchange rates, since trade and international investment were able to continue against this background. It is doubtful whether fixed exchange rates could have survived.

Commodity Prices and Inflation

We have seen that the effects of an increase in the price of oil can be dramatic. Other commodity prices were also increasing in 1972–73. The proposition that commodity prices cause world inflation cannot be accepted without qualification. An increase in the domestic price level may result from an increase in aggregate demand. Similarly, the prices of commodities may increase in response to an increase in demand. This is exactly what happened in 1971–73. When an increase in demand pushes up prices in general, the increase in commodity prices should be viewed as being part of world inflation, not an independent cause of it. To a large extent the causes of the 1973–74 oil price increase were political, not economic. Therefore, in this case it may be appropriate to think of oil prices as an independent cause of the increase in the price level. However, a single increase in the price level is not inflation.

TABLE 14.4   Current Account Balances, 1978–83

	(billions of U.S. dollars)				
	1978	*1979*	*1980*	*1981*	*1982*
Industrial countries	32.7	−5.6	−40.1	0.6	−1.2
Non-oil developing	−41.3	−61.0	−89.0	−107.7	−86.8
Oil exporters	2.2	68.6	114.3	65.0	−2.2

Source: IMF *World Economic Outlook*, 1983, p. 185.

If inflation is to result from an increase in commodity prices, prices in general must continue to increase. In the long run, this will not happen unless the monetary authorities increase the rate of monetary growth. Commodity price increases represent short run inflationary stimuli that can be neutralized by a tight monetary policy. This course of action would lead to unemployment in the short run (while real incomes are revised downward). The alternative is to accommodate the oil price increase by increasing the rate of monetary growth. (In this case real incomes fall as the price level rises.) The increase in prices and the fall in growth in 1974–75 suggest that countries pursued a policy that partly accommodated and partly offset the inflationary effect of the increase in oil prices.

The Second Oil Price Increase

A second oil price increase occurred in 1978–79, following the disruption of Iranian oil exports as a result of the Iranian revolution. The overall supply was almost unaffected because other producers increased output, but speculative/precautionary inventory accumulation pushed prices upward. The spot price rose from $16.80 in June 1978 to $44.24 on February 21, 1979, and led to higher contract prices. The average price of oil was $29 in 1980 compared to $13 in 1978.[17]

Inflation had moderated slightly in the mid seventies, but was still a problem in 1978–79 at the time of the second oil price increase. There was a move to reduce inflation at the end of the seventies. This, combined with the income effects of the oil price increase, led to a recession in 1980. The recession lasted longer than that of 1974, but inflation did not rise as much as in 1974–75 and was quickly brought under control (see Table 14.4).

Developments in the Eighties

Developments in the oil market over the last decade show the difficulty of maintaining a successful cartel. OPEC's earlier success sowed the seeds that undermined OPEC's market power. High oil prices encouraged the use

---

[17] These figures are taken from Danielsen (1982).

of other forms of energy and led to a slowing in the rate of growth of the demand for oil. Also, high oil prices encouraged other non-OPEC suppliers to enter the market. In an effort to maintain prices, OPEC cut back on production and its share of the world oil market fell. With demand remaining sluggish and oil exporters in need of export revenue, OPEC has had difficulty in reaching agreements on production quotas, and agreements have not lasted. As a result, by 1988 the oil prices had fallen to the levels of 1974 (in nominal terms).

Summary of Main Points

Following the collapse of the Smithsonian Agreement in 1973, countries have allowed exchange rates to fluctuate in response to market forces. However, exchange rates have not been perfectly free and official intervention in the foreign exchange market is common. The loose guidelines for monitoring the present system, which the IMF adopted in 1976, do little more than legalize the status quo. The IMF is supposed to exercise *surveillance* over developments, but the questions of when and how adjustment should take place have not been addressed.

Many people have argued that exchange rate changes have been excessive. Exchange rate changes have not been closely related to inflation differentials, and *real exchange rates* have fluctuated widely. There are many explanations of exchange rate volatility: overshooting, destabilizing capital flows, and unstable/different macroeconomic policies. These explanations of past behavior do little to help us predict future behavior because past behavior need not be repeated. In the absence of a consensus on how to define and measure the long-term exchange rate, measurements of past departures from the long-term rate, and predictions of future behavior, inevitably differ.

Exchange rate *volatility* has traditionally been used as an argument for intervention, and the behavior of exchange rates has led to calls for reform of the present system. Also, swings in exchange rates (taking place over a few years) have focused attention on the effects of *misaligned* exchange rates. Reform proposals include: a *wider band* of permitted fluctuation and regular exchange rate revisions. The objective of these proposals is to set guidelines for official intervention to smooth out exchange rates, while avoiding large changes in official parities that can induce speculation.

There are no signs of agreement on the costs of floating exchange rates or on the type of reform (if any) that is needed. The present (non-) system has allowed international trade and investment to continue despite major international disruptions that would have led to the collapse of a fixed exchange rate system.

The first oil price increase in 1973–74 had a significant effect on international economic relationships and helped prevent a return to a fixed exchange rate system. An increase in the price of oil tends to reduce income and increase prices in oil importing countries. The first oil price increase was followed by lower economic growth and higher inflation.

When oil prices increased again in 1978–79, inflation was already seen as a serious problem, and many countries chose to reduce inflation at the expense of a (short-term) fall in economic growth. The sequence of events was reversed in the mid eighties as lower oil prices helped non-inflationary growth in oil importing countries. The fall in oil prices illustrates the problem of maintaining a successful cartel: demand tends to fall as higher prices induce consumers to conserve energy and look for alternatives, and supply tends to increase as noncartel producers enter the market.

Study Questions

1. In 1985, many people agreed that the dollar was overvalued, but there was little agreement about the extent of the overvaluation. Why might differences of opinion arise?
2. Why might the rules governing the present international monetary system be insufficient to guide policies?
3. What arguments might be used in favor of reform of the present international monetary system?
4. What arguments might be used against changes in the present international monetary system?
5. Why are exchange rate changes inevitable if countries do not pursue similar economic policies?
6. What are the causes of exchange rate variability?
7. What are the effects of
   a. overvaluation?
   b. undervaluation?
8. Critically evaluate the proposals for reform of the international monetary system.
9. What are the effects of an increase in the price of oil on
   a. the value of the dollar?
   b. the level of real income in the United States?
10. What are the effects of a fall in oil prices on
    a. real incomes of oil importers?
    b. price levels in oil importing countries?

Selected References

Adams, J., Ed. *The Contemporary International Economy.* Second Edition. New York: St. Martin's, 1985.

Aliber, R. Z., Ed. *The Reconstruction of International Monetary Arrangements.* New York: St. Martin's, 1987.

Baldwin, R. E., and Richardson, J. D., Eds. *International Trade and Finance: Readings.* Third Edition. Boston: Little Brown, 1986.

Danielsen, A. L. *The Evolution of OPEC*. New York: Harcourt Brace Jovanovich, 1982.

Dornbusch, R. "Exchange Rate Economics: 1986." *Economic Journal* 97 (1987): 1–18.

Federal Reserve Bank of Boston. *The International Monetary System: Forty Years after Bretton Woods*. Proceedings of a conference held in May 1984 at Bretton Woods, New Hampshire.

IMF. "The Exchange Rate System: Lessons of the Past and Options for the Future." IMF Occasional Paper No. 30. 1984.

Koromzay, V., Llewellyn, J., and Potter, S. "The Rise and Fall of the Dollar: Some Explanations, Consequences and Lessons." *Economic Journal* 97 (1987): 23–43.

Meier, G. M. *Problems of a World Monetary Order*. New York: Oxford University Press, 1982.

Solomon, R. *The International Monetary System: 1945–1981*. Second Edition. New York: Harper & Row, 1982.

Williamson, J. *The Exchange Rate System*. Washington, D.C.: Institute of International Economics, revised edition, 1985.

15

COMMERCIAL POLICY IN PRACTICE

Tariffs have been used throughout the history of the United States and they are still in use. This chapter examines the history of U.S. commercial policy against the background of international commercial policy trends, and illustrates how the tariff issue has changed over the last two centuries. It is interesting that many of the arguments for tariffs that are used today were made many years ago.

Europe and America followed different courses during the nineteenth century and for this reason their experiences are examined in different sections. Then we look at the interwar years when their experience was more alike: protection increased and the collapse of world trade contributed to the depression of the early thirties. The General Agreements on Tariffs and Trade (GATT) reflected a consensus that barriers to trade were detrimental. Finally, we examine how GATT has performed and the commercial policy issues that exist today.

COMMERCIAL POLICY BEFORE WORLD WAR ONE 15.2

Mercantilism

The mercantilist era lasted from about 1500 to 1750. The objective of countries during this period was to achieve and maintain an export surplus in order to acquire precious metals, in particular gold. There were many reasons why countries sought to accumulate gold. One was that gold reserves could be used to finance wars, thus additions to the stock of gold reserves added to

299

the power of the state. Another reason was that thrift and the accumulation of wealth were thought of as good habits, and what was good for individuals was good for countries. Finally, it was thought that general economic activity could be increased by encouraging exports and discouraging imports.

The mercantilist objective of accumulating precious metals was pursued with the use of tariffs on imports and subsidies on exports. Countries had to import raw materials, but laws ensured that the materials were carried on domestically owned ships in order that the profits from transportation should be earned by domestic firms. A strong navy was needed to protect domestic shipping (and could also harass foreign vessels).

The British Free Trade Movement

The classical economists, Adam Smith, David Ricardo, and John Stuart Mill, rebelled against the mercantilist doctrine. They argued that specialization increases output and free trade increases welfare. Exports and imports were neither good nor bad in themselves, but part of the process of specialization and trade.

The free trade movement was strongest in Britain, the most important trading nation of the time. One barrier to the success of the free trade lobby was that the British government depended on tariff revenue. (Tariffs levied for the purpose of raising revenue are called *revenue tariffs.*) Thus, although a free trade movement was under way at the beginning of the nineteenth century, tariffs were increased when Britain went to war with France. After the war, British tariffs were reduced as the need for revenue decreased. With the introduction of income taxes in 1842, it became possible to make significant progress towards free trade.

The Corn Laws

However, opposition to free trade continued in Britain. British agriculture was protected by the Corn Laws under which tariffs were levied on imported wheat. Farmers opposed the abolition of the Corn Laws because protection raised the price of domestic wheat. The argument used by landowners was that English rents were so high that tariffs were needed to help domestic farmers compete with imported grain.

Ricardo argued that the proponents of tariffs did not understand the determination of land prices. In his view, the high rents were the result of protection. The Corn Laws raised the price of food and increased the revenue from farming. As a result, the demand for land increased. Ricardo assumed that agricultural land had no other uses and was fixed in supply. Thus, the increase in the demand for land was reflected in higher rents and land prices. Figure 15.1 illustrates Ricardo's argument.

Ricardo argued that agricultural protection is not necessary to ensure domestic supply. In his view, land would not disappear or be left idle if agricultural support were eliminated. It would always be better for the owner to earn as much as possible from the land. Thus, Ricardo was able to argue for

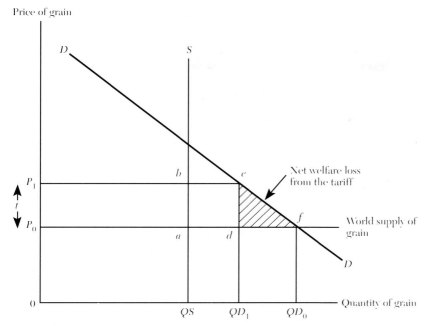

FIGURE 15.1

Ricardo's Argument against the Corn Laws

The domestic supply of grain is determined by the amount of land and is therefore perfectly inelastic, as shown by the vertical supply line at QS. The world supply of grain is shown by a horizontal line because Britain is a small country and cannot affect the world price. Under these conditions, a tariff (t) that raises the domestic price from P_0 to P_1 does not increase the domestic quantity supplied but does reduce the quantity demanded from QD_0 to QD_1. Consumer surplus falls by P_0P_1ef, farm revenue increases by P_0P_1ba, and government revenue increases by $abcd$. Thus, there is a net loss of welfare of def. Farmers gain temporarily from an increase in revenue, but as the demand for land increases, higher revenue is offset by higher rents and land prices.

the removal of the Corn Laws without worrying about the effect on the domestic supply of agricultural produce.[1] The problem for the free trade movement in the nineteenth century was that the landowners resisted the threat to the value of what they owned. A similar debate continues today. High land prices are still frequently used as a justification for agricultural support.

---

[1] Perhaps the assumption that the domestic supply of agricultural products is unaffected by changes in tariffs (because domestic supply is perfectly inelastic) is unrealistic. However, the assumption sometimes used by modern supporters of protection, that domestic supply will disappear (because domestic supply is perfectly elastic) if tariffs are reduced or not enacted, is equally unrealistic.

The Corn Laws were repealed in 1846. Their repeal was not the result of a general acceptance of Ricardo's analysis, but was because restricting imports of grain while people were starving during the Irish famines of 1845–46 led to widespread condemnation of the Corn Laws. The Crimean War (1854–56) increased the need for revenue and halted Britain's free trade movement temporarily. After the war, the movement was able to resume: the budget of 1860 removed most of the tariffs that remained and Britain became a free trade nation.

The Spread of Free Trade

Britain negotiated commercial treaties with many countries. One of the most important was the Cobden-Chevalier Act of 1860 between Britain and France. An interesting feature of Britain's commercial treaties was the inclusion of a *most-favored-nation* clause, that is, when a country signed a treaty with Britain it automatically received any concessions made by Britain to other countries. In other words, a signatory was to be accorded tariff concessions equal to those given to the most favored nation.[2] This type of clause prevents trade discrimination and turns bilateral agreements into multilateral agreements.

Britain and France negotiated treaties with other European countries. The 1862 treaty between France and the German customs union, the Zollverein, was a high point in the free trade movement. Other countries also moved toward free trade, and conventions studied ways of improving communications (canals, railways, postal services, and the like). This free trade movement contributed to a rapid increase in world trade. Over the whole period 1800–1913 trade grew by 33 percent per decade; during the shorter period 1840–1870 trade grew by 53 percent per decade.[3]

The Protectionist Trends of 1880 Onward

Toward the end of the nineteenth century, broad trends were leading towards protection. International competition, and hence demands for protection, increased as industrialization spread and communications improved. This was the era when railroads and steamships revolutionized transport. Growing nationalism added to demands for protection to help domestic industries, and tariffs provided revenue to finance new government programs and armaments expenditure. European nationalism also led to a competition for colonies. The division of Africa occurred at this time.

Against this background, two events helped stop the European free trade

---

[2] One result of Britain's free trade policy was that colonies began to lose the preferential access to the British market that they had enjoyed. Canada turned to trade with the United States and signed a trade treaty in 1854. Although this treaty did not last, it helped the development of a close relationship between the two countries that continues to this day. The Canada–United States trade agreement reached in 1987 is the most recent attempt to reduce barriers between the two countries.

[3] Kenwood and Lougheed (1983), pp. 79–80.

TABLE 15.1   Percentage of Federal Revenue from Customs Duties

1789–91	99.6
1850	91.0
1910	49.4
1920	4.9
1970	1.3

Source: U.S. Department of Commerce, *Historical Statistics of the United States: Colonial Times to 1970*, pp. 1105–6, Washington, D.C., 1975.

movement: the world depression of 1873–79, and a flow of cheap grain from the United States and Russia to Europe. Demands for protection came from both industry and agriculture. The result was that after about 1880, trade restrictions began to grow again. However, in general, trade was not seriously impaired. The countries that remained most committed to free trade until 1913 were Britain, Denmark, and Holland.

U.S. COMMERCIAL POLICY BEFORE 1913   15.3

In contrast to the European experience, the United States followed a protectionist policy throughout most of the nineteenth century. Tariffs were first used in the United States as a way of raising government revenue. In the decade after independence, states levied their own tariffs. The Constitution of 1787 ended state tariffs and gave the right to levy tariffs to the federal government. When Congress met in 1789, the first national tariff act was passed. At that time, customs duties accounted for virtually all federal government revenue. The tariff rates were generally low and changes in tariffs usually reflected the need for more revenue or the collection of too much revenue.

Revenue remained the main justification for tariffs until after the Civil War when the infant industry and cheap labor arguments began to influence policy. During the first decade of the twentieth century, tariff revenue still accounted for about 50 percent of federal government revenue. After that, tariffs declined in importance as government expenditure increased and other forms of taxation, notably the income tax, were developed (see Table 15.1).[4]

Early Tariff Arguments

The *infant industry argument* was put to Congress by Alexander Hamilton in 1791, but because American manufacturing was in its infancy and was not a powerful lobby, the argument did not have an impact on legislation at

---

[4]The Sixteenth Amendment to the Constitution in 1913 made possible the introduction of the income tax in the Underwood Tariff Act of 1913 to replace lost revenue from tariff cuts.

that time. As manufacturing grew in importance, the power of the protection-ist lobby grew. Manufacturing benefited from the disruption of trade caused by blockades during the Napoleonic Wars and the Anglo-American War of 1812–14. Following the end of hostilities and the resumption of trade, the young American industries faced competition, and protectionist pressure helped shape the Tariff Act of 1816. The pressure continued and further protectionist policies were adopted. The trend culminated in the Tariff Act of 1828, some-times known as the Tariff of Abominations. This act increased tariffs to over 45 percent. For some goods the new tariff rates were prohibitive.

The early tariff debate in the United States evolved into a conflict be-tween the interests of Northern manufacturers and Southern cotton produc-ers. The manufacturers wanted protection from imports. The Southern cotton producers opposed tariffs: they did not want to pay higher prices for manufac-tured goods to support domestic manufacturers, free trade was seen as part of the system of slavery that the South wanted to maintain, and they did not want to risk foreign retaliation that might jeopardize the export market for their cotton.

The Tariff Act of 1828 was the result of a political maneuver that back-fired. Southern members in Congress hoped to ensure that no tariff legislation would be passed. To do this, they tried to make the bill unacceptable to both North and South. The bill included high tariffs on manufactured goods that would lead to opposition from Southerners and high tariffs on raw materials used by the Northern manufacturers. To the surprise of the Southerners, the bill was passed. Opposition to the high tariffs was strong, especially in the South, and there was even talk of secession. The tariff issue was seen as a question of states' rights. South Carolina passed an act saying that the tariff would not be effective in that state. This prompted President Andrew Jackson to announce that he was prepared to use the military to enforce national laws. The dispute was resolved by the Compromise Tariff Act of 1833, which pro-vided for the gradual reduction of tariff rates.

Over the following years tariffs drifted down, in part because tariff reve-nue was too high. The downward trend was checked briefly by the Tariff Act of 1842, but the Acts of 1846 and 1857 continued the reduction of tariffs. By 1860, the United States was as close to free trade as it was to become in the nineteenth century. An indication of the evolution of tariff rates is given by Figure 15.2.

American Tariffs 1860–1914

The trend towards free trade ended when the Civil War increased the need for revenue. Tariff rates were increased with the passage of the Morrill Tariffs during 1861–63. At the end of the Civil War, the antiprotectionist lobby failed to bring tariffs down. Industries had been established, or ex-tended behind the high tariffs introduced during the war, and the people associated with these industries argued that they would be ruined by tariff reductions. It was also argued that American industries could not compete

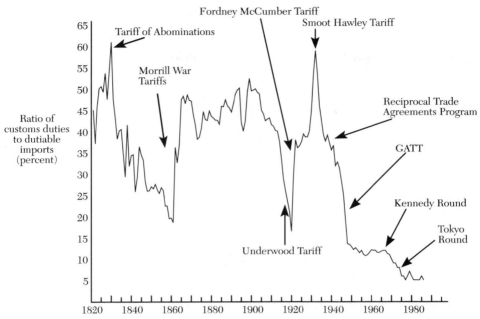

FIGURE 15.2

U.S. Tariffs, 1821–1986

Note: The ratio of tariff revenue to the value of dutiable imports is an imperfect measure of the level of protection. One problem is that goods that are free from duties are ignored, thus changes in the percentage of imports that are free from duty are not shown by the ratio. Also, prohibitive tariffs are not shown by the ratio because there is no tariff revenue when there are no imports. (*Sources:* U.S. Department of Commerce, *Historical Statistics of the United States from Colonial Times to 1970,* Washington, D.C., 1975; and *Statistical Abstract of the United States,* Washington, D.C., 1988.)

with industries in other countries that had access to cheap labor (the *cheap labor argument*).

The protection of American industries from the Civil War until 1913 shows the difficulty of removing tariff protection once it has been granted. American industries grew, but they came to depend on tariffs and the pressure for protection continued. It is interesting to note that the Republican party, which drew support from industrial areas in the East and agricultural areas in the Midwest, was the party of protectionism. Manufacturers and workers favored protection to support domestic industries, whereas farmers were persuaded that tariffs maintained higher incomes in industrial areas and meant better markets for them. The Democratic party was split on the issue, but was more in favor of free trade than the Republican party. For example, Southern farmers favored free trade, but there was strong support for protection from Democrats representing manufacturing interests in Pennsylvania.

The split in the Democratic party resulted in the failure of an attempt to reduce tariffs in 1886. This prompted President Grover Cleveland (a Democrat) to devote the whole of his annual message in December 1887 to the issue of tariffs. He argued that high tariffs were generating too much revenue and pointed to the inequity of taxing consumers to support manufacturers.[5] The tariff issue figured prominently in the 1888 presidential election, but although Cleveland won more votes Harrison (a Republican) received a majority of the electoral college. The Republican party's success was followed by higher tariffs with the passage of the McKinley Tariff Act in 1890. President Cleveland was returned to office in 1892 with Democratic control over both houses of Congress, and slightly lower tariffs were achieved with the passage of the Wilson-Gorman Tariff Act of 1894.

The Republican party led by William McKinley was returned to power in 1896, and the following year tariffs were increased by the Dingley Tariff Act. Tariff rates remained high until 1913 when the Underwood Tariff Act was passed. Again, the tariff reduction was carried out by Democrats. However, although tariffs were eventually reduced, the American market effectively remained closed to international competition because World War One disrupted international trade and provided greater protection than tariffs.

15.4 COMMERCIAL POLICY FROM 1918 TO 1945

Protectionism began to take hold before World War One, but after the war protectionist pressures increased internationally as countries concentrated on national economic interests. The international trend towards protectionism led the League of Nations to convene a conference in 1927 to address the issue. After temporary success in reducing protectionism, the problem increased significantly in the early thirties.

U.S. Policy in the Early Twentieth Century

When World War One ended, protection was adopted before international trade had recovered. In part, postwar protection reflected desires for self-sufficiency and security that had grown during the war. Also, industries that had prospered while trade had been disrupted now demanded protection. The victory of the Republican party in 1920, still the party of protection at this time, paved the way for an increase in tariffs. Agricultural prices were

---

[5] Ratner (1972) contains many important historical readings, including the text of Cleveland's message.

declining and representatives of agricultural states were willing to support any measures they thought would strengthen domestic markets.

The Fordney-McCumber Tariff of 1922 raised American tariff levels to 38 percent.[6] This act made use of the principle of the *scientific tariff* by giving the president the authority to increase or decrease tariff rates by up to 50 percent to compensate for differences between foreign and domestic costs. The term "scientific tariff" might lead one to guess that such tariffs are desirable. This would be a mistake. Tariffs determined in this way could virtually eliminate trade by removing one of the reasons for trade: differences in production costs. Only products that the domestic country cannot produce at all would continue to be imported. For example, imports of natural resources that are not available domestically would not be affected, and imports of some agricultural products requiring special climates could continue (unless the climate could be duplicated domestically at higher cost).

The Smoot-Hawley Tariff of 1930

The protectionist climax was reached with the passing of the Smoot-Hawley Act in 1930, which drastically curtailed American imports. Originally designed to provide moderate support to farmers, the proposed tariff levels were increased during the passage of the act in response to the stock market crash of 1929 and the onset of the Great Depression. The proposed tariffs escalated as votes were traded in Congress: members supported tariffs to help other members' regions in return for tariffs to help their own regions. In particular, Western support of tariffs for manufactured goods was conceded in exchange for Eastern support of agricultural tariffs. The act raised the level of tariffs to over 53 percent, the highest level in U.S. history. Over one thousand American economists signed a petition asking President Herbert Hoover to veto the bill, and other countries made strong protests against it. The strength of these protests reflected the importance of the American economy in the world. American commercial policy was no longer purely a domestic issue.

The Spread of Protectionism

The effect on imports of the U.S. depression and the Smoot-Hawley tariff was devastating: merchandise imports declined from $4.3 billion in 1929 to $1.3 billion in 1932. Although tariff rates increased, duties collected declined from $580 million to $260 million (because of the fall in imports). Other countries retaliated against American protectionism with their own tariffs; over sixty countries increased their tariffs within two years. (The policies adopted by foreign countries were also a response to their own unemployment problems.) For example, Britain passed the Import Duties Act in 1932, which

---

[6]This act, and the Smoot-Hawley Tariff of 1930, made it difficult for countries to repay money they had borrowed from the United States. Some present policies such as the Multifiber Agreement (see below) have a similar effect.

established a 10 percent *ad valorem* tariff on all imports except for food and raw materials and goods from countries in the Empire. Some countries, in particular France, resorted to import quotas.[7] Another problem was a proliferation of exchange controls, which can have effects similar to barriers to trade. Exchange controls were widely used by Germany.

The escalation of barriers to trade had a disastrous effect on world trade: between 1929 and 1933 the volume fell by one third. American merchandise exports fell from $5.2 billion in 1929 to $1.6 billion in 1932. The escalation of protectionism in the thirties did not cause the Great Depression (which started slightly before the protectionist shift); however, there is no doubt that protectionism worsened the depression.

Rolling Back Protectionism

The dangers of protectionism were recognized and a movement away from tariffs began. The first step to bring down tariffs was taken in 1934 when the first Reciprocal Trade Agreements Act was passed by the United States. The act gave the president the power to negotiate tariff reductions of up to 50 percent. This action was supposed to take tariff policy out of the political arena. It was hoped that protectionism would not be used to support special interests, as had happened when Congress passed the Smoot-Hawley tariff. In requesting the authority from Congress, President Franklin Roosevelt emphasized the gain from increased exports and said that American producers would not be hurt. Although an overall gain from trade was to be expected, it was inevitable that opening up the American market to more competition from imports would hurt some producers.

Under the Reciprocal Trade Agreements Act, the United States negotiated bilaterally with the chief supplier of a product. Agreements reached under the act included the most-favored-nation clause whereby a tariff reduction negotiated with the chief supplier of a product was extended to imports of the product from other countries that signed commercial treaties with the United States. Between 1934 and 1945, the United States negotiated treaties with twenty-seven countries. These treaties covered almost two thirds of American dutiable imports and reduced tariffs by an average of 44 percent.[8] The success of the Reciprocal Trade Agreements Act may be explained partly by the high tariff levels that were in place after Smoot-Hawley.

For the United States, the mid thirties marked the beginning of a new era. The dangers of protectionism were recognized and the United States began to pursue a policy of free trade for the first time in her history. The experience of the thirties still influences economic policy. For example,

---

[7] By 1937, 58% of French imports were subject to quotas. (Pollard, S., *Peaceful Conquest: The Industrialization of Europe 1760–1970*, Revised Edition, New York: Oxford University Press, 1982, p. 302.)

[8] Evans (1971), p. 7.

the 1988 *Economic Report of the President* uses this period as an example of the dangers of protectionism: "The lesson from Smoot-Hawley is that passage of protectionist legislation by the United States will increase protectionist activities in the rest of the world, poison the international climate for trade diplomacy in general, and slow the process of trade liberalization for years to come. Since the United States is a major trading nation, it could suffer major economic losses in the event of increased global protectionism" (p. 149).

THE GENERAL AGREEMENT ON TARIFFS AND TRADE   15.5

The First GATT Agreement

The experience of the thirties convinced most countries that trade was mutually beneficial. In 1944, the Bretton Woods agreement was signed establishing a fixed exchange rate system. It was hoped that exchange rate stability would encourage international trade. However, the Bretton Woods agreement would have been insufficient by itself: international trade could not have flourished if countries had maintained trade barriers. The problem of barriers to trade was addressed by the *General Agreement on Tariffs and Trade (GATT)*.

GATT is an international organization based in Geneva, Switzerland. It began in 1947 with a meeting of a group of countries that wanted to reduce trade barriers.[9] The agreement went beyond tariff concessions and included a code of conduct and procedures for the resolution of trade disputes by negotiation. Subsequent agreements have reduced tariff barriers further and included codes of conduct relating to non-tariff barriers to trade. More than 90 countries are now members of GATT and more than 80 percent of international trade is covered by GATT agreements.

Principles

One of the most important principles of the GATT is that of *nondiscrimination*. This principle is reflected by the incorporation in the GATT of the most-favored-nation clause, that is, if the tariff on imports from one country is reduced, the tariff on all imports of the same good from other GATT members must be reduced.[10] The tariff concessions resulting from bilateral negotiations at the 1947 conference automatically became multilateral as a result of the application of this principle. There are two exceptions to the principle of nondiscrimination. First, when a free trade area or customs union is formed,

---

[9]The original GATT treaty was to have been a step toward the creation of an International Trade Organization (ITO), which would have monitored international trade as the International Monetary Fund monitors international monetary developments. The ITO charter was never ratified because of fears that the charter would interfere with the independence of domestic policies.

[10]The United States gives most-favored-nation status to most countries, an exception being the Soviet Union.

countries may apply lower tariffs on trade with members than on imports from nonmembers. Second, lower tariffs may be applied to imports from less developed countries.

A second important GATT principle is that in general quotas are not permissible. One reason is that they violate the principle of nondiscrimination: it is difficult to allocate a quota without discriminating between alternative sources of supply. Which producers get the quota? Also, the degree of protection given by quotas is often difficult to judge. The GATT signatories were anxious that international trade disputes should be avoided by making barriers to trade "transparent," that is, ensuring that the nature and degree of protection be clear. Quotas are allowed when countries are experiencing balance of payments difficulties or when the quotas are part of an economic development program. At the request of the United States, another exception was made for quotas that are needed as part of a domestic agricultural program.

GATT in Practice

The 1947 negotiations achieved an average reduction in tariffs of 35 percent covering 54 percent of dutiable imports (giving a weighted average reduction of 18.9 percent).[11] The following four rounds of tariff reductions were not so successful, and it seemed that there was little prospect of significant benefits from further bilateral bargaining for tariff cuts on particular products.

The Kennedy Round

The creation of the European Economic Community and development of its policies led to fears that access to the European market would be lost and prompted further efforts to control trade barriers. At the request of the Kennedy administration, the Trade Expansion Act of 1962 gave the president the power to negotiate multilaterally for across-the-board tariff reductions of up to 50 percent.[12] After lengthy negotiations, agreement was reached in 1967 on tariff cuts of 35 percent on manufactured goods.[13] These tariff negotiations affected 64 percent of American dutiable imports and came to be called the *Kennedy round.* This round succeeded in reducing the average tariff rates for the major industrial countries to less than 10 percent.

Trade Adjustment Assistance

An interesting aspect of the legislation authorizing the U.S. administration to negotiate on tariff issues was the allocation of funds to compensate workers who became unemployed as the result of trade and to help them retrain for other activities. The logic was that *trade adjustment assistance (TAA)*

---

[11] Evans (1971), p. 12.

[12] The common external tariffs of the European Economic Community reflected compromises among the members. Across-the-board tariff reductions were less likely to upset the balance of national interests than tariff reductions that varied from one good to another.

[13] Evans (1971), pp. 281–3.

would help people accept changes caused by trade and allow society to enjoy the gains from trade. However, TAA did not have an important impact because few workers qualified for the programs, and where they did qualify the funds were usually used for income support rather than retraining.

The logic of TAA was dubious. Why should workers who become unemployed through trade be treated differently from workers who become unemployed for other reasons? Also, in practice it is difficult to tell whether trade was the cause of an industry's decline. Which came first: the industry's poor performance or the imports? For example, poor performance might be caused by compensation increasing faster than productivity.[14] TAA expired in 1985 and was not renewed. The Reagan administration felt that benefits paid to unemployed workers provided an incentive to delay their search for new positions.[15] Also, it was said that TAA was not needed because there were already programs to help retrain and relocate unemployed workers.[16]

The Tokyo Round

Another successful round of negotiations, the *Tokyo round*, began in 1973 and was completed in 1979. The Tokyo round was a surprising achievement in view of the uncertainty and instability in the international monetary system at the time. In this round, a formula was adopted that ensured that the higher the tariff, the greater the cut in the tariff would be. This approach was intended to achieve more uniformity of tariff rates. The negotiations covered about 90 percent of industrial trade among developed countries and, for the United States, resulted in an average tariff cut of 31 percent on manufactured goods. Tariff rates before and after the Tokyo round are shown in Table 15.2.

Since many tariffs had already been reduced to low levels by earlier agreements, one of the most significant aspects of the Tokyo round was that the problem of non-tariff barriers was tackled. Agreements were reached in six areas: subsidies and countervailing duties, antidumping procedures, government procurement, technical barriers to trade, customs valuation, and import licensing. The codes that were negotiated are general agreements that it is hoped will be replaced by more specific regulations. Although the Tokyo round made some progress towards tackling non-tariff barriers, not all GATT members have agreed to the codes.[17] Also, many important non-tariff barriers, such as voluntary export restraints, are not covered by the codes. Non-tariff barriers remain one of the main obstacles to the growth of trade (see

---

[14] Some economists argued that the reason the automobile and steel industries face strong competition from imports is because of excessive wage settlements.

[15] This logic would seem to justify the abolition of all benefit payments to the unemployed.

[16] The administration's views are summarized in the 1986 *Economic Report of the President*, pp. 126–8.

[17] The United States is a signatory of all six codes. A list of the signatories to each code and descriptions of the codes are given in Morrison, A. V., "Tokyo Round Set Rules for Nontariff Measures," *Business America*, July 7, 1986, pp. 11–13.

TABLE 15.2   Tokyo Round Tariff Cuts by Stage of Processing, Selected Countries

(percent)

Country and Period	All Industrial Products	Raw Materials	Semi-Manufactures

Finished
Manufactures

United States:			
Rates before Tokyo	6.5	0.9	4.5	8.0
Rates after Tokyo	4.4	0.2	3.0	5.7
Percent cut	31	77	33	29
European Community:			
Rates before Tokyo	6.6	0.2	5.1	9.7
Rates after Tokyo	4.7	0.2	4.2	6.9
Percent cut	29	15	27	29
Japan:			
Rates before Tokyo	5.5	1.5	6.6	12.5
Rates after Tokyo	2.8	0.5	4.6	6.0
Percent cut	49	67	30	52
Canada:			
Rates before Tokyo	13.6	1.0	14.8	13.8
Rates after Tokyo	7.9	0.5	8.3	8.3
Percent cut	42	48	44	40

Note: Observe that the tariffs are higher on manufactured goods than on raw materials. This results in higher rates of effective protection for manufactures in developed countries than the rates that would result from a uniform tariff structure.
Source: Reproduced from the 1989 *Economic Report of the President*, p. 156. (See original for sources of data.)

below). One reason there are now more non-tariff barriers is that GATT has been a victim of its own success: countries have turned to non-tariff barriers because GATT agreements prevent them from using tariffs.

15.6 RECENT ISSUES IN COMMERCIAL POLICY

The Uruguay Round

The *Uruguay round* of GATT negotiations was launched in Punta del Este, Uruguay, in 1986. It is too early to say what the outcome of the Uruguay round will be, but there are many issues that need to be addressed. In particular, earlier rounds have failed to control trade barriers in the agriculture and service sectors, and non-tariff barriers have escalated.

Agriculture and Commercial Policy

GATT agreements have done little to promote free trade in agriculture. Protection has helped Europe and the United States become self-sufficient in most of the products that do not have tropical climate requirements. Not only have these markets been denied to other countries, Europe and the United States dispose of their surplus produce by dumping it on world markets or donating surpluses as food aid. The result is that world prices of agricultural products are unstable and artificially low. Also, export markets have been lost for other countries. The recent resurgence of interest in agricultural issues might arise from a genuine desire to enjoy the benefits of freer trade. A plausible alternative explanation is that the agricultural policies of Europe and the United States have become so expensive that reform can no longer be avoided.

Services

Another omission from GATT that has begun to attract attention is that of trade in services. The service sectors of developed countries have grown rapidly in recent years. For example, services have grown from 31 percent of U.S. output in 1950 to 50 percent in 1985. International trade in services accounts for more than 20 percent of world trade. Although the importance of the service sector is clear, removing obstacles to trade in services raises problems that freeing trade in goods does not.[18]

Goods can be allowed to enter a country without the producer operating within the country. Some services, such as construction, require labor and capital to be located near the consumer. Other services, such as banking and insurance, may be provided from a distance, but local companies often have a competitive advantage over foreign companies (for example, because they have lower communications costs and can be more responsive to the needs of their consumers). Increasing trade and competition in services implies relaxing rules that prevent foreigners from establishing companies or which restrict labor and capital mobility between countries. Countries adopt rules governing foreign access for cultural, economic, and political reasons, and it will be difficult to achieve widespread agreement that these rules should be relaxed.

Developed countries are likely to have a comparative advantage in capital-intensive services using modern technology, for example, communications and financial services. Agreement to allow greater trade in this type of service is possible. Developing countries do not feel that they will gain from these changes because many of their service industries are in their infancy and would not be able to compete. Also, the comparative advantage of developing countries probably lies in labor-intensive services where the barriers are related to immigration issues. It may be difficult to reach agreements allowing trade

---

[18] The following comments draw on the World Bank *World Development Report 1987*, New York: Oxford University Press, 1987.

in labor-intensive services. For example, is the United States ready to accept Korean and Indian construction teams?

Regional Trade Agreements

Although restrictions affecting particular sectors are a problem, another more general problem facing developing countries is the formation of customs unions between rich countries. Customs unions and free trade areas are permissible exceptions to the GATT principle of nondiscrimination. When a group of countries forms a free trade area or a customs union, member countries may levy tariffs on imports from nonmembers even though they do not impose tariffs on imports from other member countries.

Two famous groups that have made use of this provision are the *European Free Trade Area (EFTA)* and the *European Economic Community (EEC)*. The members of the EEC are: Belgium, Denmark, France, Germany, Greece, Ireland, Italy, Luxembourg, the Netherlands, Portugal, Spain, and the United Kingdom. The members of EFTA are: Austria, Finland, Iceland, Norway, Sweden, and Switzerland. Over the years EFTA has lost members as countries have switched to the EEC. Austria may be the next country to switch.

The Canada–United States Free-Trade Agreement

The 1987 free trade agreement between the United States and Canada is a recent example of rich countries extending free trade to rich neighbors and excluding poor countries from the agreement. The Canada–United States agreement seeks to reduce both tariff and non-tariff barriers to trade and investment. The desire for an agreement is not hard to explain: Canada and the United States are each other's largest trading partners. The importance of their trade is shown in Table 15.3.

The New Protectionism

International agreements have reduced the importance of tariffs, but protectionist pressure has led to an expansion of non-tariff barriers. These barriers are one of the most significant problems preventing the growth of

TABLE 15.3   Shares of Merchandise Trade in 1986

	United States	Canada
Canada	18.9	—
United States	—	71.1
Japan	18.6	5.6
Mexico	5.0	0.7
Other Western Hemisphere	7.5	2.0
Rest of World	50.1	20.6

Note: Trade shares are calculated from the sum of bilateral exports and imports in dollars. *Source: Economic Report of the President, 1988,* p. 129.

international trade. One of the causes of the increase of non-tariff barriers was the growth of competition faced by developed countries in world markets from Japan and the newly industrialized countries (Brazil, Mexico, Hong Kong, Singapore, South Korea, and Taiwan). These countries often export labor-intensive products such as clothing, textiles, footwear, and sports goods. The slowing down of the world economy in the early eighties made it more difficult for displaced workers in developed countries to find alternative employment. Protectionist pressure has resulted in the use of exceptions to GATT agreements.[19]

Escape Clause Action

Escape clauses in GATT agreements allow countries to restrict trade if increased imports have caused or threaten to cause serious unforeseen injury to a domestic industry.[20] Escape clauses reflect the desire of governments to secure markets for exporters without accepting that some domestic industries will suffer because freer trade may lead to more imports. Unfortunately, significant tariff concessions are bound to hurt some sectors. Since serious injury is not defined by GATT and potential injury rather than actual injury can be grounds for protection, there is wide scope for abuse of this provision. At the midterm review of the Uruguay round in December 1988, countries were unable to reach agreement on appropriate "safeguards" for domestic producers who are seriously affected by imports.

Dumping and Countervailing Duties

Under GATT rules, countries may use tariffs in cases of *dumping*. Dumping is deemed to have occurred if a product is sold abroad for less than its production cost or price in the exporter's domestic market. Government subsidies may allow a product to be sold at an artificially low price. In this case, "countervailing" duties may be levied to offset the effects of foreign government subsidies to exporters.

There are two main problems raised by dumping and by foreign subsidies on goods. First, cheap imports may reduce competition by driving some domestic firms out of business. Second, if cheap imports are only available for a short period, unnecessary adjustment costs are incurred (domestic firms close and then reopen when the price returns to normal). The argument that tariffs can promote competition is very weak. Tariffs are designed to reduce competition. Although many economists believe that there is a valid argument for protection from temporarily low prices, the validity of the case rests on the low prices being temporary. The argument against cheap imports simply because they are cheap is not economically valid. If foreigners are kind enough

---

[19]The IMF's *Annual Report on Exchange Arrangements and Exchange Restrictions* provides a useful summary of commercial policy developments.

[20]A similar provision is the U.S. national security clause under which protection can be given to industries that are necessary for national security.

to subsidize our consumption, why should we refuse? To illustrate the problem more dramatically, suppose that the Japanese government wanted to give us free Honda cars, should we refuse them? (A possible solution would be to accept the cars and then sell them for their true value on world markets.)

One problem that arises in assessing cases of dumping is the assessment of what is a fair market price, particularly when a good is produced solely for export. For example, Poland produces golf carts for export to the United States, but there is no domestic market or market price for golf carts in Poland because there are no golf courses. Polish production costs cannot be used because costs and prices in Poland are not market determined. To assess whether Polish golf carts were being dumped in the U.S. market, the Treasury used Spanish production costs.[21] The justification used was that Spain and Poland were at similar levels of economic development. However, there is no reason why Spain's relative prices should resemble those of Poland. Would we expect Canada, Japan, and the United States to have the same prices? In this case, dumping was not proved, but the decision could easily have gone the other way.

The provisions of GATT agreements allowing antidumping duties, countervailing duties, or escape clause actions have been used to justify the erection of trade barriers. However, these provisions have also affected other trade indirectly because investigations or the threat of investigations to assess whether action can be justified on these grounds have sometimes forced foreign manufacturers to accept "voluntary" export restraint. The United States makes more extensive use of investigations and actions against (what it sees as) unfair trade than other countries.[22] This has led to charges that the United States interprets GATT rules unilaterally, and has not acted in the spirit or letter of GATT agreements. The passage of the Omnibus Trade and Competitiveness Act in 1988 has heightened international concern because the legislation requires the U.S. government to respond to what American law defines to be unfair foreign trade practices.[23]

Voluntary Export Restraint

Voluntary export restraints (VERs) are one of the most common non-tariff barriers. VERs, like other forms of non-tariff barrier, violate the basic principles of GATT: they inevitably discriminate between alternative suppliers and the level of protection given to domestic producers is not transparent. The cost of VERs falls mainly on consumers in the importing country: foreign exporters are able to charge a higher price because of the artificial scarcity that

---

[21] Requests for antidumping duties are now evaluated by the Department of Commerce; the International Trade Commission determines whether a U.S. industry has suffered injury.
[22] See Kelly et al. (1988).
[23] One of the reasons Canada wanted to reach a free trade agreement with the United States was to avoid the costs associated with defending against investigations of unfair trade practices. The European Community now produces an interesting annual report giving its view of U.S. trade policy, for example see: EC Report on U.S. Trade Barriers, *European Community News*, No. 13/89, distributed by the EC Office of Press and Public Affairs, Washington, D.C.

is created. For example, the costs to American consumers of the restriction of imports of Japanese automobiles from 1981 to 1985 have been estimated at over $4 billion, and the costs per job protected in the automobile sector are put at over $200,000 per year.[24] Two other sectors where VERs have had a significant impact are steel and textiles.

Steel

More VERs pertain to trade in steel than to any other product. Both the European and American steel industries are protected. For example, the European Economic Community negotiated agreements with its major suppliers to limit the growth of imports to 3 percent in 1986. The American steel industry requested protection because it faced increasing competition and a declining domestic market (due to a recession during the early eighties). VERs were negotiated in 1982 with European exporters after a Department of Commerce investigation had shown that countervailing duties could be justified by European government subsidies. In 1984, the president rejected a recommendation from the International Trade Commission for escape clause action to protect the steel industry, but VERs were negotiated with sixteen countries. In reporting these events, the 1986 *Economic Report of the President* commented that: "Several countries have requested agreements to ensure themselves a share of the U.S. market and to obtain immunity from unfair trade actions" (p. 116). So much for free trade!

The U.S. steel sector was protected even though, as the economic report pointed out, some of the difficulties it faced were clearly not caused by unfair competition from imports. For example, wages in steel rose from 45 percent above average weekly earnings in 1969 to 95 percent in 1979, and this change occurred while labor productivity in steel was growing less than in manufacturing (productivity in steel was practically unchanged between 1973 and 1979).

Textiles

The Multifiber Agreement (MFA) is an important example of a non-tariff barrier that adversely affects developing countries. The original agreement was supposed to be a temporary arrangement to provide for the orderly expansion of the world textile market. In practice, it has been used by developed countries to restrict the access of developing countries to their markets and seems to have become a permanent policy. Exporters are assigned quotas representing shares of developed countries' markets. Through time the restrictions have been gradually extended as new fibers and new exporters have entered the market. This agreement is particularly odious because the countries that suffer are some of the poorest countries in the world. For example,

---

[24]These figures are in 1983 dollars and are taken from Tarr, D. G., and Mokre, M. E., *Aggregate Costs to the United States of Tariffs and Quotas on Imports: General Tariff Cuts and Removal of Quotas on Automobiles, Steel, Sugar, and Textiles,* (Washington, D.C.: Federal Trade Commission, December 1984). See also Organization for Economic Cooperation and Development, *The Cost of Restricting Imports: The Automobile Industry* (Paris, 1987).

the MFA was extended to cover exports from Bangladesh, a country with an annual per capita income of only $140 in 1984.[25] The textile sector is not the only sector that suffers from the MFA: textiles could be an export-led growth sector in developing countries, with higher incomes spilling over to other sectors.

Developing Countries and GATT

Developing countries have not been active in GATT, partly because they rejected the principle of reciprocity. They had little to offer in return for tariff concessions and felt that the disparity between rich and poor countries justified concessions without reciprocity. Also, they wanted to be able to use tariffs to help development of their industries. During the Kennedy round they succeeded in obtaining a modification of the most-favored-nation clause to allow developed countries to levy *preferential* (lower) tariff rates on imports from developing countries than on imports generally. However, the preferential tariffs that have been granted do not cover all goods and the concessions include escape clauses that allow the concession to be removed if there is serious injury to domestic industries. (In other words, the concessions only last as long as the developing country is not too successful!) As a result, the system of preferences has done little to help developing countries.

The experience of developing countries in sectors such as textiles has contributed to widespread pessimism. It is felt that developed countries are not sincere in their declared support for free trade and that developing countries have little to gain from attempts to increase their exports of other products. It is not hard to imagine the feelings of developing countries with large foreign debts when they are told by rich countries to export more but cannot do so because of trade restrictions.

How to Stop the New Protectionism

Slow international economic growth contributed to the growth of non-tariff barriers. Rapid growth is probably the single factor most likely to prevent the growth of non-tariff barriers. Unfortunately, slow growth may lead to further protectionism and even lower economic growth. The lesson of the thirties is relevant today: recessions intensify protectionist forces, which, if they are successful, deepen the recession. But whether this lesson has been learned remains to be seen. The Uruguay round may succeed if governments can bring themselves to believe that freer trade is desirable.[26] However, the unwillingness to reduce barriers unilaterally and the escalation of non-tariff barriers may lead us to wonder about the commitment of governments to free trade.

---

[25] See World Bank (1987), p. 160.

[26] The attempts of the European Economic Community to achieve a unified market by 1992 have created fears that the European market will be lost to nonmembers (see Chapter 17). This may push negotiations forward. (Recall that the Kennedy round was at least in part a reaction to the development of the EEC.)

Summary of Main Points

During the nineteenth century, tariffs in Europe and the United States were often *revenue tariffs*. The benefits of free trade were recognized by European countries and the development of other forms of taxation (such as the income tax) allowed governments to reduce tariffs. Growing competition and nationalism checked the European free trade movement at the end of the nineteenth century.

The United States did not participate in the nineteenth century free trade movement. Moderate revenue tariffs were replaced by high tariffs in 1828 when a plan by supporters of free trade backfired. They had hoped that the inclusion of high tariffs on a wide range of inputs and final products would lead to general opposition and prevent the Tariff Act of 1828 from being passed. However, the act was passed and became known as the *Tariff of Abominations*. Strong opposition to the high tariff rates and excess tariff revenue led to tariff reductions. Tariffs were increased to raise revenue during the Civil War. The *cheap labor argument* and the *infant industry argument* were used to justify continued protection after the war.

After World War One protection grew and culminated in the *Smoot-Hawley Tariff* of 1930. This act led to protectionist policies in other countries and a decline in world trade. The *Reciprocal Trade Agreements Act* of 1934 allowed the president of the United States to negotiate tariff reductions with the major supplier of a product. The incorporation of the *most-favored-nation* clause helped reduce barriers by ensuring that tariff concessions were extended to other countries.

The experience of the interwar years led to the formation of the *General Agreement on Tariffs and Trade (GATT)*. This is an organization that coordinates negotiations to reduce trade barriers, interprets rules governing the conduct of commercial policy, and administers procedures for negotiated settlements of trade disputes. GATT is based on the principles of nondiscrimination, the resolution of disputes through negotiation, and the avoidance of quotas. GATT has helped reduce major countries' tariff rates for manufactured goods to insignificant levels.

The latest round of GATT negotiations, the *Uruguay round,* was launched in 1986. Two sectors that are being discussed, agriculture and services, have been virtually ignored in previous GATT negotiations. Action is also needed to stop the proliferation of non-tariff barriers and to ensure that developing countries' access to markets in developed countries is increased. Progress in these areas is more likely if rapid economic growth is sustained.

Study Questions

1. Ricardo was not concerned about the effects of the repeal of the Corn Laws on the supply of domestic agricultural products. Consider the role of the domestic elasticity of supply of import substitutes in the assessment of the effects of protection.

2. What were the major reasons for the use of tariffs by the United States during the nineteenth century? When and why did the United States begin pursuing a free trade policy?

3. What are the economic principles on which the GATT is based? What is the economic rationale for these principles?

4. Give three examples of non-tariff barriers to trade. Why did such barriers increase in the early eighties?

5. Why do infant industries that have grown into efficient industries continue to argue for protection?

6. What are the most important international commercial policy problems today? Which problems are being addressed by the Uruguay round?

7. What are voluntary export restraints? Give an example. Why are VERs inconsistent with GATT principles?

8. What legally constitutes a case of dumping? What is the economic argument for protection against dumping? What difficulties may be encountered in assessing whether a product is being dumped?

9. "If foreign countries have tariffs, we should impose them." Comment on this view with reference to the experience following the Smoot-Hawley Act.

Selected References

Coughlin, C. C. and Wood, G. E. An Introduction to Non-Tariff Barriers to Trade, *Review,* Federal Reserve Bank of St. Louis, 71 (January/February 1989), 32–46.

Dam, K. *The GATT: Law and International Organization.* Chicago: University of Chicago Press, 1970.

Dobson, J. M. *Two Centuries of Tariffs: The Background and Emergence of the International Trade Commission.* Washington, D.C.: U.S. Government Printing Office, 1976.

Evans, J. W. *The Kennedy Round in American Trade Policy: The Twilight of the GATT?* Cambridge, MA, Harvard University Press, 1971.

Kelly, M., et al. *Issues and Developments in International Trade Policy.* International Monetary Fund Occasional Paper No. 63. Washington, D.C.: IMF, December 1988.

Kenwood, A. G., and Lougheed, A. L. *The Growth of the International Economy: 1820–1980.* Boston: George Allen and Unwin, 1983.

Ratner, S. *The Tariff in American History.* New York: Van Nostrand Company, 1972.

Taussig, F. W. *The Tariff History of the United States.* Eighth Revised Edition. New York: G. P. Putnam's Sons, Capricorn Books Edition, 1964.

Tussie, D. *The Less Developed Countries and the World Trading System: A Challenge to the GATT.* London: Frances Pinter, 1987.

World Bank. *World Development Report 1987.* New York: Oxford University Press, 1987.

PART THREE

TOPICS IN INTERNATIONAL ECONOMICS

16

THE

EUROCURRENCY

MARKET

INTRODUCTION 16.1

The rise of the Eurocurrency market is one of the most significant developments in international finance since World War Two. The rate of growth of the market has been spectacular. During the sixties and seventies the market grew by more than 20 percent per year. The Eurocurrency market is now a far more important source of international loans than official institutions such as the IMF. It is not surprising that the market has attracted a great deal of attention. Some argue that the market is beneficial because it increases the efficiency of the world capital market and thereby increases world income; others have blamed the market for causing inflation and exchange rate instability. In this chapter we shall describe the nature and functions of the market and critically evaluate the major arguments used by those who argue that the market should be regulated.

THE NATURE OF THE MARKET 16.2

The *Eurocurrency market* is an international banking market, with the major center in London.[1] Loans and deposits are made in many currencies, but most transactions are made with dollars. Hence, the market is sometimes

---

[1] London accounts for about a quarter of the Eurocurrency market. Eurocurrency banking centers also include: other European countries, the Bahamas, Bahrain, Canada, the Cayman Islands, Japan, Hong Kong, Singapore, and the United States. See the discussion of IBFs (Section 16.4) for comments relating to the share of the United States in the market.

referred to as the *Eurodollar market*. A *Eurodollar* is a dollar deposit held by a bank located outside the United States. Similarly, a *Eurocurrency deposit* is a deposit with a bank located in a country outside the country from which the deposited currency originates. For example, a Euromark is a mark-denominated deposit held with a bank outside Germany and a Eurofranc is a franc-denominated deposit held with a bank outside France. The country of residence of the deposit holder is not important. Because the banks in one country deal in the currencies of other countries, the market is sometimes referred to as an *offshore banking market*. We shall refer to Eurocurrencies and the Eurocurrency market unless specifically referring to deposits in a particular currency.

The Size of the Market

The Eurocurrency market is by far the larger of the two sectors of international banking. The other sector provides domestic currency banking for nonresidents. Table 16.1 shows the size of these two sectors and the overall size of the international banking market. The gross figures represent total deposits and are an overestimate of the credit provided by the market because a deposit in one bank may be loaned to another bank before being loaned to a final user. The net figure represents the size of the market after adjustment for interbank transactions and is a more accurate indication of credit provision. Even after adjusting for interbank deposits, the market is large. By way of illustration, the American money supply in 1987 was about $750 billion, approximately 30 percent of the net size of the international banking market.

The Creation of a Eurodollar Deposit

Table 16.2 shows the currency composition of bank liabilities to nonresidents. The table shows clearly the importance of the U.S. dollar in the Eurocurrency market: Eurodollars account for about three quarters of Eurocurrency

TABLE 16.1   The Size of the Eurocurrency Market

| | (liabilities at end of period in billions of U.S. dollars) | | |
	Gross Eurocurrencies to Residents and Nonresidents	*Gross Domestic Currencies to Nonresidents*	*Gross International Banking*	*Net International Banking*
1981	1,954	263	2,217	1,155
1982	2,168	250	2,418	1,285
1983	2,278	260	2,538	1,382
1984	2,386	280	2,666	1,430
1985	2,846	377	3,223	1,676
1986	3,683	489	4,172	2,076
1987	4,509	737	5,246	2,584

Source: Morgan Guaranty Trust Company, *World Financial Markets*, April 1987 and September 1988.

TABLE 16.2   The Currency Composition of Liabilities to Nonresidents

Stocks at End of 1987		(billions of U.S. dollars)
U.S. dollars	A	1,377.9
	B	477.4
Other foreign[a]	A	996.2
	B	517.2
Of which		
Deutsche mark	A	338.8
	B	80.7
Swiss franc	A	181.5
	B	25.3
Japanese yen	A	137.2
	B	223.8
Pounds sterling	A	67.0
	B	94.0
ECU		69.4

A = Eurocurrency positions; B = external positions in domestic currency
Note: The data in this table refer only to cross-border positions of banks in industrial countries within the BIS reporting area. Therefore, the sum of the Eurocurrency liabilities of these countries is less than the size of the Eurocurrency market shown in Table 16.1.
[a] Excluding positions of banks in the United States.
Source: Bank for International Settlements, *Fifty-Eighth Annual Report (1 April 1987–31 March 1988)* (Basel, 1988), p. 119.

liabilities. The Eurodollar market allows nonresidents to trade ownership of dollar deposits held in banks in the United States. For example, when a dollar deposit is made with Barclays Bank International in London, Barclays deposits the dollars in its account with a bank in the United States. Barclays has an asset, a claim on an American domestic bank, and a liability to the depositor. The dollar deposit in London is a Eurodollar deposit. When Barclays makes a loan, it transfers ownership of the deposit with the American bank. Therefore, a necessary condition for the operation of the Eurodollar market is that the United States does not restrict nonresident holdings or transfers of dollar deposits, that is, *nonresident convertibility* must not be restricted. Another condition is that foreign countries must not restrict their citizens from holding or transferring foreign currency deposits.

Why Dollars?

These two conditions allowed the Eurodollar market to grow, but why were dollars chosen? The use of the dollar in the Eurocurrency market is a reflection of the role of the dollar in the international economic system. The dollar is used as the currency of denomination for most international contracts. Why are international contracts between residents of other countries usually expressed in dollars and not in the currency of one of the contracting parties? The reason is that by using one currency people reduce the amount of information they need. When contracts are negotiated in dollars, all traders need to know is the value of their currencies relative to the dollar. (During the Bretton Woods period, the dollar was a natural currency for people to choose because countries fixed the values of their currencies against the dollar.) Also, some contracts tend to take place in dollars because the United States is the world's most important trading nation.

The Availability of Loans in Other Currencies

Although most Eurocurrency loans are made in dollars, loans in other currencies are easily obtained. There are two ways of obtaining a loan in another currency. The first is to borrow the currency directly from a Eurobank. The second is to borrow dollars from a Eurobank, sell the dollars for the required currency in the foreign exchange market, and cover the price of dollars needed to repay the loan in the forward exchange market. Because people can borrow other currencies directly or obtain the currencies via dollar loans, arbitrage ensures that the costs of these loans are virtually identical. For example, arbitrage ensures that the forward premium between dollars and marks is almost identical to the difference between the interest rates charged on Eurodollars and Euromarks.

The Eurobond Market

The *Eurobond market* is much smaller than the Eurocurrency market. To avoid regulations, a Eurobond is usually sold outside the country that issues the currency in which the bond is denominated. A Eurobond is sold in a number of national markets and is underwritten by an international syndicate of banks. The Eurobond market differs from the Eurocurrency market because Eurodeposits are nonmarketable claims against financial intermediaries (banks), whereas Eurobonds are marketable claims against borrowers (governments or corporations) that are held directly by the lenders. Also, whereas Eurocurrency loans are usually made at flexible interest rates, Eurobonds usually have fixed interest rates.

16.3 FUNCTIONS OF THE EUROCURRENCY MARKET

The Functions of the Market

In order to understand the reasons for the growth of the Eurocurrency market, we must appreciate the services it performs. Essentially, Eurobanks perform the same services as banks in the domestic money market, that is, they act as financial intermediaries and engage in maturity transformation.

Financial Intermediation

Banks act as *financial intermediaries* by taking funds from people who want to lend and making loans to people who want to borrow. Banks reduce the transaction costs of loans because borrowers and lenders do not have to "find each other." Another aspect of the service is that a bank substitutes its creditworthiness for that of the borrowers. For example, a customer holding a deposit with Barclays has a claim on Barclays, not on the person who borrows the money from Barclays. Banks can do this because they have experience and information that allow them to assess risk more accurately than individuals. Also, the scale of their operations means that losses on some loans are expected and are accepted because they are offset by profits on other loans. It is less likely that the number of transactions undertaken by an individual would be large enough to average out risk in this way.[2]

It is clear from Table 16.1 that interbank transactions are an important part of the market. Interbank transactions are partly a reflection of the role of banks as financial intermediaries. When a bank takes a deposit it does not need to have a borrower waiting because it can lend the funds to other banks who are in need of funds. But interbank transactions have other important functions. For example, they allow banks to alter the composition of their balance sheets to take account of factors such as currency composition and loan maturity. Also, interbank trading provides banks with information about the market and maintains contacts with other banks.

Maturity Transformation

Eurocurrency deposits are time deposits, that is, depositors cannot withdraw their funds at will. The deposit period may be as short as one day, or six months, or more. The majority of deposits are for less than six months. These funds are often loaned out for much longer periods, however, sometimes for years. When banks borrow for short periods and lend for longer periods this is known as *maturity transformation*. Banks can do this because many deposits that are made for short periods are reinvested at the end of the deposit period. Thus, the banks can behave as though the funds had been invested for a longer period.

National Banking and the "Need" for Eurocurrency Banks

National banks dealing in the currency of the country in which they are located can and do provide these services to the international community, as Table 16.2 shows. Thus, in a sense, the Eurocurrency market is not strictly necessary. This observation may lead us to wonder why people bother with Eurobanks. Why not use an American bank for dollar banking services? Eurobanks can compete with national banks because they are able to pay higher rates on deposits and charge lower rates on loans. The difference or *spread* between the deposit and loan rates is one way banks make money.[3] Figure 16.1 shows the normal relationship between the spread for a Eurobank and an American bank.[4]

---

[2] Some loans are even too large for individual banks. A group of Eurobanks may form a syndicate to provide such a loan and spread the risk.
[3] A bank may also charge a fee when a loan is made.
[4] Dufey and Giddy (1978) discuss the comparability of interest rates in the Eurocurrency market and the American money market, pp. 52–54.

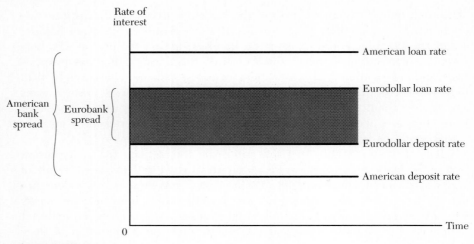

FIGURE 16.1

Spreads in the Eurodollar and American Markets

The difference between the rate paid to depositors and the rate charged to borrowers is called the spread. Banks make money from the size of the spread. Because Eurobanks are not regulated, they are able to operate with a smaller spread than American banks.

The main reason why Eurobanks can operate with a lower spread is that Eurobanks are not subject to regulations, in particular, there are no reserve requirements in the Eurocurrency market. The larger the percentage of deposits that a bank is able to loan out, the larger the revenue of the bank. Domestic banks are required to maintain minimum ratios of reserves to deposits, which prevents them from lending out all the money deposited with them. Reserve requirements foster confidence in the banking system and ensure that there are adequate funds available to meet day-to-day withdrawals. Eurobanks only handle time deposits and do not need to maintain reserves to meet withdrawal requests. Therefore, because a higher percentage of their deposits are loaned out, they can operate with a lower spread. Another reason for the narrow spread, which is often quoted, is that Eurobanks usually deal in large sums of money ($5 million or more). The paperwork is similar for transactions of $1 thousand or $5 million. Thus, the margin needed to cover the costs of the transaction declines as a percentage as the size of the transaction increases. However, this explanation of the narrow spread offered by Eurobanks is not convincing because there is nothing to prevent national banks from reducing spreads by dealing in large sums.

Political Risk

The Eurocurrency market would be able to attract funds even if there were no financial incentive to use it. The reason is that it allows customers to reduce *political risk*. When a person invests in a country, the investment falls within the political jurisdiction of that country. Taxes may be imposed, the assets may be seized, or controls may be introduced by the government to deprive the investor of the right to withdraw the funds. This is exactly what happened in 1979 when Iranian assets in the United States were frozen following the siege of the American embassy in Tehran and the taking of the American hostages. Iranian dollar deposits with banks outside the United States were outside the political jurisdiction of the United States and were not affected.[5]

The risk that a government will seize the assets of a Eurobank is small. Eurobanks do not maintain reserves, and their assets and liabilities are usually with nonresidents. Thus, there is virtually nothing to seize in a Eurobank. Also, since only one branch of an international bank is likely to be affected, the bank would merely need to announce that its bookkeeping had moved to another branch.

THE GROWTH OF THE EUROCURRENCY MARKET   16.4

Soviet Gold

Many people suggest that the origins of the modern Eurocurrency market can be traced to the early fifties, when the proceeds from Soviet gold sales were deposited by the Moscow Narodny bank with European banks. It would have been somewhat strange for the leader of the Communist world to invest its funds in the largest and richest capitalist nation.[6] Also, the funds would have been under the political jurisdiction of the American government, which, during the Cold War, would not have been a sensible investment. In other words, the Soviet Union sought to avoid political risk by investing dollars outside the political jurisdiction of the United States.

The Importance of Regulations

Although deposits of revenue from Soviet gold sales are an interesting explanation of the origins of the Eurocurrency market, two regulatory changes at the end of the fifties were more important. The first concerned the international role of sterling. After World War Two, London resumed its role as a center of international finance and British banks provided sterling finance for

---

[5]This incident contributed to the growth of Arab banking in centers such as Bahrain.
[6]Eurobanks often loaned the funds to the United States, therefore, the Soviet Union was lending indirectly to the United States.

trade between third countries. When the Bank of England restricted the provision of sterling credit to nonresidents (during a period of speculative capital flows in 1957), people turned to the use of dollars and British banks tried to maintain their international business by dealing in dollars. The second change occurred in 1958, when European countries reduced restrictions on their citizens holding dollars (as part of the return of their currencies to convertibility). These two regulatory changes set the stage for the growth of international dollar banking.

American banks might have provided dollar banking services to the world, had American regulations not prevented them from doing so. The explosion of the Eurodollar market that began in the mid sixties was largely the result of regulations imposed by the United States. One famous regulation, Regulation Q, limited the interest rates that could be paid to depositors in the United States. Eurobanks were not subject to this regulation and were able to offer higher rates of interest to attract deposits of dollars. Eurodollar deposits were sometimes loaned back to American banks or American customers because the interest rate ceiling resulted in a shortage of funds in the American money market.[7] American banks were also restrained from providing loans for investment abroad (voluntary restraint in 1965 was followed by mandatory controls in 1968). However, it is important to note that the United States did not restrict nonresident convertibility, thus offshore banking was feasible.

The growth of international dollar banking by American banks was constrained by regulation, but the British government took steps to separate domestic banking and international banking. British banks were allowed to provide foreign currency banking services to nonresidents, and restrictions were imposed to prevent British residents from using these facilities to transfer funds into or out of Britain. In this way, Britain was able to provide international banking while retaining protection from what was thought to be the danger of destabilizing capital flows. It was feared that capital flows would undermine the stability of sterling's exchange rate and disrupt the British monetary system.[8]

More recently, American regulations have been relaxed in the hope of attracting international banking business. In 1981, the Federal Reserve allowed American banks to establish *international banking facilities* (IBFs). IBFs are exempt from domestic American reserve requirements, although they are subject to (lower) Eurocurrency reserve requirements. They can only take deposits from foreigners, and deposits and withdrawals cannot be less than $100,000. The purpose of these regulations is to allow American banks to compete in the international banking market while allowing the Federal Re-

---

[7] Borrowing by American banks from the Eurodollar market fell as a result of restrictions imposed by the Federal Reserve in 1969 and the easing of Regulation Q in 1973.
[8] Britain abolished capital controls in October 1979.

serve to retain control over banks providing funds to the domestic market.[9] Japan recently adopted similar regulations, and Japanese offshore banking has been growing rapidly.

The Eurocurrency Market and the American Balance of Payments

One early explanation of the growth of the Eurodollar market was that American balance of payments deficits increased the amount of dollars held by foreigners. In fact, the growth of the Eurodollar market is not directly related to American balance of payments deficits. American deficits are neither necessary nor sufficient for the Eurocurrency market to grow. Two facts are enough to illustrate this: (1) the Eurodollar market has grown continuously, in years of large deficits and small deficits; and (2) Euromark deposits have increased even though Germany has had a persistent surplus. It is quite easy to show how the Eurodollar market can grow without an American deficit: when an American makes a deposit in the Eurodollar market in London that finances a loan to another American, a capital outflow is matched by a capital inflow, the balance of payments is not affected, but the Eurodollar market increases by the amount of the deposit.

American balance of payments deficits did help the growth of the Eurodollar market in one way. In the early seventies, countries were trying to maintain fixed exchange rates. Faced with large American deficits, foreign central banks bought dollars in the foreign exchange markets to prevent their currencies rising in value against the dollar. Some of these dollars were deposited in the Eurodollar market, and the market expanded. Depositing international reserves in the Eurocurrency market is still a common practice.[10]

OPEC Recycling

The Eurocurrency market received a boost when OPEC oil revenue was deposited in the market following the oil price increase of 1973–74. The oil price increase had led to fears that oil-importing countries would be short of funds to finance their deficits. The Eurocurrency market played its role as a financial intermediary by quickly and efficiently recycling funds from oil exporters to oil importers, and a crisis was avoided. The size of Eurocurrency market activity in these years was unprecedented. The flow of funds from oil exporters into the market was about $24 billion in 1974.[11] This recycling was achieved without massive disruption, and is often used as an example of the usefulness and efficiency of the Eurocurrency market.

---

[9]The regulations governing IBFs are described in the *Federal Reserve Bulletin*, October 1982. At the end of 1986, IBFs accounted for under 8% of banking (measured as the stock of liabilities resulting from external positions) (Bank for International Settlements, *Fifty-Seventh Annual Report*, 1987, p. 102).

[10]The annual reports of the Bank for International Settlements describe the pattern of investment of exchange reserves.

[11]Bank for International Settlements, *Forty-Fifth Annual Report*, 1975, p. 139.

Other Explanations of the Growth of the Eurocurrency Market

Finally, the Eurocurrency market may have grown because traders and investors who use foreign currencies continuously find the proximity of Eurobanks useful. Communications between countries were not as efficient in the mid sixties as they are today, and it is understandable that Europeans would have preferred European banks to American banks.[12] Even now, although dollar banking with American banks may be technically feasible for Europeans, local banks may be more familiar with and responsive to their customers' needs. In addition, European banks keep the same hours as European investors; the minimum time difference between the United States and Europe is five hours.[13]

Although many factors contributed to the growth of the Eurocurrency market, the basic justification for Eurobanks is probably economic. When Eurobanks offer better deposit rates and charge lower loan rates, why look any further? However, the growth of Eurobanking should not be seen in isolation. It took place against a background of increasing trade and improved communication between countries. When viewed against this background, the Eurocurrency market's growth can be seen as a response to the desire of investors and borrowers to increase the international diversity of their assets and liabilities. In the eighties, the rate of growth slowed as banks and individuals became more aware of the risks of international loans.[14]

16.5 CRITICISMS AND PROPOSALS FOR REFORM

The Eurocurrency market increases the efficiency of the international market by reducing the cost of capital transfers. Therefore, we would expect the world level of income to increase as a result of a more efficient allocation of capital. Regulation of the market would increase the costs of capital transfers and reduce capital mobility, but some people have argued that regulation is needed.

---

[12] Given that Luxembourg is bordered by Belgium, France, and Germany, it is not surprising that Luxembourg has become a major banking center.

[13] This suggests that banks are more likely to compete with other banks in the same time zone than with banks in different time zones. Thus, IBFs in New York are more likely to compete with Eurocurrency centers in the Caribbean, such as the Bahamas or the Cayman Islands, than with European centers.

[14] Other factors have been at work: most large international banks have now entered the market, lending slowed as banks attempted to halt the decline in the ratio of equity to total assets, and margins have fallen in response to demands by large borrowers for easier terms and competition between banks for creditworthy customers.

The Danger of International Monetary Collapse

One of the most common arguments in favor of regulation is that the Eurocurrency market is inherently unstable. It is argued that because the participants are closely linked through interbank deposits the collapse of one bank could lead to the collapse of other banks, and international monetary chaos. This argument is plausible in the sense that the banks are closely linked by interbank deposits. However, the scenario is less convincing when we consider how a bank might collapse.

The classic scenario of a loss in confidence leading to a run on the bank, as happened during the thirties in the United States, is not possible because Eurocurrency deposits are time deposits. They cannot be withdrawn at will. Deposits could be withdrawn gradually, but the answer to falling deposits is simple: banks can prevent a gradual collapse of deposits by raising interest rates. This is possible because Eurobanks do not give fixed interest rate loans. Long-term loans include provisions to revise the interest rate at regular intervals to reflect changes in market interest rates. The loan rate is usually defined as a margin above the U.S. prime rate or the London interbank offer rate (LIBOR), the rate at which one bank can obtain funds from another bank.

A default by one or more major borrowers that leads to a loss of assets is a more serious potential source of instability. This danger seems important to observers who compare traditional national banking and Eurobanking because domestic banks are protected by the domestic monetary authorities from bankruptcy. For example, the Federal Deposit Insurance Corporation guarantees deposits up to $100,000, and ultimately the stability of the American monetary system is protected by the Federal Reserve. There is no guarantee of protection for depositors in the Eurocurrency market. This problem has received some attention recently as a result of defaults by developing countries that are significant borrowers from the market. One answer has been to set aside reserves to offset possible defaults. However, these reserves may not be enough to offset a default by a major borrower.[15]

Although there is a possibility that defaults will lead to the collapse of Eurobanks, the problem is not confined to the Eurocurrency market. The problem exists whether national or international banks have made such loans. Put simply, the danger of collapse is not a justification for regulation, because regulation of Eurobanks cannot prevent defaults by debtor countries.

There is little reason to be concerned about the risk that Eurocurrency deposits will be lost if a Eurobank collapses. That is a risk investors accept when they make a deposit. The significance of the possibility of collapse is that domestic money supplies may be disrupted. Eurobanks are overseas offices of large domestic banks. If a domestic bank is at risk, the domestic

---

[15] Setting aside reserves has stopped the downward trend in the ratio of bank equity to total assets, and reduced the ratio of LDC debt to total assets (see Section 18.5).

monetary authorities should intervene to ensure that the collapse of one or more banks does not lead to a collapse of the domestic money supply. This can be achieved by the Federal Reserve guaranteeing deposits held with domestic banks. To some extent, Eurocurrency deposits may be protected indirectly by support for the parent banks from the domestic monetary authorities in their home countries. We return to this topic in our discussion of the international debt problem in Section 18.5.

Increased Capital Mobility

It has been suggested that the Eurocurrency market reduces welfare by encouraging destabilizing capital flows. Capital flows can be accommodated by traditional national banking, but it may be that the Eurocurrency market encourages capital transfers by reducing their cost. The alleged problems caused by short-term capital mobility include a reduction in monetary autonomy and increased exchange rate instability.

Lack of Monetary Autonomy

Assume that a country attempts to reduce aggregate demand by reducing its money supply. Domestic interest rates tend to rise relative to world rates and the value of domestic currency tends to increase (as the foreign demand for domestic interest-bearing assets rises relative to the domestic demand for foreign assets). Recall that under fixed exchange rates, as the value of domestic currency tends to rise, the monetary authorities must intervene in the foreign exchange market and sell domestic currency for foreign currency. In this case, the initial reduction in the money supply tends to be offset by an expansion of the money supply caused by the foreign exchange market intervention. Thus, under fixed exchange rates, the effectiveness of monetary policy is reduced by capital flows.

There is less reason to be concerned about monetary autonomy being undermined by capital flows under the present exchange rate system, because the authorities do not have to intervene to prevent the value of domestic currency from increasing. Thus, changes in the money supply are not offset by the effects of intervention in the foreign exchange market. On the contrary, under the present system, the effectiveness of domestic monetary policy may be increased by capital flows. (We might expect a reduction in the money supply to be accompanied by a higher domestic interest rate, an appreciation of domestic currency, and a fall in aggregate demand caused by lower net exports.)

Exchange Rate Stability

Under the present exchange rate system, one of the main issues is the effect of capital flows on exchange rate stability.[16] There seems to be some evidence that capital flows may have increased exchange rate variability, but

---

[16] See Section 14.3.

there is little agreement on the size of the costs of exchange rate variability. Also, some people have argued that unstable capital flows reflect unstable economic policies, that is, they are not an independent source of instability. It may be that restricting capital flows would have little effect on economic stability. Although the benefits of reduced capital mobility are disputed, the costs of reduced capital mobility are clearer. Restricting capital flows prevents some productive investments from being undertaken and reduces real income. This result is inevitable because it is impossible to distinguish between short-term speculative capital flows and flows of capital that finance productive investments.

International Inflation

The view that the growth of the Eurocurrency market leads to world inflation is usually based on the idea that the market creates money in the same way as the domestic banking system. It is true that the Eurocurrency market can lead to an increase in total bank deposits. For example, when a person withdraws dollars from an American domestic bank and deposits them with a Eurobank, the Eurobank deposits the dollars with an American bank. In this case, American bank deposits remain unchanged and the Eurocurrency market has grown, thus total bank deposits have increased. A broad measure of money (such as M3, which includes long-term time deposits) would show an increase in the world money supply.[17]

However, if a narrow definition of money is adopted (such as M1, which focuses on the role of money as a medium of exchange), the Eurocurrency market does not lead to an expansion of the money supply. This is because Eurocurrency deposits cannot be spent. They are time deposits and Eurocurrency checks do not exist. In other words, Eurocurrency deposits are a store of value, not a medium of exchange. Therefore, it is more appropriate to think of Eurocurrency deposits as investments rather than money. Returning to the example of the creation of a Eurodollar deposit, there is only one sum of dollars to be spent. When the Eurobank makes a dollar loan, it transfers ownership of these dollars; it does not create money.[18] Therefore, monetary policy can still be used to control inflation by controlling the supply of dollars.

Two qualifications must be added. First, companies may hold their working balances in the form of short-term Eurocurrency deposits rather than demand deposits. If so, funds that would otherwise have been left idle are loaned out through the Eurocurrency market. Therefore, the velocity of circulation of money is increased, and this may have a small inflationary effect. Second, future institutional developments in the market may lead to easier access to deposits and blur the distinction between investment funds and money. To

---

[17]The overall American money supply would stay the same because American money supply figures include holdings of dollars by nonresidents. The figures would show a transfer of ownership of an American deposit.

[18]In contrast, when a domestic bank makes a loan, it creates a new deposit, which is a form of money because checks can be drawn against the deposit.

the extent that such developments make it easier to conduct transactions with Eurocurrencies, there is a potential inflationary effect.

One simple argument against the view that the Eurocurrency market causes inflation is that the rate of inflation has not been related to the growth of the market. It is true that during the seventies inflation accelerated while the Eurocurrency market was growing, but international inflation fell during the early eighties as the Eurocurrency market continued to grow. Therefore, the argument that the growth of the market necessarily causes international inflation is unacceptable. However, the Eurocurrency market may have had an inflationary effect on some countries.

The Eurocurrency Market and International Adjustment

During the seventies, countries in balance of payments difficulties were able to avoid IMF conditions on loans by borrowing from the Eurocurrency market. This may have contributed to international inflation by allowing some countries to pursue inflationary policies. For example, international loans allowed governments to finance budget deficits and maintain overvalued exchange rates. Opponents of regulation point to the ease with which petrodollars were recycled. Loans made to finance oil imports added to the debts of developing countries, but, at the time, there was probably no other way to pay for imported oil. Oil imports could not be cut quickly, and it would have been difficult for a country to pay for imported oil by reducing its consumption of other imported goods. Moreover, if all oil-importing countries had attempted to pay for oil imports by cutting back their consumption of other imports, there would have been a collapse in world trade and a world recession. Therefore, it was desirable that oil imports be financed to some extent by debt.

The international debt problem, rather than international inflation, led to a recognition that Eurocurrency loans may have been too easily obtained. As a result, banks now often require that countries secure IMF funds and agree to IMF conditions before new bank loans are made. This procedure is sometimes criticized, in part because there is substantial controversy over the appropriate conditions (if any) that the IMF should attach to international loans.

Arguments against Regulation

The most important argument against regulation is the most simple: it is unlikely to happen. The major reason is that there are wide differences of opinion over whether there is any need for regulation. Even if countries agreed on the need for reform, and the nature that the reform should take, there would always be an incentive for one country to refrain from joining in the hope that it would increase its share of the Eurocurrency market. Regulation by one country is not feasible. If one country attempted to regulate the banks, the banks would simply find a more hospitable place from which to work.

Summary of Main Points

A *Eurocurrency deposit* is a deposit held at a bank outside the country that issues the currency in which the deposit is denominated. For this reason, Eurocurrency banking is sometimes referred to as *offshore banking*. Eurocurrencies are time deposits with maturities from one day to six months or more.

The banks that provide Eurocurrency banking provide basically the same services as domestic banks: *financial intermediation* and *maturity transformation*. Because Eurobanks do not have to comply with regulations, such as reserve requirements, they can usually offer higher deposit rates and charge lower loan rates than banks making loans of domestic currency to foreigners. Also, Eurocurrency deposits allow investors to reduce *political risk* because the deposits are held outside the political jurisdiction of the country that issued the currency in which the deposits are denominated.

The modern Eurodollar market is often traced to Soviet deposits of dollar revenue from gold sales. Tight American regulation of dollar banking activities combined with relatively unregulated dollar banking in Europe was a major factor contributing to the growth of the market in the early sixties. The market continued to grow as central banks deposited international reserves and OPEC deposited revenue from oil sales. The recycling of deposits of oil revenue as loans to oil importers is an important example of the Eurodollar market acting as a financial intermediary.

The growth of the Eurodollar market can be viewed as part of the overall trend towards greater international trade and investment. The market provides international banking services to governments and international firms. Because the market is highly efficient, it reduces the cost of transactions, leads to increased capital mobility, and contributes to higher global income.

The Eurocurrency market has been criticized for contributing to exchange rate instability (by increasing capital mobility). Although there may be some truth in this criticism, restricting capital flows would tend to reduce welfare by reducing productive investments. Lack of regulation has led to fears that the Eurobanks could collapse and to proposals for regulation. However, there is little danger of a run on Eurobanks because they make only time deposits. Also, the Eurobanks make variable-rate loans, thus a gradual reduction in deposits could be halted by increasing deposit and loan rates.

To some extent, the banks are also protected because they are overseas offices of large domestic banks. Thus, the obligation of the monetary authorities to prevent domestic banks from collapsing implicitly provides some protection to the Eurobanks. The main danger to Eurobanks is that defaults by major debtor nations could lead to a loss of assets. This danger is not a justification for regulation of Eurocurrency banking, because domestic banks face the same problem and regulation of the Eurocurrency market would do nothing to prevent defaults.

The market has been criticized for contributing to world inflation. However, there is little evidence to support this criticism. The market did grow during the seventies as inflation increased, but it continued to grow in the eighties as inflation fell. Also, although the Euromarket leads to an increase in global bank deposits, the Eurobanks do not create money in the same way as domestic banks: Eurobanks do not issue checks and Eurodeposits are time deposits. However, perhaps the access to loans without conditions may have allowed some countries to pursue inflationary economic policies.

The major argument against regulation is that an international agreement to regulate the market is unlikely and regulation by one country would be ineffective because the banks could move their operations to nonregulated markets.

Study Questions

1. What is a Eurodollar? What is a Euromark? Use the regulatory changes of 1957–58 to illustrate the conditions for a currency to be used in the Eurocurrency market.

2. Explain why the growth of the Eurocurrency market has been described as a response to regulation.

3. Why can Eurobanks offer higher deposit rates and lower loan rates for dollars than American banks?

4. How can the Eurobanks operate without reserve ratios?

5. Domestic banks are regulated in order to maintain confidence in the system and to prevent collapse. How can the Eurocurrency market survive without regulation?

6. Why can't Eurobanks give long-term, fixed-interest-rate loans to developing countries?

7. In evaluating the argument that the Eurocurrency market causes world inflation, why is it important to note that deposits in the Eurocurrency market are time deposits and that Eurocurrency loans are made by transferring ownership of bank deposits.

8. Critically evaluate the arguments that the Eurocurrency market should be regulated with reference to the effects of the market on: (a) exchange rates, (b) monetary autonomy, and (c) inflation.

Selected References

Davies, A., and Ball, A. "International Banking Markets." *Barclays Review* 59 (May 1984): 37–41.

Dufey, G., and Giddy, I. H. *The International Money Market.* Englewood Cliffs, N.J.: Prentice Hall, 1978.

Frydl, E. J. "The Debate Over Regulating the Eurocurrency Markets." *Federal Reserve Bank of New York Quarterly Review*, Winter 1979–80, pp. 11–19.

Johnston, G., and Ball, A. "The Euromarkets and Monetary Expansion." *Barclays Review* 55 (February 1980): 9–12.

Karlick, J. R. "Some Questions and Brief Answers About the Eurodollar Market." In *International Trade and Finance*, Second Edition, edited by R. E. Baldwin and J. D. Richardson, pp. 516–33. Boston: Little Brown, 1981.

Lewis, M. K., and Davis, K. T. *Domestic and International Banking.* Cambridge, MA: MIT Press, 1987.

McKinnon, R. I. *Money in International Exchange: The Convertible Currency System.* New York: Oxford University Press, 1979.

Park, Y. S., and Zwick, J. *International Banking in Theory and Practice.* Reading, MA: Addison Wesley, 1985.

Throop, A. W. "Eurobanking and World Inflation." *Voice* (Federal Reserve Bank of Dallas), August 1979, pp. 8–23.

Watson, M., et al. *International Capital Markets: Developments and Prospects.* IMF Occasional Paper No. 43. Washington, D.C.: International Monetary Fund, 1986.

17

THE EUROPEAN

ECONOMIC

COMMUNITY

INTRODUCTION

The European Economic Community (EEC) is the most important example of economic integration.[1] Its twelve members are: Belgium, Denmark, France, Germany, Greece, Ireland, Italy, Luxembourg, the Netherlands, Portugal, Spain, and the United Kingdom. In 1987, community income was about $3.5 trillion compared with national incomes of about $4.5 trillion for the United States and $2 trillion for Japan. Clearly the EEC is an important market. The EEC is also the world's most important trading block. In 1986, if exports from one member of the community to another are excluded, the EEC accounted for 20 percent of world exports, the United States accounted for 13 percent, and Japan 12 percent.

At present there are basically three EEC policies: a customs union, an agricultural policy, and an exchange rate agreement. In this chapter we shall examine each of these policies. Proposals for European integration in other areas have been made but have not seen much progress. The prospects for further economic integration are considered in the closing section. First, by way of introduction, let us consider the forms that economic integration may take.

17.2 **DEGREES OF ECONOMIC INTEGRATION**

A free trade area is an area in which members remove barriers to trade between themselves but retain separate barriers to trade with nonmembers. To prevent goods moving into the area over the lowest barrier, goods are

---

[1] The proposed free trade agreement between the United States and Canada is another important example. Robson (1984) discusses other examples of economic integration.

taxed according to their origin. For example, an imported good may enter the area through a low-tariff country, but additional taxes are payable if the good then moves to a high-tariff country. The European Free Trade Area (EFTA) is an example of such an arrangement.[2]

A customs union goes beyond a free trade area with the addition of a common external tariff. The EEC is an example of a customs union. A common market adds free mobility of factors of production to the requirements for a customs union. This is the target of the EEC. In an economic union, government spending and taxation are carried out at a supranational level. (Some taxes and spending may be under the control of national governments, in the way that states have fiscal powers in the United States.) Monetary union entails the use of a single currency by the members of the union. Economic policy need not necessarily be unified, for example Belgium and Luxembourg have a single currency but separate economic policies. However, it is normally assumed that economic and monetary union go together.

HISTORY OF THE EUROPEAN ECONOMIC COMMUNITY   17.3

Early Cooperation

Proposals for European integration have been made for centuries.[3] The main driving force behind early proposals was usually the maintenance of peace, and it was for this reason that the proposals began to receive serious consideration following the experience of World War Two. There was an element of idealism in the postwar era. People thought about the type of world they would like to create. European integration was seen as the way forward; for example, Winston Churchill referred to the development of a United States of Europe. The United States helped the cause of integration by encouraging European countries to cooperate in their postwar recovery effort. It was felt that this was the only way Europe might eventually be able to compete with the United States. Also, European cooperation was encouraged for political reasons: a strong united Europe was seen as a deterrent to Soviet expansionism.

The European Coal and Steel Community

The movement that eventually led to the creation of the European Economic Community began with a proposal by Robert Schuman in 1950 to establish a body, the European Coal and Steel Community (ECSC), to plan the production and consumption of coal, iron, and steel in Europe. It was hoped that the ECSC would make war impossible by controlling the materials needed to wage war and establishing a common market in those materials. A revolu-

---

[2]The members of EFTA are: Austria, Finland, Iceland, Norway, Sweden, and Switzerland.
[3]For example, the Quaker William Penn, after whom Pennsylvania is named, proposed in 1693 that central government in Europe was a way of achieving peace.

tionary aspect of the proposal was that the body would be administered by a supranational authority with powers delegated to it by national governments. The ECSC came into existence in 1951. The six founding members of the ECSC were France, Germany, Italy, and the Benelux countries (Belgium, Luxembourg, and the Netherlands). The United Kingdom was invited to join but refused, in part because the government was unwilling to give up power to a European body.[4]

Attempts to extend economic cooperation into political integration, by developing a common defense policy and forming a European army, failed because these measures would have reduced national sovereignty. Despite these setbacks, proposals for European cooperation and integration continued and resulted in the signing of the Treaty of Rome in 1957, which established the European Economic Community.[5]

The Treaty of Rome

The objective of the Treaty of Rome was to encourage economic growth and political harmony. Free trade between the members was seen as playing a crucial role in achieving this objective, but the founding members had more ambitious plans than the mere creation of a customs union. The treaty included policies to increase factor mobility with the objective of establishing a common market. The treaty included provisions for common policies in the areas of agriculture and transport, and envisaged the development of policies to tackle regional and social problems. However, the only policy that was clearly outlined in the treaty was the Common Agricultural Policy (CAP). National economic policy remained under the control of national governments, but members agreed to cooperate and coordinate economic policies.

The Progress of Integration

European economic integration proceeded well during the sixties: the customs union was established and the agricultural policy was adopted. In international monetary policy, progress was made beyond the Treaty of Rome with the development of a community exchange rate policy. After an initial failure in the early seventies, the EEC successfully established the European Monetary System in 1979. Another development was the expansion of the membership of the community. The membership of the European Economic Community increased to nine in 1973 when Denmark, Ireland, and the United Kingdom joined. In 1981, Greece became a member, and in 1985, Spain and Portugal joined. The most recent development is the attempt to remove the

---

[4]The United Kingdom was also concerned that its links would be weakened with former colonies that were members of the British Commonwealth.

[5]The European Economic Community is now part of a wider organization: the European Community. This includes the EEC, Euratom (an organization that oversees European research and development of atomic energy), and the ECSC. Because we focus on the economic policies, we have referred to the EEC throughout this chapter.

remaining barriers to trade in goods and services, and the barriers preventing free movement of factors of production, and to create a single European market by 1992. (This objective was embodied in the Single European Act of 1987, which amended the Treaty of Rome.)

COMMERCIAL POLICY 17.4

Definition

The EEC is a customs union, that is, there is free internal trade and a common external tariff. Because there is a common external tariff, the EEC bargains as a group with other countries in international organizations such as the GATT. (An important example was the agreement between the EEC and EFTA to form a joint free trade area by abolishing tariffs on industrial goods.) To protect the customs union, the EEC's industrial policy promotes competition and regulates state support for industries. The EEC is not strictly a common market because barriers to the mobility of factors of production have not been eliminated, although negotiations to remove these barriers are under way as part of the policy of creating a single European market by 1992. We shall return to this question at the end of this section.

The Effects of the Customs Union

The economic effects of a customs union were discussed in Section 5.6. The reader may recall that one of the difficulties in assessing the impact of a customs union is that a customs union promotes trade by lowering trade barriers between members, but trade between members may grow at the expense of trade with more efficient nonmembers. In practice it is virtually impossible to say whether trade between EEC members has grown at the expense of trade with nonmembers because we cannot be sure how trade would have grown in the absence of the customs union. Table 17.1 shows the

TABLE 17.1   The Growth of EEC Trade

	(Imports and exports as a percentage of GDP)		
	Intracommunity Imports	*Extracommunity Imports*	*Extracommunity Exports*
1960	6.3	10.4	9.1
1965	7.6	9.3	7.5
1970	9.2	9.1	7.9
1975	10.4	10.6	9.5
1980	12.3	12.6	9.7
1985	14.1	12.3	11.4

Source: Commission of the European Communities, *European Economy*, No. 34 (Nov. 1987).

growth of the trade of members of the EEC. Imports from other members (intracommunity imports) have increased as a percentage of national income. But, because overall trade has grown so rapidly, it has also been possible for imports from nonmembers (extracommunity imports) to grow as a percentage of income.

The problem of what might have been plagues empirical studies of the effects of tariffs. Therefore, estimates of the effects of the formation of the EEC cannot be perfect. Given this qualification, estimates of the static welfare effects of the formation of the EEC have generally suggested small welfare gains (less than 1 percent of the combined national incomes of the members). Why have studies suggested only small welfare gains?[6]

One reason is that the formation of a customs union only affects traded goods. For example, the output of the construction sector and a large part of the output of the service sector are not traded and are not directly affected by the removal of trade barriers. Another reason may be that tariffs are usually small to begin with (because countries avoid costly protection), so the creation of a customs union entails the removal of small barriers.[7] Perhaps the most important explanation is that many of the benefits of a customs union are long-term benefits (such as economies of scale) resulting from an increase in the size of the market and increased competition. Studies of the short-term welfare effects of customs unions miss these long-term gains. (However, it must be acknowledged that many of the perceived benefits from membership of the EEC are political and not economic.)

The Common External Tariff and EEC Revenue

Tariffs paid for about one third of the budget of the EEC in 1986. It may seem strange that we should find a revenue tariff used by a group of developed countries, since there are more efficient methods of taxation. The use of tariffs to fund the EEC's activities is partly because agreement cannot be reached on establishing a community tax. Members of the EEC have agreed to use value added taxes, part of the revenue of which is used to help finance the EEC. However, the rates and the goods covered vary among member countries.

Establishing a Single European Market[8]

The EEC has not yet achieved its objective of removing all barriers to trade. An obvious sign that the European market is not free from restriction is that there are still customs posts between member countries. Although

---

[6]The following reasons are given by Swann (1984), pp. 118–21.

[7]One of the reasons the United States removed the VER on Japanese cars was that the large welfare costs of the policy were becoming obvious.

[8]The following discussion draws on: Commission of the European Communities, *Completing the Internal Market: White Paper from the Commission to the European Council*, Luxembourg: Office for Official Publications of the European Communities, 1985.

people traveling between countries usually face little inconvenience, goods cannot be moved without restriction. Apart from the direct costs arising from fees and taxes, customs posts act as barriers to trade because delays at borders and paperwork add to the costs of shipping goods across borders. Before customs posts can be removed, ways to tackle noneconomic issues such as public security, immigration, and drug control must be found.

Economically, customs posts are necessary because of differences between members' technical standards and fiscal systems. Also, support (intervention) prices for agricultural products differ when converted at market exchange rates. To prevent differences in support prices acting as an inducement to trade, customs posts collect taxes and subsidies (monetary compensatory amounts) on agricultural goods. Finally, customs posts enforce bilateral agreements members of the community have negotiated with nonmember countries, such as voluntary export restraints for cars and textiles.

Differences between Tax Rates and Technical Standards

People have an incentive to engage in cross-border shopping if indirect taxes differ significantly. For example, in the United States it is sometimes worthwhile shopping in a nearby state to avoid sales tax. Consumers living along the Canadian or Mexican borders often find a shopping trip over the border worthwhile. Taxes levied at borders can prevent this, but do so by weakening the unity of the market. Asking national governments to give up their rights to determine national tax rates seems unrealistic, but if customs posts are to be removed, fiscal systems must at least be approximated. This is one of the main challenges that the community faces in the next few years. For some people, approximation of fiscal systems is seen as a step on the road to economic and monetary union.

Another problem is that technical standards differ between the member countries. In order to promote market integration, the Commission attempts to replace national regulations, such as safety standards or packaging rules, by community regulations.[9] This often creates controversy, such as when Germany was instructed to permit the sale of foreign beers that did not conform to the historical definition of beer.[10] Writing and revising regulations is a continuous process because regulations must be updated and amended to take account of technical progress.

Factor Mobility and the Common Market

The Treaty of Rome obligates members to reduce restrictions on capital flows "to the extent necessary to ensure the proper functioning of the common market." In practice, member states have retained restrictions on capital

---

[9]The Commission of the European Communities is the civil service of the EEC, Euratom, and the ECSC. It is responsible for formulating policy proposals to ensure that the aims of the Treaty of Rome are achieved.
[10]The sixteenth-century *Reinheitsgebot* required that beer be made only from barley, hops, yeast, and water.

TABLE 17.2   Migrant Workers as Percentage of Employees (1979)

	From Other Members	From Third Countries
Belgium	4.9	3.6
Denmark	0.7	1.5
France	1.4	8.0
Germany	2.1	7.3
Ireland	0.1	0.3
Italy	0.2	0.2
Luxembourg	23.5	13.3
Netherlands	1.3	0.9
United Kingdom	2.8	4.5
EUR 9[a]	1.9	4.8

[a]The EEC membership in 1979 included the nine countries listed here.
Source: Commission of the European Communities (1982), p. 64.

flows and regulated their capital markets in different ways. Fortunately, the costs of such barriers to capital mobility have been reduced by the development of a private international capital market, the Eurocurrency market. The members have agreed that capital movements will be unrestricted as part of the general movement to a single market by 1992. At the time of writing, this target seems optimistic.

Labor mobility is permitted in theory, but in practice labor mobility is not significant. Table 17.2 shows that migrant workers from other member countries make up less than 2 percent of the community workforce. At first sight this may seem surprising because wage levels and social security benefits differ greatly among members. Unskilled labor faces few official obstacles. It takes time to transfer welfare and pension rights, but it can be done.[11] Skilled labor cannot move freely around the EEC because qualifications earned in one member country are not automatically accepted in other member countries. Also, cultural differences and the fact that nine different languages are used in the EEC are sufficient to limit labor mobility.

The Customs Union and Regional Policy

Lack of labor mobility contributes to regional differences between per capita incomes. The Treaty of Rome states that the objectives of the EEC are to be attained by reducing disparities between regions, but does not outline a policy. Some people feel that an effective regional policy should accompany

---

[11] Reciprocal agreements ensure that migrants eventually receive the same welfare rights as nationals.

a free trade policy because some regions may suffer as a result of free trade. For example, funds could be used to retrain workers. When Britain and Ireland joined the EEC they pressed for the development of a regional fund. Although such a fund was established, in terms of resources regional policy at the community level is practically nonexistent. With the entry of Greece, Portugal, and Spain, pressure for a meaningful policy may grow. However, the community does not have sufficient resources to fund a regional policy, and there is resistance to a large increase in the EEC's budget, especially while the CAP continues to soak up most of the funds.

The Effects of 1992

Whether or not the policy of creating a single European market by 1992 is achieved, the policy has focused attention on barriers within the European community. Measures are being taken to reduce barriers. However, as barriers within the community are brought down, there is a possibility that trade between members will take the place of trade with nonmembers. Nonmember countries have expressed concern that the EEC is embarked on a policy that will close the European market to foreign firms.[12] (Critics of the policy have dubbed it "Fortress Europe.")

The Commission has argued that an expanding European market offers an excellent export opportunity for foreign firms. Also, the Commission points out that European countries favor and must maintain an open world trading system: a large percentage of community output is exported and the community will continue to depend on foreign markets after 1992. Not everybody shares this optimistic view; some companies have decided to shift plants to Europe to ensure that they have a foothold within the tariff barrier. Only time will tell whether the attempt to create a single European market by 1992 has led to a more or less open world trading system.

THE COMMON AGRICULTURAL POLICY (CAP)   **17.5**

The objectives of the CAP as outlined in Article 39 of the Treaty of Rome are:

    a. to increase agricultural productivity
    b. to ensure a fair standard of living for the agricultural community
    c. to stabilize markets
    d. to ensure the availability of supplies
    e. to ensure that supplies reach consumers at reasonable prices

---

[12] In other words, the fear is that trade diversion will be stronger than trade creation.

In practice, the operation of the CAP is dominated by the objective of producer support: over 90 percent of agricultural spending is devoted to producer support. In this respect, the CAP is similar to the agricultural policies of most other countries. Farm support is the usual objective. The primary method by which farmers in the EEC are supported is by the maintenance of high market prices for agricultural products. Two policy instruments are used: a tariff and intervention buying.

The Variable Levy

Agricultural production in the EEC is protected by a tariff wall, the *variable levy*, which raises the price of imported products to a chosen community price. As the world price rises or falls, the variable levy is reduced or increased to ensure that the post-tariff price of imported agricultural products remains the same.

The effects of the variable levy are an excellent example of the inefficiency of tariffs. Figure 17.1 shows the effects of the variable levy. The vari-

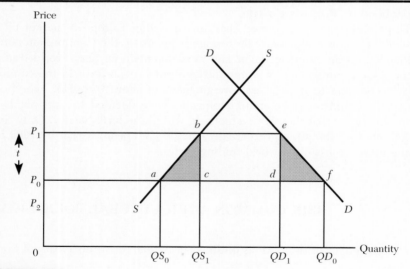

FIGURE 17.1

The Effects of the Variable Levy

EEC demand and supply are shown by DD and SS, respectively. At the world price of imports P_0, QD_0 is demanded, QS_0 is supplied domestically, and imports equal $QD_0 - QS_0$. A tariff (t) raises the EEC price of imports to P_1. Demand falls to QD_1, community supply rises to QS_1, and imports fall to $QD_1 - QS_1$. Consumer surplus falls by $P_0 P_1 ef$, producer surplus increases by $P_0 P_1 ba$, and tariff revenue of $cbed$ is collected. The net loss from the tariff equals $abc + def$. If the world price were to fall, say to P_2, the tariff would be increased to ensure that the EEC entry price (P_1) remains the same.

TABLE 17.3   EEC Prices for Agricultural Products as a Percentage of World Prices

	1970	1975	1980	1985	Average
Beef	123	121	95	100	111
Sugar	204	81	82	391	180
Butter	225	169	130	124	172
Maize	151	124	144	149	155
Wheat	151	80	115	137	126

Source: Rosenblatt (1988). Reprinted with permission of the International Monetary Fund.

able levy raises the price of imported agricultural products from P_0 to P_1. Community producers benefit because the tariff raises the prices they receive. The benefit to producers is shown by the increase in producer surplus (P_0P_1ba). Consumers suffer because they must pay higher prices for food. The loss to consumers is shown by the decline of consumer surplus (P_0P_1ef). In addition, the Commission of the European Communities receives tariff revenue, shown by the rectangle (*cbed*). There is a net welfare loss (*abc + def*) from the tariff because the loss to consumers is greater than the sum of tariff revenue and the welfare gain to producers.

The discussion in Chapter 4 showed that a tariff can be thought of as the equivalent of a consumption tax and a producer subsidy. The tax consumers pay is shown by the difference between world prices and community prices. How much does the CAP increase prices above world levels? The answer depends on the product. Table 17.3 shows the relationship between community prices and world prices. It suggests that community consumers pay much more than world prices.[13] The revenue generated by the external tariff indicates that the consumer tax is more than the producer subsidy.

In effect, taxes on food finance producer subsidies and help finance the activities of the European Economic Community. One view that is popular with economists is that if the true costs of the CAP were publicized, the CAP would not be acceptable to the electorate. To put it more bluntly, the CAP allows governments to give in to the agricultural lobby and buy votes in agricultural regions by a method that is accepted only because the true costs of

---

[13] If EEC tariffs on food were abolished, consumers would gain from lower prices for both imported food and EEC produce. The Commission argues that world prices overestimate this gain because they do not show the prices at which the community could buy large quantities of food (because purchases by the community would push up world prices). This argument presumes that lower EEC prices would lead to a large reduction of agricultural output in the community. Although some reduction might take place, it is also possible that much of the fall in price support would be offset by lower land prices and rents. The smaller the fall in EEC output, the smaller the increase in world prices would be.

the policy are hidden. How many people would vote for farm income subsidies financed by taxes on food?

Estimates of the effects of the CAP typically lead to the result that transfers from consumers and taxpayers to producers are around 3 percent of GDP. The net welfare loss (after deducting the tarriff revenue generated and the gain to producers) may be around 1 percent of GDP. However, these estimates assume that the alternative to the CAP is no agricultural support at all. As the Commission has pointed out, this is probably a "politically implausible" scenario.[14]

Intervention Buying

Community prices are stabilized by *intervention buying*. Ideally, produce purchased at low prices is sold when prices are high, and the market price is stabilized around the intervention price. In practice, lobbying by producers has succeeded in pushing intervention prices up so high that the authorities buy more than they sell. Surplus stocks are sold on world markets, but, because community prices exceed world prices, exports must be subsidized. For example, the EEC regularly sells subsidized butter to the USSR. In effect, price supports lead to overproduction and high prices for consumers, and taxpayers are faced with the cost of storing or disposing of the surplus output. Some people find this aspect of the CAP rather strange.

The Effects of the CAP on Nonmembers

The CAP has an adverse effect on the welfare of countries outside the EEC that export agricultural products. There are three reasons. First, these countries lose sales because the CAP encourages community production and discourages EEC imports of agricultural products. Second, they receive lower prices for their exports because world prices would be higher if the EEC imported more. Third, the CAP contributes to an unstable world market for agricultural products. The larger the size of the market for agricultural products, the more stable prices are likely to be (because low output in one area will sometimes be offset by high output somewhere else). The CAP closes off a major section of the world, thus price fluctuations are greater than they would be otherwise. The practice of selling community surpluses on world markets further disrupts the world market.

Reform of the CAP

The CAP is clearly in need of reform. In Section 4.4 it was shown that subsidies are preferable to tariffs. That conclusion is appropriate in the case of agricultural support. Some farmers' incomes are low, and direct income subsidies could address this problem. At present, high prices reward farmers

---

[14] See Commission of the European Community, *European Economy*, No. 35 (March 1988), p. 80.

regardless of need, and encourage overproduction. Moreover, there is strong reason to believe that the present CAP will never achieve the objective of raising farm incomes. Price support does little to increase agricultural incomes in the long term because high prices eventually lead to higher prices for inputs. For example, price support encourages people to pay more for land, thus the effects of price support on farm income are eroded by higher land costs. This view is supported by the fact that farm incomes have remained low relative to incomes in other sectors despite decades of farm support.[15]

INTERNATIONAL MONETARY POLICY   `17.6`

The Treaty of Rome was not directly concerned with international monetary issues. However, because trade between the members of the community was a major objective, the treaty recognized that national economic policies and currency values were matters of common interest. The members soon realized that exchange rates were a potentially important influence on trade, but little action was taken because the international monetary system of the early sixties was reasonably stable. Serious interest in the possibility of an EEC exchange rate policy dates from the late sixties when the underlying weaknesses in the Bretton Woods system were becoming obvious.

The Development of a Community Exchange Rate System

Three issues were important to the members of the EEC. First, they feared that international monetary instability would act as a deterrent to trade and undermine the gains from the creation of the common market. Second, currency fluctuations made the operation of the CAP difficult because it was based on the principle of common and stable agricultural prices. If support prices are to be the same in all member countries, they must change to reflect changes in the relative value of member currencies.[16] Thus, exchange rate instability could be a source of agricultural price instability.[17] Third, they felt that the role of the dollar in the Bretton Woods system had not always been beneficial to other countries.

---

[15] In Britain, at the beginning of the 1800s, it was generally thought that high land prices caused high grain prices, and that tariffs were necessary to protect domestic farmers from cheap imported food. Ricardo pointed out that tariffs on imported grain were the cause of high domestic grain prices, and high domestic prices increased the demand for land and led to high land prices. His argument that Britain should remove tariffs on imported grain was eventually successful. Often when agricultural policy is discussed it appears that Ricardo's analysis has been forgotten. Ricardo's argument is examined in Section 15.2.

[16] Domestic agricultural support prices in domestic currency must fall as domestic currency becomes more valuable relative to other currencies, and rise as domestic currency becomes less valuable.

[17] The member states have sometimes chosen not to revise support prices when exchange rates have changed. This created the need for tariffs and subsidies on agricultural products to prevent trade taking place merely to exploit differences in support prices.

The heads of state of the member countries of the EEC agreed in 1969 to pursue the objective of increased economic and monetary cooperation and requested the Commission to draw up a plan for the eventual establishment by stages of an economic and monetary union.[18] The Werner Plan that resulted recommended that in the first stage members limit exchange rate flexibility. Further integration was envisaged in the plan, but, partly because exchange rate stability was the most important objective of the members, agreement was only reached on the adoption of the first stage. Another reason for the limited nature of the agreement was that members were not willing to accept the supranational implications of agreeing to the automatic progression to a full economic and monetary union. (Although members have said that the "eventual" creation of an economic and monetary union is desirable, they have never agreed on any firm measures that might lead to this being achieved.)

The Snake

The implementation of the agreement to limit exchange rate flexibility had to be postponed because of international monetary instability accompanying the collapse of the Bretton Woods system. When the Smithsonian agreement (December 1971) temporarily restored stability, the members were able to proceed (in April 1972). The agreement was called the *snake* because the pattern traced by a group of currencies rising and falling together through time might resemble the movement of a snake. The founding members were France, Italy, Germany, and the Benelux. Members limited the divergence between their parities to 2.25 percent. The parities used were those of the Smithsonian agreement and were defined in terms of the dollar. Against the dollar, members maintained the Smithsonian parity band of ± 2.25 percent.[19]

Over the next two years, the snake operated as well as might be expected given the uncertainty that surrounded the international monetary system. Britain, Ireland, and Denmark joined on May 1, but speculation forced them to withdraw less than two months later (Denmark returned in October). During 1972 it became clear that the Smithsonian parities on which the snake was based were not sustainable. Speculation built up in early 1973. Italy was forced to withdraw from the snake and the remaining snake members floated against the dollar. For a while, realignments allowed the snake to struggle on. In January 1974, France withdrew. The snake continued in name until 1979 because a few countries (Germany and the Benelux) found that it was possible to maintain fixed exchange rates. This group had similar economic policies and was closely linked by trade. However, the zone was essentially based on the German mark and was not a European system.

---

[18] It is significant that the members agreed that monetary cooperation should be based on the "harmonization" of economic policies, not the unification of economic policies.

[19] Member currencies could change by ± 2.25% against the dollar. Therefore, the width of the band against the dollar (4.5%) was twice the width of the band against a snake currency. The dollar band was called the "tunnel" because the narrow snake could wiggle within the wider tunnel.

Why Did the Snake Die?

There are four reasons why the snake collapsed. First, the members were experiencing different economic conditions and pursued policies that were not consistent with the maintenance of fixed exchange rates. The Marjolin group investigating the reasons for the failure of the snake said: "Europe is no closer to EMU than it was in 1969. . . . The relatively harmonious economic and monetary grouping that was Europe during the 1960s has been coming apart in recent years; at no time during the past 25 years have national economic and monetary policies been more discordant, more divergent, than they are today."[20] In particular, the inflation rates differed greatly. Second, the exchange rates chosen were the Smithsonian parities. As a result of lack of exchange rate flexibility or adjustment during the Bretton Woods period, some currencies were overvalued and others were undervalued. It was only a matter of time before this became obvious. Third, the international monetary system was in a state of flux. People had seen the Bretton Woods system and the Smithsonian agreement collapse. Under these conditions, it would probably have been impossible to defend any regional fixed exchange rate system. Fourth, there may have been a lack of political will. Following the collapse of the Bretton Woods system and the onset of the oil crisis, members were probably more concerned with national problems than the success of the snake.

The European Monetary System

The *European Monetary System (EMS)* was created in 1979 in response to dissatisfaction with the performance of flexible exchange rates, and to a continued preference for fixed exchange rates. The basic characteristic of the EMS is that a member agrees to intervene in the foreign exchange market to stabilize the value of its currency against other member currencies. The value of a currency is expressed in *European currency units (ECUs)* and converted into a set of bilateral parities using the declared parities of other currencies. A currency is maintained within 2.25 percent of its declared parities against other currencies. (The margin for the Italian lira is 6 percent.) For example, if there are 40 Belgian francs per ECU, and 2 marks per ECU, there are 20 Belgian francs per mark. In this example, intervention would be required to maintain the franc-mark exchange rate between 20.45 and 19.55. Intervention is only required at the limits, but central banks have often tried to keep exchange rates well within permitted limits. This helps foster confidence in the exchange rate and avoids the buildup of speculation in favor of a parity change that may occur when a currency is at its limit. Flexible arrangements provide for a member to borrow funds for intervention from other members.

The United Kingdom has not joined the EMS. One stated reason is that influences on the value of sterling are sometimes different from the influences on other currencies' values. For example, the United Kingdom is a net exporter of oil whereas other community members are oil importers. Also, trade

---

[20] Quoted in Commission of the European Communities (1982), p. 55.

with other members is not quite as important for the United Kingdom as it is for other members, thus stable exchange rates with other community members are less important. However, the main reason for Britain remaining outside the EMS was ideological: the British government, and in particular Britain's prime minister, Margaret Thatcher, felt that exchange rates should be determined by market forces and not maintained by official intervention. At the time of writing, the other EEC members which are not members of the EMS are: Greece, Portugal, and Spain.

The ECU

As shown, the ECU serves as the *numeraire* of the EMS. It has two other functions: it serves as a means of settlement between monetary authorities, and it can be used as a divergence indicator. Because it is made up of a "basket" of European currencies, it helps show which currency is out of line with other currencies.[21] For example, if the mark is at the limit against the franc, but the franc has remained stable against the ECU, this suggests that it is the mark that is out of line.[22] Having said this, it may be worth emphasizing that the intervention requirements (margins) are specified in terms of bilateral exchange rates between pairs of national currencies.

The use of the ECU as a unit of account by private banks is growing. The reason is that the ECU tends to be stable because its value is determined by the average value of the currencies of nine members of the community, and most currency values are stabilized within the EMS. In 1986, the Bank for International Settlements agreed to operate a clearing and settlement bank for ECUs. This should allow ECU banking to increase.

Performance of the EMS

In its early years, parity changes were needed because the economic performance and inflation rates of the members differed.[23] Parity changes are difficult to negotiate because often members' interests conflict. However, the members showed that they could reach agreement on revised parities. Later, as inflation rates were brought down and became more alike, parities had to be changed less often. From March 1983 to April 1986 there was only one parity change (a devaluation of the lira in July 1985).

When realignments do take place, they are often insufficient to compensate for differences between members' inflation rates. Further changes may be needed, but this is not a source of great concern. Partly, the small changes

---

[21] In 1988, the currencies of Greece, Spain, and Portugal were not included in the basket.

[22] As a divergence indicator, the performance of the ECU is less than perfect. One reason is that the ECU is a weighted basket of currencies, with the weights reflecting each country's GNP and foreign trade. When a currency rises in value against the ECU, the value of the ECU rises. The amount by which the ECU rises is determined by the currency's weighting, thus the ECU does not react in the same way for all changes in currency values.

[23] There were two parity changes in each of the following years, 1979, 1981, and 1982, and one change in 1983. There were twelve parity changes during the first decade of the EMS (March 1979–March 1989).

reflect the purpose of the EMS, which is to avoid exchange rate instability. Also, small regular changes are less likely to encourage speculation. Finally, it must be acknowledged that, in the absence of an objective method for determining the sizes of parity changes, it would be difficult to reach agreement on one large realignment.

Differences between the EMS and Earlier Systems

The main difference between the EMS and the snake or the Bretton Woods system is that the EMS is much more flexible. Members have shown a willingness to modify domestic policies and adjust exchange rates when necessary, to avoid the development of fundamental disequilibria. The EMS has shown that a system to limit exchange rate variability is workable, and it is tempting to attempt to translate the features of the EMS into an international system. This would be a mistake for three reasons. First, trade between the members of the EEC is more important than it is between other countries. Thus, the members have more to gain from stable exchange rates. Second, members are willing to cooperate and compromise because the EMS is accompanied by other policies—members accept losses in one area because they expect gains in other areas. Third, the EMS is a symbol of European unity, and the members are committed to the success of the venture for political reasons.

The Future of the EMS

An interesting question is whether the EMS should be seen as an end in itself or as a step towards monetary union. In a monetary union, exchange risk and political risk are absent because there is a single currency and a single monetary authority. Exchange risk may be reduced by a system of fixed exchange rates, but fixed exchange rates can never generate the same degree of confidence as a single currency. While separate currencies exist, there is always the possibility that exchange rates will change. Moreover, attempting to maintain fixed exchange rates may lead countries to adopt policies that reduce the degree of monetary integration between members. For example, national monetary authorities may use capital controls to defend fixed exchange rates. (The possibility that capital controls will be imposed is an example of political risk.) At present there are no signs that monetary policy will be transferred to a supranational authority and a common currency adopted, therefore the EMS should probably be interpreted as an end in itself.

THE FUTURE OF THE EUROPEAN ECONOMIC COMMUNITY   17.7

The future development of the EEC is uncertain. The Commission is fond of suggesting that the option facing the EEC is to go forward or back, but it is more likely that the community will attempt to consolidate and improve existing policies. One of the main barriers to further significant economic integration is political: the EEC has probably reached the point where further economic integration cannot take place unless national governments hand over more power to the EEC.

Another problem is that there are few policies that benefit all members (free trade is probably the main exception), and present EEC policies are not sufficient to guarantee that gains are shared. As a result, members often block policies that would hurt their interests, even when the policies would benefit the community.[24] Also, the countries that have recently joined the community do not participate fully in all the policies of the community. Even without any new policies, a financial problem will develop for the community as existing policies (in particular the CAP) are extended to cover the new members. This will make new policies difficult to achieve.

Finally, significant economic integration cannot take place without major changes in the institutional structure of the EEC. The decision-making process in the EEC is not designed to wield power democratically at a community level. At present, there is nothing at the community level that resembles a national government to control economic policy and be held accountable.[25] This brings us back to the first point: it is difficult to imagine member countries sacrificing national sovereignty and establishing a European government.

Conclusion

Is the EEC a success or a failure? Probably the customs union and the EMS may be counted as successes of the EEC, but it is difficult to view the CAP favorably. However, in assessing the EEC we must keep in mind that the primary objective of the founders was to make a European war impossible. No one now considers a European war likely. To the extent that the EEC has contributed to this achievement, for the founders of the EEC this alone would be sufficient to justify its existence.

Summary of Main Points

The European Economic Community grew out of postwar economic cooperation and was established by the Treaty of Rome in 1957. There are three main policies: a free trade agreement, an agricultural policy, and an exchange rate stabilization system.

In a customs union, trade between members is free of tariffs or quotas, and a common tariff surrounds the union. Although tariff barriers and quotas between members have been removed, trade between members is not free of restriction. Tax rates differ between countries and there are differences between regulations and standards in the member countries. These differences act as barriers to the free movement of goods. Customs posts act as further barriers to trade because they lead to higher costs from paperwork

---

[24]The most notorious example is the repeated failure of the Commission to secure agreement to proposals to reform the CAP.
[25]The EEC Parliament is directly elected, but has little effective power.

and delays at borders. Plans have been put forward to remove non-tariff barriers to trade and unify the European market by 1992.

The common agricultural policy of the community is a classic example of an agricultural policy designed to benefit farmers with little attention to consumer interests. A tariff is used to increase the price of imported food and maintain high food prices within the community. Farmers have responded to high prices by increasing production; surpluses are purchased by intervention agencies to prevent the community price from falling. These surpluses are often sold on world markets.

The members of the community are closely related by trade and have an incentive to maintain stable exchange rates. The first attempts to establish a European exchange rate system in the seventies, the *snake*, failed. The *European Monetary System (EMS)* was established in 1979 and has survived surprisingly well. The EMS is an agreement to stabilize exchange rates within bands around target rates. These target rates are revised when needed, and with sufficient regularity so that major realignments of exchange rates are avoided.

The *European Currency Unit (ECU)* is an accounting unit based on the values of the European currencies. It is used to indicate which exchange rates should be revised. Because it is made up of a basket of currencies, and many of the currencies are participating in the EMS, the ECU tends to be reasonably stable. This has led to its use as an international unit of account.

Prospects for the adoption of significant new policies by the community do not seem strong because the budget of the European Economic Community is already under pressure, members have different interests, and few policies benefit all countries. Also, further progress can only occur if national governments surrender power to authorities at the community level.

Study Questions

1. In what ways is the EEC customs union incomplete?
2. What are the economic reasons for customs posts between countries?
3. What are the possible effects of the creation of a single European market (with virtually no barriers to trade) on members of the EEC? What are the possible effects on countries outside of the EEC?
4. What are trade diversion and trade creation? Explain why attempts to measure these are difficult, and usually fail to capture the full effects of customs unions.
5. Using the CAP as an example, discuss the effects of tariffs on food.
6. What are the effects of the CAP on nonmembers of the EEC?
7. What are the main features of the EMS? In what ways does it resemble the Bretton Woods system, and in what ways is it different?
8. Can and should the world attempt to establish a system like the EMS?

9. In what ways are fixed exchange rates and monetary union similar? How do they differ?

Selected References

Boltho, A., Ed. *The European Economy.* New York: Oxford University Press, 1982.

Cecchini, P., et al. *The European Challenge, 1992: The Benefits of a Single Market.* Commission of the European Communities, 1988. Distributed by Gower Publishing, Brookfield, VT.

Commission of the European Communities. *European Economic and Monetary Union.* Second Edition. Luxembourg: Office for Official Publications of the European Communities, 1981.

Commission of the European Communities. *The Economy of the European Community.* Luxembourg: Office for Official Publications of the European Communities, 1982.

Fratianni, M., and Peeters, T. *One Money for Europe.* London: Macmillan, 1978.

Robson, P. *The Economics of International Integration.* Second Edition. Boston: George Allen and Unwin, 1984.

Rosenblatt, J., et al. *The Common Agricultural Policy of the European Community: Principles and Consequences.* International Monetary Fund Occasional Paper No. 62. Washington, D.C., 1988.

Swann, D. *The Economics of the Common Market.* Fifth Edition. New York: Viking Penguin Inc., 1984.

Ungerer, H., et al. *The European Monetary System: Recent Developments.* International Monetary Fund Occasional Paper No. 48. Washington, D.C., December 1986.

Ypersele, J. van. *The European Monetary System.* Brussels: Commission of the European Communities, 1985.

18

LESS DEVELOPED

COUNTRIES

The theory of comparative advantage suggests that countries gain from specialization and trade. Less developed countries have participated in international trade, but have remained poor. This has led some people to question the idea that countries gain from trade. In this chapter we examine the relationship between trade and economic growth.

We begin by considering the characteristics of less developed countries and the importance of international trade for these economies. The long-term trend in the terms of trade of less developed countries has attracted a great deal of attention. We descibe the issues involved and comment on their significance. Then, we consider the role of international trade in economic development. Finally, we examine the international debt problem.

THE CHARACTERISTICS OF LESS DEVELOPED COUNTRIES   18.2

The basic characteristic of a less developed country is the obvious one that its people are poor. Although there is not a clear dividing line between rich and poor, for simplicity in most of this chapter countries are classified as either *advanced countries* (*ACs*) or *less developed countries* (*LDCs*). LDCs are sometimes referred to as *developing countries*.[1] Communist countries and the richest oil exporters are excluded from the analysis. ACs include the industrial market economies of North America, Western Europe, Australia, New Zealand, and Japan. In 1986, most of these countries had per capita incomes above $7,500. LDCs make up the rest of the world and include most of the

---

[1] In this chapter we have used the term *LDC* because, unfortunately, most of these countries are not developing economically, or are developing very slowly.

TABLE 18.1   Per Capita Incomes in Large Countries

Country	Population (millions, 1986)	GNP per Capita (dollars, 1986)
Ethiopia	43.5	120
Bangladesh	103.2	160
India	781.4	290
Pakistan	99.2	350
Indonesia	166.4	490
Philippines	57.3	560
Nigeria	103.1	640
Egypt	49.7	760
Thailand	52.6	810
Turkey	51.5	1,110
Brazil	138.4	1,810
Mexico	80.2	1,860
Italy	57.2	8,550
United Kingdom	56.7	8,870
France	55.4	10,720
Germany	60.9	12,080
Japan	121.5	12,840
United States	241.6	17,480

Source: From *World Development Report 1988.* Copyright © 1988 by The International Bank for Reconstruction and Development/The World Bank. Reprinted by permission of Oxford University Press, Inc. Compiled information from pp. 222–23.

countries in Africa, Asia, the Middle East, South America, and Oceania (excluding Australia and New Zealand). Most of these countries had per capita income levels below $2,000 in 1986. By way of illustration, Table 18.1 shows the income levels of some of the larger countries in the world and Table 18.2 gives average income levels for some classifications of countries used by the World Bank.[2]

Problems Associated with Poverty

Poverty is associated with problems such as lack of education, poor health, and malnutrition. These problems exist in all LDCs, but are worst in the poorest LDCs, the so-called low income economies, which had annual per capita incomes below $425 in 1986. In these countries live 1.4 billion people.[3] The level of education in low income economies is reflected in an adult liter-

---

[2]Although the qualitative conclusion that LDCs are relatively and absolutely poor is correct, too much weight should not be given to the figures. LDCs do not have the resources needed to collect accurate data. Also, nonmarket transactions are more important in LDCs.

[3]China is a low income country but is excluded from the analysis. In 1986, its population was 1,054 million and its per capita income level was $300.

TABLE 18.2   Income and Population

	Population (millions, 1986)	GNP per Capita (dollars, 1986)
Low income		
India	781.4	290
Other	657.4	200
Middle income	1,268.4	1,270
Industrial market		
economy	741.6	12,960

Source: From *World Development Report 1988*. Reprinted by permission of Oxford University Press, Inc. Compiled information from pp. 222–23.

acy rate of 38 percent compared to 99 percent in ACs. Malnutrition is common in LDCs; often they do not have enough food even to meet the average daily calorie requirements of their people. A more accurate assessment of malnutrition, taking into account the distribution and the nutritional value of the food, would show an even worse problem. Poverty, disease, and malnutrition lead to short life expectancies in LDCs. Life expectancy is 55 years in low income economies, 63 years in middle income economies, and 76 years in ACs. Table 18.3 compares values of these indicators of health and welfare for some LDCs with the average figure for ACs.

Incomes, Growth, and the International Economic System

Some countries have grown rapidly over the last two or three decades, in particular the *newly industrialized countries (NICs)*: Brazil, Mexico, Hong Kong, Singapore, South Korea, and Taiwan.[4] Others have grown more slowly. As Table 18.4 shows, growth has been slowest in the low income economies. One result, over the last two decades, is that the differences between per capita incomes in some poor and rich countries have widened. This is not true of all LDCs, but, whether increasing or not, the income disparity does seem large. For example, per capita income in the United States is almost 60 times higher than per capita income in India. This disparity of incomes is often used as an indictment of ACs and the world economic system as a whole. For example, the United Nations Declaration on the Establishment of a New International Economic Order states:

> The greatest and most significant achievement during the last decades has been independence from colonial and alien domination of a large number of peoples and nations which has enabled them to become members of the

---

[4]Krueger (1985) describes the performance of the "gang of four"—Hong Kong, Singapore, South Korea, and Taiwan—and considers the lessons to be learned.

TABLE 18.3   Health and Welfare Indicators for LDCs and ACs

Country	Adult Literacy (percentage, 1980)	Life Expectancy at Birth (years, 1986)	Calorie Supply (1985)
Ethiopia	15	46	1,704
Bangladesh	26	50	1,804
India	36	57	2,126
Pakistan	24	52	2,180
Indonesia	62	57	2,476
Philippines	75	63	2,260
Nigeria	34	51	2,139
Egypt	44	61	3,275
Thailand	86	64	2,399
Turkey	60	65	3,218
Brazil	76	65	2,657
Mexico	83	68	3,126
Industrial market economies (ACs)	99	76	3,357

Sources: From *World Development Report 1983 and 1988.* Copyright © 1983 and 1988 by the International Bank for Reconstruction and Development/The World Bank. Reprinted by permission of Oxford University Press, Inc.

TABLE 18.4   The Growth of Per Capita Incomes, 1965–86

Group of Countries	Average Annual Growth of Per Capita GNP (percentage)
Low income LDCs (below $425 in 1986)	
India	1.8
Other low income economies	0.5
Sub-Saharan Africa	0.9
Middle income LDCs (above $425)	2.6
Industrial market economies	2.3

Source: From *World Development Report 1988.* Reprinted by permission of Oxford University Press, Inc. Compiled information from pp. 222–23.

community of free peoples. Technological progress has also been made in all spheres of economic activities in the last three decades, thus providing a solid potential for improving the well-being of all peoples. However, the remaining vestiges of alien and colonial domination, foreign occupation, racial discrimination, *apartheid* and neocolonialism in all its forms continue to be among the greatest obstacles to the full emancipation and progress of the developing countries and all the peoples involved. The benefits of technological progress are not shared equitably by all members of the international community. The developing countries, which constitute 70 percent of the world's population, account for only 30 percent of the world's income. It has proved impossible to achieve an even and balanced development of the international economic community under the existing international economic order. The gap between developed and developing countries continues to widen in a system which was established when most of the developing countries did not even exist as independent states and which perpetuates inequality.[5]

Although the disparity between countries' per capita incomes is a source of concern, especially in view of the limited attempts made by ACs to foster international economic development, we must be careful when attempting to blame ACs for causing low per capita incomes in LDCs. The growth of LDC income has often been very rapid, sometimes far greater than growth in ACs. But, as Table 18.5 shows, income growth has been offset by population growth.

TABLE 18.5   Growth Rates of Population and Income

	1955–1970			1970–1980		
Group	Population Growth	GNP Growth	Growth of Per Capita GNP	Population Growth	GNP Growth	Growth of Per Capita GNP
Low income						
India	2.2	4.0	1.8	2.1	3.4	1.3
Other	2.4	4.4	2.0	2.7	2.7	0.0
Middle income	2.4	6.0	3.5	2.4	5.6	3.1
Industrial market	1.1	4.7	3.6	0.8	3.2	2.4
Europe	0.7	4.8	4.1	0.2	2.6	2.4
Japan	1.0	10.3	9.2	1.1	5.4	4.2
United States	1.4	3.4	2.0	1.0	3.1	2.1

Source: From *World Development Report 1984.* Copyright © 1984 by The International Bank for Reconstruction and Development/The World Bank. Reprinted by permission of Oxford University Press, Inc. Compiled information from p. 82.

---

[5]The text of this declaration and a summary of the discussion that accompanied its adoption is contained in the *Yearbook of the United Nations, 1974,* New York: United Nations. Extracts of the declaration are reprinted in Adams (1985), p. 468–77.

**TABLE 18.6   The Destination of Manufactured Exports, 1986
(in percent)**

	Industrial Market	Nonmarket Economies	High-Income Oil Exporters	LDCs
India (1985)	59	10	7	24
Other low income economies	66	4	8	22
Middle income economies	60	7	3	31
Industrial market economies	74	2	2	22

Sources: From *World Development Report 1987 and 1988.* Copyright © 1987 and 1988 by The International Bank for Reconstruction and Development/The World Bank. Reprinted by permission of Oxford University Press, Inc. Compiled information from p. 228 (1987) and pp. 248–49 (1988).

It is difficult to see how ACs are responsible for this problem. Differences between the performance of LDCs also cast doubt on the view that there is an inherent bias in the international economic system. We must look for other explanations of both growth and stagnation. A useful starting point is to consider the structure and composition of LDC trade.

The Trade and Production of LDCs

Table 18.6 shows that LDCs trade mainly with ACs. This is not surprising because they export mainly *primary products.*[6] There is limited scope for trade between countries that only produce a few primary products. Exports of manufactured products by LDCs have increased over the last two decades, but the gains have largely been recorded by a small group of countries, in particular the Asian NICs. For some countries, one or two primary products account for more than 80 percent of exports (see Table 18.7). As a result, LDCs are heavily influenced by fluctuations in the prices of primary products. For this reason, some development proposals have focused on the prices of primary products. However, it would be wrong to think that LDCs are the only exporters of primary products; some ACs (such as Australia, Canada, and New Zealand) export large quantities of primary products.

The structure of production in LDCs is different from that in ACs (see Table 18.8). Agriculture is more important and services and industrial production are less important to LDCs. Long-term economic growth typically includes a shift from agriculture to industry. However, in the early stages of economic development, its size makes the performance of the agricultural sector an important part of economic growth. This sector is also of special

---

[6]Primary products are those products in categories 0–4 of the Standard International Trade Classification (SITC). They include agricultural products, metals, minerals, and fuels.

TABLE 18.7   Examples of Export Concentration (1985)

Country	Products	Percentage of Exports
Bangladesh	Jute Goods (42), Raw Jute (13)	55
Botswana	Diamonds (76), Copper (9)	85
Burma	Rice (24), Teak (38)	62
Burundi	Coffee (84)	84
Chile	Copper (46), Iron Ore (2)	48
Colombia	Coffee (50), Cotton (2)	52
Costa Rica	Coffee (32), Bananas (21)	54
Ghana	Cocoa (55), Wood (3)	59
Guatemala	Coffee (43), Cotton (7)	49
Guyana	Sugar (32), Bauxite (48)	80
Jamaica	Alumina (38), Bauxite (15)	54
Liberia	Iron Ore (64), Rubber (18)	82
Malawi	Tobacco (41), Tea (20)	61
Rwanda	Coffee (71), Tin (6)	78
Somalia	Live Animals (73), Bananas (15)	88
Tanzania	Coffee (40), Cotton (8)	49
Uganda	Coffee (92)	92
Zambia	Copper (79)	79

Source: IMF *International Financial Statistics*, April 1987.

TABLE 18.8   The Structure of Production

| | (percentage of GDP originating in each sector) | | |
	Agriculture	Industry	Services
India	32	29	39
Other low income economies	38	20	41
Middle income economies	15	36	48
Industrial market economies	3	35	61

Source: From *World Development Report 1988*. Reprinted by permission of Oxford University Press, Inc. Compiled information from pp. 226–27.

concern because many of the poorest people in the world live in agricultural communities. Unfortunately, government policies have often been biased against this sector.[7]

---

[7] See Chhibber, A., and Wilton, J., "Macroeconomic Policies and Agricultural Performance in Developing Countries," *Finance and Development* 23 (Sept. 1986), pp. 7–9.

18.3 THE TERMS OF TRADE PROBLEM

One "explanation" of underdevelopment is so common that it is worth examining in detail. The argument is that LDCs suffer from a declining long-term trend in their terms of trade.[8] It is said that LDCs are poor because they must export increasing amounts for a given amount of imports. Since LDCs are poor, by definition, it may seem unnecessary to evaluate the terms of trade argument. However, if there truly is concern about the plight of LDCs, an attempt must be made to identify the true causes of poverty. Faulty diagnosis can lead to incorrect policy prescriptions: at best, we might end up treating the symptoms, not the disease; at worst, we could prolong or worsen the disease.

In order to assess the validity and significance of the terms of trade argument, three things must be considered:

1. the products that are important
2. the period over which to examine price changes
3. the implications of these price changes for economic welfare

The Choice of Products

LDCs often export primary products, so it is natural to focus on these products. Some are oil exporters, but oil prices are often excluded as being a special case (either because oil rose in price dramatically during the seventies or because oil prices are subject to special influences). It is arguable that products that have experienced abnormal decreases in price should also be excluded as being special cases. However, if some products are excluded as being atypical, the objectivity of the measurement of the terms of trade is brought into question.[9]

The Sample Period

The problems of measurement multiply when a sample period is chosen because the choice of the sample period has an important influence on the results. Ideally, the period should begin with a base year when prices were neither abnormally high or abnormally low (otherwise the return to "normal" prices may be confused with the trend in prices). The significance of the base year is illustrated by Figure 18.1, which shows changes in the real price of

---

[8]The terms of trade may be defined as the ratio of the price of exports to the price of imports. The following discussion focuses on the long-term trend of the terms of trade. Plans to stabilize or increase primary product prices are examined in the next section.

[9]Because LDCs often export a narrow range of primary products, changes in the average price of primary products are usually less important to individual LDCs than changes in the prices of particular products. For example, the dramatic fall in oil prices in early 1986 helped LDC oil importers but hurt LDC oil exporters, which had come to rely on the revenue from oil.

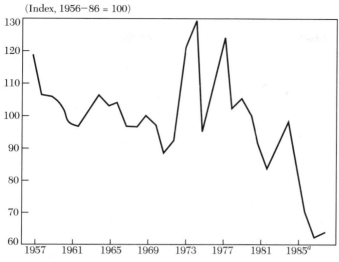

Real Non - Oil Commodity Prices, 1957 87

(Index, 1956−86 = 100)

*a*Data after end-1986 are estimates

FIGURE 18.1

Real Non-Oil Commodity Prices, 1957–1987

Note: Prices of nonfuel primary commodities exported by developing countries are deflated by the prices of manufactures. (Diagram taken from *IMF World Economic Outlook*, April 1987, p. 94)

primary products over the last three decades.[10] Given the drop after 1980, a downward trend seems possible, but it is difficult to measure the size of the trend. Choosing 1973 or 1976 as the base year makes the decline in prices look far worse than if we choose 1961 or 1971. Also, it is impossible to say whether the data from the last few years of the sample represent part of a trend or a temporary fluctuation. Only time will tell.

Welfare and the Terms of Trade

Finally, we must assess the significance of the results. A decline in price does not necessarily imply lower welfare. The prices of digital watches and color televisions have declined relative to prices in general, but these changes are not viewed as a problem. If prices decline because of technological improvements that reduce the costs of producing primary products, LDCs may still be better off after a price fall than they were before. (In fact, improve-

---

[10] The real price of commodities measures changes in the price of commodities relative to manufactured goods.

ments in technology have reduced production costs and increased the supply of many primary products.) Therefore, lower prices do not necessarily imply lower welfare.

The Issue of Exploitation or Bias

If it could be shown that there is a significant long-run downward trend in the prices of primary products relative to manufactured goods, would this prove that the world trading system is biased against LDCs? The answer is simple: no. There are many plausible reasons why commodity prices might decline in price relative to manufactured goods. The prices of primary products reflect structural changes that have little to do with the international trading system. Technological progress has reduced the costs of production of primary products, provided substitutes for primary products, and enabled producers of manufactured products to economize on the inputs they use. Another influence has been that the demand for some primary products by rich countries has weakened as they have shifted away from heavy manufacturing toward light manufacturing and services. Finally, a long-term downward trend in the relative price of primary products can be explained by changes in the nature of manufactured products. The quality of manufactured products is improving and the degree of technological sophistication is increasing continuously. In contrast, primary products have changed little over the past few decades (coffee is coffee and doesn't change noticeably from one decade to another).

The Significance of the Terms of Trade Issue

The controversy over the terms of trade results from the choice of which facts to present and the interpretation put upon them. The controversy is important because we should attempt to diagnose the trade problems of development correctly, but the question of the terms of trade may have received unwarranted attention. Exports of primary products usually account for less than 10 percent of a country's national income. Doubling the prices of these commodities would do little to change the disparity between rich and poor countries, even allowing for some generous multiplier effects. Historical experience also suggests that LDCs are not likely to get rich exporting such products. Countries that have diversified their economies and exported manufactured goods have grown far more rapidly.

Why are the prospects limited for producers of primary products? Part of the explanation is that (in the short run) the demand for primary products is inelastic with respect to price. Therefore, when the supply of primary products increases, the price of primary products falls so much that producers receive less revenue than they did initially.[11] This is illustrated in Figure

---

[11]The reverse is also true, a reduction in supply leads to an increase in revenue, as OPEC discovered in 1973–74. See Section 14.5.

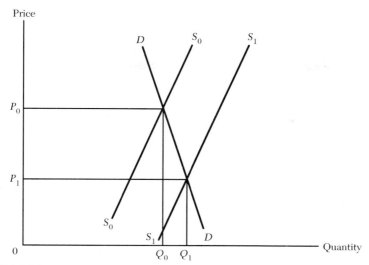

FIGURE 18.2

The Effects of an Increase in Supply When Demand Is Inelastic
When demand is inelastic, the percentage change is quantity is less than the percentage change in price. Thus, when the quantity increases from Q_0 to Q_1, the fall in price is proportionately larger than the increase in quantity, and producers' revenue falls.

18.2. Also, as real incomes rise over time, consumers demand more manufactured goods incorporating the latest technology, they do not demand more primary products. Thus, the demand for primary products does not increase with income as much as the demand for manufactured products. The conclusion that suggests itself is that rather than focus on the prices of primary products, it may be more fruitful to encourage exports of manufactured products.

REFORM PROPOSALS AND THE NEW INTERNATIONAL 18.4
ECONOMIC ORDER

In 1964, the first United Nations Conference on Trade and Development (UNCTAD) was convened in Geneva. UNCTAD has since become a permanent part of the United Nations representing the views of LDCs. During the sixties the main objectives were to secure preferential tariffs for LDCs and increased aid. Some success was achieved in the pursuit of the first objective. During the early seventies, the objectives broadened to include fundamental changes in the international economic system.

In 1974, a resolution was passed in the United Nations General Assembly calling for the creation of a *new international economic order* (NIEO), and plans for the implementation of a NIEO were the subject of the UNCTAD IV conference in Nairobi, Kenya, in 1976. The flavor of the proposed NIEO can be appreciated by consideration of its four basic recommendations relating to:

1. market access and the trade policies of ACs
2. cartels to maintain and increase commodity prices
3. commodity price stabilization
4. increased flows of aid

Market Access and the Trade Policies of ACs

LDCs doubt whether ACs are really serious in their promotion of free trade. Manufacturing in ACs is protected by tariffs that increase as higher stages of production are reached. Escalating tariffs are seen as barriers to development because they prevent LDCs from competing in AC markets.[12] *Tariff preferences* are sometimes conceded in the form of a lower tariff on imports from LDCs than applies to imports from ACs. However, the concessions often include limits on the amount an LDC can export. Also, LDCs have faced trade barriers in products in which they are competitive. Two of the most glaring examples of trade barriers that hurt LDCs are the barriers that ACs maintain on imports of textiles and steel, which are particularly odious because these are products that LDCs can produce competitively. Production of steel and textiles does not require high technology and LDCs have a competitive advantage in these products because they have lower labor costs.

Participation in GATT

LDCs do not participate in GATT. One reason is that they do not accept the principle of reciprocity in GATT negotiations: they feel that tariff concessions by ACs should not be conditional on the removal of their own tariff barriers. Another reason is that some LDCs are not convinced that they have a lot to gain from free trade. Unfortunately, it seems that the danger LDCs face from an escalation of tariff barriers is usually ignored. Given that preferential tariffs apply to a limited range of products and often include quantity limits, LDCs have probably gained far more from the reduction in general barriers to trade under the auspices of GATT than they have from preferential tariffs.

Coverage of GATT

The coverage of GATT agreements has been a source of concern. In particular, LDCs complain that agricultural products are excluded. This grievance is clearly justified. In general, developed countries have encourged domestic agricultural production and used trade barriers to separate domestic

---

[12] See Table 5.1, 5.2, and the related discussion. Also, see Table 15.2.

and international markets.[13] The result has been overproduction and a decline in world food prices. Also, dumping surplus output on world markets may have destabilized world food prices. The cost of agricultural policies has led some countries to express the view that reform is needed in this area. Although gains from lower trade barriers in agriculture are clearly possible, the tradition of government intervention to support domestic agriculture might lead us to be skeptical about the prospects of specialization in agricultural products leading to long-term economic growth in LDCs.

Raw Material Prices and Producer Cooperation

The importance of primary products to LDCs is reflected in the NIEO's objectives of stabilizing and increasing primary product prices. Let us begin by considering the objective of increasing primary product prices.

The oil price increase of 1973–74 created problems for LDCs but also seemed to offer a solution to their problems, that is, it led countries to hope that they would be able to follow the example of OPEC and push up the prices of their exports. One reason why such action is needed, it is alleged, is because the control of primary product markets exercised by companies from ACs leads to artificially low prices.[14] We do not need to spend time discussing such allegations of exploitation. The major argument against producer agreements does not concern the underlying motives—it is simply that such agreements are not sustainable.

If the price of a product is to be raised by a cartel agreement, all the major producers of the product must join so that supply can be restricted in order to push up the price. Overproduction is prevented by the allocation of production quotas. It is possible that some major producers may refuse to join, for example, because they want to be able to take advantage of technological developments and do not want their output to be limited by the cartel. Also, some producers may not join because they have different political or economic objectives from the other producers. (Recall that ACs are often major producers of primary products.)

The problems do not end there. If the cartel succeeds in raising the market price, the standard problem is that the higher price acts as an incentive to members to "cheat" by overproducing or to withdraw from the agreement. Also, higher prices may eventually lead to competition from alternative sources of supply. Few markets have the characteristics that allowed OPEC to be successful for so long: an inelastic product demand and a long period needed before alternative sources of supply can be developed. During the seventies, oil producers were able to increase the price of oil by restricting supply, but even OPEC could not succeed for ever. The development of new sources of

---

[13]The CAP is a good example; see Section 17.4.

[14]See Diaz-Alejandro, C. F., "International Markets for LDCs—The Old and the New," *American Economic Review* (Papers and Proceedings) 68 (May 1978), pp. 264–9; reprinted in Adams (1985), pp. 487–95.

supply and a fall in the rate of growth of demand for oil eventually led to a fall in oil prices during the mid eighties.

Cartels may also be undermined by technological advances leading to the development of synthetic substitutes that are cheaper or of higher quality than natural materials. UNCTAD's recommendation that "in cases where natural materials can satisfy the requirements of the market, new investment for the expansion of the capacity to produce synthetic materials and substitutes should not be made" is reminiscent of the calls of the Luddites to stop the spread of mechanization.[15]

Export Prices and Export Earnings

LDCs have unstable export earnings because of fluctuations in the price and quantity of exports. Part of the problem is that because LDCs often rely on a few commodities, price and quantity fluctuations are not averaged out as much as when exports are diversified. One of the objectives of UNCTAD has been to secure agreement on bufferstock schemes to stabilize the prices of important commodities. The idea of using bufferstocks to stabilize prices of important commodities seems attractive because a small number of commodities accounts for a large proportion of LDC trade. Ten commodities are often the focus of these proposals: cocoa, coffee, tea, sugar, cotton, jute, sisal, rubber, copper, and tin.

Bufferstocks

Essentially, a *bufferstock* can be used to stabilize commodity prices in the same way that international reserves are used to stabilize an exchange rate. When prices are low, the intervention agency increases the demand for the product and pushes up the price by adding to the bufferstock. When the price is abnormally high, sales are made from the bufferstock.

Attempts to stabilize prices in this way have generally been unsuccessful. The initial problem is that funds must be available for the creation of a bufferstock. LDCs do not have the required funds and ACs have been reluctant to provide the funds needed. A second problem concerns the selection of the target price to be used by the intervention agency. Producers have an incentive to push for a high intervention price. But, if the price is too high, an excess supply results and the intervention agency must continuously add to the bufferstock. Moreover, the excess supply created by too high a price is likely to get worse because high prices attract new producers and lead consumers to look for substitutes. Eventually, the intervention agency runs out of money and the bufferstock agreement collapses.

If a bufferstock is to stabilize prices, it must buy when prices are low and sell when prices are high. In other words, leaving storage and operations costs aside, the agreement should run at a profit. Requests by LDCs for substantial

---

[15]The Luddite riots began in Britian in 1811. Machines were smashed in an attempt to stop the mechanization of the woolen industry.

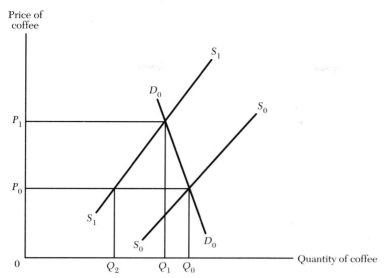

FIGURE 18.3

Bufferstocks and the Stability of Earnings

The demand for a primary product (coffee) is shown by the demand curve D_0D_0. Initially, export revenue is $P_0 \times Q_0$. Assume that the supply of coffee falls from S_0S_0 to S_1S_1 because of a bad harvest. In the absence of a bufferstock, the price of coffee increases from P_0 to P_1. The tendency for export earnings to fall because of the fall in quantity is offset (to some extent) by the increase in price. Revenue is $P_1 \times Q_1$ after the fall in supply. Price stabilization prevents this offsetting price effect. Producers sell Q_2 at P_0 and $Q_0 - Q_2$ is sold from the bufferstock. Revenue is only $P_0 \times Q_2$. Thus, price stabilization leads to a greater fall in export earnings.

resources to run such schemes suggest that the object is price support not price stability. If so, the schemes are probably doomed to failure. Also, if price support is the object of a bufferstock, it is not surprising that ACs have been reluctant to spend money on schemes designed to increase the prices of the products they buy.

Even if a bufferstock can stabilize prices, this does not guarantee that export earnings will be stabilized. When price changes result from demand fluctuations, export earnings will be stabilized by a bufferstock that stabilizes market prices. But, when price changes result from supply fluctuations, fixing prices may destabilize export earnings. For example, export earnings tend to fall when there is a fall in supply. If prices are allowed to increase as supply falls, this can help maintain earnings. Price stabilization prevents the price increase and leads to lower export earnings. Therefore, for some products, bufferstocks destabilize export earnings. This is illustrated in Figure 18.3.

TABLE 18.9   Official Development Aid as a Percentage of Donor's GNP

	1965	1975	1986	Dollar Amount, 1986 (millions)
Australia	.53	.65	.47	752
Belgium	.60	.59	.49	549
Canada	.19	.54	.48	1,695
Denmark	.13	.58	.89	695
France	.76	.62	.72	5,105
Germany	.40	.40	.43	3,832
Italy	.10	.11	.40	2,404
Japan	.27	.23	.29	5,634
Netherlands	.36	.75	1.01	1,740
Norway	.16	.66	1.20	798
Sweden	.19	.82	.85	1,090
United Kingdom	.47	.39	.32	1,750
United States	.58	.27	.23	9,564

Source: From *World Development Report 1988.* Reprinted by permission of Oxford University Press, Inc. Compiled information from p. 262 (with errata).

Resource Transfers

The United Nations established a target for ACs of official development aid to LDCs of at least 0.7 percent of an AC's GNP, but few countries have reached this goal. In fact, as Table 18.9 shows, over the last two decades aid has declined as a percentage of some donors' incomes.

If past official aid had had a clearly demonstrable effect on income disparities, for many people the case for transfers from rich to poor countries would be overwhelming (in view of the disparity between incomes). In fact, the record of aid has been patchy at best. Individual projects have been successful, but foreign aid has not reduced overall disparities between countries. Whether this is because aid has been wasted or because it has been too small is a matter of debate. We shall not examine this issue further because there are no signs that a massive increase in aid is likely. Also, because aid takes so many different forms, space does not permit an examination of this debate.[16]

SDR Allocations

One proposal that crops up regularly is that IMF special drawing rights (SDRs) should be allocated to poor countries as a form of aid and not (as at present) on the basis of IMF quotas.[17] It is sometimes mistakenly argued that

[16]Meier (1984, pp. 281–309), OECD (1985), and Cassen (1986) are useful introductions to the major issues.
[17]SDRs are described in Seciton 13.2.

helping LDCs in this way is virtually costless because SDRs cost nothing to create. True, SDRs cost nothing to create, but when a country uses SDRs (to pay for goods or settle debts) the recipient in effect accepts SDRs rather than real resources. Thus, there is a resource cost from the acceptance of SDRs even if there is not a cost of creation. If ACs are not willing to make direct payments of aid, or write off debts, why should they be expected to agree to allocations of SDRs that have the same resource cost?

Other Recommendations

Other recommendations include: the development of appropriate technology and its transfer to LDCs; the adoption of a set of rules to regulate the behavior of multinational corporations; the cancelling of the debts of LDCs; the formation of LDC customs unions; a share in the profits (if any) of seabed mining; compensation for skilled workers from LDCs who choose to remain in ACs.

The numerous proposals reflect the plight of LDCs: we are left feeling that LDCs are asking ACs to do anything, but at least do something.[18] The challenge is to help LDCs succeed in the present international economic system, if demands for a new order are to be abandoned. Perhaps the most important step for ACs in meeting this challenge is to reduce the barriers to trade on imports from LDCs. This policy would increase incomes in ACs as well as in LDCs. One significant difficulty is to overcome the power of pressure groups representing the groups in ACs who would lose. The next section considers the policies that LDCs might adopt to increase economic growth.

STATEGIES FOR TRADE AND DEVELOPMENT   18.5

Broadly speaking, two types of trade strategy have been used by LDCs: a policy of restricting trade in an effort to concentrate on domestic production (import substitution), and increasing exports in an attempt to increase domestic income through international trade (export promotion).

Import Substitution

The rationale for *import substitution* is that the demand for primary products is inelastic with respect to price and income. Therefore, increasing the supply of primary products has an adverse effect on price (as Figure 18.2 shows), and long-term growth of income in ACs does not lead to a significant increase in the demand for these products. LDCs also feel that trade barriers and lack of technology prevent them from competing with ACs in manufactured products. Therefore, protection is needed in order to develop an industrial base.

---

[18]The different proposals also reflect differences between the interests of the LDCs.

Export Promotion

The proponents of export promotion argue that *export promotion* is preferable to import substitution because production is not limited by the domestic market. (The reader may recall that the benefit of an expanded market is one of the basic arguments in favor of trade.) Although proponents accept that governments may encourage exports, they take a more market-oriented view of the world than the proponents of import substitution. For example, Krueger (1985) says: "Policies assisting those attempting to export have a high probability of success; policies determining what commodities shall be exported are probably destined to failure" (p. 208). To encourage export-led growth, other government policies should seek to maintain a stable economy, free trade, and a realistic exchange rate (a rate that changes gradually to reflect differential inflation rates and does not overvalue domestic currency).

Import Substitution versus Export Promotion

The policies of export promotion and import substitution have been extensively studied. The consensus that has emerged from empirical studies is that export promotion is a more effective policy for promoting growth than import substitution. For example, Figure 18.4 and Table 18.10 show the results of a World Bank study of the relationship between trade strategies and

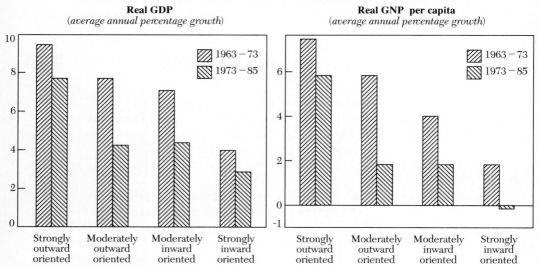

FIGURE 18.4

Outward- and Inward-Oriented Trade Strategies

Note: These bar charts summarize the performance of countries shown in Table 18.10. (*Source: The World Development Report, 1987*, p. 84. Copyright © 1987 by The International Bank for Reconstruction and Development/The World Bank. Reprinted by permission of Oxford University Press, Inc.)

TABLE 18.10 Outward-Looking and Inward-Looking Strategies

Average Annual Percentage Growth Rate of Real GNP per Person

1963–73

Outward-oriented				Inward-oriented			
Strongly		Moderately		Moderately		Strongly	
Singapore	9.0	Brazil	5.5	Yugoslavia	4.9	Turkey	3.5
S. Korea	7.1	Israel	5.4	Mexico	4.3	Dominican	
Hongkong	6.0	Thailand	4.9	Nigeria	4.2	Republic	3.4
		Indonesia	4.6	Tunisia	4.0	Burundi	3.2
		Costa Rica	3.9	Kenya	3.9	Argentina	3.1
		Malaysia	3.8m	Philippines	2.2	Pakistan	3.1
		Ivory Coast	3.5	Bolivia	2.0	Tanzania	2.7
		Colombia	3.3	Honduras	1.9	Sri Lanka	2.3
		Guatemala	2.7	El Salvador	1.4	Ethiopia	1.9
				Madagascar	1.1	Chile	1.7
				Nicaragua	1.1	Peru	1.5
						Uruguay	1.5
						Zambia	1.2
						India	1.1
						Ghana	0.4
		Cameroon	−0.1	Senegal	−0.6	Bangladesh	−1.4
						Sudan	−1.9

1973–85

Outward-oriented				Inward-oriented			
Strongly		Moderately		Moderately		Strongly	
Singapore	6.5	Malaysia	4.1	Cameroon	5.6	Bangladesh	2.0
Hongkong	6.3	Thailand	3.8	Indonesia	4.0	India	2.0
S. Korea	5.4	Tunisia	2.9	Sri Lanka	3.3	Burundi	1.2
		Brazil	1.5	Pakistan	3.1	Dominican	
		Turkey	1.4	Yugoslavia	2.7	Republic	0.5
		Israel	0.4	Colombia	1.8		
		Uruguay	0.4	Mexico	1.3		
		Chile	0.1	Philippines	1.1		
				Kenya	0.3		
				Honduras	−0.1	Ethiopia	−0.4
				Senegal	−0.8	Sudan	−0.4
				Costa Rica	−1.0	Peru	−1.1
				Guatemala	−1.0	Tanzania	−1.6
				Ivory Coast	−1.2	Argentina	−2.0
				El Salvador	−3.5	Zambia	−2.3
				Nicaragua	−3.9	Nigeria	−2.5
						Bolivia	−3.1
						Ghana	−3.2
						Madagascar	−3.4

Source: The Economist, July 4, 1987. Copyright 1987 The Economist Newspaper Ltd. Reprinted with permission.

economic growth for forty-one developing countries. The growth rates of the countries that pursued outward-oriented policies were greater than the growth rates of countries that pursued inward-oriented stategies.

The case for import substitution is a general version of the infant industry argument, and has the same weakness: protecting an industry removes the incentive for it to become competitive. Although import substitution has encouraged the growth of the protected sector, it has not been able to make the protected sector efficient. Import substitution has also had limited success in establishing manufacturing. Assembly plants have been established, but usually LDCs have not been able to manufacture components efficiently. One reason is that LDC markets are too small for efficient large-scale production.[19] Another is that manufacturing techniques and machines have been imported from ACs, where a major objective is to economize on the use of labor. These machines required skilled maintenance and skilled operators. Therefore, the technology was not always appropriate for use in LDCs.

Another problem is that import substitution has had adverse effects on the export sector. There are three reasons for this. First, import substitution encourages some domestic industries, but other industries that use the products of the protected industries, including exporters, face higher costs. Second, exporters suffer because their costs increase as resources are attracted to the import-competing sector. Third, an overvalued exchange rate is a characteristic of countries that pursue import substitution. Exporters suffer because an overvalued exchange rate encourages imports and discourages exports. The agricultural sector is hurt particularly badly because it does not usually benefit from protection and the overvalued exchange rate leads to a low price for imported food.

Overvaluation leads to the adoption of other policies that also hurt exporters. To prevent a large trade deficit, foreign exchange is rationed according to use. Such rationing leads to corruption and bureaucratic delays. This further weakens the competitiveness of exporters because they have difficulty obtaining foreign exchange to pay for imported inputs. Also, capital flight from a country is likely if it seems that the overvalued exchange rate will be abandoned (because holders of foreign assets receive a capital gain when domestic currency is devalued). In short, the policy of import substitution, which was supposed to reduce the need for foreign exchange, ends up creating a greater shortage of foreign exchange.

The success of export promotion is dependent on the ability of LDCs to penetrate foreign markets. Although a few LDCs have pursued export promotion successfully, critics of export promotion suggest that sufficient market access cannot be expected to enable all LDCs to pursue this policy. A more optimistic view is that market access will not be a problem because markets

---

[19] Some industries in Brazil, China, and India were exceptions to this generalization because the domestic markets were large enough to sustain large-scale production (IMF [1987], p. 88).

will expand. As LDCs increase their exports, they will increase their imports from ACs and from other LDCs. As a result, market penetration by LDC products will not be an issue.

Debate continues over the relative merits of the two strategies. For example, advocates of import substitution argue that export promotion often worked because it was preceded by a period of import substitution during which the foundations for growth were established. The low rates of growth when import substitution policies were in place cast doubt on the view that import substitution provided the basis for future growth by encouraging the growth of a manufacturing base. The reason why many countries abandoned import substitution in favor of export promotion was because import substitution was not working. The debate will probably never be settled completely, but it is clear that the majority of professional economists now feel that export promotion is a more effective policy for economic development than import substitution.[20]

THE INTERNATIONAL DEBT PROBLEM   18.6

Some Background to the Problem

The debt crisis began in August 1982 when Mexico announced that it could not meet interest payments. It soon became clear that other countries were also facing difficulties meeting the payments on the debt they had accumulated. Defaults by one or more of the major debtor nations could have resulted in some large banks going bankrupt. The vulnerable banks were those that had specialized in loans to a small number of the largest debtor countries. In particular, attention focused on the ten largest American banks that had loaned heavily to Argentina, Brazil, and Mexico. Loans to these countries accounted for more than 100 percent of capital for all but two of the banks.

Table 18.11 shows the growth of LDC debt. The first row shows total debt. The second row shows how debt increased as a percentage of GNP. The third and fourth rows are measures of the burden of debt in relation to export earnings (exports provide revenue to make payments on debt): the third row shows how debt has increased relative to exports, and the fourth row shows how debt service payments (interest and principal) have increased in relation to exports. The last row is of great importance because, as debt payments increase relative to exports, there is less revenue available for imports. Some imports are consumption goods, but imported goods are often imported materials or capital goods that are needed in export production. For the major

---

[20] Official policies do not always reflect this consensus. It is interesting to watch Western diplomats argue that Japan's success is attributable to its protectionist policies, while at the same time arguing that LDCs should abandon protection.

TABLE 18.11   Measures of LDC Debt

	1970	1974	1976	1978	1980	1982	1984	1985
Total debt	68.4	141.0	203.8	311.7	428.6	551.1	673.2	727.7
Debt as % of GNP	13.3	14.0	16.6	19.3	20.6	26.3	33.0	35.8
Debt as % of exports	99.4	63.7	79.6	92.9	90.0	117.6	121.2	143.7
Debt service ratio	13.5	9.5	10.9	15.4	16.0	20.6	19.5	21.4

Sources: From *World Development Report 1984 and 1987.* Reprinted by permission of Oxford University Press, Inc. Compiled information from p. 31 (1984) for 1970–78 and from p. 18 (1987) for 1980–85.

Latin American debtors in particular, export performance was hampered by high debt-service ratios. For example, in 1982 the ratios were Brazil 89 percent, Argentina 68 percent, and Mexico 57 percent.[21]

Causes of the Debt Problem

Although the debt problem was recognized in the early eighties, the origins of the problem go back much further. An early cause of the buildup of LDC debt was the 1973–74 oil price increase. Oil importers responded to the oil price increase by borrowing. The alternative, an attempt by many countries to cut back on imports of other goods, would have led to a collapse of world trade. Therefore, it was desirable that loans to oil importers should allow them to adjust gradually to higher oil prices. Unfortunately, adjustment to the adverse change in the terms of trade did not take place. Partly this was because the banks did not attach conditions to the loans they made. They recycled funds from oil exporters to oil importers, but did not ensure that the funds were used productively. In particular, some governments ran large budget deficits financed by money creation. Domestic inflation resulted, and loans were used to finance foreign exchange market intervention to maintain over-valued exchange rates.

Debt continued to increase gradually throughout the seventies. For some countries, international loans were needed to finance development projects because there was an outflow of private capital.[22] Some of these projects were of dubious economic value. Allegations have been made that banks were too eager to lend and LDCs too eager to borrow. This is too simplistic. It should be remembered that at the time LDCs seemed to have good growth prospects and they were able to service their debts. Also, governments in lending coun-

---

[21] Weisner (1985).

[22] Estimates of private capital outflows by Kahn and Ul Haque (1987) suggest that between 12% and 30% of debt can be attributed to this cause. For some countries, notably Argentina and Venezuela, capital flight was a much greater problem than for others.

TABLE 18.12   Factors Contributing to the 1982 Debt Crisis

	3-Month Eurodollar Rate	Average Crude Oil Price	Terms of Trade of Non-Oil LDCs (1975 = 100)	Trade-Weighted Value of U.S. Dollar (March 1973 = 100)
1977	6.0	13.01	115.6	93.1
1978	8.8	13.06	108.3	84.2
1979	12.0	18.91	105.9	83.2
1980	14.0	31.39	95.5	84.8
1981	16.8	35.03	90.3	100.8
1982	12.2	34.23	84.6	111.7

Sources: Barclays Review, May 1984, p. 32; Economic Report of the President, 1986, p. 373.

tries often encouraged banks to make international loans.[23] However, it is difficult to defend the exposure of major American banks in Latin America.

There are four reasons why the debt problem became much more severe in the early eighties: an increase in interest rates, an increase in oil prices, a world recession, and an increase in the value of the dollar. These developments are shown in Table 18.12. The reader may recall from Chapter 16 that interest rates on international loans are usually only fixed for short periods. At the end of the seventies, as countries adopted policies to reduce inflation, international loan rates followed domestic loan rates skyward, and interest payments on outstanding debts increased dramatically. The oil price increase of 1979 helped push the debts of oil-importing LDCs higher, and in combination with the anti-inflation policies led to a world recession in 1980–82. During this period, commodity prices collapsed, world trade stagnated, and LDC export earnings fell. Finally, because debts are usually denominated in dollars, as the dollar rose in value, the values of debt and interest payments on debt rose relative to the debtor's currencies or earnings in other currencies. The result of these influences was that debtors found that they could not meet the interest due on past debts and were forced to borrow in order to meet their debt servicing obligations.[24]

The Implications for the Lending Countries

The question is no longer whether debtor nations will default, but how many loans will be affected. The major banks recognize the possibility of defaults and have begun to set aside funds to meet this eventuality. Some banks

---

[23] The United States has continued to apply pressure because it feels that new lending is needed if debtors are to grow and pay off debts. This idea is reflected in the Baker plan, which is discussed below.

[24] A dramatic fall in oil prices in 1986 helped oil-importing LDCs but hurt oil-exporting LDCs such as Mexico, Nigeria, and Venezuela.

have stopped making loans, and claims against debtors have been sold at discounts (reflecting the possibility that payments will be suspended). This has helped large American banks reduce the absolute amount of their claims on LDCs.[25] If major defaults are avoided in the next few years, the banks should be able to deal with minor defaults and reschedulings.[26]

The implications of major defaults for ACs are interesting and usually misunderstood. At present, banks receive interest on foreign loans and hold claims against debtors as part of their assets. When debtors default, the bank loses some of its assets and interest receipts cease. This would reduce the value of bank earnings and probably of bank stocks, and in some cases the bank might go bankrupt. However, the disaster scenario that suggests that if one or more major banks collapses the domestic banking system will collapse is unlikely. The Federal Reserve can ensure that domestic monetary stability is maintained by guaranteeing that liabilities to depositors will be honored. This is what happened when the FDIC took over the operations of Continental Illinois in August 1984.[27]

The collapse of one or more banks need not be the end of the story. Freed from the burden of trying to meet interest on foreign debt, LDCs could finance new productive investments. In this case, their exports would increase, their economies would grow, and they would increase their imports of foreign goods. Of course, other countries would share in the growth of LDC imports, but American companies would be able to secure some sales. Therefore, default is not necessarily a total loss for the American economy. In fact, if it could be guaranteed that LDCs would undertake productive investments, defaults might even benefit the American economy.

The Implications for Debtor Countries

What do debtor nations have to lose from default? Two things: lack of short-term trade credits, and future access to development assistance. Trade credits bridge the gaps between receipts from sales of a good and having to pay for a good. Having to pay cash for imports, or using barter, severely increases the costs of imports, effectively preventing normal trading relations. This is not a prospect to be taken lightly. The danger of losing future foreign

---

[25] Another development has been debt-equity swaps. These are arrangements by which claims against debtor countries that have been purchased at a discount are sold to the debtor's central bank for the full price in local currency, and the currency used to purchase domestic assets. This increases the foreign stake in the country. It is hoped that further foreign investment will follow.

[26] Rescheduling agreements are complex and vary greatly. Some common features include: a lower interest rate, spreading repayments out over a longer period, and a period during which no payments need be made. See Watson, M., et al., *International Capital Markets: Developments and Prospects*, IMF Occasional Paper No. 43, 1986.

[27] The FDIC guaranteed all deposits at Continental Illinois, not only deposits of less than the $100,000 legal maximum for FDIC insurance coverage. The FDIC also took over 80% of Continental's equity and replaced the bank's top managers.

capital is not necessarily a significant problem because many countries already face great difficulties in borrowing additional funds. The reason for these difficulties is obvious: banks are reluctant to make new loans to countries that are having difficulties making payments on their present debts. There is no guarantee that the loans will be used productively or that the loans will ever be repaid. Also, when claims against debtor countries are trading in a secondary market at a discount, lenders face the prospect that the value of new loans will fall immediately to the same discount.

The Baker Plan

The plan put forward by Treasury Secretary James Baker in October 1985 attempted to address some of these issues. The main elements in the plan were:

1. The adoption by debtor countries of adjustment policies to reduce inflation, reduce balance of payments deficits, and increase growth;
2. a continuing role for the IMF and an enhanced role for the World Bank in ensuring effective use of increased lending for structural adjustment;
3. increased lending by private banks in support of adjustment programs.

The plan did not go into detail about how these objectives should be achieved, but it contained one element that is essential to a planned resolution of the debt problem: an emphasis on adjustment to ensure that new funds are not wasted.

One criticism of the Baker plan was that it did not provide an answer to the problems of the poorest debtor nations with limited growth prospects, for example, the countries of Sub-Saharan Africa.[28] The balance of the Baker plan was also attacked. For example, debtor countries were asked to open their markets to trade and asked to try to increase exports, but no commitment was given that they would be able to sell their exports in AC markets. Another source of dissatisfaction was that debtor countries felt that additional loans, which would have increased their indebtedness, were not as attractive as a reduction of interest rates on existing debt. In other words, even if the plan had worked, it would have done nothing to reduce the burden of international debt.[29]

In fact, the plan did not work. Difficulties were experienced from the beginning in persuading banks to make new loans. Private loans to developing countries fell from over $80 billion in 1981 to almost zero in 1986, and in 1988 lending was negative as developing countries repaid more than they bor-

---

[28] Sub-Saharan Africa includes the countries south of the Sahara, except South Africa.
[29] See the *Fifty-Sixth Annual Report of the Bank for International Settlements (1985–86)*, pp. 113–15.

rowed. Net private lending to the fifteen most heavily indebted countries targeted by the Baker plan was negative in 1983 and in each year from 1985 to 1988.

The Brady Proposals

The proposals put forward by Treasury Secretary Nicholas Brady in March 1989 implicitly acknowledged the failure of the Baker plan. Brady suggested that a new approach embodying *voluntary debt reduction* should be adopted. The proposal was that banks be allowed/encouraged to sell more international debts at a discount. This would enable banks to reduce their debts and debtor countries to repay loans at a discount. A role for the IMF and the World Bank was envisaged with these institutions buying debt at a discount and guaranteeing future loans. It was hoped that these proposals would encourage banks to resume international lending. However, proposals of this type face serious difficulties.

Banks have already reduced their holding of debt and have set aside reserves to protect against possible defaults. They are just beginning to recover from the loans they made a decade ago, and it is probably optimistic to assume that they will be willing to make significant new loans. Guarantees that loans remaining after debt reduction and any new loans that are made will be repaid amount to guaranteed profits for banks. Perhaps banks should not be protected from losses incurred as the result of past mistakes or losses that may be incurred from loans they make in the future? The potential role for the IMF and the World Bank is limited by lack of resources: they do not have sufficient resources to pay off debts or provide meaningful guarantees for new loans.

The basic problem is that plans to solve the international debt problem cost money. The crisis in the American savings and loan industry and the large American budget deficit suggest that major initiatives by the United States to address the international debt issue are unlikely. Other countries (notably Japan) may be willing and able to help finance debt reduction, but as yet no agreement has been reached. Banks may be able to survive minor defaults, but survival is not enough to begin a flow of new lending to poor countries. At the time of writing, the future does not look bright.

Summary of Main Points

Less developed countries (LDCs) have remained poor while taking part in international trade. LDCs trade mainly with *advanced countries* (ACs) and mainly export *primary products*. Often, a small number of products accounts for most of a country's exports.

It is often alleged that the poverty of LDCs is attributable to a long-term downward trend in their terms of trade. There are methodological problems in assessing whether a significant long-term trend exists: the result is strongly influenced by the choice of products and the period used. Also, it is not clear what significance should be attached to the results because welfare changes are not necessarily associated with changes in the terms of trade. Even if a trend could be identified, increasing the terms of trade would do little to increase living standards in LDCs.

Many reform proposals have been put forward with the intent of increasing the incomes of poor countries. Some were reflected in the call of the United Nations for the creation of a *new international economic order* (NIEO). Proposals covered issues such as increased aid to LDCs, measures to increase the prices of primary products, and improved access for the exports of LDCs in AC markets.

Some countries have succeeded in growing rapidly by adopting policies that encourage exports. Attempts to promote domestic industries by restricting imports *(import substitution)* appear to have failed. Whether *export promotion* by LDCs in general is a viable development strategy is a matter of debate. Skeptics point out that ACs do not allow market access to the products in which LDCs are competitive, for example, agriculture, steel, and textiles. Promotion of exports, it is claimed, would lead to further restrictions. Many economists argue that LDCs have suffered not from trade, but from lack of free trade.

The international debt problem has two facets. First, some countries have built up large foreign debts and now have difficulty meeting their payments. Second, some banks have made loans to a small number of countries and defaults by a few of the largest debtor nations could lead to the collapse of major banks. Some observers have argued that defaults are inevitable unless actions are taken to resolve these problems. It has been suggested that defaults could lead to the collapse of the financial system.

Although defaults by debtor nations might cause the failure of individual banks, the monetary system is not in danger provided that the monetary authorities fulfill their obligations to act as lender of last resort. The banks have set aside reserves to protect themselves against minor defaults and rescheduling problems.

The banks may be able to continue meeting minor defaults, but a continuation of the present situation is undesirable. The debtor nations face significant difficulties in trying to encourage economic growth without access to new capital. The Baker plan to tackle the debt problem called for increased lending to debtor nations, adjustment in debtor nations, and monitoring by the IMF and the World Bank to ensure effective use of resources. The Baker plan was not successful. Private investment funds dried up and official funds did not bridge the gap.

Proposals have been made for *voluntary debt reduction* with debts being traded or repaid at less than their book value. It has been suggested that IMF and World Bank guarantees for private loans could lead to an increase in private lending. A major difficulty is that banks are unlikely to make new loans to poor countries when the banks are struggling to deal with the consequeces of past loans. Also, the potential for the IMF and World Bank to play a major role is limited by their resources (which are far too small for these institutions to pay off past debts or to provide meaningful guarantees that new loans will be repaid). Agreement has yet to be reached on where the resources needed for a solution to the international debt problem will come from.

Study Questions

1. What are the characteristics of LDC trade?

2. Increasing exports is often cited as a way of encouraging economic growth. Why might this be counterproductive for producers of primary products?

3. Explain the methodological problems in measuring the long-run trend in the terms of trade of producers of primary products. Assuming that such a trend exists, can it be explained by factors other than exploitation?

4. Why has import substitution not encouraged growth?

5. Why might an overvalued exchange rate deter economic development?

6. Why is it unlikely that bufferstocks can increase long-run incomes?

7. Why do bufferstocks and cartels usually collapse?

8. In what ways can ACs help economic development without transferring resources to LDCs?

9. What were the causes of the 1982 debt crisis?

10. In view of your answer to Question 9, is it likely that the international debt problem will escalate in the near future?

11. What is the significance of the international debt problem *(a)* for the United States and *(b)* for LDCs?

12. Assuming that you were asked to represent an LDC at the next UNC-TAD meeting, what would you suggest or request.

Selected References

Adams, J., Ed. *The Contemporary International Economy.* Second Edition. New York: St. Martin's, 1985.

Bauer, P. T. *Reality and Rhetoric: Studies in the Economics of Development.* Cambridge, MA: Harvard University Press, 1984.

Cassen, R. "The Effectiveness of Aid." *Finance and Development* 23 (March 1986): pp. 11–14.

Cassen, R., et al. *Does Aid Work?* New York: Oxford University Press, 1986.

Corden, W. M. *The NIEO Proposals: A Cool Look.* Thames Essay No. 21. London: Trade Policy Research Centre, 1979. Reprinted in *International Trade and Finance*, second edition, edited by R. E. Baldwin and J. D. Richardson (Boston: Little Brown, 1981).

Dornbusch, R. "International Debt and Economic Stability." *Economic Review* (Federal Reserve Bank of Kansas City), January 1987, pp. 15–32.

Grubel, H. G. "The Case Against the New Economic Order." *Weltwirtschaftliches Archiv* 113 (1977): 284–306. Reprinted in *The Contemporary International Economy*, second edition, edited by J. Adams (New York: St. Martin's, 1985).

IMF. *World Economic Outlook*. Washington, D.C.: International Monetary Fund, 1987.

Kahn, M. S., and Ul Haque, N. "Capital Flight from Developing Countries." *Finance and Development* 24 (March 1987): 2–5.

Krueger, A. O. *Foreign Trade Regimes and Economic Development: Liberalization Attempts and Consequences*. New York: Columbia University Press, 1976.

Krueger, A. O. "The Effects of Trade Strategies on Growth." *Finance and Development* 20 (June 1983): 6–8.

Krueger, A. O. "Import Substitution Versus Export Promotion." *Finance and Development* 22 (June 1985): 20–23.

Krueger, A. O. "The Experience and Lessons of Asia's Super Exporters." In *Export-Orientated Development Strategies*, edited by V. Corbo, pp. 187–212 (Boulder, CO: Westview Press, 1985).

Meier, G. M. *Leading Issues in Economic Development*. Fourth Edition. New York: Oxford University Press, 1984.

OECD. *Twenty-Five Years of Development Cooperation*. Paris: OECD, 1985.

Weisner, E. "Domestic and External Causes of the Latin American Debt Crisis." *Finance and Development* 22 (March 1985): 22–26.

World Bank. *World Development Report*. Various issues, 1980–88. New York: Oxford University Press (for the World Bank).

19

MULTINATIONAL

CORPORATIONS

19.1 INTRODUCTION

For our purposes, a *multinational corporation* may be defined simply as an enterprise that operates in more than one country. Multinationals have been described by some people as a threat to freedom and welfare, whereas others have suggested that they contribute to the growth of world income and increase economic development. It is not possible to say which view is nearer the truth. Multinationals can have many effects and no two corporations are the same. Thus, critics and defenders of multinationals have no difficulty in finding examples to support their views.

We begin our study by examining the growth and importance of multinationals. The motives for foreign direct investment are examined. Then we consider the economic effects of multinationals at a global level and the economic effects on individual countries. A distinction is drawn between the economic effects of multinationals on host countries and source countries. A *source country* is the country where a multinational has its headquarters; a *host country* is a country where a multinational's foreign operations are located.

19.2 THE GROWTH AND IMPORTANCE OF MULTINATIONAL CORPORATIONS

Multinationals are not a recent phenomenon. Around 2500 B.C., in the earliest recorded civilization, the merchants of Sumeria found that foreign representatives were useful to handle their products.[1] The British East India Company, a trading company that operated from A.D. 1600 until 1858, is often

---

[1] This and the following examples are taken from a study by Wilkins (1970) documenting the early growth of American multinationals.

quoted as an early example of a multinational corporation. The origins of multinational corporations in manufacturing can be traced to the nineteenth century, when American manufacturing companies established foreign subsidiaries to produce goods embodying new technology. For example, in 1855, Singer licensed a French company to produce sewing machines, and, in 1867, Singer established its own plant in Glasgow. In 1882, Western Electric established a plant in Belgium to manufacture telephone equipment. In 1889, George Eastman incorporated a company in London to manufacture film for cameras he was exporting from the United States.

Although multinational enterprise has a long history, it was not until after World War Two that multinational corporations became a significant force in the world economy. Their growth was facilitated by improvements in communications and the development of computers, which made it possible to control foreign subsidiaries. Also, multinationals benefited as the international market was opened up by falling transport costs and reductions in barriers to trade and investment. Global production and marketing had become possible.

The Importance of Multinational Corporations

There is no doubt that multinational corporations are an important part of the international economic system. It is estimated that sales by multinationals account for one quarter of GNP, and sales by one firm to another firm that is part of the same company account for between one quarter and one third of world trade. Multinationals account for three quarters of American merchandise exports and almost half of American merchandise imports.[2]

Most of the large corporations shown in Table 19.1 are multinationals. It is often pointed out that the value of the sales of one of these companies is larger than the national income of many small countries. However, although national income is measured as value added, sales figures do not take account of inputs purchased by a corporation. Therefore, sales figures tend to overstate the size of corporations relative to countries. We would have to deduct the value of inputs used by multinationals to have comparable figures. However, the value added of the largest multinationals would still be larger than some countries' incomes.

A common misconception about multinationals is that they are all or nearly all American. American companies account for only eleven of the twenty-five largest companies in the world (see Table 19.1). Multinationals sell both to the domestic market and the world market. Given the size of the domestic market in the United States, it is not surprising that firms based in that market are large. Domestic market size also helps explain why firms from the two other large regional markets, Europe and Japan, account for the majority of large non-American corporations. In view of this, it may be more surprising that large companies are found from so many countries, including some LDCs.

---

[2]See Barker, B. L., "U.S. Trade Associated with U.S. Multinational Companies," *Survey of Current Business*, May 1986.

TABLE 19.1   The World's Twenty-Five Largest Industrial Corporations

Rank 1987	'86	Company	Headquarters	Industry	Sales ($ millions)	Profits ($ millions)
1	1	General Motors	Detroit	Motor Vehicles	101,781.9	3,550.9
2	3	Royal Dutch/Shell Group	London/The Hague	Petroleum Refining	78,319.3	4,725.8
3	2	Exxon	New York	Petroleum Refining	76,416.0	4,840.0
4	4	Ford Motor	Dearborn, Mich.	Motor Vehicles	71,643.4	4,625.2
5	5	International Business Machines	Armonk, N.Y.	Computers	54,217.0	5,258.0
6	6	Mobil	New York	Petroleum Refining	51,223.0	1,258.0
7	7	British Petroleum	London	Petroleum Refining	45,205.9	2,280.1
8	12	Toyota Motor	Toyota City (Japan)	Motor Vehicles	41,455.0	1,699.6
9	11	IRI	Rome	Metals	41,270.0	146.5
10	8	General Electric	Fairfield, Conn.	Electronics	39,315.0	2,915.0
11	13	Daimler-Benz	Stuttgart	Motor Vehicles	37,535.5	970.2
12	10	Texaco	White Plains, N.Y.	Petroleum Refining	34,372.0	(4,407.0)
13	9	American Tel. & Tel.	New York	Electronics	33,598.0	2,044.0
14	14	E.I. Du Pont de Nemours	Wilmington, Del.	Chemicals	30,468.0	1,786.0
15	18	Volkswagen	Wolfsburg (W. Ger.)	Motor Vehicles	30,392.7	242.1
16	19	Hitachi	Tokyo	Electronics	30,332.2	617.3
17	27	Fiat	Turin	Motor Vehicles	29,642.8	1,830.2
18	25	Siemens	Munich	Electronics	27,462.9	649.6
19	15	Matsushita Electric Industrial	Osaka	Electronics	27,325.7	862.4
20	16	Unilever	London/Rotterdam	Food	27,128.8	1,278.6
21	21	Chrysler	Highland Park, Mich.	Motor Vehicles	26,257.7	1,289.7
22	22	Philips' Gloeilampenfabrieken	Eindhoven (Neth.)	Electronics	26,021.2	316.9
23	17	Chevron	San Francisco	Petroleum Refining	26,015.0	1,007.0
24	26	Nissan Motor	Tokyo	Motor Vehicles	25,650.5	123.9
25	31	Renault	Paris	Motor Vehicles	24,539.7	613.7

Source: Fortune (August 1, 1988), p. D3. Reprinted by permission of the publisher. © 1988 Time Inc. All rights reserved.

The Geographical Distribution of Foreign Direct Investment

Multinational corporations are established by foreign direct investment. Direct investment and portfolio investment are similar in that both involve a flow of capital. In the case of *portfolio investment,* there is no attempt to gain control over the operations of the foreign enterprise, which continues to be run by local managers. *Direct investment* entails the acquisition of sufficient capital to exercise a measure of control over an enterprise. The distinction between the two is inevitably arbitrary. What percentage of equity is needed to exercise influence over operations? The U.S. Department of Commerce defines direct investment as the acquisition of 10 percent or more of a company's equity.

Table 19.2 shows the geographical distribution of American direct investment abroad and foreign direct investment in the United States. Most American direct investment abroad (three quarters) is in developed countries. This is significant because, although the activities of multinational companies in developing countries have attracted attention, developing countries are not particularly important to multinationals. Latin America accounts for over half of American foreign direct investment in developing countries.

The stock of foreign direct investment is not an accurate measure of the current value of foreign direct investment because it is based on historical costs and does not reflect increases in the market value or replacement cost of foreign assets caused by inflation. Also, the figures record the ownership of equity and do not show the resources controlled. For example, in 1986, the value of American foreign direct investment was $260 billion, whereas the value of assets of foreign affiliates of American multinationals was $932 billion.

TABLE 19.2   American Foreign Direct Investment and Foreign Direct Investment in the United States

	(stock in billions of dollars at the end of 1987)	
	American Foreign Direct Investment	*Foreign Direct Investment in the United States*
All areas	308.8	261.9
Canada	56.9	21.7
Europe	149.0	178.0
Japan	14.3	33.4
Australia, New Zealand, and South Africa	13.2	6.6
Latin America	42.3	15.3
Other	28.8	7.0
International [a]	4.3	

[a] This category refers to investment that is not allocated to a particular country, the main example being investment in shipping.
Source: Department of Commerce, *Survey of Current Business,* August 1988.

19.3 REASONS FOR FOREIGN DIRECT INVESTMENT

In order to understand the operations of multinationals and the problems they are alleged to cause, we must understand the reasons why a company undertakes foreign direct investment.

Inputs and Raw Materials

In extractive industries the reason for foreign operations is obvious: oil companies such as Exxon and Royal Dutch Shell locate where there is oil; copper mining companies such as Anaconda and Kennecott locate where there is copper. This does not explain why foreign firms exploit resources rather than local firms. A common explanation of this phenomenon is that local firms lack the capital and technology needed to find and develop natural resources.

Manufacturing firms can buy inputs on world markets, but they may have an incentive to acquire control over foreign sources of inputs. For example, a firm can guarantee its source of supply and avoid delays, it can reduce its holding of inventories, and the inputs can be designed or packaged to meet the needs of the corporation. Also, it may be possible to deny competitors access to the inputs.

Costs

Companies may invest in other countries to take advantage of lower production costs. Low wages are an important example, as are subsidized capital and low rents. However, low production costs in a country do not imply that production by a multinational is viable in that country. Multinational corporations incur costs that local firms do not. For example, communication and travel between the parent and foreign subsidiaries can be expensive. Also, a multinational may incur costs because the managers are not familiar with the language, customs, and culture of the society in which they work.

If a multinational is to be able to compete with local firms in a foreign market, it must have advantages that they do not. These advantages can take many forms. For example, a multinational corporation may possess superior manufacturing technology, managerial experience, and an international distribution network for marketing its products. Also, it may be able to borrow capital more easily than local firms because it has access to international capital markets.

International Subcontracting

Initially, foreign production by multinationals was often destined for local markets. During the late sixties and seventies there was a growth of foreign production for re-export to the home market or to other foreign markets. One reason for this development was that wage differences between countries exceeded differences in productivity. Components manufactured in the United States are now assembled in developing countries and then re-exported to other markets or back to the United States. In this way, foreign subsidiaries are incorporated into an international production process. Foreign assembly usually takes place in products that have a high value-to-weight ratio, and when assembly is labor-intensive and can be separated from other parts of the production process.

American companies are able to use foreign assembly because the United States does not levy duty on that part of a product's value that is attributable to the use of components made in the United States. This arrangement is known as the *offshore assembly provision*. Grunwald and Flamm (1985) examined the products entering the United States under this provision and found that they were mainly: "motor vehicles and parts, apparel, and various types of electrical equipment" (p. 15). In some sectors, offshore assembly is very important: they estimate that 80 percent of U.S. semiconductor production is assembled abroad.

Technology and Manufacturing

When a company has a secure domestic market position, it may own intangible assets such as managerial skills, patents, and trademarks. The company may be able to use these assets in foreign markets without jeopardizing the home market. Foreign production is sometimes preferable to exporting because minor modifications of the product can be made to suit local specifications and tastes. Also, exporting may be difficult because of high transport costs or barriers to trade.

A choice must be made between setting up foreign manufacturing facilities through foreign direct investment, or selling the right to produce a product to foreign manufacturers. Foreign direct investment may be preferred for a number of reasons. Patents can be sold, but a company cannot sell its manufacturing experience. Also, when a company licenses foreign producers, it has less control over the product. The company may want to protect its name and keep its manufacturing technology secret. Finally, foreign licensing is not an option if potential foreign licensees do not have adequate capital.

Market Access

Market access is important for companies marketing products worldwide. Market access can be limited by transport costs or by government barriers to trade. The effects of transport costs are obvious: American companies selling in Europe are more competitive if they do not have to ship their products across the Atlantic. The importance of transport costs depends on the product. For products that have a high value in relation to size or weight, transport costs are less important. Tariff and non-tariff barriers to trade can also be significant. A company can avoid trade barriers by producing within a country. For example, the possibility of import restrictions was one of the reasons why foreign automobile producers such as Honda and Volkswagen set up plants in the United States. Another example is the response of non-European firms to the plan of the European Economic Community to reduce barriers to trade within the community and establish a unified European market by 1992. This plan led to fears that the European market would be closed to foreign firms, and many responded by setting up plants within the community.

Dealer Networks

A company's activities do not always end when a product is sold. The availability of service and advice to customers is often an important part of a company's activities. Failure to provide these services can be sufficient reason to prevent a product selling. Foreign direct investment is sometimes needed in order to provide customer services, but the provision of a dealer network does not necessarily imply foreign ownership. Local franchises can be a substitute for a dealer network owned by the company itself. This solution is often adopted in the automobile industry.

Taxes

Finally, companies must consider the range of taxes that countries apply to their activities. Taxes on profits are one important example. Although taxes may influence location, it is unlikely that they are a dominant influence relative to other factors such as market proximity and economic and political stability.

19.4 THE GLOBAL EFFECTS OF MULTINATIONAL CORPORATIONS

The Allocation and Quantity of Capital

One of the basic effects of multinationals is that they increase global income. They do this by reallocating resources (mainly capital) between countries to take advantage of local cost conditions. Also, because of their size, wealth, and global connections, they are better able to recognize and exploit investment opportunities than national companies. In so doing, they increase the world stock of capital and the world income. An interesting benefit from international factor mobility is that multinationals reduce the welfare losses that might otherwise result from barriers to trade. Companies can produce in foreign markets instead of exporting to those markets.

Economies of Scale

Multinational corporations also increase world income by taking advantage of economies of scale. Resources are saved because overheads such as research and development costs can be spread over more units. Another source of economies of scale is that large firms are able to subcontract internationally to take advantage of low production costs. The Ford Escort is an interesting example of a standardized product that is marketed internationally. The components for European Escorts are produced in more than ten countries and the cars are assembled in Halewood (United Kingdom) and Saarlouis (West Germany).

Monopoly Power

The argument that multinationals improve the global allocation of resources must be qualified to the extent that multinationals are a departure from perfect competition, that is, they have monopoly power. The significance of this observation is difficult to assess. Basic microeconomic theory would lead us to expect that a monopolist will charge a higher price and produce a smaller quantity than a competitive industry with the same costs. However, if monopolistic firms have lower costs than perfectly competitive firms, as seems likely in the case of multinationals, the departure from perfect competition need not reduce welfare. Also, merely because multinationals are large does not mean that they can behave as monopolists; competition between large firms is often intense.

Multinationals and Trade Theory

Standard trade theory is based on the assumption that factors of production are mobile within countries but not between countries. This assumption implies that the resources available within a country determine the production possibilities of that country. Multinationals do not fit neatly into standard trade theory because a country's production possibilities change when the stock of capital increases as a result of a company locating within the country. The policy implication is that countries should consider not only the goods that can be produced from available resources, but also the goods that might be produced if suitable companies can be induced to move into the country. Standard trade theory might lead us to place too much emphasis on the availability of local resources.

THE ECONOMIC EFFECTS OF MULTINATIONAL ▮19.5▮ CORPORATIONS ON SOURCE COUNTRIES

Wages and Employment

It has been suggested that multinationals reduce wages and employment in the source country. There are two main ways in which this might happen. First, foreign investment may be undertaken instead of domestic investment. In this case, real wages in the source country are reduced by the export of capital (because the marginal productivity of labor declines as the amount of capital that labor has to work with decreases). Employment may also be reduced if there are rigidities in the labor market that prevent real wages from falling or labor from moving into other activities.

The second way in which multinationals can reduce wages and employment in the source country is that foreign investment can lead to the growth of foreign companies that compete with producers in the source country. For example, rather than buy from American suppliers, some American firms have established foreign plants to manufacture inputs for plants in the United States. American-owned foreign companies also compete with American firms in world markets. This leads to heated allegations that American companies are sacrificing American workers in the pursuit of profit, or that they are undertaking foreign investment because they want to weaken the power of trade unions.

There are a number of reasons for avoiding generalizations about the effects of foreign investment on wages and employment in the source country. First, the assumption that foreign investment replaces domestic investment is too simplistic. In many cases, domestic and foreign direct investment are not substitutes. The alternative to foreign investment may be no investment at all. For example, firms may undertake foreign investment to break into markets that cannot be supplied by exports, or to guarantee a source of raw materials. In these examples foreign investment is likely to increase wages and employment in the source country. Second, foreign direct investment may be financed by foreign earnings or by borrowing abroad rather than by domestic capital. In these cases, there is no reason to suppose that domestic investment will fall. Third, foreign direct investment may lead to an increase in employment in the source country as a result of sales of inputs by the parent company to foreign subsidiaries or because the foreign distribution network can be used to market other products of the parent company.

Historical experience suggests that foreign direct investment does not have an adverse effect on the economy of the source country. During the sixties, rapid American foreign direct investment was accompanied by high employment in the United States. More recently, the growth of multinationals from Japan and the newly industrialized countries of Southeast Asia took place while the economies of these countries were growing rapidly.

Loss of Tax Revenue

In principle, the source country can gain from taxes levied on the profits of multinational corporations. In fact, the gain to the United States and other source countries is usually small because of the way source countries tax the profits of multinationals. First, multinationals are allowed to defer taxes on foreign profits that are reinvested. This acts as an incentive to foreign investment. Reinvested earnings are one of the factors behind the growth of foreign direct investment. Second, if a company chooses to repatriate profits to the United States, it can deduct the taxes it has paid in the host country from its American tax liability. For example, if a company has earned $100 million in profits, at a tax rate of 46 percent it would be liable for a $46 million tax in the United States. If it has already paid $42 million to the host country, its American tax liability is only $4 million. As a result of reinvestment abroad and deduction of foreign tax payments, source countries do not in fact derive much revenue from taxes on multinationals.

The method of taxing multinationals is designed to avoid double taxation. It has an important effect: the tax rate applied to domestic and foreign earnings of domestic residents is the same. Thus, the procedure reduces the possibility that worldwide investment will be distorted by taxes.

THE ECONOMIC EFFECTS OF MULTINATIONAL CORPORATIONS ON HOST COUNTRIES 19.6

Although most foreign direct investment is from one developed country to another, in the following discussion of the effects of multinationals on host countries we shall often assume that the host country is a developing country. There are two reasons for this. First, individual multinationals are less significant in economies with high levels of income and diversified production. Second, investment flows between developed countries are largely offsetting. Although multinationals from developing countries have emerged, foreign direct investment in developing countries is much larger than foreign direct investment by developing countries.

Output and Employment

An inflow of capital increases real income because additional capital increases the productivity of labor. If there is high unemployment, which is common in developing countries, the level of employment will also increase. A commonly accepted view is that developing countries lack the capital and technology to be competitive producers. Multinationals can provide capital and technology that developing countries lack, and help them increase exports without first having to develop a manufacturing base. Drucker (1974) offers a slightly different explanation of the gains to developing countries. He attributes underdevelopment to the low productivity of resources, not the limited availability of resources. He suggests that multinationals help channel local resources into productive uses, which sets off multiplier repercussions in the economy.

The general argument that multinationals increase income and employment must be qualified. The total output of a multinational is not always an accurate representation of the scale of a company's activities in a particular market, because multinationals often use imported inputs. Particularly in the case of assembly operations, the domestic value added can be quite small relative to total output. The smaller the domestic value added, the smaller will be the contribution of a multinational to income and employment. Even if employment increases by a large amount, not all local people gain. Domestic employers who compete with the multinational for inputs find that their costs increase. In countries that are operating at or near full employment, there may be less to be gained from an inflow of foreign investment because the country experiences inflationary pressure without benefiting significantly from higher employment.

Balance of Payments

The initial effect of a multinational on the balance of payments of a host country is unambiguous: when a multinational locates in a country, there is a capital inflow that is a credit in the balance of payments. When the company's operations have begun, there are other effects. Exports by the multinational are a credit item, whereas debit items include imported materials and payments to the parent company (such as fees and royalties and profits).

A company that produces primarily for export will probably result in an overall credit. A company that uses imported inputs and sells in the domestic market will probably lead to an overall debit. However, the debit resulting from a multinational producing and selling in the domestic market will be smaller than if the goods were imported instead. To complicate matters, in some years financial transfers may outweigh the effects of a multinational's trading operations. It is impossible to say whether the overall effect on the balance of payments in any year will be a credit or a debit. Each multinational corporation must be examined individually.

Taxation

One "problem" encountered by host countries is that multinationals do not willingly pay high taxes. *Transfer pricing* is one way a company can avoid local taxes. For example, assume that a French company wants to transfer funds to an American company. It can do so by paying an abnormally high price for purchases from the American company. The excess payment over the normal cost is in effect a capital transfer. Alternatively, the transfer can be achieved by the French company selling goods to the American company for less than their true value.[3]

In order to control transfers of funds, governments may require companies to use world prices for intracompany trade. However, in some cases international prices for comparable products are not available, for example, when the company is the sole producer of a particular type of product. Also, there are no standards for fees and royalties or for services such as management. These considerations mean that it is extremely difficult for governments to control transfer pricing. Companies have difficulty fixing appropriate prices when world prices for similar products or services are not available. If a company's prices are not challenged, then the company may assume that they were appropriate.

Ultimately, if a company is forced to pay high taxes, it may decide to

---

[3]Transfer pricing also enables multinationals to avoid import duties by undervaluing imports.

leave a country. This is understandable. If a company locates in a country because it has low taxes, no one should be surprised if it leaves when taxes are increased.

Obsolescing Contracts

Early critics of multinationals suggested that developing countries inevitably faced one-sided contracts when they acted as hosts to multinationals. There are substantial costs and risks associated with locating in developing countries. Therefore, in order to attract multinationals, developing countries often had to give substantial concessions. For example, countries were induced to give tax concessions or access to duty-free imports. In cases where host countries were induced to guarantee a company a domestic monopoly, the gains to the host country have often been less than where host countries were able to maintain competition.[4]

Once the initial costs have been paid and the risks have been overcome, the company has a much safer investment. Because companies want to protect their investment and avoid relocation costs, developing countries have been able to renegotiate contracts on much more favorable terms than were possible initially. In other words, in some cases, the initial agreement has become obsolete.[5] Recognition of this possibility marked an important step forward in understanding the effects of multinational corporations.

The extraction of natural resources has provided examples of the *obsolescing contract*. In the case of the extraction of natural resources, the returns from development of deposits are often uncertain. Companies were induced to undertake exploration and development by concessions such as low taxes. When these projects were successful, resentment was felt in the host country because foreign companies were making large profits from extraction of the country's resources. As a result, tax rates were increased, and in some cases foreign firms were nationalized. To avoid losing capital, some companies now prefer joint ventures or licensing of technology to locally owned companies.

Nationalization of foreign assets is an extreme example of the obsolescing contract. In some cases, compensation has been paid at the time of the nationalization, such as in 1970 when Peru took over the 51 percent interest of Chase Manhattan in the Peruvian Banco Continental. In other cases, compensation has not been paid. An early example of expropriation without compensation was the seizure of foreign assets in the Soviet Union following the revolution of 1917. The confiscation of foreign assets by the Cuban government in 1960 was a similar case. Other examples where compensation was not paid include Peru's seizure of the assets of the International Petroleum Company in 1968, and Chile's seizure of the copper mining interests of Anaconda and Kennecott in 1971.[6]

---

[4] See Moran (1985) for examples.
[5] The theory of obsolescing contracts was put forward by Vernon (1971).
[6] In these two cases, the American government eventually reached settlements with the governments of Chile and Peru.

Transfer of Technology

It has been suggested that multinationals are a means of transferring technology from developed countries to developing countries. For example, local firms can copy the technology of the multinational or obtain it under license. Although multinationals may produce in developing countries using technology that was not available locally, the extent to which this technology is transferred to other sectors of the economy, and the usefulness of the technology to the developing country, are limited. Part of the problem is that multinationals use high technology originally designed for use in developed countries. This technology is not appropriate for local companies in a developing country. Also, multinational companies have little incentive to use low technology because this technology is more easily copied than high technology.

Another factor limiting the transfer of technology is that research and development is usually based in the source country. Host countries might like research to be carried out in their countries, but it is unrealistic to assume that the research staff and research facilities can be moved from the source country to a host country, especially in cases where the host country is a developing country. Multinational corporations may even reduce the research capacity of host countries by attracting employees back to the source country. For example, Canadians often leave Canada for the United States. This problem has been dubbed the "brain drain." Although the brain drain can be a serious problem, it is not the result of multinational enterprise, since employment opportunities with foreign national companies can induce people to emigrate. For example, universities often employ foreign academics, but universities are not usually multinational corporations.

Externalities and Safety Problems

It is often alleged that multinationals operate in an undesirable manner, by polluting the environment or exploiting natural resources at too great a rate. Companies in advanced countries are subject to many controls to prevent such problems, but in developing countries the controls are much weaker or even nonexistent. Thus, it has been said that foreign direct investment is a way for the company to avoid controls at home. In the host country, multinationals may be no better or worse than local firms (in developing countries), but, because of their size, one company may do greater harm. Unfortunately, examples of harm can easily be found: one of the worst occurred in 1984 when 2,000 people died in Bhopal, India, following the emission of poison gas from a factory owned by the American company Union Carbide. More people died later of their injuries. The *New York Times* (February 15, 1989) reported over 3,500 dead and 200,000 injured.

The Union Carbide case is interesting because in February 1989 the Indian Supreme Court ordered Union Carbide to pay $470 million as a result of the accident. This amount may seem small given the size of the tragedy. Leaving aside the question of whether Union Carbide was negligent or legally responsible (the plant was operated by an Indian subsidiary), the case shows the problem of holding a multinational company liable for damages. Union Carbide's Indian assets at the time were only worth \$30 million; thus, a larger settlement could not have been enforced by seizing assets. Perhaps a larger settlement might have eventually been reached by proceeding through Indian then American courts, but India's Supreme Court felt that immediate relief was needed rather than prolonged legal wrangling.[7]

The actions of companies can never be wholly regulated, so countries must rely on the social responsibility of firms. The failure of individual firms to recognize their responsibilities is not confined to multinational corporations. Local companies can behave irresponsibly. One of the reasons why multinationals are criticized less now than in the past is that they recognize that their long-term interests are served by generating goodwill.

Nationality and Allegiance

Early critics of multinational corporations suggested that they would reduce international competition, and that the power of corporations would weaken and replace the power of national states. In this context, because most multinationals in the early years were American, they were described as instruments of foreign domination. The emergence of multinationals from Europe, Japan, and some developing countries makes it difficult to characterize multinationals as instruments of American neocolonialism.

Sovereignty

The sovereignty of a host country can be reduced because a multinational has the option of reducing or curtailing its activities in a particular country. This option is not open to national firms. Also, some multinationals have attempted to exert political influence on the host country. For example, the United Fruit Company (now called United Brands) was criticized for conspiring to topple the government of Guatemala in 1954 (and for its abuse of monopoly power from the early part of this century until the fifties). It now prefers to work with the governments of host countries, has given up most of its land, and concentrates on distribution and marketing. However, it still has considerable influence in Central America. In 1971, the International Telephone and Telegraph Company (ITT) attempted to change the policies of the Allende government in order to avoid losing its telephone and hotel interests in Chile. ITT also sought help from the American government. Although the American government officially refused, it is generally believed that ITT and the Central Intelligence Agency (CIA) helped bring about the overthrow of the Allende government (in 1973). This incident adversely affected the position of other American companies in Latin America. Fortunately, examples of direct political interference are less common now.[8]

---

[7] The settlement is described in the *New York Times*, February 15, 1989, and the *Economist*, February 18, 1989.
[8] Other examples of "imperialist" behavior by multinationals are given by Hood and Young (1979).

The sovereignty of a host country may be reduced because a multinational may respond to pressures from the source country. For example, in 1982, the American government attempted to stop completion of a natural gas pipeline from Russia to Western Europe.[9] American firms, and European firms doing business with American firms, were instructed not to sell products for use in this project. This action was seen by European countries as an infringement of their sovereignty. European countries responded by ordering companies to honor contracts. What little sympathy there might have been for the American position was eroded when the United States signed an agreement to sell grain to Russia. Eventually, the action was abandoned. Canada has experienced similar problems as a result of American embargoes on sales to countries that Canada has friendly relations with. Although these issues are mainly political, the problem is economic to the extent that the host country is not compensated for losses resulting from these actions.

The Quality of Life

It is alleged that multinationals are responsible for the breakdown of traditional cultural values in developing countries and the spread of what is sometimes called "Coca-Cola culture." The influence of Western culture can be seen throughout the world, but is the influence due to multinationals or improved communications? And what, if anything, should be done about it? These are not economic questions, but economists can point out the costs of attempting to cure these problems by economic isolationism.

Conclusion

The main conclusion that emerges from the preceding discussion of the effects of multinationals on host countries is that we cannot say with certainty whether any particular multinational will increase welfare. We cannot even say that a particular country will always benefit from multinationals. Therefore, generalizations should be avoided. It may be reasonable to conclude that multinationals increase world income, and that individual host countries can gain from multinationals if appropriate policies are enacted. In particular, policies are needed to prevent the creation and abuse of monopoly power. Most countries recognize the gains from multinationals, and policies are often designed to attract multinationals. Therefore, we can expect multinationals to continue as a feature of the world economic system.

Summary of Main Points

A *multinational corporation* is a company with operations in more than one country. The growth of multinationals was facilitated by falling transport costs and improvements in communications. In the postwar period, many of the multinationals to attract attention were American, but American compa-

---

[9]The pipeline fiasco is discussed by Hufbauer and Scott in Moran (1985).

nies now account for less than half the largest companies in the world. Many multinationals are from Europe and Japan.

Multinational corporations are established by foreign *direct investment*. This investment is usually from one developed country to another. A company may decide to set up a foreign branch for many reasons: control over inputs, lower operating costs, access to markets, or lower taxes. Foreign companies often face higher costs than local firms that are familiar with the local language, culture, and business practices. In order to be able to compete, multinationals must have other advantages. These may include: patents and brand names, superior technology, production or management expertise, access to global capital markets, or an established global marketing network.

Multinational corporations reallocate capital between countries to take advantage of production opportunities. They also benefit from economies of scale in both production and marketing. Thus, we would expect multinationals to increase global income. Because multinationals are large, they are sometimes criticized as examples of monopoly inefficiency. This criticism presumes (unrealistically) that multinationals do not face competition or benefit from lower costs.

Multinationals may influence welfare in the *source country* where the company has its headquarters, and in the *host country* where the company invests. Multinationals are attacked as reducing employment and income in source countries. This criticism presumes that the alternative to foreign investment is greater domestic investment, but the alternative may be no investment. The relationship between foreign and domestic investment is not necessarily close, for example, foreign investment may be financed by funds raised in foreign capital markets.

The effect of foreign investment on domestic income and employment in the host country is also unclear. Foreign investment may increase domestic employment by establishing foreign companies that use the products of the parent company or by establishing distribution networks. Also, domestic producers may benefit by establishing sources of low-cost inputs. Source countries do not gain significantly from taxes levied on multinationals because foreign taxes reduce a company's domestic taxes. Also, foreign profits that are reinvested are not subject to domestic taxes.

Although attention has often focused on the effects of multinationals on developing countries, host countries are usually developed markets. Multinationals increase the available capital and thus add to employment and income in the host country. Domestic employers may lose because they must compete for labor with the multinational. However, there is often unemployment in developing countries, so competition for labor is not usually a serious problem.

The effect of multinationals on the balance of payments of host countries cannot be predicted. Although the effects of the trading activities of multinationals may be clear, the overall effect of multinationals also depends on transfers of profits, fees, and royalties. Like source countries, host countries are not able to depend on collecting taxes from multinationals. *Transfer pricing* is one way in which multinationals avoid high taxes.

Some developing countries would offer favorable contracts to companies in order to induce them to undertake large investments. After the investment had been made, these contracts would be renegotiated on terms more favorable to the host country (because the companies did not want to lose their investments). As a result, many companies now prefer to engage in joint enterprises with local producers.

Other criticisms of multinationals include allegations that they do not transfer appropriate technology to developing countries and that they avoid health and safety regulations by producing in the least regulated markets. Also, examples of multinationals intervening in the domestic politics of the host countries are used by critics who allege that they undermine the sovereignty of host countries.

Examples of good and bad conduct by multinational corporations can always be found. Generalizations should probably be avoided and each multinational corporation considered separately.

Study Questions

1. Describe briefly the importance of multinational corporations within the international economic system.
2. What were the factors that contributed to the rise of multinational corporations after World War Two?
3. Why might a multinational corporation prefer foreign direct investment (a) to exporting or (b) to licensing of foreign producers?
4. Why might multinational corporations be expected to increase the level of world income?
5. Source countries and host countries complain that they do not receive taxes from multinational corporations. How can multinationals avoid paying taxes?
6. Describe the nature of the obsolescing contract.
7. Would American employment increase if American corporations were prevented from investing abroad?
8. What are the effects of multinational corporations on the balance of payments of host countries?
9. What benefits do multinational corporations bring to host countries?
10. Why do developing countries often try to attract multinational corporations?

Selected References

Baldwin, R. E., and Richardson, J. D., Eds. *International Trade and Finance.* Second Edition. Boston: Little Brown, 1981.
Drucker, P. F. "Multinationals and Developing Countries: Myths and Realities." *For-*

eign Affairs 53 (Oct. 1974), pp. 121–34. Reprinted in Adams, J., *The Contemporary International Economy,* Second Edition (New York: St. Martin's Press, 1985).

Grunwald, J., and Flamm, K. *The Global Factory: Foreign Assembly in International Trade.* Washington, D.C.: Brookings Institution, 1985.

Hood, N., and Young, S. *The Economics of Multinational Enterprise.* New York: Longman, 1979.

Hymer, S. "The Efficiency Contradictions of Multinational Corporations." *American Economic Review* 60 (May 1970): 441–53. Reprinted in Baldwin and Richardson (1981).

Moran, T. H., Ed. *Multinational Corporations: The Political Economy of Foreign Direct Investment.* Lexington, MA: D.C. Heath and Co., 1985.

Robock, S. F., et al. *International Business and Multinational Enterprises.* Revised Edition. Homewood, IL: Richard D. Irwin Inc., 1977.

Sigmund, P. E. *Multinationals in Latin America: The Politics of Nationalization.* Madison, WI: University of Wisconsin Press, 1980.

Streeten, P. "Multinationals Revisited." *Finance and Development* 16 (June 1979): 39–42. Reprinted in Baldwin and Richardson (1981).

Vernon, R. *Sovereignty at Bay: The Multinational Spread of U.S. Enterprises.* New York: Basic Books, 1971.

Vernon, R. *Storm over the Multinationals: The Real Issues.* Cambridge, MA: Harvard University Press, 1977.

Wilkins, M. *The Emergence of Multinational Enterprise: American Business Abroad from the Colonial Era to 1914.* Cambridge, MA: Harvard University Press, 1970.

INDEX